NATIONAL GEOGRAPHIC
TRAVELER

thailand

NATIONAL GEOGRAPHIC
TRAVELER

thailand

by **Phil Macdonald** & **Carl Parkes**

National Geographic
Washington, D.C.

CONTENTS

Pages 2–3: Procession of monks with candles
Left: Umbrella painting, Chiang Mai

TRAVELING WITH EYES OPEN

Alert travelers go with a purpose and leave with a benefit. If you travel responsibly, you can help support wildlife conservation, historic preservation, and cultural enrichment in the places you visit. You can enrich your own travel experience as well.

To be a geo-savvy traveler:

- Recognize that your presence has an impact on the places you visit.

- Spend your time and money in ways that sustain local character. (Besides, it's more interesting that way.)

- Value the destination's natural and cultural heritage.

- Respect the local customs and traditions.

- Express appreciation to local people about things you find interesting and unique to the place: its nature and scenery, music and food, historic villages and buildings.

- Vote with your wallet: Support the people who support the place, patronizing businesses that make an effort to celebrate and protect what's special there. Seek out shops, local restaurants, inns, and tour operators who love their home—who love taking care of it and showing it off. Avoid businesses that detract from the character of the place.

- Enrich yourself, taking home memories and stories to tell, knowing that you have contributed to the preservation and enhancement of the destination.

That is the type of travel now called geotourism, defined as "tourism that sustains or enhances the geographical character of a place—its environment, culture, aesthetics, heritage, and the well-being of its residents." To learn more, visit National Geographic's Center for Sustainable Destinations at *www.nationalgeographic.com/travel/sustainable*.

NATIONAL GEOGRAPHIC TRAVELER
thailand

ABOUT THE AUTHORS

Phil Macdonald moved to Hong Kong from Sydney, Australia, in 1989 to continue a career in journalism that had begun eight years earlier in the west-coast city of Perth. He worked for the *Hongkong Standard* and *South China Morning Post* for a number of years before settling—by way of Laos and Singapore—in Phuket, Thailand, in 1996. He now lives in Bangkok, working as a freelance journalist and publisher, and contributing to a number of regional publications. His interests include Southeast Asian politics and recent history, and the beaches of Southern Thailand.

Carl Parkes spent his childhood in the United States and Japan, where his love of Asia first started. He now lives in San Francisco. Parkes has written several guidebooks to Southeast Asia and has contributed to numerous magazines and newspapers.

Trevor Ranges updated and wrote new features for the 2009 edition. In seeking out both the most environmentally friendly and culturally authentic Thai experiences for this edition, Ranges gave priority to those most representative of Thailand's "land of smiles" hospitality. He is also writing the upcoming *National Geographic Traveler Cambodia*.

Additional contributions to the book were made by Tim and Oi McLachlan, who live in Chiang Mai, Thailand.

Charting Your Trip

Thailand is renowned for its delectable cuisine and majestic temples, but the variety of experiences the country offers amazes first-time visitors. The capital city of Bangkok is cosmopolitan and a shopper's paradise. Chiang Mai in the north features ancient history and outdoor adventure. Thailand's beaches span two coasts with pellucid waters where you can scuba dive or receive beachside massages.

Given a week to explore Thailand, you might spend two days in Bangkok followed by four days either discovering the culture and natural beauty of the north or unwinding on the islands in the south, before returning to Bangkok to shop for souvenirs. Thailand's many corners are well served by more than 20 domestic airports and several different airlines, including Thai Airways, Bangkok Airways, NokAir (Thai Airways' budget carrier), One-two-go, and Thai Air Asia (a major player in low-cost regional service). Trains provide the most comfortable, enjoyable method of traveling around the country. The State Railway of Thailand *(www.railway.co.th)* operates four main train routes and a handful of auxiliary spurs that serve smaller towns. With the exception of chaotic Bangkok and, to some degree, Chiang Mai, Thailand is also an excellent country to tour with a rented car or motorcycle.

NOT TO BE MISSED:

Bangkok's dazzling Grand Palace and Temple of the Emerald Buddha **69–73**

Attending the Songkran and Loy Krathong festivals **21**

Seeing how Thai silk is made **57–58, 169**

Watching or learning *muay thai* boxing **61**

A visit to Ayutthaya, where Siam's golden age flourished **132–140**

Chiang Mai and its spectacular mountain setting **214–223**

A Thai cooking class **224**

A homestay in a Thai village **235**

An elephant experience **238**

Beach-hopping aboard a long-tail boat in Phangnga Bay **331–335**

Bangkok & Around

On your first day, head straight to the magnificent Grand Palace and Wat Phra Kaew—the Temple of the Emerald Buddha—in the heart of Bangkok, along the Chao Phraya river. Nearby, the National Museum and National Gallery of Art are fine places to take in some ancient culture before hopping on a *tuk-tuk* (three-wheeled motorcycle with driver) to Wat Pho to see the Reclining Buddha and receive a traditional Thai massage. A long-tail boat ride around Thon Buri's canals, where

Thai Customs & Cultural Etiquette

Visitors often misunderstand Thailand's cultural practices, usually at the expense of Thais, who are, in general, conservative and sensitive. When foreigners behave in a way they consider rude or inappropriate, Thais feel embarrassment on the offender's behalf, even when the foreigner is oblivious to his or her social faux pas. The following guidelines may help make you more etiquette savvy:

Dress: At temples, bare shoulders and exposed knees are unacceptable; however, this rule of attire also should be followed in embassies, museums, other official institutions, and while dining with Thais. Other than at the beach, bare skin is frowned upon, no matter how hot it may be.

Thai Houses: When visiting a Thai home, it is polite to bring a gift (e.g., fruit), and to remove your shoes before entering.

The Body: The head is the most sacred part of the body; the feet are the lowest. Do not touch a person's head (even a child's) or point the soles of the feet at others, including putting your feet up on a seat or table.

The King: It is both a social and legal infraction to disparage the King (or royal family) in any way.

Displays of Affection/Emotion: Thais have generally conservative sexual mores, so refrain from overt displays of affection in public. Also, dramatic expressions of anger or sorrow will leave Thais quietly shaking their heads or gracefully ignoring the outburst.

you'll glimpse traditional Thai life, should be followed by a visit to Wat Arun, with its spectacular view over the city. Finish your day with dinner at a riverside restaurant.

Day two in Bangkok could include a morning trip to Damnoern Saduak floating market; a tour of Jim Thompson's house, a beautiful old-style teak structure filled with ancient artwork; or shopping at Chatuchak weekend market or one of Bangkok's many other markets. A more relaxing day might consist of a cooking class or spa treatments. In the evening, consider watching a traditional puppet show or a *muay thai* boxing match, followed by a drink at a rooftop bar with panoramic views.

With more time, take a day trip to the ancient capital of Ayutthaya, founded in 1351. It's about 55 miles (90 km) north of Bangkok and can be visited via car, boat, or train.

Chiang Mai & the Mountains

Those interested in culture and the outdoors should journey to Chiang Mai, about an hour north of Bangkok by plane. The capital of the historic Lanna kingdom and home to 700-year-old temples, Chiang Mai is also a popular jumping-off point for mountain treks into

The "earth witness" mudra symbolizes the Buddha's enlightenment under the bodhi tree.

When to Go

Most visitors head to Thailand during the relatively cool and dry season from December to February, when rainfall is scarce and the temperature around a tolerable 84 to 90°F (28–32°C). (If you're traveling in the hills, temperatures can drop sharply in the evenings, so take a sweater.) The drawback is that popular destinations are crowded and hotel rooms can be in short supply. March to May or June is the hottest time to visit—temperatures may reach 100°F (38°C), particularly in the plains of the northeast, and the high level of humidity (around 80 percent) can make travel uncomfortable and oppressive.

hill-tribe country. Even if you're not into hiking, day trips to nearby hill tribes are enlightening experiences, as are visits to elephant sanctuaries, such as the Elephant Nature Park. A major region for handicrafts, Chiang Mai has a number of workshops along San Kamphaeng Road.

From Chiang Mai, you can experience more trekking, hill tribes, and spectacularly remote mountain scenery in Chiang Rai, hub of the Golden Triangle (about 110 miles/180 km northeast); and Mae Hong Son (220 miles/335 km northwest).

The Beaches

If you prefer sand and sun, Thailand has two coasts with gorgeous islands amid aquamarine waters. Phuket, the west coast's most popular island, about an hour south by plane from Bangkok, has beaches ranging from isolated coves harboring private resorts to crowded Patong Beach, where water activities and nightlife abound. Phuket features world-class spas, and it is a center for diving, fishing, and sailing. Nearby Krabi Province has quieter islands more suited to relaxation. Whichever base you prefer, a day trip from both to Phangna Bay, with its spectacular limestone pillars plunging into the turquoise sea, is a must. Hundreds of small islands, including James Bond Island, are best explored via kayak, and Ko Phi Phi is a popular destination for snorkelers and divers. Serious divers will want to spend several days on a live-aboard dive boat to the Similan Islands.

On the east coast, along the Gulf of Thailand, most visitors head to Ko Samui, also about an hour flight south from Bangkok. Unlike Phuket, Samui features only one golf course, but you can fill several days with a scuba certification course. If you are already certified or your primary intention is learning to dive, Ko Tao, a

Tipping

Food and drink are subject to a 7 percent value added tax (VAT), which is occasionally included in the menu price. A service charge of 10 percent may be included on the bill. Even with service included, it's polite to leave remaining coins, 20 to 100 baht, or a tip of 10 percent, depending on the quality of establishment. (Generally, Thais do not tip at lower-end venues.) Valets and porters should be pleased with 20 to 100 baht; taxi drivers will often keep the change, so small bills are preferable.

A corncob seller at Tham Phra Nang Hat, one of Phra Nang's prettiest beaches

two-hour boat ride from Samui, is the top spot. Alternatively, you can plan excellent day trips, such as a snorkeling trip to Ko Tao's neighboring Ko Nang Yuan or a kayaking trip around Ang Thong Marine Park. People who are looking to get away from it all can head to Ko Phan Ngan's spa and wellness retreats.

Off the Beaten Path

Those looking to get off the beaten path should explore the northeastern provinces—what's called Issan—for ancient Khmer temples and rural life centered on agriculture. Udon Thani, about an hour flight north of Bangkok, is a good base. Nature enthusiasts should consider Khao Sok National Park (fly to Surat Thani or Krabi—both under an hour flight south from Bangkok) or Khao Yai National Park (108 miles/175 km northeast of Bangkok via bus, car, or train), both sanctuaries for indigenous birds and wildlife—including elephants! The ancient capital of Sukhothai, a 35-minute flight north from Bangkok, has stunning ruins. The Loy Krathong festival here in November is spectacular. ■

What to Bring

Thailand is a perpetually hot country where jackets and sweaters are rarely needed (except in frigid air-conditioned interiors!). Coats, ties, and dressy dresses may be necessary in a few exclusive restaurants in Bangkok but are otherwise little more than an additional packing burden.

Clothes should be a light cotton or other natural fiber. Bring the fewest possible items of clothing and expand your wardrobe in Thailand, where the clothing selection is excellent and of international quality. Comfortable walking shoes are essential, and sandals are useful when visiting temples, where shoes must be removed prior to entry.

Other items to consider are a small medical kit, sewing kit, mini-umbrella, insect repellent, drug prescriptions, and photocopies of essential documents.

History & Culture

Above: The Reclining Buddha at Bangkok's Wat Pho. Left: The elegant art of fruit carving in Chiang Mai

Thailand Today

Thailand has the distinction among Southeast Asian countries of never having been colonized. It has not suffered civil war nor the racial conflicts that have at one time or another plagued other countries in the region. This remarkable feat in an often volatile part of the world is celebrated in its name: Thailand, or Prathet Thai. Translated, it means "land of the free."

Thailand's escape from the domination of foreign powers for any extended period of time (it did suffer invasions of Burmese and Khmers, and was briefly occupied by the Japanese during World War II) is reflected in the nature of the Thai people. They are fiercely proud and independent. These traits rarely manifest themselves in arrogance or intolerance but rather in self-assuredness, confidence, and a generosity of spirit toward foreigners. Many visitors see Thais as easygoing and fun-loving (which usually they are), but they are also a people who cherish their independence and tenaciously cling to the wonders of their past. Even as—for better or worse—the inevitable onslaught of Western cultural influence leaves its mark on the country, Thais fight to maintain their identity and their uniqueness.

Consequently, you must be prepared to encounter a paradox: an ancient culture juxtaposed against a vibrant, dynamic modern age. The result can be a mixture of exhilaration and confusion, as traditional culture stands its ground against the surge of modernity. Take a look at Bangkok, which, with eight million people, is by far the country's largest city. Here East does more than meet West—it collides with it in a thunderous explosion. You'll find traffic jams, bustling crowds, high-rise office buildings, a neon-pulsing nightlife, unashamed consumerism in gigantic shopping malls, fashion-conscious people, and a fair share of street hustlers. Then take another look: Buddhist monks in saffron robes ride the city's modern Skytrain. An elephant, being ridden by his handler, lumbers down busy Sukhumvit Road among the BMWs, colorful three-wheeled *tuk tuks,* and smoke-spewing, overcrowded buses. In quiet side streets people make food and incense offerings daily to spirits in doll-size temples set on pedestals. People still greet each other with a traditional *wai* (hands joined in a prayer-like position in front of the chest and head bowed slightly; see sidebar p. 187). Standing next to the high-rise office towers, huge, riotously ornate temples, full of gilded images, are constant reminders of the pervading influence of Buddhism in the country.

> **Standing next to the high-rise office towers, huge, riotously ornate temples, full of gilded images, are constant reminders of the pervading influence of Buddhism in the country.**

Thailand's past, represented in its art, architecture, and religion, is in itself reason enough to visit the country. But add to this a surfeit of natural beauty, an ease of traveling to all regions, safety, superb cuisine, and the traditional friendliness and hospitality of the Thai people and you end up with an exceptional country.

Two sights that will become familiar to all visitors to Bangkok are laughing children and a lavishly adorned *tuk tuk.*

Bangkok has hundreds of markets full of cheap, but notoriously fake, goods.

The Thai Personality

Perhaps better known than "Land of the Free" is the sobriquet "Land of Smiles." Visitors to Thailand are struck by the ubiquity of smiles. But all is not always as it seems. Smiles can mean many things in Thailand. In fact, Thais have managed to label 13 types of smiles, running a gauntlet of emotions from sadness to gloating and despair. There is even a smile for not smiling—*yim mai awk*, or "I'm-trying-to-smile-but-I-can't" smile. But generally smiles appear with an easygoing nature born out of a desire for *sanuk* (fun) and a quickly forgiving *mai pen rai* (never mind).

Anything worth doing in Thailand, even the most menial, laborious, and boring of tasks, must contain some element of sanuk, or it is not worth doing. This playful quality—cracking jokes, flirting, singing, playing practical jokes—does not imply that Thais do not work hard or strive to achieve their life's goals; it just means they have a bit of fun along the way. Any activity described as *mai sanuk* (not fun) is anathema.

A shrug of the shoulders followed by the words *mai pen rai* shows a determination to avoid conflict—to save face. The importance of face in Thai society (along with almost all Asian cultures) cannot be overstated. Mai pen rai is used to cool conflict, ease embarrassment, lessen stress, and defuse difficult situations. When a Thai smiles and laughs after you trip and fall down, it is an attempt to save face for all involved, including you.

The country's dominant religion, Buddhism, is a major shaper of the Thai personality, with its precepts of a detached view of life and lack of judgmental attitudes about most actions and human frailties. Buddhism traditionally values respect, quietude, and subtleness. Relationships are complex—a legacy of a complicated pyramidal social system that ranks people according to certain values. Generally, social rank is determined by age, wealth (how the wealth is obtained is not always a factor), professional rank, religious merit, and personal and political power. This may be not unlike other cultures in the world, but the difference lies in the rigid divide between the levels of social order and the set of obligations that links all members of Thai society. Forget egalitarianism; it does not exist in Thailand. It is almost automatic to defer to someone of higher status and to accord a respect that, in some cases, Westerners would liken to fawning. But in patron-client relationships, in return for respect, those of higher social status are expected to show benevolence to those of lesser rank. If an employee is loyal to a boss, then the boss will, at some stage, be obligated to grant a favor to the employee—perhaps a loan to help with his or her children's education. A Thai learns early in life where he or she stands in this social hierarchy. As a foreign visitor, you will find yourself automatically a good way up the social ladder simply because Thais are gracious and warm hosts. To stay there, you need to maintain the respect afforded you. It's easy enough to do: Simply show respect toward individuals, their beliefs, and their institutions. Voluntarily and freely compliment the country and its people, and you will find yourself even more admired.

The traditional and graceful *wai* with which Thais greet each other may appear to be simple, but this too is tied up in the complicated set of social rules touched on above. You don't need to return a wai; a simple smile and nod will do fine. Often, a hand will

EXPERIENCE: Speak Thai

Thai is a confusing language to learn; there are five tones, and words pronounced incorrectly have entirely different meanings. *Suay*, for example, means both beautiful and unlucky, depending on pronunciation.

Fortunately, Thai grammar is quite simple, and there are schools that make learning the language relatively easy. Otherwise, impromptu Thai/English exchanges with friendly Thais can be the most rewarding and fun approach to learning.

AUA Language Center *(171 Rajadamri Rd., Bangkok, tel 02-252-8170; or 110 yards/100 m west of Thapae Gate, Chiang Mai, tel 053-278407, www.aua thai.com)* With a guarantee of no books, tests, or homework, AUA Bangkok's classes are ideal for the less academically inclined visitor. Students learn by observing real-

life experiences, making learning more practical. Hour-long sample classes are available for beginners.

The Chiang Mai branch's courses are more intensive, but the atmosphere, in a breezy teak house, is more laid-back.

Chulalongkorn University *(Mahachulalongkorn Bldg., Rm. 103, Phayathai Rd., Bangkok, tel 02-218-4892, www.arts.chula .ac.th/~asc/itp.html)* The Intensive Thai Program at Chula, one of Thailand's premier universities, has courses for beginners looking to learn social Thai skills and those seeking academic levels of

proficiency. Be ready to hit the books, though: Five-week courses run 10 a.m. to 3 p.m., Monday through Friday.

Nisa Language School *(32/14-16 Yen-akart Rd., Bangkok, tel 02-671-3359, www.nisathailanguage school.com)* Nisa courses focus on "total immersion" and range from casual conversation to business language. Listening, speaking, reading, and writing are all featured in group and individual courses. Activities, such as Thai cooking, fuse culture with language studies, as do lectures on Thai holidays, festivals, and traditions.

be proffered for a handshake. Thais address each other by their first names, so don't be surprised if they do the same to you, usually preceded by the honorific *khun*. Learn a few words of Thai. The all-purpose greeting *sawadee krap* (used by males) and *sawadee ka* (females), accompanied by a warm smile, is the perfect icebreaker.

Behavior

Fist-thumping outrage and contempt will never get you anywhere in tense situations; however, an admirable Thai quality—*jai yen*, or cool heart—will. Remain calm in stressful situations. A smile will always get you a lot further than a snarl. What people in the West might regard as constructive criticism of a problem or person, when voiced in even a mildly aggressive way, labels you with *jai rorn*, or hot heart. Direct criticism is often seen as a personal attack, resulting in extreme loss of face. Thais are easygoing, but if tempers fray and face is lost, a darker side of their personality can surface.

The feet are spiritually the lowest part of the body, so it is insulting to point them directly at a Thai. Keep your feet on the ground when sitting, and never point them at anything; to do so is regarded as a grave insult. Always remove your shoes when entering a person's home. Conversely, the head is the most important part of the body; never touch a person (even a child) on the head.

> **Thais revere their royal family and will not abide any criticism of the monarchy.... Not only is criticism of the institution not tolerated, it is against the law.**

Thais & the Monarchy

Thais relish their tenuous democracy and love to gossip about their politicians' often outlandish, arrogant behavior. To a certain extent, they tolerate criticism of their culture. Many middle-class and educated Thais find the hierarchal social system anachronistic and stifling. However, Thais revere their royal family and will not abide any criticism of the monarchy. Photographs of the king are prominently displayed in many shops and homes. Not only is criticism of the institution not tolerated, it is against the law. People have been jailed for the mildest of jibes against members of the royal family. In honor of king and country, in towns and villages all over Thailand and in some areas of Bangkok, loudspeakers play the national anthem at 8 a.m. and 6 p.m. Thais stop whatever they are doing and stand still, and visitors are expected to do likewise.

Leisure Time

Thais are sociable and relish gatherings of family, friends, and colleagues. Even a work lunch can turn into a mini-party, with plenty of food, laughter, and company. They frequently have get-togethers at the end of the workday with a more boisterous aspect. If you find yourself sharing a meal with a group of locals, it will usually be by invitation with you as the main guest. On most occasions, you, as the only foreigner, are expected to pay the bill unless your fellow diners are of high or equal social status (i.e., wealthy as you are perceived to be). If in doubt, ask for the bill. If no one objects, you cheerfully pay. If others insist on sharing or paying the bill, though, don't object.

Visitors' Thailand: The first stop for most visitors to Thailand is Bangkok, a clamorous, often maddening city that can inspire a gamut of emotions—loathing, despair, humor,

Elephant trekkers take an amble in the highlands north of Chiang Rai.

Monks collect food from villagers in northern Thailand at sunrise.

and even affection—often all within minutes of each other. The country's political and commercial center, this steamy, chaotic place is challenging for visitors, but its rewards are outstanding. You'll find magnificent temples and palaces, world-class restaurants, intriguing museums, and an unrivaled nightlife. The rising sun striking temples along the Chao Phraya river—the city's main waterway—is one of Southeast Asia's great sights.

After Bangkok, head to the countryside, which both soothes and dazzles. In some cases, you'll find it an almost clichéd rendering of Southeast Asia: extraordinary temples with wildly flamboyant architectural styles; centuries-old cities of powerful, long-gone empires; fruit-laden boats gently rowed down calm canals; caparisoned elephants heading parades in northern villages; multicolored kites fluttering below clear blue skies; lush paddy fields being worked by plow-pulling oxen; and expansive plantations of rubber trees, coconut palms, and bananas. Thais turn to their rivers and waterways at the end of the rainy season and Buddhist Lent, celebrating successful harvests on the one hand with partying and raucous boat races, and, on the other, with a tender and beautiful festival, Loy Krathong (see opposite), which draws you back to the calmness and graciousness that so often defines Thailand.

In the rich, fertile plains of central Thailand (easily reached either on a guided tour or independently—ask at your hotel) are the ancient cities of the Ayutthaya and Sukhothai, remnants of past dynasties whose links to modern-day Thailand remain strong.

Just a few hours from Bangkok on the eastern gulf coast, visitors pour into the hedonistic beach resort of Pattaya. Head there with an open mind. Some travel farther along the coast to the rugged, beautiful island of Ko Charg, Thailand's second largest island and reckoned by some to be the kingdom's next tourist hot spot.

In the north of the country, mountains sweep down from the foothills of the Himalaya. Here hills, valleys, and forests present some of the most dramatic scenery in the country. On the porous borders with Myanmar (Burma), in the north and west, a rugged frontierism pervades. In the northeast, known as Issan, village and farming life remain entrenched, and life moves at a sedate pace. Here, too, lies evidence of a once great civilization, the Khmer. The masterly restored ruins at Phimai and Phanom Rung make a trip to this vast and rarely visited region well worthwhile.

South of Bangkok, the beaches and islands off the Malay Peninsula are peerless in Asia, sparkling and shimmering tropical gems that are extremely popular with foreign visitors.

Festivals: Hardly a day goes by in Thailand without some town or village celebrating something. You may want to plan your trip to coincide with major festivals (see pp. 385–386). Thais love to party, and festivals are mostly lively affairs, with plenty of food, music, dancing, and laughter, plus often a beauty contest. The Thai New Year, Songkran, celebrated in April, is perhaps the most famous, when the entire country erupts into a good-natured water fight. Others to look out for include Surin's elephant festival and Phuket's Vegetarian Festival, the country's most unusual, when young men pierce their cheeks with spears. Loy Krathong, held in November to celebrate the end of the rains, is always a delight. Candles are placed on tiny banana-leaf boats and sent by the hundreds of thousands down waterways all over the country, creating an amazing effect.

Temples: *Wats,* or temple complexes, are central to the community especially in small towns and villages. They are both places of worship and gathering spots for local people to chat and gossip. Monks have residences there, and they often contain community centers and schools. On some occasions, especially during festivals, they become retail outlets, with market stalls selling all kinds of goods. ■

Top Ten Local Phrases

Sawadee/Bye bye	Hello/Goodbye
Sabai dee mai?/Sabai dee	How are you?/I'm fine
Kawp Khun/Mai ao	Thank you/No thank you (don't want)
Kawe tote/Mai pben lai	Pardon me/Never mind
Tao lai?	How much does this cost?
Pet mai?/Kawe mai pet	Is this spicy?/Not spicy, please
Check bin	Check, please
Hawng nam tee nai?	Where is the bathroom?
Pbai nai?/	Where are you going?/
Pbai tee-ao	I'm just going out
Mee-ter dai mai?	Does your taxi charge by meter?

People & Religion

Thailand is one of the most racially homogenous nations in Southeast Asia. Of a total population of 60 million, slightly more than 80 percent are ethnic Thai. There are significant numbers of ethnic Chinese, with a smaller population of Malays found mainly in the south of the country. Cambodian, Burmese, and Vietnamese immigrants make up smaller groups, and numerous settlements of indigenous hill tribes are found in the north of Thailand.

Ethnic Thais speak four dialects, which correspond to the country's four geographic regions: Central, Northeastern, Northern, and Southern. The Central Thais of the Chao Phraya Basin compose about 36 percent of the ethnic Thai population and are the dominant social and political group. The Central Thai dialect is considered "standard" Thai language and is the language of education, television, and radio, and is used for communication between Thais from different regions. The Northeastern Thai (32 percent of ethnic Thais) of the Issan region are large in number but are perhaps the most politically and socially underrepresented in the country. Their dialect is a colorful mixture of the Thai and Laotian languages. The Northern Thais make up about 8 percent of the ethnic Thai population, while the Thai Pak Tai of Southern Thailand—from Bangkok south to the Malaysian border—consider themselves a people apart, with distinctive forms of culture and a crisp, quickly spoken native tongue. They also make up about 8 percent of the ethnic Thai population. In addition, there are about ten interregional dialects spoken by Thais in certain pockets of the country.

> Thailand's relatively harmonious society is credited to Buddhism and its inherent traditional value systems, which place great emphasis on the sanctity of family, friends, and social harmony.

Buddhism

While each regional group speaks its own language and, to an extent, practices customs unique to its area, Thai culture and social values entwine all Thais—including most of the ethnic minorities. Acceptance, albeit sometimes grudging, of ethnic minorities, and their inclusion in most aspects of Thai culture, can to a large degree be attributed to the tolerant and nonjudgmental precepts that are essential to Buddhism.

About 95 percent of the population are Theravada Buddhist, the official religion. It forms the core of modern Thai culture, dominating many aspects of daily life. Thailand's relatively harmonious society is credited to Buddhism and its inherent traditional value systems, which place great emphasis on the sanctity of family, friends, and social harmony.

Buddhism's teachings eschew the notion of an omnipotent god or gods. There is no divine ruler who decides the fate of the individual. In Buddhism, life is not a series of free choices, but rather each person's life is controlled by the karma he or she accumulated in previous lives. It is solely the action of the individual that determines the

The great majority of the Thai population is Buddhist. There are some 30,000 Buddhist temples around the country.

course of his or her life, and no god can change the effects once humankind has created the causes. Evil conduct cannot be forgiven and must reap its own punishment, while righteous deeds will reap their due rewards.

Thais believe that the fortunate, rich, or powerful obtain their status from a position of superior karma, while the poor and suffering have been cursed with their fate as a result of indiscretions in a previous existence. This notion goes a long way toward explaining the intractable social hierarchy of Thai society. A person who is rich, powerful, or influential is obviously so because of a meritorious past life. His superior karma earns him the right and privilege of deference.

Fundamental to Buddhism is the belief in the Four Noble Truths, discovered by the Buddha at the moment of his enlightenment: All life is suffering; all suffering has a cause in cravings or desire; the suffering can be overcome by eliminating the desire; and the desire can be overcome by following the Eightfold Path. This eight-step recipe for success includes right view, right intention, right speech, right action, right livelihood, right mindfulness, and right concentration. The first two principles of the Eightfold Path concern motivation, the next three address moral code, and the last three concern man's mind for right ends. Salvation occurs when the individual recognizes these eight truths and follows their guidelines to destroy desire, thereby breaking the train of reincarnation. The end result is enlightenment and entrance into a state of nirvana—the ultimate aim.

Buddhist images are cast in a limited number of poses, accorded by Buddhist scriptures.

This Eightfold Path is also known as the Middle Way, as it avoids extremes of behavior. Although an adherent does not have to live an austere life, nor should he or she move to the high-end scale of sensuality.

As a result of their belief in karma and reincarnation, Buddhists refuse to assign moral shame to the actions of an individual. Buddhists neither fear nor look forward to an eternity in heaven or hell. Thus most Thais feel free to behave without guilt, as judgment in their next life will be based on their actions and not on religious dogma.

Buddhism, unlike Christianity, refuses to answer many of the basic questions about the meaning of life, such as human origins or final disposition. Life is seen as an impermanent condition filled with contradictory forces that demand no explanation and which are experienced with little attempt at rationalization. Thai Buddhists are largely left alone to determine their own value systems and levels of morality.

To speed their path to nirvana by reducing their number of rebirths, Thais will make merit by feeding monks, giving donations to temples, and making regular appearances at temples for worship. Making merit is an intrinsic part of Thai social behavior. Wats are central to community life in many towns and villages. To be generous in your donations to your local wat not only speeds your passage to nirvana, but can also increase your social standing in the community.

Many visitors to Thailand are surprised at the large number of young men involved in monkhood. Every young man is expected to become a monk for a short period of time.

Buddhists do not keep any particular day of the week for religious observation in the way that followers of Christianity, Islam, or Judaism do. Nor do they celebrate mass or any other type of liturgy presided over by a priest or other religious leader, although they attend discourses on Buddhism given by abbots and will often seek counsel with a monk or nun to discuss life's problems. They are free to visit a wat whenever they like, and they worship personally and individually rather than in groups. Favorite days for visiting their temples tend to be every full moon and new moon, but many Buddhists will make a visit when good fortune befalls them (on winning the lottery, receiving a promotion, or getting a raise) or on their birthday.

Monks: A line of young monks clasping bowls and making their rounds from house to house collecting alms, donations, and food every morning is a common sight in towns, villages, and cities around the country.

Many visitors to Thailand are surprised at the large number of young men involved in monkhood. Every young man is expected to become a monk for a short period of time. Generally, this period falls between finishing school or college and finding a job or launching a career and marrying. Most of these young men are expected to spend about three months as monks, traditionally accepting their robes in July, at the start of the rainy season. But a majority will stay for only one or two weeks. The reason for this religious conscription is to enhance the young men's knowledge of the teachings of the Buddha and to improve their karma. It is also done to make merit for—and honor—their parents, who see even such a short tenure as a monk as an important part of their son's life. Some of these young men are ordained for a lifetime.

At any one time in Thailand's 32,000 monasteries, there are 200,000 monks. Many of these men dedicate their lives to study and become Buddhist scholars and teachers.

Life for a monk is frugal and disciplined; days are spent meditating, studying scriptures, and doing menial tasks around the temple grounds. Despite their austere lives, monks are generally friendly and welcoming to visitors. Some Buddhist monks have a tendency to stray from the path, though, boasting to gullible followers of supernatural powers assigned to them because of their position. It is common to find monks predicting lottery outcomes, practicing faith healing, selling magical charms, and charging lucrative fees in return for performing marriage and other ceremonies.

Thai boys enter the monkhood to learn about Buddhism—often for only a few months or even weeks.

Spiritualism: Beyond the world of wandering monks and glittering temples is the underlying fact that Thai Buddhism has never completely superseded earlier beliefs enshrined in Hinduism (from which Buddhism was adapted and refined) and spiritualism. Hindu ceremonies—marriages, births, and funerals—still play an important role in Thai society. Some of the most powerful religious motives are connected with animist beliefs, including the propitiation of spirits, which are called *phi* (pronounced pee).

Spirit worship in Thailand revolves around these wandering supernatural apparitions, who have the power to bring good fortune. Yet they can inflict great pain if not continually appeased with offerings of food, flowers, and incense. Among the most prevalent and powerful of all phi is the "spirit of the land," who must be provided with a doll-size spirit house (see p. 87) outside a property to compensate for the building of the house on land that belongs to the spirit.

Hinduism and spirit propitiation may not follow strictly in accordance with Buddhist teachings, yet few Thais feel any ideological conflicts between burning incense to honor the Buddha, then making food offerings to placate animist spirits.

Buddhist Iconography: Statues festoon almost every temple in Thailand. A cursory examination gives the impression that they are similar in design, with few indications of original artistry. This uniformity was crafted by Buddhist sculptors, who for centuries followed the physical descriptions of the Buddha as related in ancient Buddhist texts. Bound by tradition, sculptors sought a standard lexicon of symbolism that could easily be understood by pilgrims.

Sculptors also wanted to create reproductions of earlier images that had achieved fame as magical talismans, or were believed capable of performing miracles or providing the pious with supernatural protection. This melding of Buddhist beliefs with the power of the occult served to popularize the religion and provided the mystical link that is so beloved by contemporary Thais.

But look closely and you will see that Buddhist images throughout Thailand share a number of common body positions and hand gestures, known as *mudras* (see pp. 80–81), which symbolically represent important events in the life of the Buddha and reinforce the compassionate nature of the religion.

Buddha images are generally shown as seated, standing, walking, or reclining. The walking position, rarely employed except by the school of Sukhothai (see pp. 200–201), depicts the Buddha descending from heaven to earth. The reclining position—also rare—is often employed in very large images, to show the Buddha at the exact moment of entering nirvana. Standing and seated positions are often determined by the mudra. Standing images can show the Buddha either granting blessings or subduing evil forces. Sitting Buddha images can represent almost any important event in the life of Buddha, again as indicated by the position of the hands.

The Chinese

Several Chinese groups have migrated to Thailand during the past 250 years. The Hokkiens were the first to arrive in significant numbers, in the late 18th century, and made themselves indispensable to the monarchy as tax collectors. They were followed by the Teochews, who arrived poor and dispossessed, but soon used their entrepreurial skills in Bangkok to build their wealth. Northern Thailand opened up to substantial numbers of Hui—Chinese Muslims—in the late 19th century as they escaped religious persecution during the Ching dynasty.

Today, the Chinese make up about 11 percent of the population, and Thailand is a singular success story in Southeast Asia in terms of Chinese assimilation. Discrimination is non-existent. Ethnic Chinese have all but exclusive tenure to the top positions in government, bureaucracy, and commerce. In Bangkok, it is hard to walk the city's teeming streets without spotting a face that hints at Chinese ancestry.

Temple & Monk Etiquette

When entering a temple, always dress neatly (long trousers and shirt sleeves for men, modest dress for women, including covered shoulders) and remove your shoes. (You will find it most convenient to wear slip-on shoes while sightseeing.) Buddha images in Thailand are sacred. Never climb on an image. If you pose for a photograph in front of one, do so with respect. When sitting in a temple, keep your feet pointed away from images of the Buddha or worshippers. (Sitting cross-legged or kneeling is best.) Women are forbidden from touching or handing things to monks, sitting beside them, or entering temples when menstruating. Certain seats on public transportation are reserved for monks and marked accordingly.

The acceptance of the Chinese in Thai culture has as much to do with the Chinese desire to assimilate as with the traditional tolerance of Thais. Intermarriage has been common since the enlightened reign of King Mongkut (r. 1851–1868), who promoted immigration and intermarriage as a means of instilling a strong work ethic—for which the Chinese are famed—in the general population of his country. Rich Chinese merchants also endeared themselves to the monarchy by offering their daughters to the royal court as consorts.

Hill Tribes of the North

The remote hills of northern Thailand are home to tens of thousands of hill-tribe people. Although they make up only about 2 percent of the population, hill tribes have attracted a huge amount of interest from visitors, thousands of whom make treks to tribal villages each year. Most of the hill tribes are immigrant groups who came to Thailand from Myanmar (Burma), Laos, and China over the last century. Most are dirt-poor farmers who receive little assistance from the central government. Public services that are available to the average Thai citizen—paved roads, potable water, electricity, sanitation, medical facilities, and education—very rarely find their way to hill-tribe villages.

The people of the hill tribes are one of two groups that test the traditional and much celebrated Thai spirit of tolerance. Most Thais see them as foreign interlopers and as such afford them little respect. Many have lived in Thailand for generations and still have not been granted citizenship. Hill tribes are a marginalized people who are clinging to the very bottom rungs of the social and economic ladders.

> **Thailand's constitution enshrined equal rights for women, but in many aspects of daily life, women still face discrimination. Even so, in the past few decades they have made giant strides in gaining equality.**

The Thai government officially recognizes six major groups of hill tribes (there are about 20 groups in all), based on their languages, faith, social customs, dress, and historical lineage. The Karen, a Christian tribe that numbers about 265,000, is by far Thailand's largest hill-tribe group. While most hill tribes live solely in the northern provinces of Chiang Mai, Chiang Rai, and Mae Hong Son, the Karen trickle south as far Kanchanaburi and Tak Provinces, to the west of Bangkok.

The second largest hill tribe is the Hmong, who are called Meo by Thais. They came from Laos in the 1950s and 1960s and number about 80,000. Many Hmong in Laos allied with the U.S. military during the Vietnam War. Hmong are much in evidence at Chiang Mai's sprawling night market, where they sell finely crafted silver jewelry and exquisitely embroidered costumes.

The 34,000 Akha have been the most obstinate group as far as assimilation is concerned, preferring to hew closely to traditional ways. The group's villages are popular among foreign visitors chiefly because of the photo opportunities presented by the colorful, highly ornate headdresses that the women wear. These consist of an elaborate collection of old coins, beads, and feathers.

The majority of Lahu (numbering about 60,000) are Christian, and this group has proved the most successful in adapting to the Thai mainstream. The colorfully costumed Lisu (numbering about 25,000) are adept at commerce and they are accepted by Thais as keen businesspeople. Many Mien (also known as Yao) can trace their origins back to Yunnan Province in China. They adorn themselves with distinctive black turbans and red feather boas. Some maintain traditional Chinese customs, including Taoism and the use of Chinese script.

Hill tribes, along with Vietnamese immigrants, make up the major part of Thailand's Christian community, which accounts for about 0.5 percent of the population. For more on the hill tribes of the north, see pp. 234–235.

Muslims of the South

Thailand has more than three million Muslims, most of whom are clustered in the southern provinces of Satun, Pattani, Yala, and Narathiwat on the border of predominantly Muslim Malaysia. Significant populations also can be found in other southern provinces of Phuket, Krabi, Trang, and Songkhla. Most southern Muslims are of Malay descent. Relationships with the majority Buddhist Thais have not been smooth, and Muslims have, over the years, complained of both social and political discrimination.

More than a decade of peace here was shattered in January 2004 when Muslim insurgents launched a raid on a small military armory; they killed four soldiers and took the weapons. This foreshadowed an occasionally brutal insurgency that has continued since, causing the deaths of more than 3,000 people.

The insurgents, in Thailand's southernmost provinces of Yala, Narithiwat, and Pattani, show no signs of letting up despite earnest pleas by the Queen for peace and many, often misguided, efforts made by the government. Attacks at banks and bars in Had Yai have had foreign casualties and travel to these provinces should be avoided.

Lisu hll-tribe people harvest rice. Hill tribes are popular with visitors, but many of them live in poverty.

Women

Thailand's constitution enshrined equal rights for women, but in many aspects of daily life, women still face discrimination. Even so, in the past few decades they have made giant strides in gaining equality. More than 65 percent of university students are female, and growing numbers of women are represented in senior political and bureaucratic positions. Women of lower socioeconomic status tend to be the most entrepreneurial, operating vending stands or small businesses. It's not unusual to see women working alongside men on construction sites in Bangkok. ∎

The Land

Thais liken the shape of their country to the head of an elephant, the Malay Peninsula—extending south to the Malaysian border in the south—being the trunk. At 198,115 square miles (513,115 sq km), roughly the size of Texas, Thailand lies at the heart of Southeast Asia. It borders Myanmar (Burma) to the west, Laos and Cambodia to the east, and Malaysia to the south. Hundreds of islands are sprinkled off its lengthy coastline, which runs along the Gulf of Thailand and the Andaman Sea.

Thailand is a varied and rich country of forested mountains, deep valleys sliced by fast-flowing rivers, patchworks of cultivated areas fed by extensive waterways, thick rain forests, and vast swaths of arid land cursed with weak soil and enigmatic weather conditions.

The lush central basin is Thailand's breadbasket. This densely populated area holds nearly one-third of the country's population. The mighty Chao Phraya river, or Mae Nam (Mother of Waters), runs south through it from the confluence of the Ping, Yom, and Nan Rivers at the city of Nakhon Sawan to Bangkok and on to the Gulf of Thailand. Countless rice fields in these fertile central plains, cut by a maze of canals, produce up to three crops a year. Huge rice barges use these canals to ferry crops down to Bangkok for distribution to other parts of the country and for export. These geographic conditions have made the region the center of Thai civilization for more than 400 years, host to three successive capitals—Ayutthaya, Thon Buri, and Bangkok.

> **Roughly the size of Texas, Thailand lies at the heart of Southeast Asia. It borders Myanmar (Burma) to the west, Laos and Cambodia to the east, and Malaysia to the south.**

Above the central plains is the mountainous north. Here is the country's highest mountain, Doi Inthanon, at 8,415 feet (2,565 m). Rivers such as the Mekong, Nan, Yom, and Ping feed the spectacular tumbling waterfalls for which the region is noted. Caves, too, are plentiful—burrowed deep into limestone mountains. Varying rainfalls and rugged terrain preclude large rice crops here, but temperate fruits such as oranges, apples, and tomatoes thrive. The north was once heavily forested with teak and other handsome trees, but logging, agriculture, and slash-and-burn farming have destroyed vast areas. Logging has been banned since 1989, and many national parks have been created. But logging continues illegally—often with the compliance of corrupt officials in national parks—and remains one of Thailand's greatest environmental problems. It is estimated that 50 years ago forests covered 70 percent of Thailand; today, the figure stands at just 15 percent.

The arid northeast region, also known as Issan, sprawls across 66,000 square miles (170,000 sq km). Its dominant feature, the 655-foot-high (200 m) Khorat

Patchworks of cultivated land and mountains predominate in much of northern Thailand's landscape

Enormous karst formations typify Thailand's far south landscape.

Plateau, reaches north to the Mekong River, which forms most of the border with Laos, and south to the Dongrek Mountains, on the Cambodian border. It is harsh land, often subject to drought and floods, suitable for hardy crops such as tapioca and cotton, and for mulberry trees, whose leaves are used to feed silk worms.

Down the Malay Peninsula, much of the tropical rain forest that once blanketed the region has been lost to rubber and coconut plantations and illegal logging, but pockets still exist, mainly in the mountainous national parks that form the spine of the peninsula. The most outstanding features of the south, however, are the gigantic limestone formations that explode from the Andaman Sea; these are best seen in the provinces of Phangna and Krabi. On the east coast, the scenery is more sedate, with wildlife-rich mangrove forests. Off both sides of the peninsula are many

offshore islands, some popular tourists spots, others pristine gems of rain forest, coconut trees, sparkling white sand, and colorful coral and marine life.

Flora & Fauna

The remaining forests—almost all within national parks—are deciduous, tropical monsoon forests in central, northern, and northeastern Thailand, and rain forests in southern Thailand, where seasons are less distinct and rainfall is heavier. Relatively abundant mangrove forests exist along the coast near river mouths and amid the limestone crags of southern Thailand.

Thailand affords a wide variety of habitats for flora and fauna. Its most celebrated plant is the orchid (see pp. 246–247), with about a thousand species. Abundant tropical plants include acacia, bougainvillea, hibiscus, lotus, and frangipani. In the northern regions, rhododendrons and azaleas thrive. There are some 27,000 species of flowering plants in all.

> **The most outstanding features of the south ... are the gigantic limestone formations that explode from the Andaman Sea.**

As Thailand's forests disappear, so does much of its wildlife. Tiger numbers have plummeted, mostly through poaching. Elephants, so admired and, at times, even revered by Thais, survive in dwindling numbers in national parks and elephant sanctuaries. Of the 5,000 or so that remain, about half are domesticated. Shy Asiatic brown bears, also victims of poachers, are found only in small numbers. Gibbons remain in relatively high numbers, along with other primates, such as macaque monkeys, plus wild boar, various species of deer, and flying squirrels. Thailand is also home to the rare khun kitti bat, the world's smallest, and the tiny mouse deer. There are more than a hundred species of snake, including the poisonous king cobra. It grows up to 20 feet (6 m), but is small fry compared with the nonvenomous, reticulated python, which may grow to an incredible 50 feet (15 m). Also formidable, and sometimes tetchy, is the monitor lizard, found in the south, which can reach 7 feet (2 m).

Thailand is rich in bird life, with more than a thousand resident and migratory species, including the great hornbill, the white-crested laughing thrush, and the swiftlet, with its edible nest (see p. 333). Bird-watchers should head for Khao Yai National Park, near Bangkok, Khao Sam Roi Yot, south of the capital, and Thaleh Noi Waterfowl Park, in the far south. ■

Food & Drink

Thailand is truly blessed when it comes to food. It is quite possible to eat for a month without having to order the same dish twice (indeed, it is highly recommended that you do just that)—though once you have discovered a special favorite, you will probably find it becoming a regular choice for awhile.

Eating will be one of the highlights of your stay in Thailand. Although different regions of Thailand claim certain foods and recipes for their own, you will be able to find amazing dishes from all parts of the kingdom, wherever you are.

Staying at a good class hotel gives reasonable (though not guaranteed) assurance that the restaurant food will be of a high quality, the service will be good, and the menu will be extensive. If you want to pepper your meal with a bit of extra culture, don't be afraid to try the cleaner restaurants frequented by the locals. All restaurants must abide by health regulations as laid down by the local council (this does not apply to street vendors or temporary roadside eateries, which must be approached with caution). So eating hot stir-fried meals, curries, or soups in a clean restaurant can be regarded as safe.

Avoid dishes that are kept on display (ducks and chickens hanging in glass cabinets, for example). Don't accept seafood upcountry, and forget about experimenting with grasshoppers and locusts because the chances are they met their fate by insecticide poisoning.

Thai-style dining is a very sociable affair. Unless the food is served *jarn deeyo* as an individual meal (fried rice or *pad thai,* for example), the main dishes will be placed in the center of the dining table, or, more traditionally, laid out on a mat placed on the floor, and everybody is free to ladle small portions onto their own plate of rice as they eat.

Staples

Rice *(kow)* is the staple of the Thai diet, and most meals are served with boiled white rice *(kow suay).* There are, however, many variations. Rice porridge *(jok)* and rice soup *(kow tom)* make good breakfast dishes,

though they are often eaten late in the evening for supper as well. Sticky rice *(kow neeyao),* which is popular in the north and northeastern provinces, is eaten with the hand and dipped into soups and pastes. Fried rice is also very popular and can be ordered in many styles, including chicken *(gai),* pork *(mu),* prawn *(goong),* and vegetarian *(jay).* Also worth trying is *"kow pud American,"* a legacy of American soldiers stationed in Thailand during the Vietnam War. This is undoubtedly the mother of all fried rice dishes, made with such special additions as sausages, vegetables, and pineapple—all mixed in with ketchup and nicely crowned with a fried egg.

Noodles *(pad),* introduced in Thailand from China, also play a large role in the Thai diet and are served in many forms. One distinctly Thai variety is pad thai (literally, "fried Thai"), a favorite among Thais and travelers alike. Thin noodles are fried with a blend of sweet and bitter sauces, tofu, egg, and dried shrimp to produce a great meal, which will not be complete until you have added the complementary peanuts and a squeeze of lemon.

Another favorite dish is *pad see yoo,* often listed on menus in English as "Chinese-style noodles in soy sauce." Flat noodles are fried together with egg and *kanar* (a popular green vegetable) in soy sauce. Make use of the extra condiments that are usually provided (vinegar, sugar, dried chili powder, and the ever present fish sauce) to create a taste to suit yourself.

Regional Specialties

The following are the dishes that visitors will come across most often, classified by region.

Central Thailand: Many dishes originating from this region use coconut milk *(gati)* and

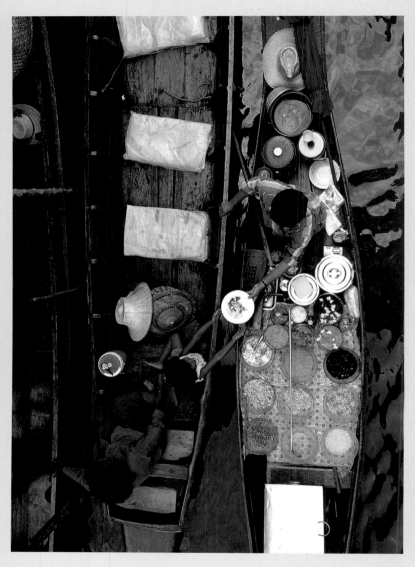

Floating markets, like this one at Damnoen Saduak, still form an intrinsic part of community life in the canals near Bangkok.

chili paste *(nam prik)* as a base to which vegetables, herbs, and seasonings are added to produce a curry. Most curries include meat.

Gai pud med mamuang himapaan (fried chicken and cashews): Cashews, chicken, and oyster sauce are the main ingredients, a bit exclusive because of the price of cashews.

Complements most Thai dishes well.

Panang (Thai red curry): Usually made with chicken (gai) or pork (mu). Other ingredients include garlic, red onion, lemongrass, chopped kaffir leaves, basil, and Thai spices.

Tom ka gai (sweet, sour, and spicy chicken soup): Plenty of mushrooms, basil, and galangal root *(kar)* are blended with other favorite sauces and seasonings to give a very distinctive Thai flavor.

Tom yum goong (sour and spicy prawn soup): In July 1999 a survey by the National Culture Commission of more than 500 Thai restaurants worldwide concluded that tom yum goong was the favorite Thai dish. Most Thais would agree with the results of that survey.

Thais use red-hot chilies to spice up many dishes. Despite their tiny size, these *prik kee noo* are the hottest peppers around.

Yum woon sen (mixed jelly noodles): *Yum* means to mix together; jelly noodles (similar to vermicelli) are mixed with peppers, lemon juice, fish sauce, scallions, parsley, onion and, usually, either minced pork (pre-boiled) or prawns.

Northern Thailand: *Gang hunglay* (pork and ginger stew): The combination of ginger, curry powder, and Thai sauces produces a sweet stew usually eaten on rice. Highly recommended.

Kow soi gai (spicy northern chicken curry): An interesting mixture of large pieces of chicken and both soft and crunchy noodles set in a smooth curry. This dish is always hot enough to tickle the back of the throat but has a nice flavor that is both sweet and spicy.

Nam prik ong (mild red chili paste with pork and tomato): You may have difficulty finding it in high-class restaurants, but nam prik ong is a favorite of locals in the north as it's convenient to eat with sticky rice and makes for a very cheap meal.

A surprising number of chili paste styles are available in the north (as well as the rest of the country), created by using different types of chili peppers with varying combinations of vegetables, meat, and seasoning. Nam prik ong tends to be one of the milder forms of these pastes, but is probably still best left to chili freaks.

The Northeast (Issan): *Larp* (spicy ground meat): Larp is made from cooked ground chicken, pork, beef, or fish and relies on a blend of mint, basil, and other herbs and spices. It is also possible to find water buffalo-flavored larp *(larp kwai)* in rural areas. (For vampires, there is even *larp lueat,* which is raw meat, usually water buffalo, minced with fresh blood and spices.)

Som tam (papaya salad): This is sometimes known as papaya *bok-bok* because of the sound produced by the striking of the pestle against the mortar as the ingredients are pounded together. The primary ingredient is shredded green papaya, mixed in with tomatoes, beans, garlic, miniature dried shrimp, a dash of fish sauce, lemon juice, and honey. This produces a tangy taste, which is characteristic of other Thai dishes. Often a whole crab or two will be thrown in *(som tam pu),* or, if you prefer something slightly less crunchy, you could order it with peanuts instead *(som tam thai).* Thais tend to prefer their som tam quite spicy; it is probably a good idea to order som tam without chili peppers, as just one rebellious pepper is enough to ruin an otherwise enjoyable experience. Som tam is eaten with sticky rice and often complemented with grilled chicken *(gai yang),* fried pork *(mu yang),* and/or larp.

Southern Thailand: *Kow yum:* The distinctive sweet, sour, and salty flavor of this dish relies on a specially prepared mix of fish sauce, roasted ground coconut, prawns, fruit, vegetables, and herbs. You stir a bowl of rice into the dish. Highly recommended.

Massaman gai: This is a spicy curry popular among Muslims, with chicken and potatoes in a thick massaman sauce. It is a very satisfying meal, eaten with rice and/or roti (flat bread).

Fruit

There is a vast array of delicious fruit in Thailand, many of which you may never have seen before. Try to visit at least one fresh fruit and produce market during your stay (they are most active in the mornings.). You'll get some great photo opportunities, and the tantalizing sights, sounds, tastes, and smells make it a truly memorable experience.

Well-known fruits that grow year-round in abundance here include bananas (kluay), coconuts (maphrao), watermelon (taeng moe), and pineapples (sap-parote). Also available year-round are other fruits that are less familiar to visitors:

Cantaloop (cantaloupe): Tropical melon, very sweet and juicy when ripe.

Falang (guava): Thais often eat guava (and mangoes) while they are still unripe, sprinkling them with a mixture of sugar, salt, and ground chili pepper.

Malakawe (papaya): The unripe fruit is used in salad (see som tam, opposite). When ripe, its orange flesh is slightly sweet and very juicy.

Mang-khut (mangosteen): Much prized, sweet white fruit in a hard, purple shell.

Ngor (rambutan): Small, hairy, bright red fruit with sweet, litchi-like flesh.

Som-oh (pomelo): The largest of all citrus fruit, not unlike a large, sweet grapefruit.

Seasonal Fruits: Lumyai (longan): A small, round, sweet fruit with a brown shell, grown in the north (predominantly in Chiang Mai) and most widely available during the northern rainy season from June to September.

Ma muang (mango): There are many varieties of mango, most of them appearing from April through the hotter months. They are often eaten as dessert with sweet sticky rice and coconut milk syrup (kow neeyao mc-muang).

Toorian (durian): This bizarre-looking fruit has the appearance of a spiky football and a smell that could lose you friends. People love it or hate it. Mostly available May to June.

Drink

Some of the fruits available in Thailand are transformed in restaurants into deliciously refreshing juices. Try naam falang, made with guava, or naam lumyai, made with longan.

Drinking alcoholic beverages is traditionally a male pastime, though it is becoming common to see young women drinking beer (usually locally brewed "import" Heineken) or wine. The men generally prefer beer or Thai whiskey, such as Saeng Thip or Mekong—or more expensive, foreign imports to show social status.

EXPERIENCE: Fruit Carving

Not content to have one of the best tasting cuisines in the world, Thais strive to make the most beautiful food as well. Through kae sa luk, fruit or vegetable carving, Thais transform carrots, chilies, and even watermelon into works of art, using only a small knife. Whether to make fruit salads more attractive, garnish a meal, or learn a new art, visitors can learn carving techniques quickly through classes or experimentation. Any cooking supply store will have the small, ornamental knives, and there are myriad books on the subject. Many cooking schools give brief classes; some offer more intense study: **The Carving Institute** (Bangkok, tel 084-932-7811, www.carvinginstitute.com) Offers a five-day course. **Samui Institute of Thai Culinary Arts** (46/6 Moo 3, Chaweng Beach, Ko Samui 84320, tel 077-413172, www.sitca.net /index.htm)

History of Thailand

From the early centuries of the first millennium, a succession of dynasties conquered and ruled various parts of Thailand. With the rise of the Sukhothai Kingdom in the mid-13th century, though, the country gained its true identity. From the 12th to the mid-20th centuries foreigners used the name Siam, but citizens called their country the name of the ruling dynasty's capital.

Archaeological evidence is sketchy, but it is thought that the Mekong River Valley and the Khorat Plateau in northeast Thailand and parts of Laos and Cambodia were inhabited more than 10,000 years ago. Farming implements dating from about 3500 B.C. have been uncovered at Spirit Cave near Mae Hong Song and at Ban Kao in Kanchanaburi. The most significant archaeological finds, however, were made at Ban Chiang in the northeast. Here, bronze tools and other implements dating from 3000 B.C.—earlier than those discovered in the Middle East, which was thought to be the center of the Bronze Age—were found. So, too, was decorated pottery as well as evidence of agriculture, which indicate that the area once supported a thriving and sophisticated culture.

....

The most significant archaeological finds were made at Ban Chiang in the northeast. Here, bronze tools ... dating from 3000 B.C.—earlier than those discovered in the Middle East ...—were found.

....

Thailand's early inhabitants were gradually displaced and absorbed by the Tai peoples moving down into Southeast Asia from China from about the first century A.D. A further, and much larger, wave of migration followed in the mid-13th century as people fled the forces of Chinese emperor Kublai Khan (r. 1260–1294). They settled in the northern reaches of Myanmar (Burma), Thailand, Cambodia, and Vietnam.

There is also conjecture that early Tai peoples originated in Thailand and moved through Southeast Asia and into China, establishing a center at Nanchao, in modern China's Yunnan Province. After the Mongol armies invaded Nanchao in 1253, these people moved south again and resettled in Thailand.

Srivijaya Period (2nd–13th Centuries)

The Srivijaya Kingdom spread from its southern capital in Sumatra in Indonesia, northward through Malaysia, gradually making its way up to Thailand's southern peninsula, and establishing centers in Nakhon Si Thammarat and Chaiya in Surat Thani Province around the eighth century. Some argue that the name Chaiya is a derivation of Srivijaya (or Srivichai, as Thais refer to it), which would point to the city's major role in the empire. Many artifacts found at Chaiya—one of Thailand's oldest cities—are Srivijayan. (They can be seen in the National Museum in Bangkok.)

Dvaravati (Mon) Period (6th–13th Centuries)

Before the tidal wave of migration of Tai peoples from southern China in the mid-13th century, the Mon had forged a loose collection of city-states with the likely

Once the main transport arteries of Bangkok, nearly all of the *khlongs*, or canals, have been filled in and replaced by roads.

Ancient murals in temples often relate tales of the Thai epic, the *Ramakien*.

capital at Nakhon Pathom, west of Bangkok. Archaeological work here has uncovered evidence of the Mon, including coins bearing Sanskrit inscriptions of the name Dvaravati. Most of the historical and cultural evidence of this mysterious kingdom, save for a few temple ruins (Wat Kukut in Lamphun is the most significant), remain lost in time. The Dvaravati Kingdom is known to have included Hariphunchai, established in 661 A.D. near present-day Lamphun, as well as Nakhon Pathom. The much traveled Chinese monk Xuan Zang mentions the area as Tuoluobodi in a description of a pilgrimage to India. At its peak, the kingdom may have extended from southern Myanmar (Burma), across Thailand's central plains, and into western Cambodia.

The Mon were originally a missionary tribe from India, sent to spread the word of Buddhism, who moved east through the mountain ranges of Myanmar. Indian records note that the religion was promoted throughout Southeast Asia in the third century A.D. by Theravada Buddhist missionaries sent by the Mogul king Ashoka in India.

The Mon presence at Nakhon Pathom and the lower Chao Phraya river basin, along with its eastern outposts, were swallowed up by the westward march of the Khmers from their capital at Angkor in Cambodia. The only Mon stronghold to survive Khmer territorial gains was Hariphunchai. It managed to hold out until 1281, when the armies of the Lanna Kingdom conquered it.

Khmer Period (8th–13th Centuries)

At its height, the Khmer Empire was the dominant power in Southeast Asia; its influence spread from its capital at Angkor, in Cambodia, west to the Myanmar border with Thailand, north to Laos, and south as far as Nakhon Si Thammarat in Thailand. It set up centers in That Phanom and Sakhon Nakhon in the central Mekong Valley; Phimai and Phanom Rung in Khorat; and Lop Buri, Nakhon Pathom, and Phetchaburi in the Chao Phraya Basin; and Sukhothai, Si Satchanalai, and Phitsanulok in the central plains.

The Khmers built grand temples and cities. Two of the best extant examples are the ruins at Prasat Hin Phimai and at Prasat Phanom Rung—both of which have been restored. Connecting these was a Royal Road, which was notable for its engineering and for the construction of rest houses, clinics, and places of worship for pilgrims along its route.

The Khmer Empire was ruled by a succession of god-kings and, up until the 12th century, worshipped the Brahmanic gods of Hinduism. The great King Jayavarman VII then adopted Mahayana Buddhism as the official religion, although Brahmanic rituals and gods were maintained. By the mid-12th century Lop Buri had become the kingdom's cultural center as leaders in the scattering of Khmer cities began to assert their independence. Angkor's authority soon diminished, and by the mid-13th century the Khmer Empire was in rapid decline.

Lanna Kingdom (1259–1558)

Before the rise of the Sukhothai Kingdom, several small fiefdoms claimed territory around the Mekong River and in Chiang Mai in northern Thailand. These were gradually overshadowed by the Lanna Kingdom, which centered on Chiang Mai and held sway in the north for some three centuries.

The most outstanding Lanna king was its founder, Mengrai (r. 1259–1317). As a young prince, Mengrai fought successful military campaigns to expand his empire and unify warring principalities. He transferred the capital from Chiang Saen to Chiang Rai and aligned with rulers from states to the south, many of whom were princes he befriended when studying at Lop Buri in his youth. Allies included the Sukhothai and Phayao, as well as the Pegu in Burma.

In 1281 Mengrai conquered the Mon at Hariphunchai. In 1292 he moved his capital again, this time to Chiang Mai, where it flourished for another 260 years. He later formed an alliance with the Pagan of upper Myanmar and repulsed an attack of Mongols from the Chinese,

who resented his choice of Chiang Mai as capital. Under Mengrai, Lanna became strong and prosperous, controlling the Shan to the west and the Lao to the north and northeast. Mengrai adopted Sinhalese Buddhism.

After Mengrai's death in 1317, the Lanna Kingdom declined as successors to the throne

EXPERIENCE: Tattoos

The tattoo traditions of Thailand date back to the Khmer Empire at Angkor. More than body art, tattoos endowed their wearers with magical properties that protected them in battle and were status symbols that no honorable man would be found without. Today, tattoos remain sacred markings that are believed to grant seductive powers, protect wearers from illness, or even stop bullets.

One place where this tradition thrives is **Wat Bang Phra** in Amphor Nakom Chaisri (tel 034-389-3333). In addition to hosting a tattoo festival in March, the temple is a popular destination for traditional Sak Yant charcoal tattoos given daily by monks. Arrive at 8 a.m., buy flowers or cigarettes as an offering to Buddha, and enter the temple, where you sit down and wait your turn. The monks manually pierce the skin with a long steel needle and blow on the completed design to endow it with magical power.

fought over sovereignty. By 1328 stability hac returned, and the kingdom began to reassert itself, especially under the rule of King Ku Na (r.1355–1385). Ku Na continued to promote Sinhalese Buddhism, which became the preeminent cultural force and religion in the kingdom (until Theravada Buddhism became the dominant religion in the next century). King Tilok (r.1441–1487) was Lanna's last great king. He warded off attacks on Lamphun, extended the empire, and fought off Ayutthaya's territorial designs. After his death, lengthy battles with Ayutthaya continued, and a succession of civil wars gradually weakened Lanna. It was finally overrun by the Burmese, who used it as a base for battles with Ayutthaya.

Sukhothai Period (1238–1360)

Thai leaders of Khmer principalities in the Mekong Valley began to seize the initiative from their autocratic rulers in Angkor as the central rule of this once great city rapidly fell into decline. In 1238 a small battalion led by Prince Indraditya routed the garrison

Several Ayutthaya kings used Wat Phra Si Sanphet as the royal temple-palace.

at the relatively unimportant Khmer city of Sukhothai and took over. Eventually, other principalities joined Indraditya to smash Khmer control and establish the kingdom of Sukhothai (Rising of Happiness), with Indraditya declaring himself its first sovereign.

During Indraditya's 40-year rule, Sukhothai remained relatively small. But by the end of the reign of Indraditya's son Ramkamhaeng, Sukhothai's second king, in 1318, the kingdom had spread from Luang Prabang in Laos, through Thailand's central plains, and on to the Malay Peninsula in the south. Sukhothai is recognized as the first true Thai kingdom. Although the Sukhothai period was relatively short, its legacy of culture, politics, and religion shaped the foundations of a new Thai identity. Most of these achievements have been credited to the rule of Ramkamhaeng (r 1279–1298).

The legend of King Ramkamhaeng began early in his life. At 19, on a military campaign with his father, he challenged a neighboring state's leader to hand-to-hand combat on the back of an elephant. His victory earned him the title of Ramkamhaeng—Rama the Bold. But Ramkamhaeng didn't always use the sword to expand his empire. He used skillful diplomacy and political wisdom to unite the Thai peoples and keep potential enemies on his side (forming alliances with the northern kingdoms of Phayao and Lanna, and establishing diplomatic relations with China). He also fostered marriages between ruling houses in his dominions to entrench loyalty and solidarity.

Golden Era: Ramkamhaeng presided over what Thais like to call their golden era. He was a visionary monarch whose contributions to Thai culture, education, and art were enormous. He is credited with inventing the Thai alphabet, borrowing elements of Khmer and Mon script and adding Thai tonal marks. One of the first examples of the new language was an inscribed stela, carved in 1292, which detailed Sukhothai life and Ramkamhaeng's achievements. These included his meritorious elephant-back victory, as well as the prosperity and progressiveness of the kingdom (free trade, abundant food, the ending of slavery, the right to inheritance, and so forth).

Ramkamhaeng showed scant prejudices in borrowing the best from other cultures and refining this to the demands of a nascent Thai identity. The architecture of his temple complexes shows influences of the Khmer and the Mon, but he added flourishes of sometimes subliminal art to both the interiors and exteriors of temples and palaces. Sukhothai artists, artisans, and architects slowly developed their own styles under his patronage to create what is now recognized as the most sophisticated Thai artistic style.

During his reign, Ramkamhaeng revived Theravada Buddhism, using its precepts as a platform of governance. This enlightened approach earned Sukhothai a peace and prosperity that was unrivaled by any of the preceding kingdoms.

Decline of Sukhothai: After Ramkamhaeng's death, Sukhothai fell into terminal decline as subsequent kings were unable to maintain political and economic power. Ramkamhaeng's son, Lo Thai (r. 1298–1347), largely neglected affairs of state, enveloping himself in religious pursuits and the construction of temples to enhance his personal merit. By the time of Lo Thai's death, Sukhothai was facing the ever increasing threat from one of its upstart dominions, Ayutthaya.

The last significant Sukhothai ruler was Ramkamhaeng's grandson, Li Thai (r. 1347–1368), who continued to surrender power to Ayutthaya but remained a strong patron of the arts. Many of Sukhothai's great temples were created during his reign. Under Ayutthaya's eventual rule, Sukhothai became little more than a regional outpost. The town was abandoned in 1438 and was all but forgotten for four centuries, until its rediscovery in the mid-19th century. It is now a popular historical park at the modern city of Sukhothai.

> The persistent Burmese continued their attacks on the kingdom. All-out war developed, and they laid siege to the capital. In 1767, Ayutthaya was overrun and destroyed.

Ayutthaya Period (1350–1767)

Late in the 14th century, after the Khmer Empire disintegrated and the Burmese Empire at Pagan was sacked by the Mongols, mainland Southeast Asia experienced a power vacuum. Lanna's power in northern Thailand was enigmatic, while Sukhothai puttered along under the leadership of Ramkamhaeng's descendants. The scene was set for a new power to hold together the Thai peoples.

The key turned out to be Suphan Buri, a relatively small Sukhothai suzerainty that had claimed independence from Sukhothai after Ramkamhaeng's death but lacked the strength to carry out its aim fully until the rise to power of U Thong (r. 1350–1369). A cholera outbreak in 1351 forced the new leader to move his population from the present-day area of U Thong to Ayutthaya, a site almost completely surrounded by rivers. He took the name Ramathibodi and declared himself king. He immediately began expanding his empire with a prolonged, bloody assault on Sukhothai and military campaigns against smaller Thai dominions in the south.

The accessible monarchy established by the kings of Sukhothai was replaced by the Khmer notion of god-kings—an absolute monarchy whose power was mandated by divine forces. Although this tradition was tempered to some extent by Ramathibodi's embrace of Theravada Buddhism as the major religion, he and subsequent Ayutthaya kings employed the Khmer rituals of royal court, carving a divide between royalty and subjects.

Other Ayutthaya Kings: After Ramathibodi's death in 1369, his son Ramasuen (r. 1369–1370, 1388–1395) became leader. He was overthrown shortly afterward by Boromraja I, who held control for 18 years, continuing attacks on Sukhothai, capturing Nakhon Sawan, Phitsanulok, and Kamphaeng Phet, claiming suzerainty over Sukhothai, and waging war against Lanna. Ramasuen regained power in 1388, captured the Lanna capital of Chiang Mai in 1390, and successfully staved off the Burmese to the west. In 1431 Ayutthaya's armies marched into Angkor, forcing the Khmer rulers to flee to Phnom Penh. Fighting with the Lanna continued for more than 100 years. The reign of King Boroma Trailokanath, known as Trailok (r. 1448–1488), gathered together the kingdom's states under centralized rule, bringing military and administrative controls to Ayutthaya. He instituted the *sakdi naa* system of land ownership, which set up rules and rankings of social status and hierarchy that were to shape Thailand's social order for another four centuries and that still exist in a similar, but less emphatic, form today. Trailok also required men to contribute their labor for a certain period of time each year. Trade was brought under royal control, and the kingdom prospered despite remaining perpetually in a state of war.

The Burmese sacked Ayutthaya in 1569. Most of the court and citizenry were captured and held as hostages in Pegu. Prince Naresuen (r. 1590–1605), who inherited the throne from his father, reversed this humiliating defeat a few years later, in 1584.

By now Ayutthaya was receiving a growing number of European visitors. Portugal had set up an embassy in 1511. A century later, others began arriving—the Dutch (1605), the

Royal barges such as these are still seen on Bangkok's Chao Phraya river.

English (1612), the Danes (1621), and the French (1662). European influence peaked during the reign of King Narai (r. 1656–1688). European traders and diplomats were awed by Ayutthaya's grandeur—it had developed into the most magnificent city in Southeast Asia. The kingdom's affair with Europe ended with the expulsion of a garrison of 600 French soldiers, which King Narai had earlier allowed to be based in the city (the Thai word for foreigner, *farang*, comes from the abbreviated name for the French, *farangset*) as fears grew about French intentions. Foreigners were subsequently shut out for 150 years.

The persistent Burmese continued their attacks on the kingdom. All-out war developed, and they laid siege to the capital. In 1767, Ayutthaya was overrun and destroyed.

Foundations of Bangkok

The destruction of its great capital might have been the end of the Thai nation had it not been for the military prowess of Praya Taksin (r. 1767–1782), a half-Chinese,

King Mongkut began the modernization of Thailand and invited Western ideas.

half-Thai general. Taksin organized an army, drove the Burmese from Ayutthaya, and regained control of the country. He abandoned Ayutthaya as the capital, moving it to a more defensible location at Thon Buri, a small fishing village on the Chao Phraya river, opposite present-day Bangkok. Despite his military success, Taksin was not an effective ruler. He neglected his administrative duties, became increasingly brutal, and slowly went insane. When he declared himself the reincarnation of the Buddha, his ministers removed him from office. He was executed in the fashion reserved for royalty—beaten to death in a velvet sack so his blood would not touch the ground.

Chakri Dynasty (1872–Present)

Another general, Chao Phraya Chakri, came to power and was crowned Ramathibodi (r.1782–1809). His original name is given to the Chakri dynasty, whose royal lineage continues to this day. Ramathibodi moved the capital to Rattanakosin island, in present-day Bangkok, in 1782. He began securing the city from the restless Burmese and restoring the grandeur of the Thai art and architecture destroyed at Ayutthaya.

Successors—King Phutthalaetia, known as Rama II (r.1809–1824), and his son King Nangklao, known as Rama III (r.1824–1851)—continued Ramathibodi's rebuilding of Thai civilization. Rama II is remembered for the construction of Wat Arun and was famed as a great poet, developing the Thai version of the Indian Hindu epic, the *Ramayana*, the *Ramakien*. Following his predecessors' tentative contacts with European powers, Rama III continued to open the doors to the West but remained suspicious of its motives. He was deeply religious and conservative, and was not highly regarded by the Europeans and Americans intent on forcing more trade with Siam.

Rama III's elder halfbrother, Prince Mongkut (r.1851–1868), who had forgone ascension to the throne in order to enter the monkhood, became the next Chakri monarch as Rama IV. Mongkut had used his 27 years of monastic life well, learning Latin and English so that he could study Western culture. He had a keen interest in the sciences, history, geography, and astronomy—all put to good use during his reign.

Modernization of Siam

Mongkut's son, Chulalongkorn, or Rama V (r.1868–1910), continued his father's work of reform and modernization. He opened Thailand's first hospital and its first post and telegraph office, and he set about linking the various parts of the country with a network of roads and rail. He built up a civil service, further improved the educational system, and ended the age-old practice of compulsory state labor.

In his battle to maintain Siam's independence—Britain had colonized Burma and Malaysia, and France had control of most of Indochina—he ceded parts of the then extended kingdom of Siam to Indochina and Burma. The French occupied Chanthaburi and Trat provinces on the Cambodian border in 1893 and did not hand them back to Siam until 1905. (More land was later ceded to the French, whose colonization continued until 1941.)

British-educated King Vajiravudh, or Rama VI (r.1910–1925), is chiefly remembered for continuing his father's modernization of the country. He introduced compulsory education and made other educational reforms, and established Thailand's first university (Chulalongkorn). His reign witnessed the first attempt to overthrow the absolute monarchy, made in 1912 by the Thai military. Coups were a feature of the Thai political scene during the 20th century.

Modern Age (1925–Present)

Prajadhiphok, Vajiravudh's brother and Chulalongkorn's 76th child and youngest son, reigned as Rama VII (r.1925–1935), the last absolute monarch of the Chakri dynasty. In 1932 democratically minded students, with the help of the military, overthrew the monarchy in a bloodless coup d'etat. When Prajadhiphok learned of the coup, he was playing golf at Hua Hin, south of Bangkok.

A civilian/military government was set up. The monarchy's absolute power was replaced by a constitutional monarchy, leaving royalty with a largely ceremonial role in state affairs. Royalist sympathizers launched an unsuccessful attempt to reinstate absolute monarchy in another coup d'etat in 1933. In 1935

King Mongkut

Mongkut was a wise, progressive leader. He was the first Thai king to realize that Siam's independence could be retained by moving his country into the modern era and encouraging contact and trade with the West. He also began reforming the legal system, promoting social reforms and modeling Siam's education system along Western lines. Mongkut died of malaria in 1868, shortly after returning from a trip to Phetchaburi, south of Bangkok, with an entourage of European diplomats who had traveled there to observe a solar eclipse—which, legend holds, Mongkut had predicted.

Prajadhiphok abdicated and went into self-imposed exile in Britain without declaring an heir. The government decided that his nephew, ten-year-old Prince Ananda Mahidol (r.1935–1946), would be king. Ananda was born in Germany and studied in Switzerland before arriving in Thailand in December 1945.

Meanwhile, the military leader Phibun (Pibul) Songkhram (1897–1964) bullied his way into leading the government in 1938. He renamed the country Thailand in 1939 and remained in power, on and off, until after World War II. Ananda was shot dead in his palace bedroom in June 1946 under mysterious circumstances. Bhumibol Adulyadej, his younger brother, became Rama IX and continues to rule as king today (see pp. 74–75). Although they were never convicted of the crime, two of Ananda's attendants—generally considered to be scapegoats—were arrested and later, in 1954, executed. The facts of Ananda's death have never been established; referring to the event remains virtually taboo in Thailand.

Out of expediency, Thailand allowed the occupation of Japanese troops during World War II and declared war on the Allies—although the Thai ambassador to the United States, Seni Pramoj (1905–1997), refused to deliver the declaration to Washington. Pibul resigned in 1944 under pressure from Thailand's resistance movement, and ambassador Seni became premier. However, he was unseated two years later in a general election as Pridi Phanomyong (1900–1983), a left-wing intellectual and one of the leaders of the 1932 coup d'etat, took control of a civilian government. But that was also short-lived. Pibul returned and led a successful coup in 1947, suspending the constitution. He took a strong anti-Communist stance, pandering to U.S. and French policies in Southeast Asia.

> **Suchinda and the leader of the protestors ... were hauled before King Bhumibol, who told them to end the madness.**

During the 1950s and 1960s, Thailand's succession of military governments ruled with an iron fist. From the mid-1960s to the early 1970s, the U.S. was allowed to set up military bases in the country to support its campaign in Vietnam. In 1973, thousands of students gathered at Thammasat University in Bangkok and demanded an end to military rule and a new constitution. The ruling generals, Thanom Kittikachorn (1912–) and Praphat Charusathien, called in troops and a bloodbath ensued.

In one of his rare forays into politics, the highly respected King Bhumibol, with another moderate, General Krit Sivara, condemned the violence. Thanom and Praphat fled the country. Democratic elections followed, and left-leaning Kukrit Pramoj (1911–1995; brother of Seni) headed a multiparty coalition government.

But democracy was short-lived. When Thanom returned to Thailand in 1976 in the guise of a monk, students again protested at Thammasat University. Police and paramilitary right-wingers attacked the students, killing hundreds. Using the unrest as an excuse, the military pushed aside the government and took control. As a result, thousands of students, intellectuals, and other disillusioned people fled to the countryside, joining the left-wing People's Liberation Army of Thailand (PLAT). By the time the moderate, military-installed leader Prem Tinsulanonda (1920–) took power in 1980, PLAT and the Communist Party of Thailand had combined forces that numbered well over 10,000.

Prem ruled for eight years, introducing political stability and reform. He reduced the ranks of the PLAT and the Communist Party of Thailand through military campaigns and offers of amnesty. In 1988, after general elections, Chatichai Choonhavan (1922–1998) became Thailand's prime minister. He oversaw the country's further democratization and its unprecedented economic growth, but did little to curb rampant corruption.

On February 23, 1991, a bloodless coup d'etat ended civilian rule; power was handed to the National Peace-Keeping Council (NPKC), led by General Suchinda Kraprayoon (1933–). A well-respected civilian, Anand Panyarachun (1932–), was appointed caretaker prime minister while a new constitution, which favored continued military participation in government, was drawn up and passed by parliament.

Elections were held in March 1992, heralding a five-party coalition as government. However, after military machinations, Suchinda took power, to the outrage of many Thai citizens. In May, tens of thousands of people took to the streets in protest. The military fired on the demonstrators, killing at least 50 people. Suchinda and the leader of the protesters, Bangkok governor Chamlong Srimuang, were hauled before King Bhumibol, who told them to end the madness. Suchinda resigned, and new elections held in September brought to power Chuan Leekpai (1938–), a man admired for his integrity.

The events of May 1992 were pivotal in the democratization of Thailand. A number of elections have been held since then without military meddling. In 2005, for the first time since the end of the absolute monarchy, a government, led by populist Prime Minister Thaksin Shinawatra, was reelected to a consecutive term. Thaksin, a telecom tycoon, created another first in Thai politics. When his party won more than 350 seats in the 500-seat parliament, he was given the luxury of ruling without the need for coalition partners.

Unfortunately, such authority may have led to his undoing. Despite passing populist policies that endeared him to rural voters, the prime minister was dogged by corruption allegations, particularly regarding the "tax-free" sale of his telecommunications giant to the government of Singapore. While attending a conference at the UN, Thaksin was deposed in a December 2006 coup that was met with open arms by Bangkokers, who overwhelmingly supported the rival Democratic Party and brought food and flowers to the soldiers.

After more than a year of peaceful protests, during which coup leaders organized a nationwide referendum to amend or replace the constitution (preventing future corruption of power, but undermining the democratic nature of the heralded 1997 constitution), the military regime, led by General Sonthi Boonyaratglin, kept its word: Elections were held. The remnants of Thaksin's party returned to power in a shaky coalition government, with the former prime minister living in exile with tax-evasion charges hanging over him. ∎

King Bhumibol, Thailand's highly respected king

The Arts

Thailand's artistic heritage was founded on an amalgam of Asian influences, but it has been crafted into a distinct style. Architecture, crafts, visual art, drama, literature, and song and dance all reveal elements drawn, at different stages, from Indian, Khmer, Chinese, Malay, and European cultures. Be prepared for a rich, startling array of Thai arts throughout the country.

Temple Art & Architecture

Religion was the prime mover behind the early development of Thai art. Thai Buddhist architects of the Sukhothai Kingdom—a period that saw the first real attempts to unify the Thai people—borrowed from Khmer temple architecture, then added their own distinctive, soaring multitiered rooftops and golden spires. Later, in the Ayutthaya period, Chinese influence predominated, with ornate decoration—particularly the use of porcelain fragments to veneer many *wat* (temple complex) buildings. This richness of ornamentation reached its peak in the first half of the 19th century, when glass mosaics highlighted gables and pillars, lacquerware and gold leaf adorned walls, and mother-of-pearl was inlaid into doors and shutters—the sum of which created a riot of color.

The most important and sacred structure within the *wat* is the *bot*, often the most spectacular building inside the temple compound.

Wat: An estimated 30,000 wats are scattered throughout the country, and they are much more than places of worship. This is especially so in smaller towns and villages, where they form an intrinsic part of the community, containing clinics, funeral homes, schools, community centers, places of entertainment, markets, and monasteries. Some even act as drug rehabilitation centers.

Inside the wats, you'll find numerous buildings that are each used for specific purposes. These include the *bot, wihan, chedi, prang, mondop, prasat,* and smaller structures such as the *sala* and *kutis.*

Wats often have names that reflect the history or religious significance of the compound. Many temples are prefixed with "Rat," "Raja," or "Racha" as a sign of respect to Thai royalty, members of whom were responsible for the construction or renovation of the buildings. Others make a more direct connection to the major benefactor by including the name of a specific king in the wat's moniker. Temples such as Wat Phra Kaeo in Bangkok are named after their central Buddha image, while those that are famed for their possession of a great *(maha)* and sacred *(that)* relic of the Buddha may include "Wat Mahathat" in their name.

Bot: The most important and sacred structure within the wat is the bot, often the most spectacular building inside the temple compound, replete with lavishly

The workmanship of temple art is often exquisitely detailed, as seen in these superb door carvings.

decorated shutters and doors and soaring roofs with gleaming towers. The bot is a meeting hall where religious ceremonies and monks' ordinations are held, and where novice monks meditate daily. Senior monks also use bots as a place to recite scriptures for Buddhist priesthood and to give sermons to supplicants.

These rectangular buildings are usually surrounded by eight sacred boundary stones known as *bai sema*. Resembling small tombstones and often enclosed within miniature tabernacles, these stones keep evil spirits outside the consecrated ground.

Intrinsic to a bot's exterior design are *chcfas*, carved finials curling up at roof extremities to represent *garudas* (mythical half-bird, half-human creatures). Interior murals follow a standard form. For example, the main mural behind the central Buddha image

Bangkok's Grand Palace and Wat Phra Kaeo exemplify Thai temple architecture.

shows the Buddhist cosmological order (see p. 140). Murals above the main entrance often show the enlightenment of the Buddha, or the devil divinity Mara, tempting the Buddha during his meditations. Murals on the side walls depict other stories from the life of the Buddha.

Wihan: This structure is the secondary assembly hall, where devotees gather to honor a wat's primary Buddha images. While there will be only one bot in a wat, there may be several wihans. The wihan is also used as a sermon hall for monks and lay worshippers.

Wihans lack the consecrated boundary stones that define the bot, but the wealth of exterior and interior murals often rivals those of the more significant building. Wihans found within larger complexes such as Wat Pho in Bangkok (see pp. 77–79) are enclosed by rectangular cloisters filled with images of the Buddha and backed by resplendent murals depicting such classic Buddhist tales as the *Ramakien*. The images inside the wihan may be repositories of ashes of devotees.

Chedi: Chedis are Indian-derived stupas—dome-shaped monuments that were originally designed to hold sacred Buddha relics such as texts, images, and bone fragments. (Many Thais believe that Buddha bone fragments have the power to reproduce themselves, so they can be distributed to thousands of other wats.) Later, chedis were built to cover and commemorate the remains of kings and saints. These days, they may hold the remains of anyone wealthy enough to afford the construction. In the hope that they will bring merit to the builder, many newer chedis are designed to replicate historic ones that contain Buddha relics.

The chedi is generally a bell-shaped structure. Raised on square or round terraces of diminishing size, it often dominates the grounds of the wat. The world's largest chedi is found at Nakhon Pathom near Bangkok (see pp. 120–121).

Mondops **are used for storing sacred texts and relics—often a Buddha footprint cast or carved in stone and much larger than life-size.**

Prang: Prangs are soaring towers; Thai prangs are modeled on those found in Khmer temples. Although they partly reflect the basic outline of a chedi, prangs are much slimmer in profile and more elegant than chedis. They are also more decorative, with imaginative rows of carved or cast demons and angels ringing the lower perimeter of the structure. Sometimes these are depicted in dancing poses, sometimes they appear to be supporting the prang. Decorative elements such as a thunderbolt, the symbol of the Hindu god Shiva, are found at the top of a prang. The stunning Wat Arun, standing on the western banks of the Chao Phraya river in Bangkok, is Thailand's best known prang.

Mondop: A mondop is a square-shaped building with a roof in the form of a stepped pyramid, topped by a slender spire. Mondops are used for storing sacred texts and relics—often a Buddha footprint cast or carved in stone and much larger than life-size. A good example is at Wat Phra Phutthabat, near Saraburi (see p. 143); highly venerated, it attracts tens of thousands of pilgrims each year.

Prasat: These sanctuary towers were adapted from those built during the Khmer era, when they were central features in a temple. The main tower of the prasat—the prang—and four smaller surrounding towers represent the peaks of Mount Meru, the center of the Hindu universe and home of the gods. In wats, prasats take on a less significant role, being used for secular functions, as well as religious ceremonies. Prasats designed for royal and secular ceremonies feature the sweeping, multileveled roofs seen on most buildings in the wat, while religious prasats take the Khmer form.

Sala: Salas are graciously styled, open-sided buildings used by pilgrims and monks to escape the heat of the day. They are also used as classrooms and community halls, and to provide over-night shelter for visitors during festivals.

Other Structures: The *hor rakang* is a small, simply constructed structure that contains a drum or bell tower used to call monks to ordinations, meals, or medita-tion. Most temples also have a *hor trai,* an elaborately carved and decorated library. It is often raised on stilts to keep insects and other pests from invading the building and damaging the texts. *Kutis* are monks' quarters, usually built behind a wall, fence, or canal to separate them from the wat's religious buildings. They tend to consist mainly of dormitories, with individual cells for only a small number of monks.

Some larger wats may have cloisters—open galleries displaying rows of Buddha images or small chedis. In many towns or villages, wats have a crematorium—its needle-like chimney is easily identifiable.

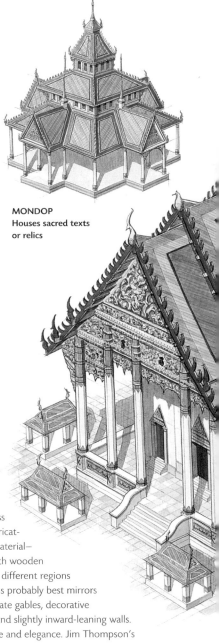

MONDOP
Houses sacred texts or relics

Domestic Architecture

Thai domestic architecture evolved from that of temple architecture, although it is less grandiose by necessity. Builders used prefabricat-ed panels of teakwood—the predominant material—attached to a framework of heavy pillars, with wooden pegs for joining. Various styles developed in different regions of the country. The style of the central plains probably best mirrors temple style, with steeply pitched roofs, ornate gables, decorative boardwalks separating different structures, and slightly inward-leaning walls. Ponds and gardens add to the sense of grace and elegance. Jim Thompson's House (see pp. 94–95) is a fine example.

Traditional Thai architecture began to decline in the early 1900s as Western tastes took over from—and in some cases blended with—local styles. In recent years some hotels have employed traditional Thai architecture with impressive results. One striking example is the Sukhothai Hotel in Bangkok, with its expansive, shallow pond and, in its lobby area, a row of small chedis built in naked brick.

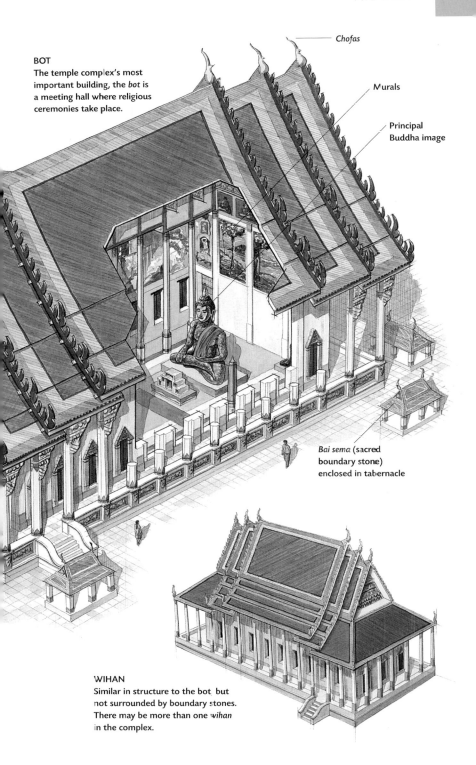

Chofas

BOT
The temple complex's most important building, the *bot* is a meeting hall where religious ceremonies take place.

Murals

Principal Buddha image

Bai sema (sacred boundary stone) enclosed in tabernacle

WIHAN
Similar in structure to the bot but not surrounded by boundary stones. There may be more than one *wihan* in the complex.

Classical Thai theater often employs masked dancers in scenes from the *Ramakien*.

Handicrafts

Many crafts, such as woodcarving, mother-of-pearl inlay, ceramics, and lacquerware, have their origins as decorative forms in temple architecture. Some crafts have inevitably declined with the modernization of Thailand and the loss of skilled craftsmen, but others have thrived because of the increase in foreign tourism and the demand for high-quality souvenirs. Woodcarving and silverwork both have maintained high standards, while woven silk manufactured in northeast Thailand has become a major export item. Ceramics, such as celadon stoneware and finely wrought nielloware bowls, can sometimes be of exceptional quality.

Most of the artifacts described below can be purchased in Bangkok. They can also be purchased at lower prices in Chiang Mai, recognized as the craft center of Thailand and one of the premier places in Southeast Asia for handicrafts.

Ceramics: Thailand produces a number of different ceramics, including lustrous green-glazed celadon pottery. The most celebrated ceramic is the delicate and highly decorated Benjarong, the manufacture of which dates back to China's Ming dynasty (1368–1644). Benjarong follows traditional patterns of intricately woven floral designs with the use of five colors—red, green, yellow, blue, and white. Benjarong items range from pots and vases to entire dinner services.

Lacquerware: Lacquerware from northern Thailand comes in two varieties: gold and black, and a matte red with black and/or green details. It is found on ornate containers and trays, wooden figurines, and woven bamboo baskets, as well as

Buddhist manuscripts. At least three coats of lacquer are applied to the object being decorated, giving it a lustrous surface. Craftsmen paint a design with a water-soluble resin and, in the case of gold and black lacquerware, the area to which the gold is to adhere is left unpainted. Gold leaf is then pressed over the entire surface. The object is later washed with water to remove the excess gold leaf.

Mother-of-pearl Inlay: Mother-of-pearl inlays are used in presentation trays and in various containers, as well as on plaques bearing classical scenes. The style of decoration dates back to the Dvaravati period. Little else is known of its evolution between then and the late Ayutthaya and early Bangkok periods, when it was used extensively to decorate doors and windows in temples, as well as furniture and drinking vessels.

Nielloware: Portuguese traders to southern Thailand probably introduced this exquisite craft to the kingdom. Nakhon Si Thammarat has been the center of niello-ware production for several centuries, and the craft has recently undergone a revival in the province, as well as nationwide. A design is incised in silver and sometimes gold, and then the background is cut away and filled with an amalgam of darker metals. This creates a dark background against which the figures stand in relief. Niel-loware items include rings, necklaces, bracelets, bowls, pedestals, boxes, and trays.

Silk Weaving: Shimmering, handwoven Thai silk is regarded as among the world's best and is much sought after by decorators and designers. Silk remnants discovered at Ban Chiang, in northeast Thailand, suggest the craft was practiced

EXPERIENCE: Handicrafts

Thailand is celebrated for its beautiful handicrafts. Here is a handful of places to learn the secrets of how to make them.

Bang Sai Arts and Crafts Centre *(Bang-sai District, Ayutthaya, tel 035-366252, www.bangsaiarts.com)* Set amid manicured gardens, a "village" of Thai shop-houses features crafts that are manufactured at nearby workshops. Training courses offered here allow Thais to learn 30 skills, including mask-making, basket-weaving, and constructing rattan furniture.

Visitors can interact with students whose finest items are sold in the neigh-boring pavilion. In the village, visitors can attempt craftmaking or dine on mats beside friendly Thais who perform onsite folk performances and dances. The Crafts Centre is under the Royal Patronage of Her Majesty Queen Sirikit.

Mooban Kruang Benjarong Homestay *(Samut Sakorn, tel 081-995-9196)* Benjarong is Thai porcelain that was historically reserved for the royal court. Nowadays the elaborately painted dishware, which fea-tures geometric patterns and Thai motifs in multicolored relief glazing, is produced for the public. Visitors can do homestays in this village and learn the process firsthand.

Umbrella Making Center *(111/2 Bo Sang, Chiang Mai, tel 035-338324)* Visitors can observe the construction of *sa* paper umbrellas and the process of painting elaborate designs. Special paints and brushes are for sale to visitors, who can craft their own creations on unpainted umbrellas when they return home.

there in ancient times. Thai-speaking migrants probably introduced other components of silk culture from Yunnan Province in China.

What is certain is that silk was woven in the first Thai capital of Sukhothai and, around that time, at several settlements in southern Thailand, including Nakhon Si Thammarat and Songkhla. During the Bangkok period, the silk industry became entrenched in the northeast of the country, where conditions are good for growing mulberry trees (essential food for silkworms). By growing mulberry trees, farmers can earn extra income between rice harvests.

Silk declined in importance in the early 20th century, as factory-produced textiles became available, but was revived after World War II by American entrepreneur Jim Thompson (see pp. 94–95).

Umbrellas & Fans: Hand-painted umbrellas and folding fans are made from pounded bark (often mulberry), silk, or cotton. The bamboo frame is split by hand, and the holes are punched with a foot-powered bow drill. The items are hand-painted with designs of birds, dragons, and village scenes, and are mostly used for ornamentation.

Silverwork

Legend holds that in the late 13th century 500 families of silversmiths fled to Chiang Mai from Myanmar (Burma) as refugees from the Mongol invaders. They settled there, and the area now produces some of the most refined silverwork in Asia. Among the best of the silverwork products to look for are classically styled bowls used as water vessels and food containers, contemporary teapots and tableware, and filigree jewelry.

Woodcarving: Thailand's once extensive forests of teak and other hardwoods were a ready source of material for woodcarvers, whose skillful handiwork can be seen in the elaborately decorative gables, doors, and roof supports that grace almost every temple in Thailand.

A ban on logging was implemented in 1989, but woodcarving is still one of the most prominent Thai crafts. The timber used these days is mainly imported from Myanmar (Burma) or taken from existing supplies that have been confiscated from illegal loggers or salvaged from dilapidated buildings. Illegal logging is still rife in Thailand, so there is little doubt that some of the products you see for sale in markets have come from this source.

Craftsmen turn out an amazing range of woodcarvings, from intricately carved screens, bedsteads, and furniture to 6-foot-high (2 m) elephants to delicate figurines, elegant salad bowls, and novelties and games. Even moderately priced woodcarvings sometimes display impressive craftsmanship.

Dance & Drama

Traditional Thai theater has developed over several centuries under royal patronage into a rich variation of classical dance, elaborate theater, and sometimes bawdy, down-to-earth folk entertainment. There are six forms: the *khon*, which depicts scenes from the *Ramakien* using masks and formal dance; *lakhon*, which employs both formal and less structured theater and carries various themes; *li-khe*, the country's most popular drama form, often employing comedic and melodramatic themes; *manhora*, the southern Thailand version of li-khe, based on Indian folklore;

nang, or shadow puppetry, a dying art form also from the south; and *lakhon lek,* which uses marionettes dressed in costumes similar to khon performers.

Khon: This classical theater includes large numbers of exclusively male dancers. Traditionally, khon was performed by hundreds of dancers in front of royalty and their guests; today, because of the expense, numbers have been reduced. Khon relates tales from the Thai epic, *Ramakien,* with performers adorned in a dazzling array of costumes, headdresses, and masks representing four types of characters—male humans, female humans, monkeys, and demons. Performers mime the dialogue provided by narrators and choruses, and the performance is backed by the Thai *pipat* orchestra. Truncated but still impressive versions of khon can be seen at Bangkok's National Theater.

Lakhon: The lakhon bases its appeal on female grace and refined dexterity. Themes derived from the *Ramakien* are expanded with folk dances from the northeast and ancient legends from the far south.

This style of theater is noted for its gilded costumes and profuse decorative elements, which greatly exceed those in other Thai performing arts. Its use of singing and dialogue make it much livelier than the khon, with its controlled strictures. In contrast to the muscular displays of the khon, the lakhon demonstrates the highly restrained and subtle use of the upper portion of the female body. The dancer employs a range of eye and hand movements to indicate emotion and the development of the storyline.

> Traditional Thai theater has developed over several centuries ... into a rich variation of classical dance, elaborate theater, and sometimes bawdy, down-to-earth folk entertainment.

Li-khe: This is the most popular form of live theater, performed at temple fairs, village festivals, and other venues in towns and villages throughout Thailand. It is good-time theater, incorporating classical and folk music, wild costumes, slapstick comedy, melodrama, and sexual innuendo. Often it is used as political satire and cutting social commentary. Traveling troupes of entertainers put on the shows, and entire villages gather for a night of boisterous fun. Over the centuries li-khe has remained hugely popular and has translated well onto the television screen. Li-khe sitcoms are now a staple on daytime Thai television.

The southern version of li-khe is known as the *ma-norah.* It is loosely based on the *Ramakien,* where, in this case, Prince Suthon travels in search of the kidnapped Manhora, a half-woman, half-bird princess. Narrators relate the story of the prince's travails in comic rhyming prose.

Shadow Puppetry: Although rarely performed these days, shadow puppetry, or nang (see p. 312), was once southern Thailand's most popular form of entertainment. There are two forms of nang. *Nang yai* uses life-size puppets, which are manipulated by skilled puppet masters using two poles. They are moved behind an illuminated white screen that is positioned between the puppets and the audience. The illumination casts wavering shadow images of the puppets out into the crowd. Nang yai puppets are still crafted but are usually sold as interior decorations rather than for use in performances. *Nang thalung* uses smaller, more maneuverable puppets with articulated joints, similar to the *wayang kulit* of Indonesia. This form of puppetry is still occasionally seen at temple fairs in southern Thailand. Traditional nang performances typically act out scenes from the *Ramakien* and can last for hours. These days, they are often given a contemporary theme by the puppet masters.

Lakhon Lek: Lakhon lek, translated as "little theater," is no longer performed. It used marionettes up to 3 feet (90 cm) high and made from paper and wire. The puppets were dressed in elaborate costumes similar to those worn in khon, and the plays carried similar themes. Puppet masters used poles to move the marionettes' arms, legs, hands, and sometimes fingers and eyes. The Bangkok National Museum has a small collection of the puppets. Another type of puppet theater using three-dimensional figures is *hun krabok*. These are hand puppets, each about 12 inches (30 cm) high, carved from wood and viewed from the waist up.

Ram Wong: Thailand's most popular traditional dance, performed at temple fairs and festivals, is the ram wong (dance circle). Movements appear simple and natural, with the dancers' emotions expressed with graceful arm and hand movements. Thais of all social classes enjoy dancing the ram wong, a very social affair.

Martial Arts

Thai Boxing: In most countries, boxing lies directly in the realm of sport, but in Thailand, *muay Thai,* or Thai boxing, infuses elements of art and ritual. The sport is a mixture of conventional boxing and eastern martial arts such as karate and

Evocative locations—such as ancient ruins—sometimes serve as backdrops for classical theater performances.

EXPERIENCE: *Muay Thai*

While many foreigners study muay Thai to test themselves physically and mentally, the sport has become increasingly popular with the growth of mixed martial arts competitions. Relentless conditioning and the use of hands, feet, elbows, and knees to strike opponents has made Thai boxing a standard technique for such fighters to learn.

Fairtex *(179/185–212 Moo 5 North Pattaya Rd., Chon Buri, tel 038-416640, www.fairtex.com)* State-of-the-art facilities in Pattaya or Bangkok offer morning and afternoon training with off-hours spent in the weight room, cardio center, or pool. One-on-one coaching by former champions and on-site lodging underscore why this muay Thai gym is internationally renowned.

Lanna Muay Thai *(161, Soi Chang Kian, Huay Kaew Rd., Chiang Mai, tel 053-892-102, www.lannamuaythai .com)* With its open-air room, corrugated roof, and concrete floor, where weathered heavy bags swing beside patchy canvas rings, this gym evokes *Rocky*. Yet the gym trains championship fighters and gives classes at the Four Seasons. Open to anyone, including visitors looking for a single day of instruction, Lanna puts an emphasis on learning, not beating each other up.

Pramote Gym *(23 Building Charter House, 124 Lad Prao, Bangkok, tel 02-934-3046, www .thaipichaiyuth.com)* With introductory courses for novices and long-term training for dedicated fighters, Pramote Gym focuses on either performance or skill. The three-day basic muay Thai course culminates in testing and certification, and five-day Krabi Krabong instruction provides an introduction to the ancient art of Thai weapons fighting.

tae kwon do. Opponents can use their fists, elbows, knees, and feet to batter their opponent in just about any part of the body where the opportunity avails itself. Watching the sport, you will find it hard to believe that it could ever be more violent—but it used to be. Up until the 1930s, the rules and regulations were few, and serious injuries were common among fighters, who also employed biting, scratching, strangling, and spitting in their repertoire. (The sport was banned in the 1920s and revived in the 1930s under new rules.)

Before the match begins, strident music erupts from a small orchestra in the stadium. Then, the fighters enter the ring wearing colored headbands and armbands, which are regarded as sacred ornaments that offer blessing and protection. They kneel and perform a quick prayer, then—with the orchestra still playing—move into a mesmerizing boxing dance around the ring called the *rom muay*. The dance, performed with heavily exaggerated movements and in slow motion, is traditionally the participants' way of paying respect to the trainer and the boxing school to which they belong.

After the rom muay, the fighter's headband is removed, but the armband, which contains a small Buddha amulet, is worn throughout the fight. The orchestra keeps on playing throughout the five three-minute rounds, with often frenzied crescendos rising and falling in tune with the action in the ring.

There are an estimated 60,000 muay Thai fighters in Thailand. Fights are held regularly at Lumphini and Ratchadamneon Stadiums in Bangkok and in towns and villages around the country.

Krabi Kabong: This traditional Thai martial art has its roots in Ayutthaya's Wat Phutthaisawan as far back as 400 years ago, when the king's bodyguards learned the skills that incorporate sword, quarterstaff, and club fighting, and hand-to-hand combat. Although the martial art is today an integral and exciting part of cultural shows for international visitors and festivals, it is nevertheless still taken seriously by its exponents, and contests continue to be held, with winners being judged on stamina and technical skills. Although sharpened swords and other weapons are used, krabi kabong fighters avoid striking their opponents.

Music

Traditional Music: Traditional classical Thai music, dating from the Sukhothai period, combines Chinese, Indonesian, and Indian influences. Initially, it may sound strange and discordant to unfamiliar ears, but the longer you listen, the more sense it makes. It is based on a five-tone diatonic scale, used long before the evolution of the contemporary Western scale. The music is performed by an orchestra that emphasizes percussion instruments—so you should expect the sounds of drums, gongs, and vibraphones, along with a range of string instruments drawn from Asian musical traditions.

> **Traditional classical Thai music, dating from the Sukhothai period, combines Chinese, Indonesian, and Indian influences.**

These tunes have long backed up performances of the khon, lakhon, and li-khe; a reduced version of the Thai orchestra is used to introduce and play backing music for Thai boxing matches (see p. 61), adding an almost surreal touch to the mayhem of fight nights.

Modern Music: Thai pop music contains the syrupy lyrics found in Western pop, but there are also some styles that have a distinct Thai flavor, using traditional instruments and biting lyrics that shed light on modern-day Thai culture. Popular music came of age in the 1980s with the crafting of a socially conscious form of song known as *pleng peur cheevit*. This gave lyrical importance to social and political issues rather than themes of young and unrequited love. The popular Bangkok-based group Carabao, which wrote and performed the 1980s hit "Made in Thailand," first forged the change. This song, and later ones from a growing number of bands, questioned the importance of Western materialism in Thai society and addressed issues of morality and poverty.

Literature

The *Ramakien,* the Thai version of the *Ramayana,* the Hindu epic, is the most pervasive of Thai classical literature, also celebrated in visual art, drama, and song. It arrived in Thailand about 900 years ago with the Khmers, who carved scenes from the epic into stone at Prasat Hin Phimai (see pp. 170–171), Prasat Phanom Rung (see pp. 174–176), and other temples. The Thai version was put down on paper during the reign of Rama I and contains 60,000 verses. The *Ramakien* remains essentially the same as the *Ramayana,* but certain characters are embellished, while others are given less emphasis. The story is an odyssey of quest, love, betrayal, and war. ∎

The vast, sprawling City of Angels, with a global reputation for splendid restaurants, nonstop nightlife, superb shopping, and magnificent temples

Bangkok

Mural detail, Wat Phra Kaeo

Bangkok

Visitors to Thailand's capital cannot help being overwhelmed by it all. The city is daunting—a steamy, modern sprawl that seems to carry on endlessly. The traffic is maddening, the din endless, and the crowds irritating. Most can't wait to escape to the beaches of the south or the jungles and mountains in the north. That's a shame, because Bangkok truly is one of Asia's great cities.

Bangkok's full name is the world's longest city name: Krungthepmahanakhon Amonratankosin Mahintharayutthaya Mahadilokphop Nophosin Ratchathaniburirom Udomrathaniwetmahasa Amonphiman Awatansathit Sakkathatiya Witsanukamprasit. This means: City of Angels, Great City of Immortals, Magnificent City of the Nine Gems, Seat of the King, City of Royal Palaces, Home of the Gods Incarnate, Erected by Visvakarman at Indra's Behest. Thais commonly call the city simply Krung Threp, or City of Angels.

Bangkok (*bang* means "riverside village" and *kok* means "a wild olive") became Thailand's capital when Ramathibodi, or Rama I, moved the city across the Chao Phraya river from Thon Buri in 1782 to ensure its fortification against the Burmese, who had sacked the capital of Ayutthaya. Magnificent palaces, temples, and canals were built. The area, known as Rattanakosin island, or the old royal city, exists today, housing the Grand Palace, the National Museum, and some of the city's most celebrated *wats* (temple complexes).

From Rattanakosin, the city spread out. Under royal orders, Chinese merchants moved eastward to form a new settlement—today's vibrant Chinatown. King Chulalongkorn (Rama V), inspired by his European travels, built wide, tree-lined boulevards and erected neoclassical buildings that are still common sights in Dusit, north of Rattanakosin.

Bangkok sprawls on both sides of the Chao Phraya river.

Unbridled development began in the late 1950s and has, more or less, continued since. Canals (khlongs), which had earned the city the appellation of the Venice of the East by early European travelers, were mostly filled in and roads built. Rows of monotonous shops were constructed. Later came the mad rush of office high-rises, hotels, and condominiums with little, if any, thought to urban planning.

Today, Bangkok hammers the senses of visitors with its controlled chaos. But scratch the surface of this metropolis—population about eight million—and you'll find pockets of surprising beauty and grace. A surfeit of grand, riotously ornate Thai architecture links the city to its past. Yet gleaming modern, at times fantastic, skyscrapers point to its future. Just off the frenetic, traffic-clogged streets are quiet, snaking sois (side streets) with rows of wooden houses and a community feel. A trip on the city's Skytrain unfolds rooftop views of parks, lush tropical gardens, and huge colonial mansions that have escaped development. The main waterway, the Chao Phraya river, reveals a tranquil side of the city; exploring it and the maze of khlongs either by public water transportation or by charter is a highlight of a visit.

Indeed, it is the dichotomy of Bangkok that is so appealing. Here, the truly shocking, horrendous, and horrible exist alongside moments of pure beauty. Sukhumvit Road, a main avenue in the eastern part of the city, is a perfect example. Sukhumvit appears to be a creation of the devil, with absurdly packed sidewalks, broken chunks of concrete, the sky blackened by the concrete pillars and tracks of the Skytrain, vendors crammed into every square inch, and a total sense of anarchy and mayhem. Yet, walk slowly and you will see the magnificence of carved fruit among vendors selling copy watches, the smiling girl selling exquisite floral baskets next to an open sewer, a Buddhist shrine at a busy intersection, and perhaps an old Hindu astrologer predicting people's fortunes in the middle of all this madness.

At night the city explodes with the liveliest entertainment in Asia. Superb Thai restaurants

---

NOT TO BE MISSED:

The dazzling spectacle of the Grand Palace & Wat Phra Kaeo 69–79

A muay thai boxing match at Lumphini Stadium 99

Beautiful Vimanmek Palace 104–105

A Chao Phraya river cruise or dinner boat 112–114

Discovering Thon Buri by long-tail boat 114

The remarkable Royal Barges Museum 110–111

The bustling activity of an early morning floating market 116

---

are found in traditional houses. International cuisine ranks with the world's best. Sophisticated nightclubs, along with raunchy bars and entertainment venues, are scattered through the city. About the only thing Bangkok doesn't offer the visitor is boredom.

Epic traffic jams are a constant source of frustration. Luckily, taxi fares are cheap. Trips around town usually costs less than $3, even in heavy traffic. (Make sure the driver turns on the meter. If he refuses, get out and catch another taxi; they are plentiful.) Many locals, and the occasional adventurous tourist, opt for the city's army of motorcycle taxis that weave expertly through traffic. It is a quick, hair-raising way to get around. Tuk tuks, colorful three-wheeled taxis—named for the noise made by their small engines—are fun for short journeys but are often more expensive (and dangerous) than taxis. Always agree on a price beforehand. The city's Skytrain and subway are the most efficient, agreeable ways to get around the city.

Tours of Bangkok and surrounding areas are inexpensive and can be easily arranged at your hotel tour desk. It's wise to take at least one of these tours. ■

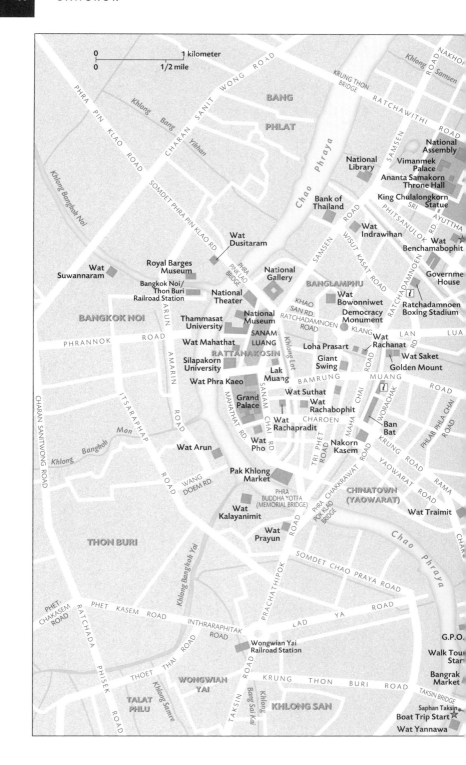

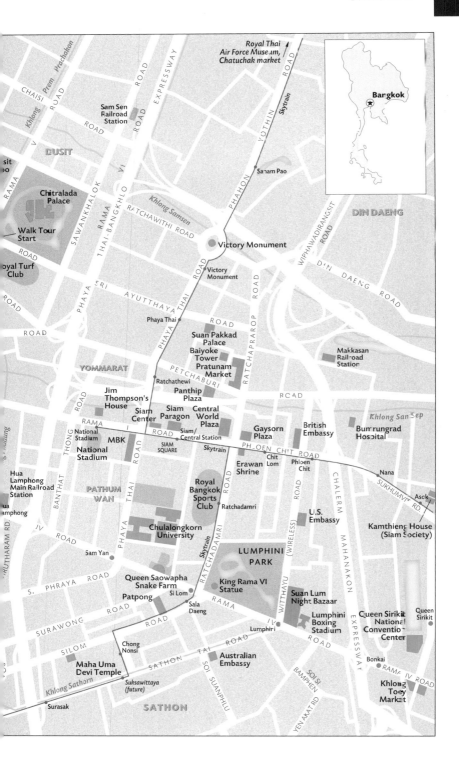

Royal Thai
Air Force Museum,
Chatuchak market

CHAISI
Khong Prem Prachakon
ROAD
EXPRESSWAY
RAMA V
YOTHIN ROAD
Skytrain

Sam Sen
Railroad
Station

DUSIT
sit
oo

SAWANKHALOK ROAD
RAMA VI
THAI-BANGKHLO
RATCHAWITHI ROAD

Chitralada
Palace

Khlong Samsen

DIN DAENG

Sanam Pao

Walk Tour
Start

Victory Monument

oyal Turf
Club
ROAD

Victory
Monument

PHAYA SRI
AYUTTHAYA ROAD

PHAHON

WIPHAWADIRANGSIT ROAD
DIN DAENG ROAD

PHAYA THAI
ROAD
RATCHAPRAROP ROAD

ROAD
ROAD

Phaya Thai

Suan Pakkad
Palace
Baiyoke
Tower
Pratunam
Market

Makkasan
Railroad
Station

YOMMARAT

PETCHABURI

Ratchathewi
Panthip
Plaza

Jim
Thompson's
House

RCAD

Khlong San Sep

Siam
Center
Siam
Paragon
Central
World
Plaza

RAMA ROAD

THONG

National
Stadium

MBK

Gaysorn
Plaza

British
Embassy

Bumrungrad
Hospital

National
Stadium

SIAM
SQUARE
Siam/
Central Station
Skytrain

PHLOEN CHIT ROAD

Chit
Lom
Phloen
Chit

Nana

Hua
Lamphong
Main Railroad
Station
ua
amphong

Erawan
Shrine

SUKHUMVIT RD.
Asck

BANTHAT

PATHUM
WAN

Royal
Bangkok
Sports
Club

CHALERM

Kamthieng House
(Siam Society)

Ratchadamri

Chulalongkorn
University

U.S.
Embassy

IV ROAD
PHAYA THAI ROAD
RATCHADAMRI ROAD
Skytrain

Sam Yan

LUMPHINI
PARK

MAHANAKON

Queen Saowapha
Snake Farm

King Rama VI
Statue

WITTHAYU (WIRELESS) ROAD

S. PHRAYA ROAD
SURAWONG ROAD

Patpong
Si Lom

Sala
Daeng

RAMA IV ROAD

Suan Lum
Night Bazaar

Queen Sirikit
National
Conventio
Center

Queen
Sirikit

NUTTHARAM RD.

Lumphini
Boxing
Stadium

EXPRESSWAY

Bonkai

RAMA IV ROAD

SILOM ROAD

Chong
Nonsi

Lumphini

Maha Uma
Devi Temple

SATHON TAI ROAD

Australian
Embassy

Khlong Sathon
Suksawittaya
(future)

SATHON

SOI SUANPHLU

SOI SI
BAMPHEN

YEN AKAT RD.

Khlong
Toey
Market

Surasak

Bangkok

Rattanakosin

The historical and cultural heart of Bangkok is Rattanakosin island, site of the old royal city. Fronting a curve on the Chao Phraya river and backed by canals (*khlongs*), Rattanakosin contains many of Bangkok's architectural and religious splendors. Here you will find the magnificent Grand Palace, the renowned temple complexes of Wat Mahathat, Wat Suthat, and Wat Phra Kaeo, the city's top universities, and the National Museum and National Gallery.

Khon figures guard a stupa at the Grand Palace at Rattanakosin, the ancient heart of Bangkok.

When Rama I moved the capital across the Chao Phraya river from Thon Buri to Bangkok in 1782, he decided to model his country's new seat of power on the architectural magnificence of the former capital at Ayutthaya. Concentric canals were built to evoke the rivers around the old capital, brick was salvaged from there to build palaces and temples, and Buddha images were collected from the ruined Ayutthaya and installed in the new temples at Rattanakosin.

Both the new Royal Palace and Wat Phra Kaeo were embellished by subsequent Chakri kings, who added their own royal temples within the confines of the Rattanakosin district, including Wat Saket and several structures near the Golden Mount. As the new capital became established, temples and government offices were constructed in outlying districts, and Bangkok spread in all directions.

Rattanakosin and Bangkok expanded further under the rule

of King Mongkut. In 1862, he ordered the building of the city's first road, to connect his palace with the commercial enclave of Chinatown. Until the road opened, all transportation had been conducted by boat on the Chao Phraya or on the canals around the centrally placed Royal Palace.

King Chulalongkorn continued to modernize the city, which developed into the kingdom's bustling political and economic centerpiece. The historical quarter remained a royal enclave, housing the royal family's quarters, government offices, and royal temples, until the overthrow of the absolute monarchy in 1932. To a large degree, however, the flavor of the original old royal city remains intact in Rattanakosin.

Wat Phra Kaeo & the Grand Palace

The most dazzling sight in all of Thailand—and one of the great wonders of Asia—is **Wat Phra Kaeo** (Temple of the Emerald Buddha), with the adjoining **Grand Palace.** The temple and palace grounds are filled with a bewildering number of other buildings and sacred structures that, taken together, provide an architectural lexicon of Thailand the single most comprehensive introduction to its physical and cultural charms.

The entrance to the grounds of the royal temple leads through a narrow gateway and directly into a scene of incredible, dazzling brilliance, a world of shimmering golden spires and extravagantly ornate pavilions, all of which is guarded by a host of garish

mythological creatures.

Rather than rushing directly to the *bot* (meeting hall) that houses the famous Emerald Buddha, you should work up to this highlight by first slowly exploring the collection of buildings within the temple grounds, starting with the *Ramakien* murals. Then, visit the structures just outside the confines of the *wat*. The clockwise walk then proceeds through a narrow gate into the grounds of the Grand Palace, before leaving the grounds through the main gate just opposite Sanam Luang.

INSIDER TIP:

Bangkok can be a nightmare to get around; simplify your life by using the hotel (free) and express river boats (cheap), or the BTS (Skytrain).

—DANIEL STILES, PH.D.
National Geographic field researcher

Ramakien Murals: The profuse and potentially confusing *Ramakien* murals cover the interior cloister's entire walls and are 2,080 yards (1,900 m) long. A professional guide is recommended to explain the story line, which begins by the north gate with the discovery of Sita, then advances through the various adventures of her consort, Rama and his assistant, the white monkey-god Hanuman. This legendary account of Rama is a Thai adaptation of the *Ramayana,*

Wat Phra Kaeo & Grand Palace
- Map p. 66
- Na Phralan Rd.
- $
- Air-con bus: 8 or 12
- Chao Phraya River Express to Chang Pier (Tha Chang)

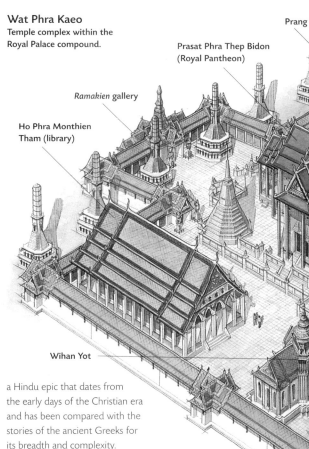

Wat Phra Kaeo
Temple complex within the Royal Palace compound.

Prang

Prasat Phra Thep Bidon
(Royal Pantheon)

Ramakien gallery

Ho Phra Monthien
Tham (library)

Wihan Yot

**The Emerald Buddha,
a symbol of power
and enlightenment**

a Hindu epic that dates from the early days of the Christian era and has been compared with the stories of the ancient Greeks for its breadth and complexity.

The murals date from the early 19th century, but the humid climate has taken its toll and they have been restored several times during the past 150 years. The quality of workmanship in the restoration varies, but the overall result maintains the basic integrity. Along with the story of Rama and Sita, the murals provide amusing insights into ordinary Thai life, from scenes of children at play and portraits of royal concubines, to depictions of grinning gamblers and souls lost to the wages of sin.

Golden Chedi: After inspecting the *Ramakien* murals, stop by **Phra Sri Rattana** (Golden Chedi), built by King Mongkut to house a piece of the Buddha's breastbone and inspired by Phra Sri Rattana Chedi in Ayutthaya. Between the Golden Chedi and the bot is a richly carved **Phra Mondop,** a library with a gleaming silver floor and a chest covered with mother-of-pearl inlay in which sacred Buddhist texts are held. This structure is usually closed to the public.

Below the mondop is a small reproduction of the Cambodian

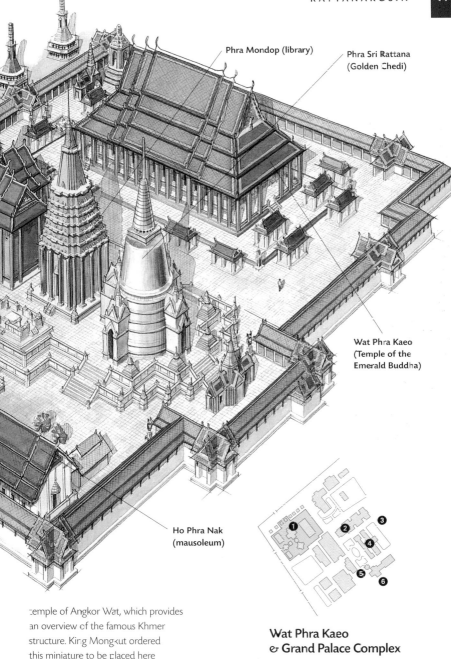

Phra Mondop (library)

Phra Sri Rattana
(Golden Chedi)

Wat Phra Kaeo
(Temple of the
Emerald Buddha)

Ho Phra Nak
(mausoleum)

temple of Angkor Wat, which provides
an overview of the famous Khmer
structure. King Mongkut ordered
this miniature to be placed here
during a period when Cambodia
belonged to the Thai Empire, as a
public reminder of his vast territorial
realm. The nearby gabled structure,
known as **Wihan Yot** and covered

Wat Phra Kaeo
& Grand Palace Complex

1 Wat Phra Kaeo
2 Amarinda Audience Hall
3 Entrance to Inner Palace
4 Grand Palace Throne Hall
5 Aphonphimok
6 Dusit Audience Hall

with ceramics and porcelains, is home to the Manangasila Stone, an ancient throne used by King Ramkamhaeng and worth a brief visit. **Ho Phra Nak,** in the northwest corner of the complex, is a royal mausoleum holding urns that contain the ashes of royal family members. It is closed to the public, though its magnificent exterior is well worth close inspection for its wealth of traditional detail.

The western facade of the **Ho Phra Monthien Tham,** the large secondary library of the temp e complex, is considered the finest of its type in the country. The doors, inlaid with mother-of-pearl, are particularly magnificent. The closed interior contains Buddhist texts and copies of the *Tripitaka.*

In an elevated position a few steps above the temple grounds stands the **Royal Pantheon** (Prasat Phra Thep Bidon), surmounted with an ocher-colored *prang* (tower). Inside are life-size statues of the early rulers of the Chakri dynasty. Look for the strange mythological creatures that surround the Royal Pantheon, such as the *kinaree,* a divine part-human, part-bird creature of Himalayan origins, and ferocious lions, known as *norasinghs,* which guard the main entrance. Hindu-derived *garudas,* the sacred animal of Vishnu, are displayed on the friezes that flank the main entrance.

Temple of the Emerald Buddha: The bot is the largest building within the wat, and Thailand's most significant religious structure. Note that visitors must show great respect, be well dressed and covered, and remove their shoes before entering. Photography is prohibited. Bangkok's Royal Temple was constructed at the end of the 18th century by Rama I to house the **Emerald Buddha** (Phra Kaeo), a most holy and powerful statue, and a symbol to the Thai people of the power, divinity,

A prime example of Buddhist architecture, Wat Phra Kaeo contains more exquisite carvings and decoration per square inch than any comparable site in the world.

and enlightenment of their country. The tiny image, which is carved from green jasper, stands just 26 inches (66 cm) tall. Its origins are obscure, but the story goes that it was discovered by accident, hidden in a lump of plaster in Chiang Rai, northern Thailand, in 1434. Transported at one point to Laos, it was restored to Thailand in 1778. It rested temporarily in Bangkok's Wat Arun

INSIDER TIP:

Grand Palace tickets cover both the palace and Emerald Buddha temple. Don't take photographs inside the temple, but sit quietly and avoid pointing your feet toward the shrine.

—SOLANGE HANDO
National Geographic writer

while a new, suitably lavish home was built. Although it is difficult to view, because of its remote and highly elevated position at the back of the temple, the Emerald Buddha draws a steady stream of pilgrims, who believe that the image represents the near mystical relationship between Thailand and its king. The king himself changes the sacred golden vestments on the statue three times yearly, as the seasons change.

The **interior frescoes** of the bot follow the classic arrangement: Those between the windows tell of the *Jataka* stories from the

previous lives of the Buddha, while the Buddhist universe is shown on the rear wall, just behind the central altar. Of special note for its hellish imagery is the fresco above the temple entrance, which depicts the Buddha resisting the temptations of Mara (see p. 76).

Just outside the Temple of the Emerald Buddha, the pair of glaring bronze lions ranks among the finest examples of Khmer art in the country.

Grand Palace: Rama VII was the last monarch to live here officially. He moved out in 1925, and now the Grand Palace fulfills a purely ceremonial function. While the palace lacks the exuberant exoticism of Wat Phra Kaeo, its curiously successful fusion of disparate Thai and Western styles makes it worth a quick inspection.

Built at the same time as the wat, the audience halls and former private royal residences adopted an unusual combination of formal Italian Renaissance styles in the main rooms and structures, with a familiar Thai roofline placed on top. Much has been altered over the centuries, and today only the Dusit and Amarinda Audience Halls are in regular ceremonial use.

Amarinda Audience Hall: Walking from the interior courtyard of Wat Phra Kaeo, you come to the Amarinda Audience Hall, part of the original private residence of Rama I and later the national Hall of Justice. Inside, the walls are painted with murals, and there is a splendid *(continued on p. 76)*

The Royal Family

King Bhumibol Adulyadej (Rama IX) was born on December 5, 1927, in Cambridge, Massachusetts, where his father was studying medicine at Harvard University. At the time, succession seemed unlikely. Bhumibol stood in the royal line behind his uncle, the reigning King Prajadhipok; his father, Prince Mahidol; and elder brother, Prince Ananda.

Images of the king are found in temples, shops, and private homes.

Fate intervened when Mahidol died unexpectedly in 1929, and Prajadhipok abdicated without a direct heir in 1935. Ananda succeeded to the throne, reigning until his mysterious death in 1946, when the crown was passed to Bhumibol, who at the time was a student at Lausanne University in Switzerland.

Bhumibol, the longest reigning king in Thai history, has his own privy council made up of 14 appointees who advise and assist with the king's royal duties. The king and his wife, Queen Sirikit, have four children: Princess Ubol Ratana (born 1951), Crown Prince Maha Vajiralongkorn (born 1952), Princess Mahachakri Sirind-horn (born 1955), and Princess Chulabhorn (born 1957).

Current law indicates that the king should follow constitutional practice, allowing him to choose his successor. The heir apparent is Prince Maha Vajiralongkorn, but in the unlikely event

that he declines ascendancy or is unable to take the crown due to illness or death, the order of ascension isn't clear, particularly as the crown prince himself now has a male heir.

Princess Ubol Ratana, the king's eldest daughter, was once next in line, but fell out of favor in 1972 when she married American Peter Jensen against palace wishes. Although her royal rank was later reinstated, her sister Princess Mahachakri Sirind-horn, widely admired because of her regular visits to the countryside and down-to-earth nature, was bestowed with the equivalent rank of her elder brother and was legally made second in line to the throne.

Although negative comments about the monarchy are punishable by law, Thais feel no inhibitions about gossiping about members of the royal family in private and many would like to see Sirindorn, who is lovingly referred to as the "princess angel," follow her father's reign, although traditional rulings make this unlikely.

King Bhumibol and other members of the present royal family have done more than any other Thai royal family to give the institution a human face. Although deference to the monarchy has a lot to do with traditional reverence and esteem, their genuine concern for ordinary, less wealthy Thais has enhanced the institution's status. During his reign, the king—more often than not accompanied by his beloved wife—has visited most places in Thailand, listening to the concerns of local officials and farmers. His travels have inspired the construction of hundreds of small-scale public works programs around the country under his patronage.

The extensive grounds of the royal family's home, Chiltralada Palace, have been turned into an agricultural research center, where scientists work on projects to improve Thailand's primary industries. Queen Sirikit works to promote the country's unique arts and crafts industry. Also on the palace grounds, there are workshops where craftsmen are passing on their skills to selected rural students in educa-tion programs set up with royal patronage.

As a constitutional monarch, Bhumibol's status is ceremonial, but he can wield great influence in political life. Two attempted coups d'etat in the 1980s were thought to have failed because they could not garner the king's implicit approval. The coup of 1991, which overthrew a woefully corrupt (even by Thai standards) gov-ernment, is believed to have had palace approval.

The most visible demonstration of the king's political influence was in May 1992, at the height of the bloody pro-democracy demon-strations in Bangkok (see p. 48–49). Bhumibol summoned the then (unelected) prime minister, Suchinda Kraprayoon, and Bangkok's governor and protest leader, Chamlong Srimuang, to his residence at Chiltralada Palace. On videotaped footage that was seen around the world, the two men—looking more like contrite schoolboys than men of power—lay prostrate before a stern-looking Bhumibol. The madness on the streets outside the palace subsequently ceased. Suchinda resigned in disgrace and, within a few months, Thais went to the polls to elect a new, democratic government.

EXPERIENCE: Respecting the King

Thai people revere their King, Bhumibol Adulyadej. Even in their daily lives, Thais engage in activities to honor the King and royal family. Visitors should be aware of common practices that they may participate in to show their respect and others, if not followed, that could result in arrest for violation of lèse-majesté criticism of the royal family.

Lèse-majesté: The law has been applied to someone foolish enough to spray paint a photo of the King and to block YouTube (www.youtube.com) for hosting an insulting video. Thais are easily offended by any criticism of the royal family or their likenesses; tearing a bank note in half, for example, would be an outrage irreparable by tape.

Standing at Attention: Prior to movie screenings, the royal anthem is played and viewers must stand and pay respect to the King. A Thai citizen who failed to do so in 2008 was arrested for the offense. When the national anthem is played at 8 a.m. and 6 p.m., people must stand or stop walking. Although technically not related to the King, most Thais associate national-ism with the King.

Yellow Shirts: In 2006 to mark the 60th year of the King's reign, Thais took to wearing yellow shirts on Monday, as Thais have colors that correspond to certain days and the King was born on a Monday. Wearing pink on Tuesday has come into vogue, as the color is thought to bring good health to the King.

boat-shaped throne. This was separated from the main hall by brocade curtains, which hid the king from his audience until, with a great fanfare, they were parted.

Just outside the hall are several red and gold painted wooden posts; these were hitching posts for the royal elephants. A small pavilion decorated with glass mosaics was the king's dressing room, where he could change his robes before setting out on a ride.

The **Inner Palace** behind Amarinda Audience Hall was once the private home of the king's

korn in 1882 to honor the 100th anniversary of the Chakri dynasty and heavily influenced by Western architecture. The *prasat* on the top helps it to blend in with its surroundings, but inside, the state rooms follow a Western neoclassical design, complete with marble pillars, gilded plasterwork, and heavy oil paintings of past kings.

Visitors are permitted only in the reception rooms flanking the main entrance, decorated with marble columns, portraits of Siamese princes and former kings, and marble busts of Western

---

Temptations of the Buddha

It may not be a great artistic statement, but the small white pavilion and its elevated female statue across from the Royal Hotel *(corner of Ratchadamnoen & Atsadang Rds.)* is worth a brief visit, since it relates an important story about the Buddha.

According to traditional folklore, Buddha once entered into a long period of meditation to discover the truths of life. During his arduous ordeal, he was subjected to a series of temptations by an evil goddess named Mara and her company of sensual dancing ladies. This story of 40 days of fasting and temptation by the devil

(Mara) is, of course, comparable to the biblical story of Christ in the desert.

Buddha refused to submit to the onslaught of hedonistic temptations and continued his meditations. His trials and tribulations were closely watched by an earth goddess known as Torani, who was so impressed with his moral fortitude that she decided to honor his courageous acts. Torani aided the Buddha by wringing out her long hair, which unleashed a tidal wave that destroyed Mara and her wicked cohorts. This extremely popular legend is retold endlessly in murals and statues throughout Thailand.

---

wives, children, and concubines. Cut off from the world, they ran their own community with their own laws. With the introduction of monogamy under Rama VI, such a place became obsolete, and today it serves only as the venue of the king's birthday party.

Throne Hall: The impressive Throne Hall (Chakri Maha Prasat) was erected by King Chulalong-

rulers. Beyond these rooms, another hall leads to the throne room, where foreign ambassadors once presented their letters of introduction to the king, and where state banquets were held. Several other reception rooms, lavishly decorated with marble urns and gilded objets d'art, are located upstairs. This was the official residence of King Ananda (Rama VIII) until his death in 1946.

Aphonphimok: Next stop is Aphonphimok, a small wooden pavilion where in earlier days King Mongkut would step down from his royal elephant and show himself to members of the court below. The building was constructed at such a height that the king could then continue directly to the royal buildings without the need to descend.

This lovely little building is considered the epitome of refined Thai architecture. It has been copied twice—once for the king's summer retreat in Bang Pa-in (see pp. 141–142), and again in Brussels for the 1892 World's Fair.

Dusit Audience Hall: With its magnificent decoration and gilded, nine-tiered spire, the Dusit Audience Hall (Dusit Maha Prasat) undoubtedly ranks as Thailand's most splendid royal building. Constructed on a cross-shaped platform of white marble, the hall was built in 1789 at the instigation of Rama I. The interior has typical late 18th-century Siamese murals; the doors and windows are heavily lacquered and gilded in abstract designs. The highlight is Rama I's original teak throne, beautifully inlaid with mother-of-pearl.

Wat Pho

Adjacent to Wat Phra Kaeo, Wat Pho (also known as the Temple of the Reclining Buddha) is the oldest and largest temple complex in Bangkok. Established in the 16th century and bustling with life and interest, it contrasts starkly with its more formal, reserved neighbor.

Officially called Wat Chetuphon,

Intricate mother-of-pearl inlays decorate the feet of Wat Pho's immense and highly revered Reclining Buddha.

it has a wonderful collection of religious structures, unusual statuary, rock gardens, painted bell towers, several significant chedis, and a magnificent central bot. Of course, its most famous inhabitant is the 150-foot-long (46 m) Reclining Buddha.

Wat Pho was established long before the rise of Bangkok as the national capital, and many of the buildings were restored in the late 18th and early 19th centuries. In 1832 the progressive Rama III opened the gates of the temple to public learning. Paintings, inscriptions, and sculptures throughout the temple deal with varied subjects, including warfare, literature, astronomy, and archaeology. The mounds of stone found throughout the grounds encouraged the study of geology. Statues of *rishis* (Indian hermits) in yoga positions guided students in the correct postures for meditation and other relaxation techniques, and murals demonstrated massage techniques. The early science of palmistry continues to be practiced at the wat.

Wat Pho

- Map p. 66
- Chetuphon Rd.
- $
- Air-con bus: 6, 8, or 12
- Chao Phraya River Express to Tien Pier (Tha Tien)

Wat Pho's **College of Traditional Medicine** was the first in the country to teach Thai massage. The eastern courtyard once housed classrooms for professional massage instruction; they were relocated off the temple grounds in 2000. Today, at the eastern end of the complex, a former classroom serves as an air-conditioned treatment room, where both graduates and current students can practice their massage techniques on

INSIDER TIP:

Don't miss the opportunity for an inexpensive, relaxing traditional massage at Wat Pho, given by massage students. You can also sign up for massage training classes and learn to give massages yourself!

—BARBARA A. NOE
National Geographic editor

visitors. Getting a massage here is highly recommended: It's inexpensive and Wat Pho's colorful, bustling atmosphere enlivens the experience. At the center of the complex, the souvenir shop is housed in the former Medicine Pavilion; look for the murals depicting massage points.

Guarding the monumental gates of the main entrance and at other parts of the inner courtyard are fearsome demons, huge stone figures bedecked with top hats. These statues were carved from stone ballast used in the rice barges

that plied the Chao Phraya.

Four tall, brightly colored *chedis* (stupas) stand to the left of the main bot, honoring the first four kings of Thailand. The most intriguing of these buildings is the blue structure at the back, the Phra Si Sanphet Chedi, which was erected by King Mongkut in memory of his wife, Queen Suriyothai. According to legend, she gave her life in battle to save her husband, an act of piety that brings her special honor among queens. Hundreds of standing Buddha images in the double-blessing pose watch from the surrounding cloister.

Eastern Bot: The eastern courtyard of Wat Pho is dominated by the Eastern Bot, famed for its elegant proportions, soaring rooflines, and profuse decoration. It is enclosed by a rare double gallery and filled with almost 400 Buddhas cast in the classical Ayutthaya style. Khmer prangs of white marble stand at each corner, balanced by four *wihans* (assembly halls), each with its own Buddha statue.

Eight stairways, each guarded by a pair of finely cast bronze lions and with bas-reliefs underneath of scenes from the *Ramakien,* lead up to the temple walkway. If all this carving and relief isn't enough to overload your senses, the superb doorways have mother-of-pearl inlays depicting scenes of Moorish traders, Chinese landscapes, and Western visitors riding horses.

Finally, you enter the bot itself through the eastern doorway. The interior is dominated by a magnificent bronze Buddha, mounted on a high, gilded pedestal at the back. Murals on the walls and above the entrance are highly decorative, including scenes from everyday Thai life, such as women bathing and children playing.

Guides

Guides, primarily college students, can be hired at the entrance of Wat Pho for a few dollars per person. Most are knowledgeable, but tend to linger too long at the Reclining Buddha. Politely suggest you would like to see more of the complex.

Reclining Buddha: The western courtyard is home to Wat Pho's biggest attraction, the huge, gilded Buddha that reclines on its elbow. The Reclining Buddha—150 feet (46 m) long and 50 feet (15 m) high—is the largest of its type in Thailand. Although mere brick and plaster underneath, on the outside it gleams with shiny gold leaf. The statue virtually fills the vihara that Rama III built to house it. Yet is a shame the vihara is not bigger, as the size makes it difficult to grasp the dimensions of this immense icon, and this can be frustrating. Since the vihara is the number one attraction at Wat Pho, it is usually crowded. However, this tends to draw you closer to the statue's exquisite detail. The statue does not represent Buddha sleeping— as many assume—but his moment of enlightenment, when he

entered nirvana. His joyous passing is represented by the reclining position and the languid, ecstatic smile on the finely modeled face of the statue.

Look closely at the soles of the feet. These are encrusted with mother-of-pearl inlays that— appropriately—describe the 108 lakshanas, or auspicious signs, that identify an enlightened one.

Wat Mahathat & Lak Muang

The Temple of the Great Relic, or Wat Mahathat, lies midway between the Grand Palace and the National Museum. Rebuilt in the mid-19th century, it's nothing special in architectural terms. Functionality takes the place of decoration, for this wat plays a central role in the study of vipassana (insight) meditation. It is also home to one of the most important centers of Buddhist teaching in the country, Mahachulalongkorn University.

The complex is the seat of the Theravada sect of Buddhism— that is, the variation of Buddhism as practiced by most Thais. Introductory lectures in English and meditation retreats take place here each month.

Even if you are not interested in meditation, visit the weekend market that is held on the grounds. Inevitably, the market specializes in Buddhist trappings such as medals, sacred images (often cast just across the river in Thon Buri), and monkish essentials—begging bowls, orange robes, and fans. This is also the place to seek out traditional herbal medicines.

(continued on p. 82)

Wat Mahathat

- Map p. 66
- Na Phra That Rd.
- Air-con bus: 8 or 12
- Chao Phraya River Express to Maharat Pier (Tha Maharat)

Mudras of the Buddha

The hand gestures *(mudras)* of the Buddha image complement the body position and give the faithful a pantheon of religious teachings in stone, not unlike the carved saints placed outside medieval Christian cathedrals.

The reclining Buddha icons represent the Buddha at enlightenment.

Meditation Mudra

The meditation mudra is a seated Buddha with both hands folded in the lap, and the legs tightly crossed in the "lotus position." Several historical references can be made to this position, including the last period of meditation, and the moment of enlightenment as the Buddha sat under the sacred *bodhi* tree. This serene position neatly summarizes the ecstatic goal of the ancient yoga, who withholds all spiritual disquiet in order to concentrate on the truth.

"Calling the Earth to Witness" Mudra

One of the most common positions depicts the Buddha with his right hand extended, the palm turned inward with the fingers extending down to touch the earth. The image is seated in a "half lotus" position or, more rarely, in a "full lotus" with both feet elevated above the knees. This mudra symbolizes the Buddha's victory over evil as personified by the demon goddess Mara. According to legend, when the Buddha was on the verge of enlightenment, he was attacked by Mara, who demanded that he demonstrate his powers. The Buddha then touched the earth and summoned the earth goddess Torani, who wrung water from her hair and washed away the evil hordes.

"Turning the Wheel of the Law" Mudra

A third seated position of the Buddha, in which both hands are raised to the chest, shows the position of the Buddha as he preached his first sermon in the deer park at Sarnath. The thumb and forefinger of the right hand are joined to form a circle, which represents the Buddhist "Wheel of the Law." This wheel symbolizes the setting in motion of Buddhist law, the endless cycle of birth and rebirth, and the principles of karma and nirvana.

at shoulder level with palms turned outward—except the palm is exposed, open, and empty.

"Triumph over Evil" Mudra

This mudra, generally depicted in a standing image, shows the Buddha with his right, left, or both hands held at shoulder level, palms turned outward, with the fingers stretched upward. According to legend, the Buddha was attacked by a mad elephant sent by his cousin to trample him, but he raised his hand and stopped the beast in its tracks. The pose is also called Giving Protection, Dispelling Fear, or Granting Fearlessness.

"Dispensing Favors" Mudra

Symbolizing Buddha's vows of assistance and gifts of truth, this mudra is almost the same as the "triumph over evil" mudra—hands held out

"Adoration" Mudra

This mudra is performed by bodhisattvas (angels) giving homage to Buddha. The hand gesture is the same as the traditional Thai greeting, the wai—open hands pressed together at chest level.

"Calling for Rain" Mudra

This noncanonical mudra is sometimes encountered on Buddha images in northern Thailand, especially Chiang Rai, Nan, and Phrae Provinces. The arms of a standing image fall downward at the sides of the body, with the palms facing the thighs. This posture and mudra signify the call for rain that will bring nourishment to rice fields.

EXPERIENCE: Thai Buddhism & Meditation

Many temples are open for foreigners to discuss Buddhism or learn meditation. Visitors to multiday retreats are normally required to bring their own toiletries and be in good health. Most retreats require a general vow of silence, other than chanting and discussions on Buddhism; willingness to follow temple routines is also required.

MCU Buddhist University (*Wat Suan Dok, Suthep Rd., Chiang Mai, tel 053-278967, ext 111*) MCU hosts "Monk Chats" (*5–7 p.m. Mon., Wed., & Fri., www.monkchat. net*) during which visitors may converse with monks and novices. Two- and three-day retreats, beginning each Tuesday, feature introductory Buddhism, insight meditation instruction, and discussions about visitors' experiences.

Wat Chedi Luang (*Phrapokklao Rd., Chiang Mai*) The former home of

the Emerald Buddha, this historic temple holds daily monk chats in the shade of its 600-year-old *chedi*. Visitors can ask questions about Buddhism, the lives of the monks, or whatever else they wish to raise in a casual atmosphere.

Wat Mahadhatu (*Maharaj Rd., Bangkok, tel 02-222-6011*) Section 5 at Wat Mahadhatu, near the Grand Palace, offers morning, afternoon, and evening meditation instruction and practice, and nightly *dharma* discussions. Visitors are

welcome to retreats on the temple grounds for as long as they wish to stay.

Wat Suan Mokkh (*Amphur Chaiya, Surat Thani, tel 077-431596, www.suanmokkh.org*) The Dharmadana Foundation organizes ten-day meditation retreats in English. Each day follows a strict schedule of discussions, meditation, chores, evening tea, and hot springs. Visitors must arrive on the last day of the month to register in person for retreats, which begin on the first of every month.

National Museum

Map p. 66

✉ Na Phra That Rd., opposite the northern end of Sanam Luang Park

☎ 02-224-1404

🕐 Closed Mon.–Tues.

💲 $

🚌 Air-con bus: 8 or 12

⛴ Chao Phraya River Express to Maharat Pier (Tha Maharat)

**www.bangkok
museum.co.th**

Lak Muang: Just opposite the Grand Palace is a moderately sized but very significant marble pavilion, housing a phallic-shaped icon that symbolizes the city's foundation stone. All distances around the country are measured from this sacred monument.

The shrine is also where Bangkok's powerful landlord-spirits reside. Many Thais believe these spirits possess the power to perform miracles, so supplicants arrive daily to make offerings in support of winning lottery numbers and the continued health of their children. It's intriguing to linger inside the pavilion to watch the pilgrims in action and to admire the performances of Thai classical dance sponsored by successful supplicants. The best times to see these are early morning and late afternoon, especially in the times immediately preceding events such as the lottery.

National Museum

The National Museum is the largest and most comprehensive museum in Thailand, and is an outstanding place to study its history and arts, as well as the religious symbolism of Buddhism. Visitors who intend to visit the ancient capitals of Ayutthaya and Sukhothai (see pp. 132–140 and 195–199) will find the museum an invaluable aid to their understanding of the country and its various schools of religious art. Complimentary guided tours in English, which start daily at 9:30 a.m., are highly recommended.

The museum is housed in several buildings around the central Wang Na Palace, including a beautiful 18th-century wat and three historic pavilions. Chronologically arranged displays range from the prehistory of the country to artistic movements of the Rattanakosin era.

After purchasing your ticket, your first stop should be the **Sivamokhapiman Hall** to the left, which functions as a quick introduction to Thai history, with dioramas and other displays on the historical epochs from Sukhothai to the modern era. The prize exhibits are the famous Sukhothai inscription, or stela, of King Ramkamhaeng, which is the earliest known representation of the Thai script, and those describing the possible origins of the Thai people.

The **Gallery of Pre-Thai History** to the rear of the Sivamokhapiman Hall

Red Pavilion

Sivamokhapiman Hall

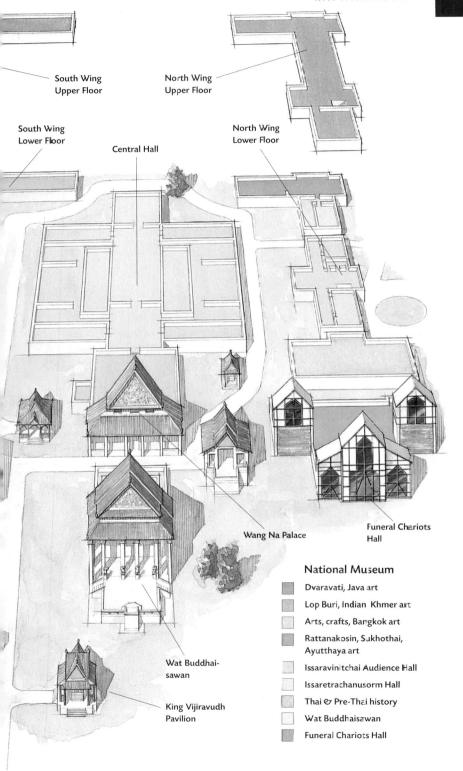

South Wing
Upper Floor

North Wing
Upper Floor

South Wing
Lower Floor

North Wing
Lower Floor

Central Hall

Funeral Chariots
Hall

Wang Na Palace

Wat Buddhai-
sawan

King Vijiravudh
Pavilion

National Museum

- Dvaravati, Java art
- Lop Buri, Indian Khmer art
- Arts, crafts, Bangkok art
- Rattanakosin, Sukhothai, Ayutthaya art
- Issaravinitchai Audience Hall
- Issaretrachanusorm Hall
- Thai & Pre-Thai history
- Wat Buddhaisawan
- Funeral Chariots Hall

displays Paleolithic artifacts from Kanchanaburi (see pp.124–127), and the famous pottery and bronze creations discovered near the town of Ban Chiang (see pp. 182).

Wat Buddhaisawan: Most important of the various examples of Thai architecture here is the centrally placed Wat Buddhaisawan, among the finest of the early monastic temples. The structure dates from 1787 and was built to contain a holy statue of the Buddha, the Phra Buddha Sing. The highlight is the spacious interior, set with richly gleaming wooden floors and superb murals in warm, vivid colors that give the room a wonderfully romantic atmosphere.

A return to the main museum route leads to the **Red Pavilion** (Taman Daeng). The former home of Rama I's sister, it is filled with the trappings of a royal resi-

dence of the late 18th and early 19th centuries.

Central Hall: Magnificent lacquered doors lead into the Wang Na Palace and the **Issaravinitchai Audience Hall,** once used by the surrogate monarch (the ruler's deputy). It now houses changing exhibits, such as recent archaeological discoveries. A small room at the back is filled with treasures discovered at Wat Ratchaburana in Ayutthaya (see pp. 136–137).

The rear section has more than a dozen rooms filled with a variety of fine arts and more utilitarian creations. Most rooms have a core theme that helps reduce confusion as you explore the labyrinth.

The first of these is the **Phimuk Monthain Gallery,** filled with splendidly decorative litters used in funerals, and howdahs carried by royal elephants. The room to the left is filled with shadow puppets and other intriguing stage properties, such as *khon* masks worn by dignitaries of the court of Rama VI.

The Central Hall also has rooms filled with European and Asian ceramics, glazed ware from Lop Buri, Sukhothai-period Sangkhalok stoneware and celadon, and

The sublime lines of a Buddha image at the National Museum, dating from the Sukhothai period

brightly colored Rattanakosin-era porcelain called Benjarong. You will also find richly carved elephant tusks and models of white elephants, elephant battle armor covered with religious symbols, antique weaponry, more royal regalia, carved teak, ancient inscribed stones, a collection of rare costumes and textiles from all regions of Southeast Asia, and Thai musical instruments, along with gamelans from Java and Bali.

South Wing: After exploring the Central Hall, take a quick look at the first flcor of the museum's South Wing. This section is dedicated to ancient artistic cultures of Thailand and its neighbors, including Cambodia and Java. The first room illustrates the importance of Indian culture on Thai art. Another concentrates on the role of various styles of Khmer art, from those known as Kompong Prae and Baphuon to the pinnacle of Cambodian heritage, Bayon.

The second floor of the South Wing includes rooms filled with art cf the Dvaravati period, and a small but worthwhile collection of images from central Java, including some exquisite examples of Hindu and Buddhist sculpture from Borobudur and Prambanan. A seventh-century stone Vishnu sculpture is a notable highlight.

North Wing: Artifacts from the later traditions of Sukhothai, Ayutthaya, and Bangkok are found in the North Wing, and are for many visitors the most impressive collections.

Among the highlights on the ground floor are printed and

embroidered textiles from the Rattanakosin period; lacquerware, inlay-work, and ceramics; Bangkok-era statuary, with its elaborate headdresses and ethereal faces; and a room filled with Buddha statues from various epochs, of which the image carved in the Dvaravati style—seated in the "European" fashion with hands on knees—is the most unusual. The numismatic gallery has displays of Thai coinage.

The upper floor of the North

EXPERIENCE:
Study Thai Culture
One of the top institutions of higher learning in Thailand, Chulalongkorn University's **Thai Studies Center** *(Faculty of Arts, Chulalongkorn University, tel 02-218-4862, www.arts.chula.ac.th/international/ thai)* offers English-language M.A. and Ph.D. programs in Thai studies. For those looking for something less intense, a nondegree program allows visitors to study different aspects of Thai culture, depending on student interest and time constraints. Available courses vary depending on the semester, but include **Modernization and Traditional Society in Thailand; Human Rights in Thai Tradition; Thai Buddhism; Thai Literature; Folklore in Thai Society; and Thai Music.**

To be considered for the semester-long program, applicants need a B.A. in any field; all applicants will be enrolled on a first-come, first-served basis. If you attend more than 80 percent of the classes, you are guaranteed a certificate of attendance.

Wing contains the richest collection of Buddha images in the museum, ranging from the small but precise Lanna and Chiang Saen figures from northern Thailand to the grander creations of the

A monk climbs the 320 steps to the top of the Golden Mount, once the highest point in Bangkok.

Wat Saket

- Map p. 66
- Boriphat Rd.
- $
- Air-con bus: 8, 11, or 12

Sukhothai Kingdom, regarded as the epitome of Thai art. Look for the magnificent bronze four-armed Vishnu and a statue of Harihara with eight arms arched in different mudras.

The final two rooms contain Buddha images from the Ayutthaya period, distinguished by their highly embellished headpieces and robes. Less interesting contemporary Buddhas complete the picture, and there are further examples of Rattanakosin craftwork.

Nearby are the **Funeral Chariots Hall,** full of magnificent chariots, and **Issaretrachanusorm Hall,** which was built for King Rama IV (r. 1851–1868), with his original European furniture in situ.

Wat Saket & the Golden Mount

At the northern end of historic Rattanakosin island is Wat Saket, undistinguished aside from its interesting carved windows. Nearby, the 260-foot (78 m) artificial hill known to Westerners as the Golden Mount, topped by a golden spire, is a clear landmark.

The temple, like Wat Phra Kaeo and Wat Pho, was constructed by Rama I in the early 19th century and therefore ranks as among the oldest structures in the city. It was originally built outside the city walls to serve as a crematorium for commoners. Later, toward the end of the 19th century, it was used as a burial site for victims of a cholera epidemic. It follows a traditional style of architecture, with a principal sanctuary surrounded by a large and peaceful courtyard—a welcome escape from the city.

The interior of the temple is covered with fairly modern frescoes. They are well restored and reward close inspection. Look for the rows of angels on the upper levels, who are praying with their heads turned toward the altar.

Just outside the main cloister is another sanctuary, with a huge standing Buddha that Rama I brought from the ruins of Sukhothai (see pp. 195–203). On the walls are paintings of Buddha's disciples. Behind the altar in the sanctuary, a seated Buddha image is surrounded by bronze statues of his disciples.

On the western side of the wat, the 320 steps leading to the summit of the Golden Mount—the highest point in Bangkok until the 1960s—wind past tombstones, myriad Buddhist monuments, small mountains erected to recall the Khmer/Buddhist co-opted Hindu heaven of Mount Meru, and clutches of monks who often engage in conversation with visitors to improve their English. This artificial hill was created from mud, brick, and teak logs after a chedi being built on the orders of Rama III collapsed because the soft soil beneath it gave way. Rama IV subsequently built another small, unimpressive chedi on the crest of the hill. The second chedi was expanded to house an Indian Buddha relic that was presented to Rama V by the British government in 1897. Each November, a festival held at Wat Saket features a candlelit parade up the steps to the summit of the Golden Mount.

It is worth the long climb to the top for the sweeping views over Bangkok—if, that is, the usual blanket of smog permits.

Wat Suthat & the Giant Swing

The large wihan (main hall) and bot (meeting hall) of Wat Suthat form one of the most impressive religious structures in Bangkok, a must-see after the splendor of the Grand Palace and Wat Phra Kaeo. Construction of the two buildings was started in 1807 by Rama I and gradually completed by his two successors.

Before entering the wihan, spend a few minutes exploring the **temple grounds,** which hold a museum of stone carvings, bronze animals, and Buddha images. Highlights include Chinese statues of American sailors and Chinese warlords, 28 hexagonal Chinese pagodas, and four magnificent bronze horses.

The wihan is the biggest in Bangkok, and whatever it may lack in terms of gaudy glitter is more than compensated for in its refined style and good taste. The structure stands on a pair of rising platforms and is entered through tall teak doors that are carved in five exquisite layers to recall the mythological forest of Himavada. In an act of piety, Rama II made one of these himself; it is in the National Museum (see pp. 82–86). The lavish interior radiates authority with a high ceiling, marble pillars, and frescoes. The 26-foot (8 m) bronze Buddha is a 14th-century masterpiece from Sukhothai.

The bot, built about 1839, is famous for its murals. Painted with pre-Western treatments of perspective, panels between the windows relate tales about the early lives of the Buddha. Frescoes on the shutters depict the heavenly city of Indra, while those on the front wall concern the Buddha's temptation by Mara (see p. 76).

Giant Swing: Near Wat Suthat's main entrance are two towering red pillars dating from 1784. They were once capped with a crossbar from which hung a long swing, part of a highly dangerous Hindu ceremony involving monks and bags of gold coins that's no longer practiced. ∎

Wat Suthat
- Map p. 66
- Bamrung Muang Rd., just SW of Wat Rachanat
- Air-con bus: 8 or 12

More Places to Visit in Rattanakosin

Loha Prasart

Behind Wat Rachanat is Loha Prasart, an unusual religious structure that resembles a large wedding cake, complete with candle-like spires. The pinkish monument, modeled on ancient temples in Sri Lanka and India, has a thousand rooms and was designed to serve as the home of Buddha and his disciples; this is the only surviving example of its type in the world. Although the exterior gate is generally locked, a resident monk will usually open it for you.

⛰ Map p. 66 ✉ Mahachai Rd.
🚌 Air-con bus: 11 or 39

Wat Rachabophit

Another unusual temple on Rattanakosin island is Wat Rachabophit, which has several buildings of interest, including a small chapel decorated in Italian Gothic style. Look for the particularly fine mother-of-pearl inlays in the doors and windows. In the royal cemetery next door, the tombs resemble miniature Asian temples or tiny European cathedrals. Best of all, you will probably be the only visitor there. The attendant monks are usually pleased to show people around the temple grounds.

⛰ Map p. 66 ✉ Atsadang Rd.
🚌 Air-con bus: 3 or 12

Spirit Houses

Many Thai buildings have spirit houses for spirits, or *phra phum*, to keep them from entering and causing trouble for the inhabitants. The spirit houses—ornate, dollhouse-size temples mounted on a pedestal in front of the main building—offer the spirits inviting daily gifts of food, flowers, and incense. The figurines inside symbolize the spirits that guard the property.

Wat Rachanat

Wat Rachanat, three blocks northeast of the Giant Swing, dates from 1846. It has some outstanding frescoes in the main sanctuary and a wihan of an unusual design (thought to be modeled on Burmese structures), with Buddhas mounted on an elevated altar. Its amulet market rivals that at Wat Mahathat (see p. 79).

⛰ Map p. 66 ✉ Mahachai Rd.
🚌 Air-con bus: 11 or 39

INSIDER TIP:

When visiting palaces, government offices, and temples, do not wear shorts or sleeveless shirts. Women should wear skirts that cover their knees.

—SUCHANA A. CHAVANICH
National Geographic field scientist

Wat Rachapradit

This peaceful minor temple is within easy walking distance of the Grand Palace and not far from Wat Suthat. Wat Rachapradit dates from the mid-19th century and was erected by King Mongkut to complement a pair of temples in Ayutthaya. It incorporates a variety of architectural styles, from older Thai traditions to Western motifs. The fascinating interior murals depict lively scenes of mid-19th-century Bangkok, including the Giant Swing ceremony (see p. 87). A prang in the courtyard has an impressive carved image of the four-faced Brahma.

⛰ Map p. 66 ✉ Rachini Rd.
🚌 Air-con bus: 3 or 12

Chinatown

Chinatown is a district south of the Grand Palace, bounded on one side by the Chao Phraya river and on the other by Charoen Krung Road. It is rarely walked by foreign visitors, though it is one of the most exciting ethnic enclaves in Bangkok.

Hidden behind the main streets, which now carry the dull look of modernization, are gaudily decorated temples filled with Taoist monks, creaky old pharmacies offering traditional Chinese medicines, gold shops piled high with chains and necklaces, and narrow alleys packed with all forms of street markets and peddlers of bric-a-brac.

Chinatown is also one of the oldest districts of the city, dating back to the late 18th century. The Chinese merchants moved their shops southward when they were cleared from the land on which Rama I intended to build his Grand Palace and Wat Phra Kaeo. The first businesses were established along narrow Sampeng Lane, which doubled as a commercial zone during the day and an opium district at night. Most of the illicit operations have long since closed down, though sufficient sights and smells remain to make this one of the most exotic corners of the city.

Chinatown, however, is not a neighborhood for the faint of heart. Nor is it a place for anyone who dislikes seething, frenetic, jam-packed quarters, where the scattered attractions and kaleidoscopic chaos make for a difficult walking tour. Probably the most convenient introduction and starting point is Ratachawong Pier (Tha Ratchawong), from where

Bangkok's ethnic Chinese patronize well-stocked herbal medicine shops.

you can walk up Ratachawong Road past several banks to visit the following attractions.

You can turn right to walk down romantic Sampeng Lane, visit the famous Golden Buddha at Wat Traimit, and return up the more commercialized Charoen Krung Road. Be prepared to make lots of trips up the side lanes to visit temples and other historic structures. Remember, it's the small details of Chinatown that make it just about the most interesting section of Bangkok—far more intriguing and culturally rewarding than the shopping centers and modern high-rises that now characterize so much of this rapidly changing city.

work painted to portray Chinese legends. Octagonal doors flanking the main altars lead into auxiliary chambers, including crypts and private rooms of worship.

The temple comes to active life once a year in the fall, during the Vegetarian Festival, to honor the nine chief deities. Traveling opera troupes perform at this time on the stage opposite the main entrance.

Sampeng Lane, also known as Soi Sampeng or Soi Wainit 1, runs parallel with the river. Built in the 1870s, it was the first street in Chinatown. It offers an authentic experience to all the senses and some unusual shops. It is far too narrow for regular traffic but

How to Haggle

The cost of products at open-air markets is negotiable. When haggling, be aware that you are often bickering over small amounts. While Thais are shrewd salespeople, they also are good-natured; maintain an air of cordiality at all times. Begin bidding at half the asking price and aim to settle at around 70 to 80 percent. If a vendor won't come down to an acceptable figure, politely decline and walk away; he or she will often offer a lower number.

Purchasing items early in the day is significantly advantageous, as superstitious vendors believe that early sales portend a prosperous day. You are likely to hand over the least baht during this time, and vendors will tap the bills on remaining products to bestow them with good luck.

Chinatown Highlights

Boonsamakan Vegetarian Hall (Soi Krai) is a small and very peaceful, old, yellow temple containing magnificent examples of Chinese woodcarving. The carvings are seen in the entrance porch and around the altars inside, and depict dragons and other mythological Chinese creatures. There are also miniature reproductions of traditional opera scenes and tile

perfect for pedestrians—who must make their way through the piles of merchandise that spill out from the intriguing old shopfronts, dodging the porters who madly haul their heavy loads. Fabric markets and clothing merchants predominate, and at the western end of the lane is the fabulous Pahurat Cloth Market, full of exotic silks and batiks.

Tang To Kang Gold Shop, a teetering but impressive seven-

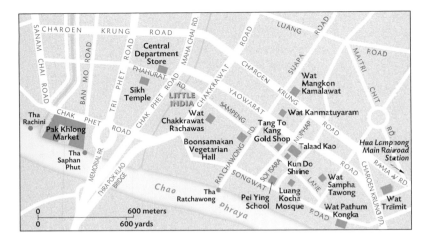

story structure designed by a Dutchman, was the original gold exchange for the neighborhood. It opened during Rama V's reign.

The **Kun Do Shrine** on Soi Isara Nuphap features a large grinning gilded horse head that is said to bring luck to those who bring him offerings of vegetables.

Talaad Kao, or Old Market, (Soi 16) is best visited in the early morning, when Chinese merchants and housewives come to trade all manner of produce, poultry, and fresh seafood. Come here before 10 a.m. to catch the best action of the day. Lantern-making, an old tradition that has now largely disappeared from Thailand, survives in the small alley off Soi Isara Nuphap.

Pei Ying School, located just off Sampeng Lane, is a large building of European design, housing a junior school founded by Chinese immigrants in 1916 to foster their language and customs. Chinatown also has a small Indian community, and Muslims gather on Friday afternoons at **Luang Kocha Mosque,** two

blocks south of Pei Ying School, to perform their weekly ablutions. Ancient Islamic tombstones in the graveyard behind the mosque are worth seeing.

Wat Sampha Tawong, also known as Wat Koh, features an impressive, modern multi-storied bot. Farther south, **Wat Pathum Kongka** straddles Songwat Road and dates from the Ayutthaya period, almost a hundred years before the founding of Bangkok.

Most visitors make the requisite stop to see the famous **Golden Buddha** inside **Wat Traimit** (Tri Mit Rd.), at the southern end of Chinatown and just across a canal from Hua Lamphong train station. The complex has the air of a rather seedy tourist trap, and the image itself, despite its claim to the biggest golden Buddha in the world, is undistinguished. Dating from the 13th century, it stands 13 feet (4 m) high, weighs an estimated 5.5 tons (5 tonnes), and is believed to be made of solid gold. According to legend, the Buddha

Chinatown

- Map above & p. 66
- Subway: Hua Lamphong station. Air-con bus: 1 or 7

had long been hidden under a disguising layer of stucco, until it was accidentally dropped from a crane in 1955, and a metallic core was revealed.

After paying your respects to the Golden Buddha, walk north up busy Charoen Krung Road, passing elaborately decorated gold stores and traditional Chinese wedding boutiques to **Soi Isara Nuphap** (Soi 16 Market), which is like a mini Sampeng Lane with its crazy bazaar atmosphere. Food is the main item sold here—everything from fresh raw ingredients to ready-to-eat Chinese snacks.

The Chinese venerate the impressive **Wat Mangkon Kamalawat,** or Dragon Flower Temple (Soi 21, off Charoen Krung Rd.). The central complex is filled with a fascinating collection of religious icons, from a fat Buddha to Taoist Star deities. ∎

Medical Tourism

Thailand has quality medical services, including modern facilities in urban centers and pharmacies throughout the kingdom. Health insurance covering overseas treatments is useful, although medical costs in Thailand are generally far less expensive than in the U.S. Subsequently, people frequently travel to Thailand specifically to receive treatments, often combining procedures with shopping trips or a week of recovery at the beach. When choosing a facility, be sure to check it out fully. Visit the Tourism Authority of Thailand (www.tourismthailand.org) for additional information.

Cosmetic Surgery: Thailand is a major destination for tourists looking for cosmetic treatments, such as face lifts, Botox and collagen injections, laser hair removal, and LASIK eye surgery.

Dental Care: Dental procedures, such as cleanings and fillings, are generally cheaper in Thailand, and more invasive procedures, such as root canals, are considerably less expensive.

Medical Procedures: Western-trained physicians, state-of-the-art medical equipment, and five-star service and facilities are primary reasons why more than one million foreigners visit Thai hospitals annually. Including airfare, proce-

dures are still cheaper than in the United States. Even cutting-edge therapies, such as stem-cell treatment, are available. The large numbers of specialists and operating theaters make scheduling easy.

Prescriptions: Most pharmacies do not require prescriptions and dispense pharmaceutical products over the counter. More serious prescriptions require a visit to a hospital pharmacy to fill.

Here are some medical facilities that offer different treatments:

Apex Profound Beauty
Emporium Department Store
3rd floor, Bangkok
Tel 02-664-8613
www.apexprofoundbeauty.com/en
Bangkok Hospital
Soi Soonvijai 7, New Petchburi Rd.
Bangkok
Tel 02-310-3102
www.bangkokhospital.com
Bumrungrad International Hospital
33 Sukhumvit 3, Bangkok
Tel 02-667-1000
www.bumrungrad.com
TRSC LASIK Center
986 Rama IV Rd., U Chu Liang Bldg.
6th floor, Bangkok
Tel 02-733-2020
www.lasikthai.com

A dragon dance winds through Chinatown during New Year festivities.

More Places to Visit in Chinatown

Hua Lamphong Station

The city's major train station, built by Dutch architects shortly before World War I, is Bangkok's most impressive art deco building, with huge vaulted ceilings, massive skylights, and wide entrances. The inexpensive bars and restaurants on the mezzanine floor have the best view.

Map p. 91 Rama Rd. IV Subway: Hua Lamphong station. Air-con bus: 1, 7, or 29

Little India

Purely Hindu neighborhoods are now rare in Thailand, with the exception of this small district between Chakkrawat and Chak Phet Roads, and pockets of Hindu culture near Silom and Charoen Krung Roads.On **Chak Phet Road,** which runs from the Central Department Store down to the river, shops sell traditional wedding gear for Hindu ceremonies as well as elaborate Thai dance costumes. The white **Sikh temple** stands seven stories high. Dozens of inexpensive food stalls and cafés line both sides of Chak Phet.
AMap p. 91 Between Chakkrawat & Chak Phet Rds. Subway: Hua Lamphong station. Air-conbus: 1 or 7

Pak Khlong Market

The city's largest wholesale fruit and vegetable emporium. Come early in the morning to see it at its best. Visitors love the displays of flowers and the colorful arrays of exotic fruit.

Map p. 91 Chak Phet Rd. near Memorial Bridge Subway: Hua Lamphong station. Air-con bus: 3 or 9 Tha Rachini

Wat Chakkrawat Rachawas

Chinese funerals are held here every day, it seems. The most notable feature of the wat is its crocodile pond, located just off the main courtyard.

Map p. 91 Chakkrawat Rd. Subway: Hua Lamphong station. Air-con bus: 1 or 7

Wat Kanmatuyaram

This interesting little temple on a side street opposite the Cathay department store dates from 1864 and is chiefly visited for its striking chedi designed in the Sri Lankan style. The temple has some of Thailand's most important murals, untouched since they were first painted. To see them, ask a monk to unlock the door to the interior.

Map p. 91 Mangkorn Rd. Subway: Hua Lamphong station. Air-con bus: 1 or 7

Eastern Bangkok

Beyond Chinatown, the mad sprawl of Bangkok continues eastward. Office towers, hotels, and condominiums rise from a seemingly endless urban landscape. Traffic clogs the roads with more intensity than elsewhere, and people crowd the potholed sidewalks, dodging motorcycles and muscling past myriad food and trinket vendors. Beyond all this, there are numerous—albeit dispersed—attractions, many of them easily accessed by the modern, air-conditioned Skytrain.

Colonial-style architecture, including the East Asiatic Company building, lines the Chao Phraya.

The line begins at the Chao Phraya river at the end of Sathorn Road near the gracious old farang (foreigner) quarter (see pp. 98–99). It heads northeast along the financial and entertainment district on **Silom Road,** home to world-famous **Patpong** and its side streets of go-go bars, massage parlors, restaurants, and night market It then crosses Rama IV Road, passing by leafy Lumphini Park, the exclusive **Royal Bangkok Sports Club,** and the popular Erawan Shrine (see p. 96), coming to Sukhumvit Road.

With the Skytrain gliding high above, Sukhumvit Road spears the length of eastern Bangkok, tunneling through the daunting sprawl of the metropolis, with much of the city's version of suburbia hiding beneath the continuous row of shops and small buildings that line it. At the rail crossing near the Marriott Hotel, Sukhumvit Road becomes Ploen Chit Road, a perpetually congested section that edges its way for about 2 miles (3 km) to the shopping district at Siam Square (see p. 93). Here it again changes names—this time to Rama I Road—before heading west toward Rattanokosin and the Chao Phraya river.

At the Skytrain's northern limits sprawls the **Chatuchak** weekend market *(Skytrain: Morchit station,*

INSIDER TIP:

Sirocco, a restaurant on top of State Tower, is the best place in town for a sunset cocktail. Go to the side overlooking the river for the best views.

—KRIS LEBOUTILLIER
National Geographic photographer

Subway: Chatuchak Park station), an absolute must for shoppers. You'll find antiques, clothing, paintings, kitchenware, and assorted novelties. To get a perspective, get a map at the market's tourist center. It's best to arrive mid-morning on Saturdays.

Siam Society

Established in 1904, the Siam Society is Thailand's premier cultural organization. It publishes books and the scholarly *Journal of the Siam Society,* and works to preserve all facets of traditional Thai culture. For those seeking a serious foray into Thailand's history and culture, a visit to its headquarters can be rewarding.

An excellent research library and archive is maintained on two floors at the society's headquarters in the Chalerm Phrakiat Building. Anything you need to find out about Thailand is housed here. There is also an art gallery and lecture and performance hall in the building, with lectures given by both Thai and Western scholars. Perhaps best of all are the regular excursions offered by the society to places of historical and cultural importance, including temples and archaeological sites, and to festivals around Thailand. Guided tours head deep into detail and incisiveness, and visitors can join in.

On the grounds of the society's headquarters is 175-year-old **Kamthieng House.** The society dismantled this traditional Thai wooden stilt house in Chiang Mai in Northern Thailand in the 1960s, then moved to Bangkok, and reassembled the building here. It houses an ethnological museum that provides a fascinating record of rural life in Northern Thailand, with exhibits that include woodcarvings and an assortment of northern hill-tribe costumes.

Shopping Around Rama I Road

Back on Sukhumvit Road, take the Skytrain west from Asoke station to **Siam Square,** beneath the Skytrain station of the same name *(near the junction of Rama I and Praya Thai Rds.).* Here you'll find shopping centers, movie theaters, hotels, street vendors, restaurants, and coffee shops—along with students, shoppers, and tourists. BTS Siam links with the jewel of Thai shopping malls, **Siam Paragon,** and its neighbor, **Siam Center.** From the eastern

Kamthieng House (Siam Society)

- ✉ 131 Soi Asoke
- ☎ 02-661-6410
- 🕐 Closed Sun.–Mon.
- 🚌 Air-con bus: 1, 8, 11, or 13. Subway: Sukhumvit station. Skytrain: Asoke station

Siam Center, Siam Paragon, Siam Square, Central World Plaza

- 🗺 Map p. 67
- ✉ Rama I Rd.
- 🚌 Air-con bus: 1, 8, 11, or 13. Skytrain: Siam station

Jim Thompson's House

🅐 Map p. 67

✉ Soi Kasem San 2, Rama I Rd.

☎ 02-612-3742

💲 $

🚌 Air-con bus: 1 or 8. Skytrain: National Stadium station

exit of BTS Siam, a sky-bridge leads to the Central World and Gaysorn plazas, past the Erawan and Intercontinental hotels, and terminates at BTS Chitlom.

Just south of Siam Square stands **Mahbonkrong shopping center** (also known as MBK), popular with tourists looking for bargains.

Jim Thompson's House

This is the modest but attractive former home of American architect and military officer Jim Thompson (1906–1967), who settled in Bangkok at the end of World War II. Credited with reviving Thailand's ailing silk industry (see pp. 178–179), Thompson disappeared in 1967 while hiking in the Cameron Highlands in Malaysia; no trace of his body was ever found, despite a massive search.

Thompson was an avid collector of Southeast Asian art and antiques, and his interconnecting maze of seven old teak houses is now a private museum full of assorted antiques, pottery, and other valuable curiosities. Highlights include the sixth-century headless Buddha that stands in the garden, Thompson's collection of Ming dynasty blue and white porcelain, and early 19th-century paintings of tales from the *Jataka*.

EXPERIENCE: Learn All About Gemology

Bangkok is an international hub for the distribution of gemstones, and it is considered the colored stone world capital. The high ratio of skill to cost for cutting, polishing, and setting stones has made gems one of Thailand's top foreign exchange businesses.

Subsequently, Bangkok is ideal for studying the art and science of gemology, both for professional and personal purposes. Students can learn to evaluate a gem's value or even disprove its authenticity, a valuable skill considering that Thailand is also a world leader in the manufacture of synthetic gemstones.

Asian Institute of Gemological Sciences (33rd fl., N. Tower, Jewelry Trade Center, 919/1 Silom Rd., Bangkok, tel 02-267-4315, www.aigst hailand.com)

In addition to field trips to ruby and sapphire mines, regional gem markets, and precious stone dealerships, students are given hands-on access to thousands of individual stones in order to practice their skills. An introductory course provides practical buying tips; the Accredited Gemologist Diploma is a month-long intensive program for professionals; and Basic Gemology is a four-week intermediary program. Jewelry design courses are also available.

Gemological Institute of America (12th fl., Thailand Campus Bisco Tower, 56/12 Sub Rd., Bangrak, Bangkok, tel 02-237-9575, www.giathailand.com) One of 14 international campuses, GIA Bangkok allows you to study in the classroom or via DVD instruction, which you can watch prior to your trip and then attend a five-day lab class upon arrival in Thailand. Novices can also study jewelry design, while professionals may enroll in seven weeks of focused diamond, colored stone, and gemologist "graduate" coursework.

The house (opposite MBK and the National Stadium) stands on the banks of an attractive canal, Khlong Saen Saeb, with a simple entrance courtyard and finely crafted gardens. The wooden houses were dismantled and brought here from the countryside, and all have been carefully preserved to retain their traditional charm, complete with the high and slightly curved roofs and polished teak floors that are typical of central Thailand. The overall effect is of an intimate and stylishly decorated residence.

In his quest for authenticity, Thompson adhered to particular customs of the early Thai builders, such as the elevation of the houses a full story above the ground (a practical precaution to avoid flooding during the rainy season). Thompson also had roof tiles made in Ayutthaya, employing a design that was common centuries ago but now is rarely seen. The house's exterior walls were painted in a red preservative paint once commonly used on old buildings.

Thompson also insisted that traditional religious procedures be followed during construction. Even the date of dedication was chosen by local astrologers as one that was auspicious. Within a few years of its completion in the spring of 1959, the house and art collection had become such a point of interest in Bangkok that Thompson opened his residence to the public, donating proceeds to local charities.

Suan Pakkad Palace

Don't be put off by the literal translation of this palace's name; *suan pakkad* means "cabbage patch." This collection of five traditional pavilions set in richly landscaped gardens forms one of the finest examples of traditional domestic architecture in Bangkok. The principal house was originally the residence of a wealthy northern family. Prince Chumbhot, a notable art collector, dismantled it and had it moved south from Chiang Mai.

The most striking building on

Suan Pakkad Palace

- Map p. 67
- 352 Sri Ayutthaya Rd.
- 02-245-4934
- $
- Air-con bus: 4. Skytrain: Phrya Thai station

www.suanpakkad.com

The home of Jim Thompson, the man who revived Thailand's silk industry after World War II, is now a museum.

the grounds is the 450-year-old **Lacquer Pavilion,** which was rescued from Ayutthaya (see pp. 132–140). It was originally the library of a temple located between Ayutthaya and Bang Pa-in.

The glossy black and gold structure is a unique example of Siamese decorative art, the only example of its kind to survive the ravages of time and warfare. Today it is admired not only for its fine

Erawan Shrine

  Map p. 67

✉ Phloen Chit Rd.

🚌 Air-con bus: 1, 4, 5, 8, 11, or 13. Skytrain: Chit Lom

proportions, but also for its remarkable lacquerwork murals, ornamented with intricate designs in gold. These panels, executed with great ingenuity, show thousands of minutely observed people in stylized surroundings. Around the pavilion, formal gardens provide welcome relief from the heat and pollution of Bangkok.

The other pavilions—once a bedroom, reception area, chapel,

Lumphini Park offers the perfect escape from Bangkok's noisy streets.

and dining room, respectively—hold a wide assortment of Thai artifacts. Highlights are Bronze Age pottery uncovered at Ban Chiang (see p. 182), Khmer sculpture, Sangkhalok ceramics, and multicolored Benjarong ceramics. Other artifacts include musical instruments, finely crafted reproductions of royal state barges, and antique drums that date back to the Dong Son era of ancient Vietnam. The pavilions also house antique Thai furniture, bronze and stone statues (of which those from the Dvaravati and Khmer periods are considered particularly fine), Chinese and

Thai porcelain, swords that once belonged to Siamese warriors, and delicately crafted fans used by priests in Buddhist rites.

The prince's family lived here for several decades. After his death the site was converted into a museum. Most of the collection is displayed in an informal style that reflects the former owners' tastes.

Erawan Shrine

The small but highly regarded Erawan Shrine, on one of the city's busiest intersections and just outside the Erawan Grand Hyatt hotel, is an extraordinary spot dedicated to the mysterious and all-pervasive forces of animist spirits and Hindu deities.

The shrine was erected in the 1950s to honor the Hindu god Brahma and to halt the string of disasters that had occurred during the construction of the original hotel at this site (including the sinking of a ship carrying marble for the lobby and the deaths of several construction workers). Along with spiraling costs, these disasters threatened to stop completion of the hotel. Hindu Brahman priests were summoned to lift the curse; the shrine was built on their advice and the hotel's troubles ended.

In 2006, a deranged man attacked the shrine, smashing the Brahma image. Two witnesses violently killed the man. The shrine was closed for a brief period, after which a new statue, including pieces of the original, was installed in its place.

Today, the shrine is a madcap scene of religious frenzy. Devotees arrive with gifts of flowers and smoking incense. Wooden effigies of elephants are left for Erawan, the veneratec three-headed elephant god who carried Brahma. Pilgrims ask for blessings or give thanks for good fortune. Those whose prayers have been answered may pay for traditional dancers to perform.

The nearby **Bayoike Tower** has an observation deck on the 77th of its 85 floors from which you can take in Bangkok's urban sprawl and—on clear days—the Gulf of Thailand.

Lumphini Park & Around

Lumphini Park, once little more than rice fields on the edge of town, covers 140 acres (56 ha)

Buddha Amulets

Thais believe that Buddha amulets worn around the neck can protect them from evil spirits, danger, and misfortune. The small icons, found at all markets, can cost hundreds of dollars, depending on their perceived power—attained by being blessed by a monk or by being issued by a powerful organization such as the army or police. Taxi drivers wear them to protect against accidents; thieves don them to ward off arrest; soldiers clench them between their teeth before entering battle.

---

of some of the best real estate in Bangkok. As the city's most popular park, Lumphini offers an easy escape from the incessant crowds, noise, and pollution of Bangkok's streets.

The park is named after Bud-

dha's birthplace in Nepal, reputedly an enchanted garden. Its central feature is the large artificial lake, where you can hire boats for a row or a paddle. The city's health conscious run on the jogging trail during the early morning hours, use the tennis and basketball courts, or play afternoon games of badminton and *takraw*. An intriguing structure is a Chinese pagoda-style clock tower. Chinese philanthropic organizations were responsible for its construction—and for many other buildings in public venues.

A ten-minute walk east of the park along Rama IV Road brings you to the **Lumphini Boxing Stadium,** the ramshackle theater of *muay Thai*. There is nothing fake about the raucous, beer-swilling crowd, the clanging, high-pitched instruments, or the fierce, often brutal antics of competitors—the country's best *muay thai* athletes. Matches are held Tuesdays and Fridays beginning at 6:30 p.m., and Saturdays between 5 and 8 p.m. and after 8:30 p.m.

Near the boxing stadium is the Joe Lou s Theatre, where the **Traditional Thai Puppet Theater** (*1875 Rama IV Rd., Lumphini, tel 02-252-9683, www.thaipuppet .com, $$$$$) performs scenes from the *Ramakien*. Puppets are each controlled by three puppeteers, all of whom are experienced khon dance performers. The family-run theater is under royal patronage, having single-handedly revived the ancient art, about which there is a preperformance documentary. An on-site restaurant allows for a dinner-theatre experience; nightly performances begin at 7 p.m. ∎

Bayoike Tower

 222 Ratchaprarop Rd., Skytrain: Phraya Thai station

Lumphini Park

 Map p. 67

 Bounded by Rama IV Rd., Sarasin Rd., Witnayu Rd., & Ratchadamri Rd. Main entrance: corner of Rama IV Rd. & Ratchadamri Rd.

 02-252-5348

 Air-con bus: 4, 5, or 7. Subway: Silom station. Skytrain: Saladaeng station

Lumphini Boxing Stadium

 Map p. 67

 67 Rama IV Rd ,near Lumpini Park & junction of Sathorn & Rama IV

 02-252-8763 or 02-251-4303

 $

A Walk Around the Old *Farang* Quarter

A fairly short but interesting walking tour can be made along the Chao Phraya river, around the attractive old commercial and diplomatic enclave that once comprised the original *farang* (foreigner) community within the city of Bangkok.

Authors' Lounge, located in the original part of the Mandarin Oriental hotel

Start at the world-famous **Mandarin Oriental** ❶, where you can spend some time exploring the palm-filled **Authors' Lounge** (early 20th-century luminaries such as Joseph Conrad, Noël Coward, and Graham Greene stayed here), or enjoy breakfast on the veranda overlooking the Chao Phraya. Just where Oriental Avenue terminates at the river, a Dutch flag flies over the whitewashed former headquarters of the **East Asiatic Company** ❷, built in 1901. Founded by Dutch investors in 1897, this mercantile firm was one of the first to set up permanent offices in the city.

Pass through the arch of the East Asiatic Company building and walk parallel to the river. Follow the alley around to the left to reach the pink and white **Assumption Cathedral** ❸. There has been a Catholic cathedral on this site since the first Europeans settled here in 1822, though the present structure dates from 1910.

NOT TO BE MISSED:

Authors' Lounge, Mandarin Oriental hotel • Assumption Cathedral • French Embassy • Old Customs House • Harun Mosque • Antiques at River City Shopping Complex

The brightly painted rococo interior has a marble altar imported from France. Visitors are welcome.

Turn left on Oriental Lane, and bear left onto Oriental Avenue, then immediately right, to pass the Oriental Hotel on your left. Tucked on the next corner, just beyond the hotel, is the lovely old **French Embassy** ❹, built in the mid-19th century and the second oldest embassy in Bangkok. With its spacious rooms, shuttered windows, and upper verandas overlooking a well-tended garden, this building evokes a more elegant age.

Turn left down Soi 36 toward the river, then take a right to pass by the finely proportioned **Old Customs House ⑤**. Built in the 1880s, this was Bangkok's primary customs house until more modern port facilities were developed downriver at Khlong Toey. Today the building is used by the Bangkok Fire Brigade, which docks several fireboats along the waterfront.

Beyond the Customs House, turn right away from the river, and weave through the narrow alleys to reach the **Harun Mosque ⑥**. Bangkok's small community of Muslims gather here on Fridays to worship. Paths lead on, away from the river, toward the **General Post Office ⑦**, through a neighborhood where many Indians and Pakistanis live. Small cafés provide fine opportunities for a stop on your walking tour.

You might want to make a quick visit to the post office to wander around its cavernous interior and purchase some Thai commemorative stamps, or check your mail at Poste Restante.

A few steps up from the post office is the **Portuguese Embassy ⑧**, which dates from 1820 and is the oldest foreign embassy in Bangkok. The Portuguese were the first Europeans to open trade relations with Siam in the 16th century, from their base in the Malaysian city of Melaka, and the first to be granted land for a trading post and then a consulate in Bangkok during the reign of Rama II. You can peer over the embassy walls to see portions of the original construction.

One block beyond the post office, narrow alleys wind back to the river and the **Royal Orchid Sheraton** hotel, and then continue to the nearby air-conditioned **River City Shopping Complex ⑨**. River City is Bangkok's premier outlet for Southeast Asian antiques, best picked up at the monthly auctions (check details in the *Bangkok Post*). Art exhibitions also are held here.

River City makes for a convenient finish to your walking tour, though a handful of other sights are within a few blocks up the river. The **Holy Rosary Church ⑩** stands on the site of a church built in 1787 by Portuguese

Catholics, who had fled the destruction of Thon Buri by the Burmese. Known locally as Wat Calavar, this small but elegant Gothic-style church features some fine stained glass.

From here, you could also continue along the riverside for the short distance (0.5 mile/ 0.8 km) to **Wat Traimit,** the temple of the Golden Buddha (see p. 91), and then to the restored **Hua Lamphong** train station (see p. 93) and Chinatown (see pp. 89–93).

ⓐ	See area map pp. 66–67
▶	Oriental Hotel
↔	1 mile (1.5 km)
⏱	1.5 hours
▶	River City Shopping Complex

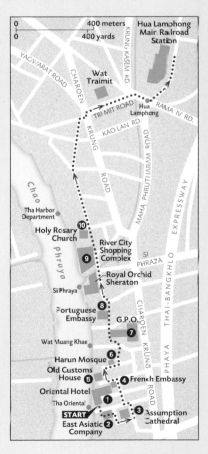

More Places to Visit in Eastern Bangkok

Ban Bat

Rama I established three villages in Bangkok to house the artisans who made bowls for the local community of monks. Only a single village remains, Ban Bat, near Wat Saket and the Golden Mount. A handful of craftspeople continue to fashion bowls of polished silver, each traditionally and laboriously made from eight separate pieces of metal. These can be seen in use by local monks making their morning rounds to collect alms of rice and other food. You also can buy the monks' bowls at Wat Suthat.

🅰 Map p. 66 ✉ Soi Ban Bat, near Bamrung Muang Rd. 🕐 Bowl production most days until around 6 p.m. 🚌 Air-con bus: 8, 11, or 12

Patpong

Once Bangkok's most notorious street, Patpong has been sufficiently diluted during the past decade or so and no longer deserves that title. Its main feature these days is a dominating market that sells overpriced counterfeit goods to tourists; getting from one end of the street to the other is an onerous navigational feat.

🅰 Map p. 67 ✉ Silom Rd. at Pan Pan Rd. 🚌 Air-con bus: 2, 4, or 5. Subway: Silom station. Skytrain: Saladaeng station

Queen Saowapha Snake Farm

One block from Lumphini Park is the former Pasteur Institute, Thailand's leading facility for the development of vaccines against diseases such as cholera, smallpox, typhoid, and rabies. More interesting for visitors, it is also a center for education about the local poisonous snakes, and anti-snakebite serum is made here.

More than a thousand snakes are kept at the Queen Saowapha Snake Farm by the Thai Red Cross for both research and education. Snake demonstrations are held twice a day (once a day on weekends). After watching a 20-minute slide show about the center, visitors are led into a circular room. Handlers bring out a variety of snakes, including the mesmerizing Siamese king cobra, and "milk" them spectacularly, waving them within inches of the audience.

The snakes' fangs seep poisonous venom harmlessly into glass jars, providing some highly unusual shots for photographers. More indigenous venomous and non-poisonous snakes are displayed in the adjacent vivarium.

🅰 Map p. 67 ✉ Rama IV Rd. ☎ 252-0161 💲 $ 🚌 Air-con bus: 4, 5, or 7. Subway: Silom station. Skytrain: Saladaeng station

INSIDER TIP:

Don't hesitate to eat from street food vendors—most of the dishes are stir-fried at high temperatures (killing germs). For starters try *pad see yu* (noodles with soy sauce) or mango with sweet sticky rice.

—BARBARA A. NOE
National Geographic editor

Royal Thai Air Force Museum

Strictly for fans of military aircraft, the Royal Thai Air Force Museum includes rare examples of a Japanese Tachikawa trainer, a Spitfire, and several Breguets. This is one of two such collections in the country; the other is the Warbirds Museum at Chiang Mai International Airport (see p. 221).

🅰 Map p. 67 ✉ Don Muang Airport, Wing 6 🕐 Closed weekends 🚌 Airport Bus: A1, A2, or A3. Skytrain: Morchit station. Subway: Chatuchak station

Dusit

In the northern part of Bangkok, this fascinating neighborhood is home to many of the important government offices and royal residences that were moved here at the beginning of the 20th century, away from the more crowded area around the Grand Palace (see pp. 73 & 76–77). The broad, tree-lined avenues and spacious mansions and public buildings give this leafy section of Bangkok, also known as the New Royal City, a curiously European flavor.

Dusit is one of the few districts in Bangkok that shows signs of urban planning; green spaces between the government buildings provide a calm dignity that has been lost in the rest of the capital. Public offices, universities and private schools, palaces, and parks dominate the area. Although land speculation and the construction of modern houses and high-rise offices have inevitably changed it, Dusit is one of the few places where you can get a glimpse of the city's garden aspects, which made it so remarkable to early travelers.

The most popular attractions are Chitralada Palace (where King Bhumibol Adulyadej lives today), the beautiful wooden Vimanmek Palace, the outstanding Marble Temple (Wat Benchamabophit), the National Assembly (Parliament) building, and Dusit Zoo. These are all found close together, making Dusit surprisingly convenient to explore.

Ratchadamnoen Nok Road leads past the headquarters of the Tourism Authority of Thailand (T.A.T.), then the Ratchadamnoen Boxing Stadium, and finally the Khlong Phadung Krung Kasem, before reaching the old National Assembly building. Just before this, look for an impressive equestrian statue of King Chulalongkorn, the

This 105-foot-high (32 m) Buddha statue at Wat Indrawihan offers great views of Dusit.

man responsible for the planning and construction of Dusit. Amporn Park is opposite the statue, while Vimanmek Palace and Dusit Zoo flank the National Assembly. Chitralada Palace is a few blocks east, on the far side of the zoo.

With its 80 rooms, Vimanmek Palace is believed to be the largest golden teak building in the world.

Dusit Zoo

Map p. 67 & p. 107

✉ Ratchawithi Rd.

$ $

🚌 Air-con bus: 10

Vimanmek Palace

Map p. 66 & map p. 105

✉ Ratchawithi Rd.

$ $; English-language tours available

🚌 Air-con bus: 10

Dusit Park

On the grounds of Dusit Park are a clock museum, a display of King Bhumibol's photographs (he is an avid photographer), and the Royal Carriage Museum, which houses an eccentric array of ceremonial vehicles. Highlights are the zoo and Vimanmek Palace.

Dusit Zoo: With its modest but growing collection of animals from across Southeast Asia, Thailand's largest zoo provides a welcome change from a steady diet of historical buildings. It has large mammals such as rhinos, monkeys, elephants, tigers, and bears, plus deer and other indigenous species, including serow (antelope) and gaur (a species of ox). Visitors can also enjoy hundreds of birds and the extensive reptile collection.

The zoo has a playground, several small cafés, and an artificial lake with recreation facilities. It is a shady place bisected by decorative waterways, which provide the setting for a competition of floats for

the Loy Kratong festival in the fall.

As with so much else in Dusit Park, the zoo was created by King Chulalongkorn, who was inspired by zoological gardens in Europe. In 1909 the king traveled to Indonesia, where he purchased a handful of star deer; they were allowed to roam the private royal botanical gardens. After the coup of 1932, the new government petitioned the king to transfer the gardens and park to the municipality of Bangkok for the people's use.

The zoo opened to the public in 1938 but was still limited to a handful of animals. Authorities added representative species of Thailand; within a few years it also had white monkeys, bears, and a crocodile pond. The zoo was greatly expanded after the founding of the Zoological Organization of Thailand in 1954. This organization opened another zoo in Chiang Mai (see p. 222) and an "open zoo" in Khao Khieo, Chonburi Province.

Vimanmek Palace: If Bangkok has one house filled with memories, serene, beautiful Vimanmek Palace must be it. This gracious building was once the royal residence of King Chulalongkorn, one of Thailand's most beloved and progressive monarchs.

It also survives as a delicate architectural balance between the last gasp of the 19th century and the modernization of the early 20th century. The original structure was started in 1893 on the resort island of Ko Si Chang under orders from Chulalongkorn, who named the teak pavilion Mundhat Ratanaroj. It was designed by a German architect and built without a single nail. Construction came to a halt the following year, after a diplomatic crisis brought French warships sailing into the Gulf of Siam, rendering further royal visits to Ko Si Chang impossible.

The unfinished structure lay abandoned until 1901, when the king ordered that it be dismantled, hauled to Bangkok, and fashioned into the present structure, renamed Vimanmek, or "castle in the clouds." Incredibly, it took only seven months to complete the world's largest golden teak building. With open galleries, gingerbread fretwork, charming porticoes, grand stairways, and spiral staircases, the building shows European and Victorian architectural influences. Daily tours *(English available)* include fewer than half of the 80 rooms but give a good flavor of this extraordinary home.

The king and his family (and concubines) lived here until they could move into nearby Chitralada Palace. Closed up and neglected, Vimanmek was on the point of collapse when Queen Sirikit came to its rescue in 1982; it was beautifully restored as part of Bangkok's bicentennial celebrations. Today it is a museum housing royal artifacts and Chulalongkorn's personal items, from antique photos of the last elephant hunt to the first shower installed in Thailand. ∎

Ordering & Eating Like a Thai

Many visitors avoid local eateries and street stalls, and miss out on the most authentic Thai cuisine. In general, the more popular a restaurant, the more fresh ("safe") the food will be; follow the crowd.

Many street stalls specialize in certain dishes. See what other diners are having, whether it's shared dishes with rice or bowls of noodles. *Ba mee mu daeng* vendors, who display slabs of red pork *(mu daeng)*, almost exclusively serve noodles with spicy pork (try the one at the corner of Silom soi Convent, by 7-11). Vendors with chickens on display will primarily serve *khao mun gai*, oily rice with chicken (Sukhumvit Rd. between Emporium Shopping Center & Soi 24 is a good bet).

At restaurants, diners typically collaborate on ordering meat, fish, or vegetable dishes and individual plates of rice and then share. Considering the low prices, you could order a few more dishes than your number of diners and discover your individual preferences. Experimentation is part of the fun, but remember to order *mai pet* ("not hot") if you can't handle spicy Thai!

When dining, Thais use a fork and spoon, using the fork to push food onto the spoon, from which they eat. Knives are basically unavailable and chopsticks are reserved for dishes of Chinese origin, particularly noodle soups, though a soup spoon is also then used and Thais often use the chopsticks to transfer noodles to the spoon.

A Walking Tour of Dusit Park

Dusit Park and its environs provide a number of worthwhile sights within a small area. The sights are varied: a glorious temple, seats of government, royal palaces, both outlandish and exquisite architecture, a zoo, and cool parks and gardens.

Many consider Wat Benchamabophit the most impressive example of modern Thai architecture.

Start your walk at **Wat Benchamabophit** ❶ *(corner of Rama V & Sri Ayutthaya Rds.),* one of the most elegant and refined pieces of modern religious architecture in Thailand. It was commissioned by King Chulalongkorn in 1899, to the designs of his half brother, Prince Naris, and Italian architect Hercules Manfredi. The Italian white Carrara marble facing gave the temple its nickname—the Marble Temple.

Proceed down the side road that runs parallel to Rama V Road for about five minutes and turn right onto Thanon Luk Luang. The tree-lined boulevard is separated from a parallel road by the wide Khlong Phadung Krung Kasem; laughing children may well be seen splashing in the canal. Both roads run past the sprawling complex at **Government House** ❷, dominated by the Gothic Thai Koo Fah Building. With an exterior of extravagantly ornate arches, domes, pillars, and eaves, this extraordinary building looks

NOT TO BE MISSED:

Wat Benchamabophit • Abhisek Dusit Throne Hall • Vimanmek Palace

more like a European palace than the office of Thailand's prime minister. The surrounding area is often filled with resilient protesters: a mixture of farmers from the country's impoverished northeast, trade unionists, and activists who spend months at a time in makeshift shelters.

At the corner of Thanon Luk Luang and Ratchadamnoen Nok Road, a small bridge curves over the canal. Its green wrought-iron barriers run to thick columns veneered in marble and streetlights wrapped in intricately worked wrought iron top patterned steel and concrete poles. Turn right, down leafy Ratchadamnoen

Nok Road for about five minutes to Dusit Park (take care crossing busy Sri Ayutthaya Road).

Dominating the **Royal Plaza ❸** at the park's entrance is an equestrian statue of King Chulalongkorn. Every December 5, the plaza bursts forth with pomp and ceremony for the Trooping of the Colors, when the Royal Guard Regiment affirms its oath of loyalty to the King and Queen, who attend the event.

Behind the plaza is the **Ananta Samakorn Throne Hall ❹**. Overdone in Italianate architecture, it almost appears as a parody. A huge green dome supported by a ring of Roman columns crowns the building (rarely open to the public). Its former stables, reached by a path to the left off

Uthong Nai Road, house the **Royal Elephant National Museum.** Exhibits include the gigantic tusks of the elephants of Ramas III, IV, and V.

Farther down the path, over a tiny bridge, is the **Abhisek Dusit Throne Hall ❺**. The facade features a veranda carved in exquisite timber latticework. The building now houses the **SUPPORT Museum,** displaying traditional crafts such as nielloware, woodcarving, and textiles.

Beyond the museum is the extraordinary **Vimanmek Palace ❻**, a marvel of traditional architecture and the world's largest teak building (see pp. 104–105). A little farther up Uthong Nai Road is the concrete, bunker-style **National Assembly,** built in the 1970s. Backtrack to the **Dusit Zoo ❼** (see p. 104), and rent a paddleboat for a trip around the zoo's delightful lake.

Adjacent to Dusit Zoo, across busy Rama V Road, is **Chitralada Palace ❽**, the king's official residence (closed to the public).

🗺	See area map pp. 66–67
▶	Dusit Park
↔	1.6 miles (2.6 km)
⏱	2 hours
▶	Dusit Park

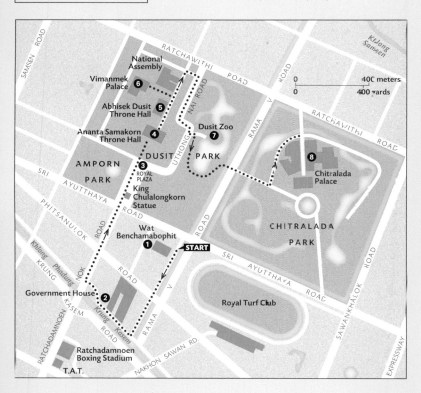

More Places to Visit in Dusit

Democracy Monument

The rallying point of Thailand's democracy movements over the past 30 years, the Democracy Monument was built in 1939 to commemorate the overthrow of absolute monarchy in 1932. The imposing 78-foot (24 m) monument's sharp lines, reliefs of diligent, muscular citizens carrying out their duties with pride, and military hardware evoke overblown fascist and communist architecture more than democracy. Still, the monument remains a potent symbol and city landmark. Ratchadamnoen Road, between the monument and Royal Field, has been the scene of many public protests, including the Black May pro-democracy demonstrations in 1992 (see p. 48), when at least 50 protesters were killed by the military.

🅰 Map p. 66 ✉ Pracha Thipatai & Ratchadamnoen Klang Rds. 🚌 Air-con bus: 11, 12, or 44

Khao San Road

The area around Khao San Road in Banglamphu has evolved from a backpacker's haven with cheap guesthouses into a lively neighborhood of trendy bars and restaurants popular with locals and tourists. You'll even find a boutique hotel and a Starbucks here.

Budget travelers are not ignored, though: Roadside vendors sell bottles of beer for less than a dollar and mixed drinks for $1.25. Outdoor cafés provide some of the best people-watching in Bangkok, and stalls selling clothes and trinkets line the road.

Wat Bowonniwet

On the northern edge of Rattanakosin, Wat Bowonniwet holds an important place in Thais' hearts, for this is where many royal princes studied and served their monkhood, including the current King, Bhumibol.

The architecturally unremarkable temple dates from the mid-19th century. Yet it was saved from obscurity by the popularity and status of the future King Mongkut, who served part of his monkhood here and became the chief abbot.

Today, the *wat* is the residence of Thailand's Supreme Patriarch, the recognized leader of Buddhism in the country. It is also the headquarters of the Thammayut sect of Buddhism, a small, strict order that inspires great respect; it is widely thought to be purer than the Theravada branch.

The great golden *chedi* at the wat's heart enshrines sacred relics and ashes of Thai royalty. The two *wihans* are closed to the public. The unusual T-shaped *bot* holds a magnificent Sukhothai-period Buddha, cast in 1257 to celebrate freedom from the Khmers.

The temple's most impressive features, however, are the imaginative three-dimensional murals on the bot's interior walls. Murals were traditionally light and cheery, strictly limited both in their subject matter and style. Monk-artist Khrua In Khong, court painter to King Mongkut, introduced Western perspective, bringing a sense of realism to traditional Buddhist topics, and preferred mysterious, moody shading over the more commonly seen bright hues.

🅰 Map p. 66 ✉ Phra Sumen Rd. 🚌 Air-con bus: 11

Wat Indrawihan

A 20-minute walk north of Wat Bowonniwet, Wat Indrawihan is in a peaceful residential area. Stroll down the smaller alleys for an insight into the lifestyle of the average Thai. This minor temple is dominated by a standing Buddha statue created in 1830, which you can enter and then climb *(donation: $)* for terrific views.

🅰 Map p. 66 ✉ Wisut Kasat Rd. 🚌 Air-con bus: 3, 6, or 9.

Thon Buri

The former capital of Thailand spreads down the western shore of the Chao Phraya river, linked to the newer city by bridges and ferry boats. Thon Buri was the original Bang Kok ("riverside village of the wild olive"), and lent this name to its newer neighbor. Much of the old capital retains its traditional charms and is built on a network of rivers and canals (*khlongs*), all in a state of bustling activity.

Long-tail boats can be chartered for trips along the Chao Phraya river and the nearby canals.

Thon Buri was founded in 1757 and served as the capital of Siam for 15 years after the fall of Ayutthaya. Then Rama I moved his court across the river for safety. Over the ensuing two centuries, while Bangkok became a bustling commercial center, Thon Buri was allowed to sleep on, almost completely untouched by the forces of modernization. The first bridge between the two was not built until 1932. Other bridges followed, as did the construction of roads and shops. In the 1980s and 1990s, condominiums sprang up. But development in this surprisingly peaceful and rarely visited part of Bangkok has not greatly affected its ancient canal network, and much of it still remains intact.

Highlights of Thon Buri include the world-famous Wat Arun (Temple of the Dawn) and the Royal Barges Museum, as well as the *wats* of Suwannaram, Kalyanimit, and Dusitaram.

Exploring Thon Buri can be tricky, as the smaller roads that lead to the most interesting temples are often little more than patchy lanes without formal demarcation. However, wandering around the alleys and planked walkways can be an excellent experience, as the people are friendly and invariably hospitable to the visitors who find themselves off the beaten track. In fact, getting lost is almost a blessing here, as locals are more than happy to point out the correct direction to the temple of your choice.

The best way to explore Thon Buri is via a combination of water transportation, such as a motor-powered long-tail water taxi, and travel on foot through the maze of alleys. Long-tail boats can be hired at most of the piers on the Bangkok side of river, but be aware that few boatmen speak enough English to serve as adequate guides. Be sure to negotiate a price beforehand; a fair rate is 300 to 400 baht per hour.

Royal Barges Museum

This remarkable collection of more than 50 elaborately decorated longboats is displayed in a vast, covered dry dock near Khlong Bangkok Noi. Painted, carved, and gilded, the boats were modeled after various mythological creatures from the epic *Ramakien,* and come out only on the grandest of ceremonial occasions—for example, a procession on the Chao Phraya in December 1999 to celebrate King Bhumibol's 72nd birthday, the start of his sixth 12-year cycle of life, an auspicious age in Buddhism.

The tradition of royal barge processions dates back to the heyday of the Ayutthaya Kingdom, when King Narai the Great led a flotilla of 147 boats along the Chao Phraya to accompany a diplomatic delegation sent to Siam by the great French king Louis XIV (r. 1643–1715). At this time the royal barges served a dual purpose, both as decora-

Ornate barges are used in royal ceremonies.

tive and ceremonial means of transportation and as the naval fleet. The barges were also used in boat races for entertainment and in religious rites such as the annual festival of Tod Kathin.

During the war of 1767 with the Burmese, which destroyed Ayutthaya, the royal barges were

INSIDER TIP:

If you want to learn more about the Buddhist religion and traditions, many temples offer "monk chats" that give you the opportunity to talk with a monk.

—RUSS BAHORSKY
National Geographic Books

wrecked along with other treasures. Fortunately, when Rama I ascended the throne in 1782, he regarded the renewal of national arts and crafts as a priority, and initiated the construction of new barges. By the mid-19th century, the royal barge procession had expanded to 269 boats, which required more than 10,000 oarsmen. The barges sustained severe damage during the bombing of Bangkok in World War II but were reconstructed and restored by King Bhumibol.

The most significant barge, known as **Supphanahongsa,** is 165 feet (50 m) long and weighs more than 15 tons (13.5 tonnes). The vessel is carved from a single piece of teak, with the exception of the gilded figurehead that depicts the mythical golden swan, Hamsa.

This enormous boat requires the services of 54 oarsmen to pull it through the water, along with two helmsmen, two officers, one flagman, and a rhythm keeper who taps the butt of his silver spear on the deck to keep the time for the chanting of ancient songs.

One of the best times to see the boats in action is during the royal Kathin ceremony at the end of Phansaa—the Buddhist rains retreat—during the October or November new moon. The festival features the magnificent *Anantan-agaraj,* a 145-foot-long (44 m) barge with a multiheaded *naga* serpent on its prow. The vessel is used to carry new robes that are offered to monks.

Wat Arun

Wat Arun, also known as the Temple of the Dawn, looms 286 feet (86 m) above the west bank of the Chao Phraya in an unmistakable silhouette that has become a striking symbol of Bangkok itself. It is even found on the 10-baht coin. The towering *prang,* built in the rather solid Khmer style, dates from the reign of Rama I and represents Mount Meru, mythological home of the Hindu gods. It was constructed on the grounds of an Ayutthaya temple, Wat Makok, which was at one time the home of the Emerald Buddha. When Taksin and his army reached the monastery following the destruction of Ayutthaya, the king renamed it Wat Jang (*jang* means "dawn") after the moment of his arrival—exactly at dawn.

(continued on p. 115)

Royal Barges Museum

- Map p. 66
- Arun Amarin Rd.
- $
- Ferry to Tha Fot Fai in Thon Buri, then a short walk

A Boat Trip on the Chao Phraya

Exploring the Chao Phraya river by boat is one of Bangkok's greatest pleasures. The inexpensive Chao Phraya River Express, a commuter ferry, makes stops up the river's east bank as far as Nonthaburi. To visit the west bank, however, you'll have to take shuttles across the river. A more leisurely option is to visit the east bank sites by commuter ferry one day, then visit the west bank sites by long-tail boat the next.

The sun sets behind Wat Arun.

The white-and-red Express boats run every 20 minutes, from 6 a.m. to 6 p.m.; you pay the fare once aboard. Start at **Tha (Pier) Sathon,** where Sathon Road meets the Chao Phraya at Taksin Bridge, and head upriver.

The Express soon makes its first stop, at Tha Oriental, named after the venerable hotel (see p. 100). The nearby Old Customs House, the East Asiatic Company building, and, a little farther north near Tha Mueng

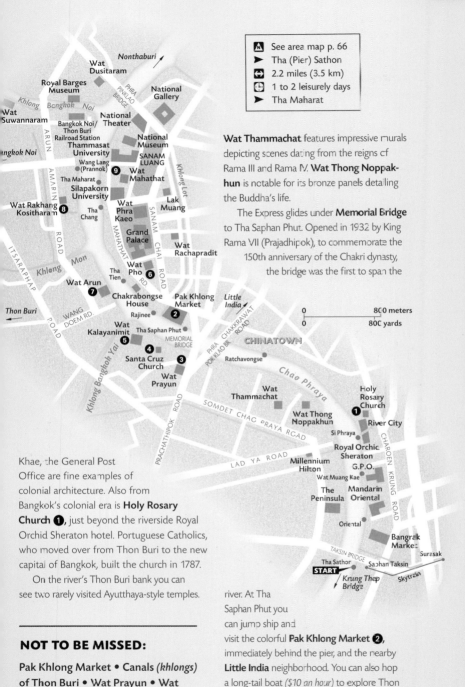

▲	See area map p. 66
►	Tha (Pier) Sathon
⟷	2.2 miles (3.5 km)
⏱	1 to 2 leisurely days
►	Tha Maharat

Wat Thammachat features impressive murals depicting scenes dating from the reigns of Rama III and Rama IV. **Wat Thong Noppakhun** is notable for its bronze panels detailing the Buddha's life.

The Express glides under **Memorial Bridge** to Tha Saphan Phut. Opened in 1932 by King Rama VII (Prajadhipok), to commemorate the 150th anniversary of the Chakri dynasty, the bridge was the first to span the

Khae, the General Post Office are fine examples of colonial architecture. Also from Bangkok's colonial era is **Holy Rosary Church ❶**, just beyond the riverside Royal Orchid Sheraton hotel. Portuguese Catholics, who moved over from Thon Buri to the new capital of Bangkok, built the church in 1787.

On the river's Thon Buri bank you can see two rarely visited Ayutthaya-style temples.

NOT TO BE MISSED:

Pak Khlong Market • Canals *(khlongs)* **of Thon Buri • Wat Prayun • Wat Rakhang Kositharam**

---

river. At Tha Saphan Phut you can jump ship and visit the colorful **Pak Khlong Market ❷**, immediately behind the pier, and the nearby **Little India** neighborhood. You can also hop a long-tail boat *($10 an hour)* to explore Thon Buri's maze of *khlongs* (see p. 114).

At Tha Rachini shuttle boats carry

passengers to Thon Buri and three notable sites. **Wat Prayun ❸**, built in the early 19th century under Rama III, is memorable for its central hillock planted with small *chedis* and frangipani trees. Around the hill is a pond full of

INSIDER TIP:

Don't take a pricey tourist boat. For a baht, anyone can ride on the old wood commuter boats that ply the stops up and down the river. Just jump on and the ticket seller will find you.

—KRIS LEBOUTILLIER
National Geographic photographer

turtles that are regularly fed by worshippers to gain merit. The temple's two *wihans* have doors inlaid with mother-of-pearl and extensively ornate gables (see also p. 116). Just north of Wat Prayun is **Santa Cruz Church ❹**, another place of worship constructed by Portuguese Catholics fleeing the Burmese invaders of Ayutthaya. **Wat Kalayanimit ❺**, next to Santa Cruz

Church, houses an immense Buddha image and more murals from the time of Rama III (see p. 116). Just before Tha Tien, near Wat Pho and the Grand Palace is **Chakrabongse House.** Built in 1909 by Rama V, it is one of the last royal residences on the Chao Phraya. From Tha Tien you can explore **Wat Pho, Wat Phra Kaeo,** and the **Grand Palace ❻** (see pp. 69–73 & 76–79), and take a shuttle boat across the river to **Wat Arun ❼** (see pp. 111 & 115–116).

Farther upriver, on the Thon Buri side, the Express stops at Tha Rakhang, near **Wat Rakhang Kositharam ❽**. This little-visited temple is noted for its superb library consisting of three late 18th-century timber buildings, the residence of Rama I before he became king. From here, you get a fine view of the Grand Palace, Wat Phra Kaeo, and Wat Pho.

Exit at Tha Maharat for **Wat Mahathat ❾** (see p. 79), the **National Museum** (see pp. 82–86), and **Thammasat University.** Thammasat is the most prestigious university in Thailand after Chulalongkorn. It's seen its share of unrest: In 1973 students led protests that overthrew the military government, and in 1976 it was the awful scene of right-wing revenge, when paramilitaries and vigilantes murdered more than 200 students.

Canals (Khlongs) of Thon Buri

Leading off the western banks of the Chao Phraya river and into Thon Buri is a fascinating network of canals where you see stilted wooden houses and ancient temples set among rice fields, vegetable gardens, and orchards.

Three primary canals lead west from the Chao Phraya and arch around Thon Buri: Khlong Bangkok Noi, Khlong Bangkok Mon, and Khlong Bangkok Yai. These are bisected by many smaller arteries that reach otherwise hidden communities. Khlong Bangkok Noi river taxis leave from Tha Maharat, cross the river by the Royal Barge Museum, and into the khlong; the farther you go, the more rustic the scene.

From Tha Tien, river taxis go up Khlong Bangkok Mon for similar sights. Most head up the canal and then turn off into smaller ones before terminating. Stay aboard to return to Tha Tien. Water taxis to Khlong Bangkok Yai leave Tha Tien or Tha Rachini, and pass Wat Intharam, unusual for its *bot's* gold and black lacquerwork doors and a chedi housing the ashes of assassinated King Taksin.

River taxis ply these routes every 30 minutes from 6 a.m. to 6:30 p.m. *(less than 50 cents).* Or long-tails can be hired from river piers *(a one-hour excursion should, depending on bargaining skills and number of passengers, cost around $10).*

Rama II was responsible for initiating the building of the tall central spire, but he did not live to see it completed. This was done by Rama III in 1842, and King Mongkut, who finished off the structure by covering it with thousands of donated fragments of Chinese porcelain. He also renamed the shrine Wat Arun

prangs at each corner. Giants and monkeys of traditional Thai design encircle the lower sections of the first terrace, along with images of other gods and Siamese mythological creatures.

The second terrace has a lovely pavilion, with four statues that illustrate important events in the life of the Buddha—his birth,

Wat Arun

Map p. 66
Arun Amarin Rd.
$
Ferry from Tha Tien to Wat Arun Pier

Wat Arun's soaring prang is made of a brick core covered with plaster and embedded with broken bits of Chinese porcelain.

Rajavararam. Arun is more precise than jang, and it also reflects the Hindu god of the dawn, Aruna.

The huge central prang, surmounted by a Hindu *vagra* (thunderbolt), rests on three levels of terraces, surrounded by four smaller corner prangs, interspersed with four *mondops*. The combination of central prang, trident, and four lesser prangs represents the Buddhist universe and the four great seas of the physical world. Eight sets of stone steps, guarded by fierce Chinese figures, lead up to the first terrace, with the minor

enlightenment, first sermon, and moment of entering nirvana at his death. Visitors can only climb to the third terrace, from where there are great views back over the river to the Oriental Hotel. Above, the symbolic layers continue, with the Traiphum representing existence across the three worlds of the Buddhist universe; the Tavatisma Heaven, guarded at all four corners by additional vagras; and right at the top, the Devaphum, which symbolizes the peak of the seven realms of happiness. ∎

More Places to Visit in Thon Buri

Floating Market

For generations, the people of lower central Thailand conducted much of their commerce on the network of canals that crisscrossed their land. It is only in the past few decades that roads have replaced the functionality of the canals.

Wat Suwannaram & Wat Dusitaram

Wat Suwannaram, near the Thon Buri train station, is architecturally significant as it represents an evolution from the forms favored at Ayutthaya to the more extravagant styles of contemporary Bangkok. The temple was finished in 1832 and is chiefly noted for its superb interior murals, some of the most original and refined in the city.

The works of Luang Vichit Chetsada and Krua Khonpae, the murals are full of lively detail, depicting *Jataka* tales as well as the Buddhist cosmology and the defeat of Mara. Frescoes of great sensitivity, telling the traditional tales from the life of the Buddha, can also be seen inside Wat Dusitaram, near the Royal Barges Museum.

Bangkok had an active floating market once, but this largely disappeared in the 1960s as roads were constructed and vendors moved into modern shopping centers. The demise of the traditional floating market within the city limits inspired tour operators to create an artificial market, hiring local women to paddle around each morning and pretend to bargain for their produce. Although this attraction has more in common with the theme park than authentic experience, visitors with limited time might consider a half-day tour of this market, which also includes opportunities to shop in the attached souvenir stalls. For an authentic floating market, head south to the town of Damnoen Saduak (see pp. 122–123).

🖂 Khlong Bangkok Yai 🕐 Closes at noon 🛐 $ 🖾 Organized tours only

Wat Kalayanimit & Wat Prayun

Two interesting temples are situated near the banks of the Chao Phraya and can be easily toured in a morning with a rented long-tail boat. The Chinese-influenced Wat Kalayanimit is located near the opening of Khlong Bangkok Yai and is therefore easily accessible by public or private boat. This vast *wihan* houses a huge sitting Buddha, but the temple is best known for the giant bronze bell, the biggest in Thailand, that hangs in its white tower. Both the wihan and the *bot* have reasonably well-preserved frescoes

INSIDER TIP:

Thais believe that the release of animals is considered good karma. Don't be surprised when you see birds in cages being sold for this purpose along the side of the road.

—SUCHANA A. CHAVANICH, PH.D.
National Geographic field scientist

dating from the mid-19th century.

Nearby Wat Prayun is much more modest but features some intriguing exterior details, such as a hill—reputedly modeled on melted wax from Rama III's candle—covered in miniature temples and a pool with turtles and carp. The turtles are bought and released here as a way of gaining merit for a future life.

🅰 Map p. 66 🖂 Soi Wat Kanlaya
⛴ Ferry from Rachini pier

An array of top attractions within a few hours of Bangkok that exemplify Thailand's natural beauty, culture, and history

Around Bangkok

Dome, Phra Pathom Chedi

Around Bangkok

The areas to the west and north of Bangkok offer plenty of cultural, historic, and natural sites to keep visitors occupied. Indeed, places such as the magnificent old Thai capital of Ayutthaya, the immense Phra Pathom Chedi at Nakhon Pathom, and the beautiful and evocative Kanchanaburi Province are regulation stops on a trip to Thailand.

Tourists take part in an elephant show at Samut Prakan Crocodile Farm.

All the sites described in this chapter are within easy reach of Bangkok. Visits to all of them can be arranged as part of organized excursions booked through the tour desk at your hotel.

A good way to get to Ayutthaya—the great cultural center and capital of Thailand from 1350 to 1767—is to take a leisurely cruise up the Chao Phraya river from Bangkok by luxury boat. At Ayutthaya switch to a long-tail boat for a trip along the waterways that surround the old city. Then move ashore to take in the city's magnificent buildings.

North of Ayutthaya is the historically important center of Lop Buri, one of Thailand's oldest cities, which has been continuously occupied since the sixth century.

Just 30 miles (50 km) west of Bangkok is Nakhon Pathom, famed for its *chedi* (stupa): the tallest Buddhist monument in the world and one of the most revered in Thailand. The chedi is the centerpiece of some other wonderful Thai monuments, including a number of impressive Buddha statues.

West of the capital, Kanchanaburi is a place with a surfeit of natural attractions, making it a popular weekend getaway for Bangkok residents. Among visitors the area is famous for its Khwae River bridge and the Thailand–Burma Railway, otherwise known as the Death Railway, built for the Japanese during World War II by Allied and Asian prisoners of wars at a terrible cost of human life. ■

Area of map detail

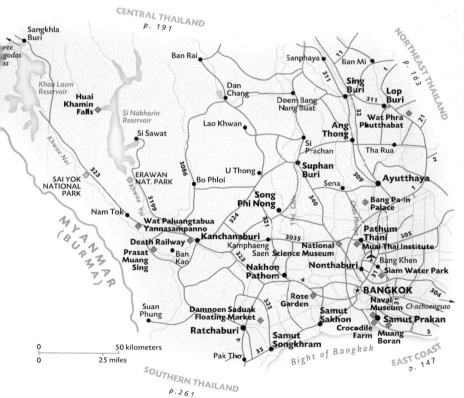

Nakhon Pathom

One hour west of Bangkok, this provincial city is visited almost exclusively for its towering Phra Pathom Chedi, the tallest Buddhist structure in the world. Nakhon Pathom is believed to be one of the oldest settled sites in Thailand; according to tradition, it was founded several centuries before the Christian era as a seaport for the mythical kingdom of Suwannaphum.

The golden Phra Pathom Chedi is considered the most sacred Buddhist site in Thailand.

Nakhon Pathom is revered as the birthplace of Buddhism in Thailand. It is believed that during the reign of King Asoka the Great (r. 272–232 B.C.), two senior monks were sent from India to introduce Theravada Buddhism to the residents of the lower Chao Phraya plains. They probably traveled through the Three Pagodas Pass on the border of Myanmar (Burma) and Thailand, and made their first converts in the villages around Nakhon Pathom. A stupa was built around this time.

In the sixth century, the site flourished as a capital of the mysterious Mon people (whose Dvaravati Empire dominated central Thailand from the 6th to 13th centuries). Several stone inscriptions survive, along with small stupas and a coin inscribed with the words "Lord of Dvaravati."

In the early 11th century Nakhon Pathom was conquered by Khmer King Suryavarman (r. 1011–1150) and became part of the Khmer Empire. The city fell again in 1078, to Burmese invaders, who abandoned it soon after. Its potential as a defensive outpost against Burma was recognized, and the town was reestablished in the 17th century by the Siamese. It was King Mongkut, however, who realized the importance of the stupa built by the converts to Buddhism. He ordered the stupa's preservation and restoration in 1860, encasing it in the bulbous Phra Pathom Chedi, which dominates the town today.

Phra Pathom Chedi

Nakhon Pathom's magnificent chedi, rising almost 395 feet (120 m) into the skies, is covered with golden-orange tiles. It is sometimes compared to the Shwedagon in Yangon, Myanmar, but it is taller and is surrounded by an intriguing complex of bots, Buddha images, and other curious substructures. The tower is topped by a gold trident, symbol of the Hindu god Shiva, with a superimposed Royal Crown of Thailand highlighting its national status and importance.

The monument is best approached from the north side, which faces the train station, across a long field flanked by minor religious sites and usually thronged with pilgrims. Left of the main entrance are amulet salesmen, toothy old palmists who can divine the future for both Thais and Western tourists, and stalls serving refreshing glasses of iced coffee.

Past the two ceremonial halls and up the Grand Staircase into the **north wihan,** is the revered **Phra Ruang Rochanarit,** or standing Buddha. Its modern bronze body matches the much older stone hands, feet, and head. In the nearby temple offices a mural shows the principal features of Phra Pathom Chedi. The restoration of the chedi is chronicled in a public hall.

The circular **cloister** that separates the chedi from the walkway houses a series of impressive bronze Buddha statues, in various positions, set into its walls. At the **east wihan,** an enlightened Buddha at an altar is shaded by a mural of a spreading *bodhi* tree. Beyond the wihan, the east terrace contains the **Dvaravati seated Buddha,** skillfully carved in white quartzite, and positioned in the "European" seated fashion—a closed-kneed posture believed to have been developed from Greco-Roman statues. A European influence is discernible in robe contours and facial expressions. Nearby are a *sala,* a Chinese temple, and a museum with Dvaravati-period relics.

In the courtyard at the southern entrance, a model of the original stupa has been surmounted by a Khmer-style *prang.* Next to the prang is another large Dvaravati seated Buddha. The wihan here has a Buddha in an earth-touching pose, surrounded by disciples. In an inner chamber a Khmer-style Buddha receives shelter under a hooded *naga.* At the **west wihan** is a highly venerated 29-foot-long (9 m) reclining Buddha. An interior chamber is generally crowded with pilgrims paying homage to a smaller Buddha. In the courtyard are monks' quarters built in timber.

INSIDER TIP:

Allow plenty of time to wander the grounds of Phra Pathom Chedi. Be sure to see the Reclining Buddha and have your fortune told for fun and a small fee.

—SOLANGE HANDO
National Geographic writer

Surrounding the huge chedi are 24 bells, often rung by pilgrims.

About 1 mile (1.6 km) west of Phra Pathom Chedi is **Sanam Chan Palace,** built by Rama VI at the end of the 19th century (entry is not permitted into the palace buildings). The palace is a collection of generously proportioned buildings in Thai and European design, surrounded by neat gardens. One curious aspect is a statue of Vajay, Rama IV's beloved pet dog, who was poisoned by palace staff because of his fierce nature. ∎

Nakhon Pathom
- Map p. 119
- Frequent buses from Southern Bus Terminal, Bangkok; train from Hua Lamphong Station, Bangkok

Visitor Information
- Fangchootoa, Banneum Muang, Kanchanaburi
- 034-512500, ext. 2199

Phra Pathom Chedi
- Ratchadamnoen Rd.

Around Nakhon Pathom

A number of attractions can be found west of Bangkok en route to Nakhon Pathom. They are best explored as part of tour packages—easily arranged at your hotel—from the capital. These provide an excellent reason to escape Bangkok for the day.

Dancers at the Rose Garden carry *krathongs*, which are floated on waterways during the Loy Krathong festival in November.

Damnoen Saduak Floating Market

- Map p. 119
- Sukhaphiban 1 Rd., Damnoen Saduak
- Market active daily sunrise–noon
- Bus: 78 from Southern Bus Terminal, Bangkok

Damnoen Saduak Floating Market

The image of a traditional Thai floating market is a powerful one for visitors. While those in Bangkok have been re-created to serve the tourist trade, the Damnoen Saduak floating market remains the real thing.

The town lies between Nakhon Pathom and Samut Songkhram, some 68 miles (109 km) southwest of Bangkok, and in fact has several floating markets in different neighborhoods. Most visitors head directly to the biggest one, at Ton Kem.

The best way to experience the floating market is to stay overnight in a hotel in nearby

Damnoer Saduak, but you could rise early and hire a taxi from Bangkok. The market is at its busiest and best in the early morning—before the tour groups arrive. The "stalls" are the traders' open sampan boats, which bustle up and down the narrow canals selling a range of deliciously fresh produce, mainly fruit and vegetables. The boats are paddled mostly by women, who wear lampshade hats and the blue shirts that are typical of the farming community.

Visitors can watch the parade of sampans, piled high with produce and flowers, either from the bridge that crosses over the canal or from the produce shed on the right.

Rose Garden

The Rose Garden is in a lovely setting on the banks of the Nakorn Chaisri River. This well-designed resort complex has landscaped gardens set around a large lake, an aviary with more than 300 species of exotic birds, orchid and rose nurseries, a championship 18-hole golf course, and a model village where craftsworkers demonstrate weaving, carving, and basketry.

The highlight is the twice daily **cultural show** (11 a.m., 2:45 p.m., www.rosegarden riverside.com), when a hundred performers delight the crowd with their displays of traditional dance, music, and martial arts. This is one of the best such shows in Thailand, squeezing a wedding, the ordination of a Buddhist monk, sword-fighting, and boxing into the space of one nonstop hour.

Close by are the **Thai Human Imagery Museum** (43/2 Moo 1, Boromratchanchonni Rd., Pinklao-Nakhonchaisri Rd., Km 31, Kunkaew, Nakhonchaisri, Nakhonpathom, tel 03-433-2607), with fiberglass models of historical figures, and **Samphran Elephant Ground & Zoo** (see p. 146).

EXPERIENCE:
Authentic Floating Market

There are two floating markets in the greater Bangkok area: **Damnoen Saduak** market, a major tourist destination in Ratchaburi Province (see opposite), and **Amphawa Market,** a more authentic venue in Samut Songkhram Province, approximately one hour south of the capital. Visiting each of these in the early morning provides a glimpse into traditional Thai life.

But the way to truly experience the floating market is with the **Headman of Thongyip Village,** who shows guests the ins and outs of Amphawa Market, as well as life on the Mae Klong river. He allows visitors to stay in his home, or in a neighboring property. Guests learn to make Thai desserts that they sell at the floating market, as well as explore the area via boat, learn Thai cooking, and visit fruit and vegetable farms. Find more information at **Samut Songkhram Homestay** (34 Moo 9, Tambon Muangmai Amphawa, Samut Songkhram, tel 034-375073).

Phra Phutta Monthon

Also southeast of Nakhon Pathom, on the Bangkok road, this Buddhist "theme park" has re-creations of Buddha's journey from birth, enlightenment, and first sermon to nirvana. A 133-foot (41 m) walking Buddha dominates the park. ∎

Rose Garden
- Map p. 119
- 20 miles (32 km) W of Bangkok, off Hwy. 4
- 02-295-3261
- $; extra for show
- Bus: 83 & 997

Phra Phutta Monthon
- Map p. 119
- Hwy. 3310, between Hwys. 4 & 338
- Bus from Southern Bus Terminal, Bangkok

Kanchanaburi & Around

This relaxed town to the west of Bangkok sits in a beautiful setting of forests and picturesque hills. It is best known for its connections with the notorious Thailand–Burma Railway, also known as the Death Railway, which was built during World War II with forced Allied labor. Kanchanaburi is the site of a bridge over the Khwae (Kwai) Yai River, made famous by David Lean's Oscar-winning 1957 film.

Waterfalls enhance the natural beauty of the countryside around Kanchanaburi.

More recently, Kanchanaburi became the focus of world attention when proposals for a massive dam threatened to destroy significant areas of wildlife habitat. After environmental outcry, the project was scrapped.

The first inhabitants of this area were neolithic tribespeople, and fragments of their lives—pottery and simple tools—are displayed at the **Ban Kao Museum,** 22 miles (35 km) west of Kanchanaburi (see p. 130).

The main historic trade route to India, via the Three Pagodas Pass, lies along the Khwae Yai Valley. During the 13th century the area fell under the control of the Khmer Empire, and a magnificent fort was erected at Muang Sing. Khmer rulers were replaced by Ayutthayans, who constructed a military citadel to the west of Kanchanaburi (both sites have been restored and can be visited). In 1548 the Burmese invasion army marched into Siam through here. It was Rama I who set up a military camp at Kanchanaburi, however, and the town grew up as a major defensive center.

The main focus of a visit to Kanchanaburi is likely to be the notorious **Khwae Yai River Bridge,** 2 miles (3 km) north of the town.

INSIDER TIP:

If you have a little extra time and want to learn about elephant conservation, visit the Elephant Conservation Network (www. ecnthailand.org) that works in the forests near Kanchanaburi.

—DANIEL STILES
National Geographic field researcher

center. For a fuller understanding of the story behind its construction, the men who worked on it, and the bridge's part in the wider history of the Thailand–Burma Railway (see pp. 128–129), it is well worth visiting some of the associated sites first.

JEATH War Museum

An excellent place to start is the JEATH War Museum, in Kanchanaburi. The title is an acronym formed from the names of some of the nations involved in the building of the railway: Japan, England, Australia/America, Thailand, and Holland.

The museum is informal, with three bamboo huts revealing something of the feel of the original prison camps. Memorabilia displayed inside the huts includes paintings and drawings by the prisoners of war that graphically depict the horrors of camp life, and letters written by the POWs, telling of sacrifice and deprivation on the railroad and grisly tortures inflicted by the Japanese.

JEATH War Museum may be modest in scale, but it is a moving and unforgettable memorial to the 12,000 Allied prisoners of war and 100,000 Asian laborers who died here under such appalling conditions in the construction of the Thailand–Burma Railway.

Kanchanaburi War Cemetery

This vast graveyard, situated midway between downtown Kanchanaburi and the famous bridge, is the final resting place for nearly 7,000 Allied POWs (mainly British and Australian) who died building the railroad. The graves are immaculately maintained by a dedicated team of gardeners under the auspices of the Commonwealth War Graves Commission in London. Simply reading the inscriptions on the tombstones brings a lump to the throat. At Chung Kai there is a smaller cemetery. (See also Konyu Cemetery, Hellfire Pass, p. 130.)

Kanchanaburi

⬛ Map p. 119

🚌 Bus from Southern Bus Terminal in Thon Buri. Train from Bangkok Noi station (also Thon Buri); frequent service on weekends (reserve seats); limited service during the week

Visitor Information

✉ Tourism Authority of Thailand, Saeng Chuto Rd., Kanchanaburi

☎ 034-511200

JEATH War Museum

✉ Pak Phrack Rd., Kanchanaburi

💲 $

Kanchanaburi War Cemetery

✉ Saeng Chuto Rd., Kanchanaburi

Khwae Yai River Bridge

✉ Saeng Chuto Rd., Kanchanaburi.

EXPERIENCE: Help Save Tigers

An estimated 150 to 200 Indochinese tigers live in the wild in Thailand. Encroachment on their land by farmers and developers and illegal poaching, however, threaten the dwindling population. Furthermore, there are a number of tiger "zoos" that require tigers to perform tricks or live in unnatural environments. Short of catching a rare glimpse in the wild, there are few ways to get close-up experiences with tigers, fewer still to help preserve their diminishing numbers.

One of the best ways is at **Wat Paluangtabua Yannasampanno** (Sai Yok District, Kanchanaburi, tel 034-531557 or -8, www.boonheng.com). In 1999 a tiger cub was brought to the temple, the start of a project to help preserve these endangered animals: an effort that has successfully bred and raised a number of tigers. It has also become a refuge for sick and injured domestic and wild animals.

The adult tigers are taken for daily walks to a small canyon, where visitors can touch and pose for photos with them (an exhilarating/terrifying experience). The temple also accepts volunteers, who are responsible for cleaning cages, feeding cubs, and handling visitors, among other activities. One such activity is helping construct "Tiger Island," a 12-acre (5 ha) forest reserve that will allow the tigers to live in a more natural environment and permit researchers to study their adaptation behavior.

Khwae Yai River Bridge

The present bridge and railroad are largely modern constructions that replaced the original work of the Japanese. The Thai government eventually took over responsibility for it all after the end of the war, tearing down some of the bridge and the railroad as far as Nam Tok for the scrap iron. The government later requested help from the Japanese in the form of war reparations, and these included the replacement of the central girders with the present flat, boxy structures.

Although the story of the construction and destruction of the bridge is charged with emotion (see pp. 128–129), the modern-day crossing can be a disappointment—just a seemingly run-down wood and iron bridge mounted on ungainly concrete pillars. It comes to life when the twice-daily train departs Kanchanaburi and slowly makes its way across the rickety structure, on its way north to the terminus at Nam Tok. You can walk onto the wooden planks of the bridge, but it's also used by local motorcyclists, so be careful.

Around the Bridge

Several minor but worthwhile sights are located near the famous bridge. These include an old steam engine, which dates from the 1940s, and a curious Japanese supply truck that could run on both road and rails. Just south of the bridge, cafés overlook the river, and there are souvenir shops. An art gallery nearby is notable for its contemporary murals.

A Japanese memorial in the area, raised in 1944, is euphemistically dedicated to those who "died through illness during the course of the construction."

Buddhist Temples

Several Buddhist temples to the south of Kanchanaburi are worth a brief visit, if only to experience their sense of kitsch and unbridled commercialism

INSIDER TIP:

A great excursion from Kanchanaburi is to the town of Sangkhla Buri. Stay in a floating cabin overnight at Songkalia resort, on Khao Laem Reservoir. A boat brings coffee and donut-like *patongo* **for breakfast.**

—ALISA TANG
National Geographic Traveler magazine writer

(which seems to characterize an increasing number of temples in the country). **Wat Tham Monkam Thong,** or Cave Temple of the Golden Dragon, features a Buddhist nun and her disciples, who float in water while meditating and whistling—the steady stream of pilgrims consider this a neat trick. Behind the temple complex, steps lead to an series of limestone cliffs filled with exquisite Buddha images and providing fine views over the river.

Near the town of Tha Muang, a pair of very striking temples perch on the edge of the valley on a limestone outcrop. The temple on the left, **Wat Tham Sua,** is chiefly noted for its Chinese pagoda and spacious courtyard, which is dominated by a rotund Buddha. **Wat Tham Kao Noi** has been constructed in classic Thai style, with a massive *wihan* holding an immerse Buddha image. ∎

Wat Tham Monkam Thong

- ✉ Chukkadon Rd., Kanchanaburi
- 🚐 Miri-truck from Kanchanaburi

Songkalia River Hut & Resort

- ✉ 34/1 Mu 2 Tambon Nonglu, Amphoe Sangkhla Buri, Kanchanaburi Province
- ☎ 034-595024 or 02-896-2346 (Bangkok office)

Wat Tham Monkam Thong employs such gimmicks as this floating, meditating Buddhist nun to attract pilgrims.

Death Railway

Kanchanaburi's chief attraction, and one of the most famous World War II memorials in Southeast Asia, is the simple girdered bridge at the north end of town. The original wooden bridge was part of a much more ambitious project, which gained notoriety at the center of one of the most terrible and tragic stories of the war.

A train still runs along the remains of the Thailand–Burma Railway.

The Japanese conceived a plan in the fall of 1942 to build a 255-mile (414 km) railroad across Thailand to Thanbyu-zayat in Burma (now Myanmar). Allied operations around Singapore and in the Straits of Malacca had effectively blocked sea routes used by the Japanese between mainland Southeast Asia and points west, such as Burma and—the final goal—India. The Japanese had quickly conquered Burma at the beginning of the conflict and

badly needed to provide supplies to their bases and troops.

The construction time of the serpentine rail line, through jungle and over mountain passes, was initially estimated at five years, but this was overruled by the Japanese High Command, who ordered that the link be completed in just 12 months (in fact, it took 16 months). Allied prisoners were brought in from Singapore, Hong Kong, and other British territories, while Asians were shipped in from all corners of the region under Japanese control. The forced labor was essential to the success of the scheme, and men were treated as expendable—the appalling treatment, working and living conditions, malnutrition, and tropical diseases such as malaria, cholera, and dysentery killed thousands of laborers. The cost in human lives across the most difficult sections was later dubbed "a life for every sleeper"—a dead man for every railroad tie.

INSIDER TIP:

A visit to Kanchanaburi's JEATH museum, housed in a rickety walled bamboo hut similar to the POW accommodations, provides a sobering look at the atrocities the soldiers suffered while building the railway.

—BARBARA A. NOE
National Geographic editor

Building & Rebuilding

The first bridge built by POWs over the Khwae (Kwai) Yai River was a rickety affair of wood, replaced in 1943 by a stronger iron structure imported from Java, which remains today. The bridge was the regular target of United States B-24 bombers, which knocked out the central span in 1945. It was rebuilt after the war with Japanese cooperation as reparation. The railroad itself operated for just two years—today only the 47-mile (77 km) stretch between Kanchanaburi and Nam Tok remains in regular use.

The Cinematic Version

Most visitors' views are colored by the famous Academy Award–winning movie (it won seven awards) *The Bridge on the River Kwai* (1957), by English director David Lean (1908–1981). The epic film is based on a novel by French author Pierre Boulle

(1912–1994) called *Le Pont de la rivière Kwai (The Bridge on the River Kwai)* and takes a number of liberties in its retelling of history.

The central character of the movie—Colonel Nicholson, played so movingly by Alec Guinness (1914–2000)—never existed and was invented for the purposes of the story. The film also suggests that the Allied prisoners were responsible for the engineering of the bridge, but in fact it was highly trained Japanese engineers who designed the project.

The film hinges on Nicholson's obsession with constructing a perfect bridge that will be a tribute to its builders, but in reality the prisoners sabotaged and delayed the project at every possible turn.

The film also weaves an imaginative story about an American maverick, played by William Holden (1918–1981), escaping from the POW camp and then making his way to Ceylon (Sri Lanka), before returning to Kanchanaburi to blow up the bridge. The true story is that no one escaped the Japanese internment camp at Kanchanaburi and lived to talk about it. Perhaps the most tragic aspect of the book and the film was not the liberal retelling of the saga, but the fact that neither medium made much mention of the tremendous loss of Asian lives during the construction of the railroad bridge.

About 7,000 Allied soldiers who died during the construction of the Death Railway are buried in Kanchanaburi.

On the Road to the Myanmar Border

Highway 323, running 150 miles (250 km) northwest from Kanchanaburi to the Myanmar (Burma) border at Three Pagodas Pass, takes you through some stunning scenery. Lush mountain outlooks prevail along the route, which cuts through the Khwae Noi river valley and follows the trail of the "Death Railway" (see pp. 128–129) line to Myanmar, passing the enormous man-made Khao Laem Reservoir.

Along the road from Kanchanaburi to Myanmar (Burma)

the Khwae Noi River, was at the western extremities of the Khmer Empire and was most likely set up as a trading outpost. The remains of ramparts still guard the complex; four entrances (*gopura*) lead to the main shrine in the center.

Back on Highway 323, about 50 miles (80 km) from Kanchanaburi, is **Hellfire Pass,** so named by the Allied and Asian POWs building the Death Railway because of the light thrown onto the bare rock by the workers' torches at night. At the pass is a memorial to the hundreds of Australian and British soldiers who died constructing this section of the railroad and who are buried at the nearby **Konyu Cemetery.**

A trail follows the remains of the track through the pass, then up a hill to an overlook. A quaint train still runs along a section of the railroad from Kanchanaburi to the town of **Nam Tok** near the pass. From Pak Sang pier at Nam Tok, long-tail boats can be hired for a journey upriver to **Sai Yok National Park,** about 24 miles (38 km) from Nam Tok, where you will find peaceful stands of forest on the Khwae Noi River. Follow the signs from the information center to the suspension bridge to see Sai Yok Noi waterfall.

Highway 323 continues north-

Ban Kao Museum

- Map p. 119
- 22 miles (35 km) from Kanchanaburi on Hwy. 323, then Hwy. 3229 & 3455 to the museum
- Closed Mon.–Tues.
- $

About 22 miles (35 km) west of Kanchanaburi, the small **Ban Kao Museum** houses a fascinating collection of neolithic tools and utensils collected from nearby digs and dating back 3,000 to 4,000 years. Four miles (7 km) farther west along Highway 3455 are the remains of the 13th-century Khmer temple at **Prasat Muang Sing.** The 170-acre (70 ha) site, attractively set on the banks of

east along the vast **Khao Laem Reservoir** (Krung Kravia Lake), dammed to power a huge hydroelectric turbine, to **Sangkhla Buri,** 137 miles (220 km) from Kanchanaburi, at its northern end. The charm of this small town, mainly populated by Mon, Karen, and Burmese, lies in its isolation. Its major attractions are a colorful morning market, and a Mon village on the reservoir's banks *(from the center of town, go E over an impressive wooden bridge).* Arrange boat tours of the reservoir at guesthouses in the town.

Three *chedis* mark the Thai / Myanmar (Burma) border at the **Three Pagodas Pass,** the historical transit point of invading Burmese armies into Thailand. These days the pass is a major point for cross-border smuggling, and rebel activities sometimes result in temporary closure of the border crossing.

Erawan National Park

The superb waterfalls at this national park are Thailand's most popular. A rock formation at the top of one cascade recalls the shape of the sacred elephant Erawan and gives the park its name. The superior, higher falls are almost deserted, while those at the bottom are usually busier; swimming is possible in the lowest pools. Erawan is best visited during the rainy months *(July–Nov.),* when water is at its most plentiful.

Stretching north of these spectacular falls is the vast reservoir **Si Nakharin**. The lake is popular with Bangkok residents, who arrive on weekends in great numbers to fish, hike, enjoy boat tours, or relax in the raft hotels—some of which are luxurious—on the shoreline. ■

Prasat Muang Sing

- 🅰 Map p. 119
- ✉ Hwy. 3455
- 💲 $
- 🚌 Bus from Kanchanaburi

Sai Yok National Park

- 🅰 Map p. 119
- ✉ Off Hwy 323
- 🚌 Bus, train from Kanchanaburi
- 🚤 Boat from Pak Sang pier, Nam Tok

Erawan National Park

- 🅰 Map p. 119
- ✉ On Hwy. 3199, 50 miles (80 km) N of Kanchanaburi
- 💲 $
- 🚌 Bus from Kanchanaburi

EXPERIENCE: Teaching English

Being an *ajarn,* the Thai word for teacher, earns great respect. *Kru,* or tutor, is also an honorable title. There are a plentitude of opportunities for a farang to teach, both in Bangkok and in rural villages throughout the kingdoms. Here are some ideas on how:

www.Ajarn.com is the premier Web portal for information regarding Teaching English as a Foreign Language (TEFL) certification, job listings, visas, and teaching in general. Useful FAQs and discussion boards from the teaching community are invaluable resources for new teachers in Thailand.

Language Institute *(Chiang Mai University, 239 Huay Kaew Rd., Chiang Mai,*

tel 053-943756, www .teflcmu.com) To teach English legally in Thailand, most teachers require a TEFL certification. Four-week courses at the Language Institute CMU consist of lectures and discussion groups that provide instructors with the skills and qualifications to teach.

Mirror Foundation *(106 Moo 1 Ean Huay Khom, Chiang Rai, tel 053-737425,*

www.mirrorartgroup.org) The foundation runs volunteer programs to assist the villagers of Mae Yao district. Teaching English is one of the fundamental tasks for volunteers, although working in the fields and playing with children are typical activities. Experiencing a genuine cultural exchange is the reward for 4 to 5 days of work with a team of other volunteers.

Ayutthaya

This romantic ruined city, surrounded by a modern town, is one of Thailand's national treasures. It attests to the power and splendor of an empire that dominated Southeast Asia for almost 400 years. In the bloody aftermath of a Burmese onslaught, most of the city was destroyed by fire, its people killed or taken to Burma as slaves. It was a catastrophic loss on a scale now hard to imagine.

Ayutthaya reigned as the Thai capital from circa 1350 to 1767.

The city began as a Khmer military and trading outpost. Ramathibodi I made it his capital about 1350. Ayutthaya was ideally located within the protective surroundings of several rivers, which were diverted and channeled into smaller canals, to create a waterbound and almost impregnable fortress.

Ramathibodi named Ayutthaya after a mythical kingdom that is portrayed in the *Ramakien*. At the king's behest, the building of royal palaces and temples soon got

For those with a sweet tooth, *roti saimai*—a candy floss wrapped in cooked dough—is a popular local dessert.

—SUCHANA A. CHAVANICH
National Geographic field scientist

under way. To honor his belief in Theravada Buddhism, he invited monks from Sri Lanka to direct most religious activities in his royal city.

During its four centuries of existence, Ayutthaya was ruled by a succession of 33 kings, each of whom erected new, and embellished existing, temples and palaces, while maintaining large armies to increase the national borderlands. Ayutthayan kings conducted almost continual warfare against Burma, as well as fighting with the Cambodian, Laotian, and Muslim empires to

the south. By the end of the 15th century Ayutthaya controlled most of Southeast Asia.

Ayutthaya developed into an important commercial center for mainland Southeast Asia and was visited by international trading groups from all over Europe. Dazzled emissaries of French king Louis XIV compared the city to European capitals.

Finally, after four centuries of power and glory, Ayutthaya slipped into decline. For two years it withstood a Burmese siege but fell at last in 1767.

Highlights of Ayutthaya

A traveler from Europe at the end of the 17th century estimated Ayutthaya's population at over a million, with some 1,700 temples, some 30,000 priests, and more than 4,000 Buddha images, all of them cast in gold or covered with golden gilt. Tragically, most of

(continued on p. 136)

Ayutthaya
Map p. 119

Visitor Information

Tourism Authority of Thailand, 108/22 Mu 4, Pratu Chai, Ayutthaya

035-246076

Bus from Northern Bus Terminal, Bangkok. Train from Hua Lamphong Station, Bangkok

River boat from Bangkok

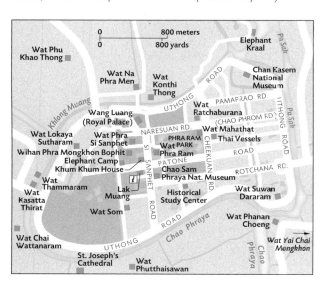

Architecture & Sculpture of Ayutthaya

The four centuries of the Ayutthayan period were an important era for art and architecture, encouraged and patronized by wealthy temple-building kings who saw themselves as the cultural inheritors of previous Southeast Asian empires. The result was an architectural gold mine, plus a high level of achievement in sculpture, painting, and other fine arts.

Central to the Hindu belief in many separate, parallel universes is the image of the magical Mount Meru, mythical home of the gods—the Mount Olympus for Asian religions. Ayutthaya was therefore constructed as a giant mandala, surrounded by ramparts and moats to symbolize great seas, with the royal palace as the heavenly center and lesser buildings and even cities spread around it in cosmological order.

Architecture

If sculpture marked the high point of the Sukhothai Kingdom, then Ayutthaya's crowning glory was its architecture. European visitors reported that the city had more than 600 major monuments and temples of extraordinary design. Construction of most of the monuments was initiated during the founding reign of King Ramathibodi (r. 1350–1369) and completed during the next 150 years.

When looking at these remarkable structures, it helps to understand that, throughout Southeast Asia, it had long been the fashion to construct temples in stone, while royal palaces and utilitarian structures such as homes and businesses were made of wood. This is the chief reason why only religious structures have survived the ravages of time.

Ayutthayan architects borrowed forms from the Khmers (such as the cob-shaped *prang*) and from Sri Lanka (notably the bell-shaped *chedi*). These foreign designs were modified and refined into unique expressions of Siamese style. Thus squat Khmer prangs and heavy unadorned Ceylonese chedis with an elongated elegance combined to form a new definition of Asian religious architecture.

Sculpture

Ayutthayan sculpture is not in the same league as that of Sukhothai but is still important. Early artists continued the traditions of

---

EXPERIENCE: Biking Through History

Touring the ruins of Ayutthaya is a must, and there are many different ways to go about this, ranging from tour buses to following a guide with a bullhorn. But to cover the most ground without sacrificing the details, the best way to see the city is by bike. Take the train from Bangkok and rent a bike from **Lung Piak** (tel 08-9037-0143) or **Ban Chantha Guesthouse** (tel 08-9785-4216), or pick up a bike at the **Chao Prom Market** opposite the train station. You can start at the TAT Tourist Information Center and hire a guide for the 7.5-mile (12 km) route through the city. The route is paved, and it is relaxed enough for children and mediocre cyclists alike. The different sites are marked, and with a bike, you will have ample time to see them all. As you ride by Wat Thammikarat, make a wish. It will come true, provided that you lift a 22-pound (10 kg) bronze elephant with one finger. Better start practicing.

Frangipani trees frame one of the main *chedis* at Ayutthaya's ruined Wat Phra Si Sanphet.

the Uthong school of art, which was inspired by the Mon and Khmers. Later sculpture was influenced by the Sukhothai; some of the most successful work dates from this time.

As the artistic influence of Sukhothai waned, late Ayutthayan images became over-ornamented, lacking the sensitivity of earlier styles. Yet Ayutthayan sculptors also introduced remarkable innovations—such as the depiction of the Buddha in a wider variety of poses—and proved themselves masters of casting bronze images on a large scale.

Chan Kasem National Palace
- Map p. 133
- Uthong Rd.
- Closed Mon.–Tues.
- $
- Tuk-tuk from Ayutthaya city center

the temples and icons were destroyed by the Burmese, but around 50 temples remain in various states of repair and restoration, along with monuments such as giant reclining Buddhas. Three excellent museums are filled with smaller Buddha images and other important archaeological discoveries.

Chan Kasem National Palace: Ayutthaya's oldest museum is inside a palace originally built as the future home of King Naresuan (r. 1590–1605), one of Ayutthaya's most powerful kings. Like so much of the city, it was destroyed in 1765 but was reconstructed in the 19th century.

The displays are somewhat modest, though the complex of buildings has architectural interest. To the left of the main entrance, the Chantura Mukh Pavilion houses an impressive standing Buddha. Behind this, the Piman Rajaja Pavilion is filled with rare Thai shadow puppets and smaller Buddha images. The nearby Pisai Sayalak Tower was an astronomical observatory.

Wat Ratchaburana: One of Thailand's great archaeological discoveries took place in this unremarkable temple, constructed in 1424 by King Borommaracha II (r. 1424–1448) to honor his brothers, who had killed each other in a fight for the throne. The central *prang* was built shortly after the king had conquered and looted the great Khmer capital, Angkor Thom.

Borommaracha apparently hauled his plunder back to Ayutthaya and stored it inside a secret crypt below the prang. In 1957, a fabulous treasure trove of priceless gold objects, bronzes, Buddhas,

A tree encases the head of a Buddha at Ayutthaya's dilapidated Wat Mahathat.

and other items, both from Angkor Thom and created by the craftsmen of Ayutthaya, was discovered by accident when thieves broke in. Much of the surviving treasure is now displayed in the Chao Sam Phraya National Museum (see below). Steps still lead down into the crypt where the artifacts lay hidden for so many centuries.

INSIDER TIP:

Check out the Tha Prachan amulet market—near the Sanam Luang grounds and Wat Mahathat— where you can find good-luck charms, love potions, and unusual trinkets. Just don't buy ivory, please.

—DANIEL STILES, PH.D.
National Geographic field researcher

Wat Mahathat: This Khmer-influenced temple was constructed in 1374 by King Borommaracha I (r. 1370–1388). Known as the Temple of the Great Relic, Wat Mahathat was leveled by the Burmese and today largely lies in ruin. However, the scale of the floor plan suggests the impressive size and relative importance of this central temple complex. Look for the broken Buddha head in the southeast corner, which appears to be growing out of a tree trunk (*Naresuan/ Cheekuan Rds.*).

Wat Phra Ram: This modest temple dates from 1369 and was built on the funeral site of King Ramathibodi (r. 1350–1369), by his son, Ramasuen (r. 1369–1395). The extraordinary corncob prang, adorned with mythical figures and Buddhas, was added around a hundred years later. Wat Phra Ram is less impressive than some of the larger temples at Ayutthaya, but it is in a stunning location—on a grassy peninsula that extends into a pond covered in giant water lilies (*Si Sanphet Rd.*).

Chao Sam Phraya National Museum: The funds for this major museum, formally known as the Chao Sam Phraya, were raised from the sale of less important artifacts discovered in the haul at Wat Ratchaburana (see opposite). The collection, spread over the two floors of the main building, is representative of all the major movements in Thai art. Highlights to watch for during your tour of the museum include golden treasure from the Wat Ratchaburana hoard and a massive bronze Buddha head. As with many Thai museums, the displays are arranged in chronological order.

Ayutthaya Historical Study Center: This academic center, opened in 1990, promotes research into the history of Ayutthaya. Its principal building serves as a museum, open to the public, while other buildings to the rear are reserved for students, researchers, and academics. Exhibitions range from

Chao Sam Phraya National Palace

- 🅰 Map p. 133
- ✉ Rotchana Rd.
- ⊕ Closed Mon.–Tues.
- 💲 $
- 🚖 Tuk-tuk from Ayutthaya city center

Ayutthaya Historical Study Center

- 🅰 Map p. 133
- ✉ Rotchana Rd.
- ☎ 035-245123
- ⊕ Closed Mon.
- 💲 $
- 🚖 Tuk-tuk from Ayutthaya city center

**Lak Muang
& Khum Khum
House**

🗺 Map p. 133

✉ Si Sanphet Rd.

🚕 Tuk-tuk from
city center

Royal Palace

🗺 Map p. 133

✉ Si Sanphet Rd.

💲 $

🚕 Tuk-tuk from
city center

the history of ancient Ayutthaya to the role of the Ayutthaya Empire in international relations. Miniatures of seafaring vessels include a Chinese merchantship, and scale models of various structures depict older incarnations of Ayutthaya, including a reconstruction of Wat Phra Si Sanphet (see below) and a typical Thai village.

St. Joseph Cathedral

During Ayutthaya's heyday, Western merchants and emissaries lived outside the city walls, and could only enter with official permission. As a result, various European communities grew up beyond the river boundary, and the 17th-century Catholic cathedral belongs to this time. Rebuilt in the 19th century, it continues to operate as a church *(Bung Phra Ram Rd., across the river, south side of city).*

Lak Muang & Khum Khum House: Ayutthaya's city pillar, Lak Muang, stands by the National Museum and is believed to be the home of ancient spirits that live in the ground under the modern city. This means it is an animist or Hindu shrine, rather than a religious structure dedicated to the Buddha.

Nearby Khum Khum House was built in 1894 as the city jail, and it remains an outstanding example of traditional domestic architecture. It is now home to the

Fine Arts Department, and visitors are welcome to explore the grounds.

Wihan Phra Mongkhon Bophit: One of Thailand's largest and most highly revered Buddhas is located inside this unimaginative building *(Si Sanphet Rd.),* immediately south of the far more elegant Wat Phra Si Sanphet. The original building on this site was erected during the Ayutthaya period but collapsed in 1767. It was reconstructed in 1951. Head inside to enjoy the power of the immense image, covered with a thick black coating and gilded with gleaming mother-of-pearl eyes.

Wat Phra Si Sanphet: Similar in purpose to Wat Phra Kaeo in Bangkok (see pp. 69–77), this famous trio of 15th-century *chedis* once formed the core of the most important temple complex in Ayutthaya. The *wat* was both the private chapel and ceremonial courtyard for royalty, who would arrive on gilded palanquins from the nearby Royal Palace. The finely proportioned, symmetrically domed chedis stand on a long central platform, separated by square *mondops*, and are an image used widely on film—from Thai television commercials to American movies. The chedis were built to enshrine the ashes of important kings. The ruins are overgrown but one of the great sights of Ayutthaya.

Royal Palace: At no other place in Ayutthaya is the destruction of the city more evident than on the grounds of the old Royal Palace, where nothing remains but some scattered foundations connected by a series of small paths. It was built in the mid-15th century by King Borommatrailokanat (r. 1448–1488) and expanded over the following centuries. Today, there is little that hints at its former opulence.

Wat Na Phra Men: One of the few great monuments to escape the destruction of 1767 is this soaring monastery on Khlong Sabua, opposite the Royal Palace. Believed to date from the late 15th century, it has been restored several times. Rarely visited by tourists, Wat Na Phra Men features a large *bot* beside a small but significant *wihan.* The larger building boasts magnificent Ayutthayan architectural details in its gateways, elaborate porticoes, and refined pediments. The interior, with its gilded supports, gleaming floors, and roofs carved with lotus buds, is just as remarkable. A gilded, Ayutthaya-style Buddha sits at the center.

The smaller wihan is noted for its extraordinarily rare Dvaravati Buddha, which is seated, with spread feet and hands curiously placed on the knees—a powerful image that richly deserves its reputation as a masterpiece of Mon art *(north part of town off Uthong Rd.).*

Wat Lokaya Sutharam: The site of this wat, to the west of Ayutthaya's main attractions, is marked by the 67-foot (20 m) figure of a reclining Buddha. The somewhat ungainly image was once protected by a wooden wihan, of which only the octagonal pillars survive—now a coat of whitewash is all that keeps him from the elements. Reclining Buddhas are usually associated with the Buddha's entry into nirvana, but this one relates to a particular story about the Buddha's growing huge in order to defeat an enemy.

Little remains of the Royal Palace's original grandeur.

Wat Phanan Choeng: One of Ayutthaya's oldest and largest temples, Wat Phanan Choeng was constructed in 1324 specifically to house a massive seated Buddha, the gift of a Chinese emperor. The powerful and inspiring image has been restored many times, and a steady stream of Thai and Chinese pilgrims arrive daily to make offerings. An adjoining wihan to the left of the main temple has several rare and valuable Sukhothai statues *(south of town at ferry crossing).*

Cosmic Symbolism in Thai Architecture

To visitors, Thai architecture may at first appear to be confusing and haphazard, but in fact nearly every religious structure has been carefully designed to follow traditional elements that symbolize Theravada Buddhism and the underlying belief in Hindu cosmology. Almost every aspect of ancient and modern Thai architecture can be traced back to Hindu architectural concepts, which borrowed from the Khmers and were adapted by Thai builders.

Thai temples are filled with numerous Buddha images, which follow Hindu symbolism. This may seem a strange combination, but animism underpins Buddhism in Thailand. Thus, while Thai kings honored

Buddhism in their spiritual beliefs, they followed the animist traditions of Hinduism in their building designs.

Hindu cosmology dictates the architectural structure of all Thai temples. A massive tower that represents Mount Meru must always be the centerpiece, with 33 tiers that symbolize the 33 levels of heaven. *Prangs* were surmounted by a thunderbolt trident, the heavenly symbol of Indra, while *chedis* were capped with a circular orb to represent the core of nirvana. Moats symbolized ancient oceans separating the human race from the home of gods. Interpreted with the Thai love of curvature and extravagance, the results are an outstanding architectural triumph.

Elephant Kraal

 Map p. 133

✉ Old Lop Buri River Rd., in Ban Phaniat

💲 $

🚕 Tuk-tuk from city center

Wat Yai Chai Mongkhon:

Southeast of town, toward the train station, is a monastery established in 1360 for local monks who, in the spirit of the new Buddhism, wished to emphasize meditation rather than the study of the Buddhist canon. Today it is home to a large community of Buddhist nuns *(mae chi),* who maintain the lawns and buildings. The wat's main feature is a huge reclining Buddha, exposed to the skies.

Wat Suwan Dararam: This

small temple on Uthong Road in the southeast quarter of the old city is worth seeking out for its magnificent interior murals, which date from the reign of Rama II. They depict events from the *Vessantara* and *Suvanasama Jatakas.* More modern murals commissioned by Rama VII show scenes from the life of King Naresuan.

Wat Phu Khao Thong: Situ-

ated in rolling countryside some 3 miles (5 km) west of town is the gigantic chedi of Phu Khao Thong, the "golden mountain." The soaring 266-foot (80 m) structure was erected by the Burmese but later modified into a Thai style. Renovation projects over the centuries have not been kind to the chedi, but visitors who make the tiring hike to the summit will be rewarded with outstanding views over the plains.

Elephant Kraal: Ayutthaya's

elephant enclosure—one of the last surviving teak stockades— was built to hold and train wild elephants for military use and was not abandoned until the mid-19th century. The stockade has been restored but is rather unexciting without its chief inhabitants. The shrine at the center is dedicated to the elephant guardian Ganesha. ■

Bang Pa-in Palace

Monarchs worldwide have sought a retreat from the confines of their royal capitals since time immemorial. So Philip II of Spain (r.1556–1598) built his Escorial palace, and Louis XIV of France his Versailles. For centuries, Siamese kings chose to escape the worst of the hot season in the riverine town of Bang Pa-in.

The habit of maintaining retreats and summer palaces started in the 17th century with King Narai (r. 1656–1688), who received French envoys not only in his royal palace in Ayutthaya, but also at his great upriver retreat at Lop Buri (see p. 144). Narai also maintained a summer palace downriver at Bang Pa-in, a site established by his father, King Prasat Thong (r.1629–1656) in honor of Narai's birth. The royal family used this summer palace until the fall of Ayutthaya in 1767, and the site lay neglected until its revival by King Mongkut in the mid-19th century.

Mongkut and his successor, King Chulalongkorn, enjoyed the site, revitalizing the area with new construction that can be seen today. Bang Pa-in could be reached by boat up the Chao Phraya or, later, via the railroad that ran from Bangkok to Chiang Mai.

Bang Pa-in is of secular rather than religious importance. The small collection of royal buildings that make up the palace are an easy stopover between Bangkok and Ayutthaya, and most reflect Chulalongkorn's fascination with European architecture. The overall impression is a mixture of French neoclassic, Victorian Gothic, imperial Chinese, and traditional Thai styles. The lovely grassy parklands are, in turn, formal French, rustic English, and classic Chinese.

Most of Bang Pa-in's buildings date from 1872 to 1899—the swansong of European monarchy, but for Siam an era that embraced both traditional culture and Western innovations. The architectural range from château to summer-house, pagoda to lighthouse, and Chinese mansion to Thai *sala* may sound like a 19th-century

Bang Pa-in Palace

🔺 Map p. 119

✉ Hwy. 32

💲 $

🚌 Bus from Northern Bus Terminal, Bangkok

Royalty retreated from the duties of Bangkok at Bang Pa-in Palace.

Disneyland, but the reality is a place of charm and dignity.

Phra Thinang Aisawan Thippa-at

The highlight of Bang Pa-in Palace is this pavilion, which appears to float in the shimmering pool that surrounds the complex. Translated as "the divine seat of personal freedom" and designed in Rattanakosin style, the delicate Phra Thinang Aisawan Thippa-at is an icon of Thai architecture—and a great place for photos. The building is, in fact, a copy of a pavilion in Bangkok's Grand Palace (see pp. 73–76) and houses a statue of King Chulalongkorn in the uniform of a field marshal.

Phra Thinang Wehat Chamrun

Nicknamed the Peking Palace, this mansion is a copy of a monument in the Beijing Imperial Court, presented to King Chulalongkorn in 1889 by Chinese merchants and imported lock, stock, and barrel from China. It is one of the few buildings open to the public, with interesting displays of lacquer tables, Chulalongkorn's fantastically carved bed, Ming porcelain, and a superb collection of jade.

Phra Thinang Warophat Phiman

The "excellent and shining abode" is a European-style palace set between the lake and the river, erected by King Chulalongkorn to replace King Mongkut's two-story royal residence. A grand porticoed structure, it was Chulalongkorn's official residence and throne hall. Memorials honor important events in national history.

Ho Withun Thasana

This curious Royal Observatory tower is where avid astronomer King Mongkut spent his evenings observing the stars. The tower is what remains of a wooden palace destroyed by fire in 1938.

INSIDER TIP:

Take the cable car from Bang Pa-in across the river to Wat Nivet Thamaprawat—as far off the tourist track as you can get.

—BARBARA A. NOE
National Geographic editor

Queen's Monument

Chulalongkorn's first queen is honored with a white marble memorial across a small bridge, inscribed with Thai and English eulogies composed by the king. Queen Sunandakumariratha tragically drowned in 1880, within reach of would-be rescuers who were absolutely forbidden to touch the royal personage.

Wat Nivet Thamaprawat

A small cable car takes you over the river from the main group of buildings to this neo-Gothic-style temple that looks more like a Christian church than a Buddhist temple. A stained-glass window feature King Chulalongkorn (the builder). ∎

Wat Phra Phutthabat

Located between the towns of Saraburi and Lop Buri (see pp. 144–145), north of Bangkok, this *wat* is one of the country's most revered. The temple was constructed by King Song Tham about 1620–1628, to honor a wandering hunter's miraculous discovery of a footprint left by the Buddha during his time on Earth. The hunter reported that scars and wounds across his face and body vanished immediately after he bathed in the waters held within the immense footprint.

A *naga*-lined staircase leads to a *mondop* housing a Buddha footprint thought to have healing powers.

The miraculous powers assigned to the footprint over the centuries have turned it into a sort of Lourdes of Thailand, attracting a steady stream of pilgrims. Today the wat s one of the holiest shrines in the country, along with the temples at Chiang Mai, Nakhon Phanom, and Nakhon Si Thammarat.

An elaborate *mondop* shelters the 5-foot-long (1.5 m) gilded footprint, which is reached via a walkway guarded by mythological snakes. The hall is impressive inside—it was restored in the 18th century. Pilgrims throw coins into the footprint to improve their karma and toss in special sticks to divine their fortune. Electronic fortune-telling machines have also been installed in the mondop and other buildings within the temple complex.

Wihan Luang, within the same complex, is a museum of assorted religious relics. Smaller *chedis* and *bots* are dedicated to the Buddha and the Hindu god Kala.

Phra Phutthabat is the focus of two festive pilgrimages each year, in February and late March. Held for more than 400 years, the festivals draw up to 800,000 people. ■

Wat Phra Phutthabat

- Map p. 119
- Saraburi
- 036-321667, 036-321668, or 036-321669
- Closed Fri –Sat. & holidays
- Bus from Northern Bus Terminal, Bangkok

Lop Buri

Some 102 miles (164 km) north of Bangkok, this is the site of one of Thailand's most ancient cities, continuously occupied since the sixth century. Lop Buri, originally known as Lavo, is thought to have been the capital of the Dvaravati Empire. The Khmers took over the town in the 11th century but permitted it to continue the cultural and religious traditions of the Dvaravati Empire. It was during this period that most of the major monuments were built.

Resident monkeys are the guests of honor for a feast at Wat San Phra Khan.

After the fall of the Khmer Empire, the city lay abandoned until its revitalization in the 17th century by Ayutthaya's King Narai. He transformed the ancient city into an alternative capital, where he invited Europeans to visit and help create his summer "Versailles of Siam." French architects assisted in the building of his new residence, and exquisite gifts were exchanged with Louis XIV of France. This golden era ended with Narai's death in 1688, and Lop Buri slipped into the backwaters of history. Today, a lively modern town has grown up to the east of the ancient city.

Phra Narai Ratchaniwet

Narai's enormous **royal palace** complex displays a strong blend of traditional Khmer and European architecture.

To the right of the main entrance is the Chanthara Phisan Pavilion, built in 1665 and now the Lop Buri National Museum, with an interesting collection of Buddhas, and displays of Uthong, Khmer, and Ayutthayan art. The Audience Hall to the left of the museum was a reception hall. Now little more than teetering stone walls, it was once lined with grand mirrors in imitation of Versailles.

Wat Phra Si Rattana Mahathat

This 12th-century Khmer temple, located on Naprakan Road, is the city's most significant piece of architecture. The towering central prang, decorated with elaborate stuccowork, survived clumsy renovations during the Ayutthaya and Sukhothai periods, and is an outstanding site. A brick wihan was built for King Narai, and its unusual pointed window arch clearly shows European and Persian influence.

INSIDER TIP:

When in Lop Buri, you can't miss the monkeys. They are cute but can be aggressive and are attracted to hats and bags.

—SUCHANA A. CHAVANICH
National Geographic field scientist

Wat San Phra Kan

Also known as the Kala Temple, the site, located on Wichayen Road, includes the remains of a tenth-century Khmer prang, a smaller temple with a particularly ornate doorway, and a modern temple built in 1953, with a gilded statue of the four-armed Hindu god Kala. Visitors come here to see the monkeys that have been allowed to take over the temple.

Chao Phraya Wichayen

This European-style palace on Wichayen Road was built by King Narai for a French ambassador of Louis XIV but later gained fame as the residence of a Greek, Constantine Phaulkon (d. 1688). He exerted considerable influence over the king and hoped to convert him to Christianity. Upon the king's death, however, Phaulkon's rivals promptly had him executed. The palace was demolished at the same time. ∎

Lop Buri

▲ Map p. 119

Visitor Information

✉ Tourism Authority of Thailand, Narai Maharat Rd., Lop Buri

☎ 036-422768 or 036-422769; fax 036-424089

🚌 Bus from Northern Bus Terminal, Bangkok

www.tat7.com

Phra Narai Ratchaniwet (Royal Palace)

✉ Sorasak Rd.

🕐 National Museum closed Mon.–Tues. (palace open daily)

$ $

EXPERIENCE: Meeting Up With Monkeys & Apes

If you happen to dislike monkeys and apes, you might want to stay away from this part of the country. But if you can't get enough of their howling, bug-picking, hat-stealing ways, there are many ways to enjoy the company of our evolutionary in-laws. Here are a couple:

Highland Farm (*Amphur Mae Sot, Tak, tel 089-958-0821, www.highland-farm.com*) Nestled in the hills of Tak Province near the Thai-Burmese border, Highland Farm runs a sanctuary for more than 40 gibbons. Visitors may attend afternoon feedings, stay for several days, or volunteer for at least one month. Volunteers do various chores associated with gibbon care, including cleaning, feeding, and providing TLC.

Lop Buri Monkey Festival (*Lopburi Inn, 28/9 Naraima-harach Rd., Lop Buri, tel 036-412300, www.lopburi innhotel.com*) The Lopburi Inn hosts a monkey festival on the last Sunday of November. Located on the grounds of an ancient Khmer ruin, nearby the temple where the town's monkeys reside, the festival's theme changes annually, and thousands of monkeys attend a feast that is laid out in their honor. It's quite the spectacle to see.

More Places to Visit Around Bangkok

Chachoengsao

Despite encroaching urban sprawl, this town, about 90 minutes from Bangkok, has managed to retain its charm with narrow streets lined with teak shop-houses and restaurants, and its lovely old market in the town center. 🔼 Map p. 119 🔁 Inter-provincial bus from Eastern Bus Station, Sukhumvit Rd., Ekamai

Crocodile Farm

A few miles from Muang Boran is the world's largest reptile farm, established in 1950 to protect endangered crocodiles. The 30,000 crocodiles here include species from around the world. The crocodile-wrestling show is popular; feeding time is 4:30–5:30 p.m. 🔼 Map p. 119 ✉ Old Sukhumvit Hwy., Samut Prakan ☎ 02-703-5144 or 02-703-5145 💲 $$ 🔁 Bus: 7, 8, or 11 to Samut Prakan

Muai Thai Institute

This institute promotes the culture and gives instruction in the martial art of *muay Thai*, or Thai boxing. Muay Thai courses for foreigners emphasize the sport's culture. Call ahead. www.muaithai-institute.net 🔼 Map p. 119 ✉ 336/932 Prachathipat, Thanyaburi, Pathum Thani ☎ 02-992-0096

Muang Boran

Also called Ancient City, this outdoor historical and architectural park features 65 reproductions of significant Thai buildings, such as the Grand Palace of Ayutthaya. 🔼 Map p. 119 ✉ 20 miles (33 km) SW of Bangkok, at Sukhumvit Rd., Bangpu Samut Prakan ☎ 02-226-1936 💲 $ 🔁 Bus: 7, 8, or 11 to Samut Prakan

National Science Museum

The museum is the first part of a huge "technopolis" that, when completed, will also include the Natural History Museum, Ecology and Environment Museum, and Aviation and Telecommunications Museum. Six floors cf exhibits cover the history of science and technology. www.nsm.or.th 🔼 Map p. 119 ✉ Klong 5, Klong Luang, Pahum Thani ☎ 02-577-9999 🕐 Closed Mon. 💲 $

Naval Museum

The museum chronicles the history of the Royal Thai Navy and its important battles. It also features scale models of ships, including the warship H.M.S. *Phra Ruang* and H.M.S. *Matchanu*, the first submarine in the Thai Navy, and the glorious Royal Barges. www.navy.mi.th/navalmuseum 🔼 Map p. 119 ✉ Sukhumvit Rd. Km 10, Bang Nang Keng, Pak Nam, Samut Prakan ☎ 02-394-1997 💲 $ 🔁 Bus: 7, 8, or 11

Nonthaburi

Six miles (10 km) north of Bangkok, this small town retains some of old Siam's charm, with its riverside market, royal boathouse, and temple ruins amid breadfruit trees. Best reached by river, the town is also the home of the Singha Brewery. 🔼 Map p. 119 ✉ Hwy. 305 🔁 Bus: 5 or 6 ⛴ Chao Phraya River Express from Bangkok

Samphran Elephant Ground & Zoo

Crocodile wrestling and animal-themed magic shows are part of this small farm's appeal. But it is the elephant games that are the most unusual, including the re-creation of a historical battle fought on elephant-back. Shows at 1:45 p.m. and 3:30 p.m. www.elephantshow.com 🔼 Map p. 119 ✉ Km 31, Hwy. 4 ☎ 02-284-1873 💲 $ 🔁 Bus: 83 or 997 from Southern Bus Terminal, Bangkok

Siam Water Park

The sprawling park offers plenty of watery fun, including an artificial wave pool, water chutes, and fast waterslides. 🔼 Map p. 119 ✉ Min Buri ☎ 02-919-7200 to -19 💲 $$$$$ 🔁 Bus: 26 or 27 from Victory Monument, Bangkok

A rambunctious and famous international resort, beach towns where locals spend their weekends away from Bangkok, and peaceful, idyllic islands on Thailand's east coast

East Coast

Fishing boat in Rayong harbor

East Coast

Thailand's eastern coastline is an almost unbroken stretch of sand running from south-east of Bangkok to Hat Lek, a village on the Cambodian border in Trat Province. The coast closer to Bangkok is the industrial heartland—manufacturing, oil refinery, and power plants predominate. Where the factories end, the famous resort city of Pattaya begins. Beyond Pattaya, unspoiled islands attract visitors seeking quieter locations.

All towns along the east coast lie on or near Sukhumvit Highway (Highway 3), which stretches 399 miles (638 km) from the heart of Bangkok as far as the Cambodian border. After cutting through the urban southeast of Bangkok, Sukhumvit Highway emerges into traces of countryside before it reaches the coastline, a narrow strip of land wedged between the Gulf of Thailand and the Don-grek Mountains, which rise abruptly just a few miles inland. Here government planners have set in motion a package of schemes that could transform this section of the eastern seaboard from a collection of fishing villages to Thailand's major industrial zone.

While deepwater ports, natural gas and oil refineries, and industrial estates may have little appeal for the visitor, the resort city of Pattaya certainly does. The honeypot of the east coast, Pattaya provides an enormous range of activities for visitors, from superb golf

---

NOT TO BE MISSED:

---

courses and excellent scuba diving to theme parks for children. Reasonable diversions can be made from Pattaya to the modest beach at Bang Saen and to the island of Ko Si Chang, just a short boat ride from Si Racha.

The coast beyond Pattaya unveils a couple of island gems—Ko Samet and Ko Chang—and a number of towns with varying degrees of appeal.

Rayong is an unremarkable town, though it provides the gateway to the nearby island of Ko Samet. This is a favorite stop for Thai students, who bring their guitars with them and stay in the moderately priced bungalows that flank the island.

Farther east again is the large town of Chanthaburi, located in an area famed throughout Thailand for the sheer perfection of its tropical fruits, including rambutan and durian. Chanthaburi has a thriving gem industry, and it is situated near the beautiful waterfalls and national parks of the Dongrek Mountains.

From Trat, in the southeastern corner of Thailand, some people head farther south and over the border into Cambodia. Others turn toward the coast and the beautiful islands of the Mu Ko Chang Marine National Park. Dominated by the rugged and heavily forested major island of Ko Chang, the group provides a more downbeat way to enjoy the pleasures of tropical islands. The only accommodations on these island are simple bungalows, and the amenities are sparse. ■

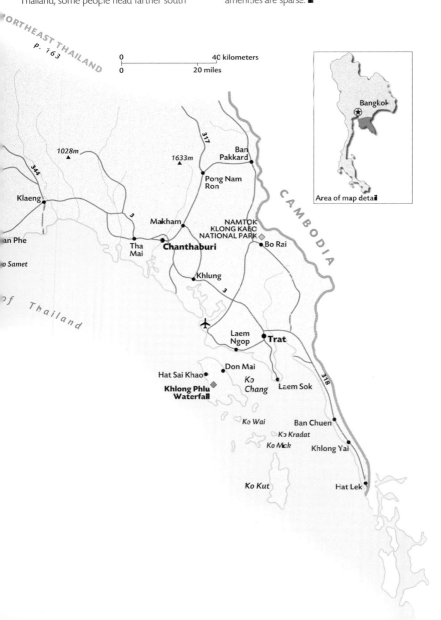

NORTHEAST THAILAND
P. 163

0   40 kilometers
0   20 miles

Bangkok

Area of map detail

CAMBODIA

1028m
1633m
344
Klaeng
an Phe
o Samet
of Thailand
3
Makham
Tha Mai
Chanthaburi
NAMTOK KLONG KAEO NATIONAL PARK
Ban Pakkard
Pong Nam Ron
317
Bo Rai
Khlung
3
Laem Ngop
Trat
318
Don Mai
Hat Sai Khao
Ko Chang
Laem Sok
Khlong Phlu Waterfall
Ko Wai
Ban Chuen
Ko Kradat
Ko Mak
Khlong Yai
Ko Kut
Hat Lek

Bang Saen

Sukhumvit Highway cuts across what little remains of the rice fields that once characterized the area southeast of Bangkok, until it reaches the large industrial city of Chon Buri, known on the tourist circuit only for its annual waterbuffalo races. A few miles beyond is one of the oldest beach resorts in Thailand, the modest stretch of sand and casuarina trees at Bang Saen.

Stonemasons are in high demand for creating sculptures for theme parks and other tourist attractions.

Bang Saen
🅰 Map p. 148
🚌 Bus from Ekamai (Eastern) Bus Terminal, Bangkok

Before the completion of the road to Pattaya in 1969, Bang Saen was the kingdom's most popular weekend beach escape.

Even today it attracts big crowds of Thais, who appreciate its proximity to Bangkok and its almost total lack of tourists.

The beach here is clean, but the waters on any particular day can vary from clear to murky. Vendors are always on hand to rent umbrellas and bamboo furniture to go along with the mats on which families spread out picnics. Visitors are a rarity, so you can expect to be invited to join a group of Thais, who will probably be cracking open mussels and consuming prodigious quantities of Mekong whiskey.

Khao Khieo Open Zoo (Rte. 3144, tel 038-298270), 12 miles (18 km) inland from Bang Saen, opened in 1973 to provide overflow facilities for the cramped Dusit Zoo in Bangkok (see p. 104). ■

EXPERIENCE: Getting to Know Water Buffalo

Considered traditional Thai tractors, buffalo were once an essential aspect of Thai rural life, responsible for sowing fields, providing milk and meat, and even participating in battle. Today, machines have all but replaced the buffalo, yet you can still experience the days of yore and gain appreciation of this once integral part of agricultural life.

One of the best places is the **Chon Buri Water Buffalo Racing Festival,** held each year in October or November in downtown Chon Buri (west of Pattaya). In the 427-foot (130 m) race, a bareback jockey urges a water buffalo to sprint down the street.

Or kick off your shoes and sow the fields behind a giant buffalo at the **Mae Rim Buffalo Training Camp** (Chiang Mai, tel 081-882-2331). Here, too, you can jump behind the horns for a ride upon these peaceful beasts. Watch buffalo perform traditional activities, as well as tricks normally associated with elephants!

Si Racha & Ko Si Chang

The small but active fishing village of Si Racha is famous as the production center of a pungent fish concoction called *nam phrik si racha*—the most popular sweet and spicy sauce in Thailand. The town itself has little of great interest, but it is the launching point for boats across to the historic island of Ko Si Chang.

While waiting for the boat for Ko Si Chang, spend an hour wandering around Si Racha, visiting a few temples and exploring the colorful waterfront (look for the unique motorcycle trishaws).

The only attraction of note is the famous island of **Ko Loi**, linked to the mainland by a 1-mile (1.5 km) bridge. Thai tourists flock to Wat Ko Loi to honor the memory of a deceased monk. According to local folklore, the monk possessed miraculous healing powers. You can see his wax statue at the temple.

Ko Si Chang

This island, 8 miles (13 km) offshore from Si Racha, became popular with wealthy Thais and royalty in the mid-1800s—so popular that King Chulalongkorn built a summer palace here in 1892. The end result—you can see it to the right as you arrive on the island from Si Racha— was impressive: The two-story Wattana Palace, the eight-sided Phongsri on a nearby hill, and the Aphirom with dual porches were part of a compound that included 14 royal domiciles and four throne halls built in teak, plus a hillside *chedi*. Wells were dug, a lighthouse was constructed to aid passing ships, and roads were built to connect the residences.

The palace fell into disrepair

after the French occupied the island from 1893 to 1904. One of the four throne halls was moved to Bangkok in 1901, where it now serves as Vimanmek Palace (see pp. 104–105). Its foundations and stairway remain at Ko Si Chang. Other surviving palace buildings, or what's left of them, are partly overgrown, but still appealing.

Shrimp Farms

Shrimp farms proliferate in Thailand's coastal areas. Mangroves are cut down and wetlands dredged to make way for the farms, destroying these important habitats and exposing the coastline to erosion. Local species are affected and migratory birds—which once came in the thousands—no longer return.

Another site worth searching out is a Chinese temple called **San Chao Por Khao Yai**, a gathering point for thousands of Chinese Thais who come every year during Chinese New Year. The temple, at the top of steep climb, has a number of shrine caves. The views over the island are spectacular.

The best beach is **Hat Tha Wang** at the island's western end, 1.25 miles (2 km) from the main pier near the palace. ■

Si Racha

- Map p. 148
- Bus from Ekamai (Eastern) Bus Terminal, Bangkok

Visitor Information

- 609 Mu 10 Phra Tham Nak Rd., Tambon Nongpue, Amphoe Eang-Lamung, Chon Buri
- 038-427657 or 038-428750

Pattaya

Fifty years ago, Pattaya was a somnolent fishing village accessible only by boat from Bangkok or other towns near the estuary of the Chao Phraya. The town's chief claim to fame was that it served as a resting place for King Narai during his military campaign to oust Burmese forces from his country.

A rare quiet moment in Pattaya, Thailand's busiest beach resort

In 1959 a group of American GIs from a U.S. military base in Nakhon Ratchasima (Khorat) arrived in Pattaya, renting houses in the southern part of town. On their return to Khorat, they spread the word about the white sands and clear waters of Pattaya beach. The visit jump-started Pattaya's tourism drive. More U.S. servicemen from military bases throughout northeast Thailand used the town as a rest and recreation spot during the Vietnam War. By the 1970s locals and tourists were starting to discover its charms. Hotels were built along the shoreline, together with restaurants, nightclubs, and bars. By the 1980s Pattaya had become one of Thailand's most popular tourist resorts.

Today, three million visitors flood this rambunctious resort every year to enjoy its high-rise hotels, simple guesthouses, roaring

INSIDER TIP:

Head to the Tiffany Club for an evening cabaret show. The "girls" do amazing performances, and it's some of the best theater in Thailand.

—KRIS LEBOUTILLIER
National Geographic photographer

discos, fine restaurants, souvenir shops, and countless nightclubs, which complement several world-class golf courses and every imaginable ocean-related activity. Those who seek perfect quiet on a lonely tropical island should skip Pattaya and head down to Ko Chang (see pp. 160–161). But visitors who desire comforts and pleasures, along with nonstop entertainment, will love Pattaya, one of Southeast Asia's great party towns.

The most accessible beach resort near Bangkok, Pattaya is in the process of changing itself from a rather seedy destination for single men into a highly varied retreat favored by couples and families. But no one can hide the problems that Pattaya faces. Because of reckless development over the years, its main beach became so polluted that people were warned not to swim there. For a long while, the city was probably the only beach resort in the world where the beach was out of bounds. Pattaya also suffers from its image as a sex center and is a favorite haunt for men from abroad looking for sex.

City fathers face a constant battle with the resort's image,

launching campaign after campaign to try to convince people that it has cleaned up its act. And to some extent it has. You can now swim at Pattaya Beach. The city has become one of Asia's premier golf centers, with a dozen quality courses attracting people from all over the region. There is a myriad of water sports, and on nearby offshore islands, sparkling beaches and gardens of coral are great for diving and snorkeling. There are amusement parks and plenty of other tourist sites in and around the town. And—if you keep an open mind—you will encounter a lively and enjoyable nightlife.

Pattaya Beach is narrow and

Pattaya
- Maps p. 148 & below
- Bus from Ekamai (Eastern) Bus Terminal, Bangkok

Visitor Information
- Tourism Authority of Thailand, 382/1 Mu 10 Chaihat Rd., Pattaya City
- 038-427667 or 038-428750

Tiffany Club
- Pattaya 2 Rd., Pattaya

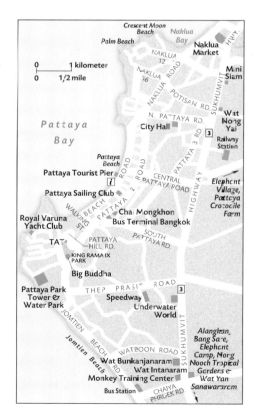

Young Thais congregate in one of Pattaya's many beer bars.

Around Pattaya

Pattaya Crocodile Farm *(Siam Country Club Rd., tel 038-249347)* has rare animals, as well as crocodiles and a botanical garden. In Pattaya, turn off Sukhumvit Highway at the Kilometer 140 signpost to Chaiyaphonwithi Road (Highway 3024) for 3 miles (5 km).

Mini Siam *(Sukhumvit Hwy., tel 038-421628)*, on the left of Sukhumvit Highway traveling south, at the Kilometer 143 signpost, features almost a hundred miniature models of famous Siamese temples and other historical structures, including Wat Phra Kaeo (see pp. 69–73), the bridge over the Kwai (Khwae; see p. 125), and the Khmer temple at Phimai (see pp. 170–171). The park also has models of international icons such as the Eiffel Tower and the Statue of Liberty.

INSIDER TIP:

If you're looking for snorkeling or scuba diving but don't have time to go to southern Thailand, the islands around Pattaya are an excellent option.

—SUCHANA A. CHAVANICH
National Geographic field scientist

From Mini Siam, head south on Sukhumvit Highway, past North Pattaya Road; then turn left on Pornprapanimitr Road toward the Siam Country Club to the popular **Pattaya Elephant Village** *(Siam Country Club Rd., tel 038-428645)*.

less impressive than beaches in southern Thailand. However, a few hours relaxing under an umbrella, munching on Thai snacks, makes for a pleasant diversion.

For excellent views overlooking Pattaya, head up Pattaya Hill Road, at the southern end of town, to Wat Pra Yai. While you're there, check out its **Big Buddha** statue.

Off Pattaya Hill Road, not far from Wat Pra Yai, at the northern Jomtien beachfront on Thapphraya Road, is **Pattaya Water Park** *(Jomtien Beach, tel 038-251201)*. With its waterslides and whirlpools, this is a place the entire family will enjoy. Next door is **Pattaya Park Tower** *(Jomtien Beach, tel 038-251201)*, which features a revolving restaurant on the 53rd floor. After a buffet lunch, you can ride the elevator down to the ground or jump out of the window and descend to earth on the seemingly perilous "sky shuttle."

See demonstrations of the unique skills of the Thai elephant, and take a two-hour ride through the adjacent jungle. An elephant ride, jungle trek, and river-rafting package is also available.

Bira International Circuit *(Hwy. 36, 038-936085)* is on Highway 36—the main Pattaya-Ranong road—about 9 miles (14 km) north of town. It sponsors international motor-racing events and is home to a popular race school. Rental choices range from go-carts to Formula 3 models.

About 10 miles (16 km) south of Pattaya off Sukhumvit Highway, **Wat Yan Sangwararam** features seven unique structures in various Asian and Western styles, and a magnificent museum filled with Chinese paintings, scrolls, bronzeware, carved wall reliefs, and a small-scale model of the excavated tomb in Xian, China.

A few miles south, still on Sukhumvit Highway, turn left at the Kilometer 163 signpost to **Nong Nooch Tropical Gardens** *(Rte. 3, tel 038-709358)*, another well-managed tourist resort, with gardens, a small zoo, an orchid house and aviary, several restaurants, and a daily cultural show that ranks among the better of its kind.

Bang Sare, a small fishing village 3 miles (5 km) south of Nong Nooch Tropical Gardens, is the departure point for many fishing trips.

Ko Lan

After visiting some of the more commercialized attractions of Pattaya, many visitors choose to spend a day out on one of the nearby islands, where the sand is much cleaner and more inviting than at the municipal beach. Of the half-dozen islands offshore, the most popular is **Ko Lan** ("coral island"), which has several beautiful beaches, clear water, and an abundance of coral. You can view the coral from a glass-bottom boat, snorkel, or orga-

Golf Courses

The three most highly regarded golf courses around Pattaya are **St. Andrews 2000** *(9/36 Moo 7 Samnakthon Banchang Rayong, tel 038-893838),* **Amata Spring Country Club** *(700/5 Moo 6 Nongmaidang, Chon Buri, tel 038-468888),* and **Laem Chabang International Country Club** *(106/8 Moo 4, Beung, Sriracha, Chon Buri, tel 038-372273).*

nize a trip at one of the dozen scuba-dive centers in Pattaya.

Tour boats from Pattaya head to **Ta Waen Beach** on the northeast coast of Ko Lan, the island's best and most popular beach (avoid weekends, when it gets packed). Restaurants and outlets offering water sports line most of the beach. Besides glass-bottom boat tours of the nearby coral crops, you can hire snorkeling gear, try parasailing, go waterskiing, or rent a water scooter. At the southwestern end of the island is the clean and tranquil (on weekdays) **Laemtien Beach.** South again are the smaller, more secluded Samae and Nual beaches. ∎

Ko Samet

Ko Samet is a small, wedge-shaped island located just offshore from Ban Phe. Graced with fairly nice sandy beaches and calm, swimmable waters, it sits below rocky headlands that are typical of the arid interior. Samet's appeal also lies in its relatively close proximity to Bangkok and in its simple, rustic lifestyle, which provides a marked contrast to the livelier atmosphere of Pattaya.

Formerly called Ko Kaew Phitsadau ("vast jewel isle"), a reference to the island's glorious white sand, Ko Samet takes its present name from the abundant *samet*, or cajeput, trees.

Foreign visitors know Ko Samet for its unpretentious charms, but Thais associate the island with their greatest poet, Sunthorn Phu (1786–1855), who based his earliest and most famous epic poem, *Phra Aphaimani*, on his experiences while living on the island. Sunthorn wrote this in the mid-19th century, at a time when Samet functioned as the last customhouse for junks and other ships sailing between China and Siam. The island and its adjoining straits were also the haunt of brigands who raided the cargo-laden vessels. Captured pirates were executed near the customhouse on the north side of Samet.

Ko Samet lay largely off the tourist trail until the early 1970s, when young Thais seeking quiet and solitude traveled down from Bangkok to live in simple shacks on the deserted beaches. An attempt was made to develop the island with resorts, but the outcry from local environmental groups forced the National Parks Division of the Forestry Department to declare the entire island a national park in October 1981, effectively halting large-scale development. Despite these legal measures, developers continued to encroach on the island without permits, and local authorities did little to stop the building of bungalows and resorts, water-sports facilities, and even a few small nightclubs.

The confrontation between private resort developers and government officials peaked in May 1990, when a special police task force raided the island and closed dozens of bungalows as illegally constructed facilities. Although the blitzkrieg was short-lived and ultimately doomed to failure, it helped raise a national consciousness about the preservation of the environment and the threatened overdevelopment of a once unspoiled paradise.

Despite the political controversies that continue to swirl, the island remains an essentially quiet and easygoing destination, without the high-tech thrills of other commercially developed islands in the kingdom.

Visitors arrive on converted fishing trawlers, which leave hourly from the creaky pier at Ban Phe. Most of the boats are chartered by the more upscale resorts and proceed directly to their destinations.

The **Na Dan ferry landing** on the north shore of Ko Samet is the most professionally developed enclave on the island, with hotels and resorts in all price ranges, and water sports that cover the whole spectrum, from windsurfing and boat excursions to snorkeling and scuba diving.

Ko Samet's finest beaches and cleanest waters are found along the east coast, starting with **Hat Sai Kaeo** ("diamond sand beach") at the northeastern tip of the island and just a ten-minute walk from the Na Dan ferry landing. Hat Sai Kaeo has the longest and most impressive beach, and has become the favorite stop for many of the families with children and moderately affluent travelers who come down from Pattaya for a day visit.

South of Hat Sai Kaeo are a number of smaller beaches and coves packed with everything from primitive wooden huts to deluxe resorts with swimming pools and air-conditioned restaurants. **Phai Beach,** also known as Paradise Beach, is a typical small cove with a handful of small bungalows to rent, and basic services including a travel office and a post office with general delivery facilities. **Tub Tim** and **Pudsa Beaches,** farther south, offer a quieter atmosphere plus relatively easy walking access

What's Next for Ko Samet?

Today Ko Samet remains in a quandary about its future. Whether large-scale development will overrun the island or controlled simplicity will remain the common theme are questions that remain unanswered, as they do on many other small islands. The completion of a large freshwater reservoir in 2000 has given credence to the claims of local resort owners that their historic rights must supersede those of the Forestry Department. Today, the island receives almost 30,000 visitors per month; its roughly 50 illegal resorts have more than 1,500 rooms.

to the near-deserted beaches of the west coast—the perfect place for dramatic sunsets. **Wong Deuan, Candlelight, Wai,** and **Kui Beaches** round out the possibilities on the lower stretches of the east coast. ■

Ko Samet

⚐ Map p. 143

🚌 Bus to Rayong from Ekamai (Eastern) Bus Terminal, Bangkok

Visitor Information

✉ Tourism Authority of Thailand, Ban Gon Ao Tambon Pae, Rayong

☎ 038-65303

www.dnt.co.th/samet

Chanthaburi

Chanthaburi ("city of the moon"), a busy commercial enclave on the highway to Cambodia, makes an interesting stop on the long drive to Ko Chang (see pp. 160–161). It has a thriving gem industry, durian plantations (the smelly fruit so loved by many Thais), and a significant population of Vietnamese Christians who fled Vietnam in the late 19th century.

Fruit and vegetable vendors in Chanthaburi vie for customers with more modern retail outlets.

Chanthaburi

- 🗺 Map p. 149
- 🚌 Bus from Ekamai (Eastern) Terminal, Bangkok

Visitor Information

- ✉ Tourism Authority of Thailand, 153/4 Sukhumvit Hwy., Amphoe Muang, Rayong
- ☎ 038-655420 or 038-655421

www.tat-rayoung
.com

With its utilitarian architecture and modern conveniences, Chanthaburi appears unremarkable. In fact, it figured prominently in battles with the French, who occupied this section of Thailand between 1893 and 1904.

Chanthaburi's riverside district and lush parks are relaxing places to watch the local people and visit the limited range of attractions that reflect the region's history. Top draw for most visitors is the historic Catholic **Church of the Immaculate Conception,** constructed in French style between 1906 and 1909 by Vietnamese immigrants who escaped the religious persecution of Emperor Gia Long. The delightfully cheerful color scheme on the exterior seems very French, an impression borne out by details of the interior, from the stained-glass windows (imported from Europe) to the shellwork chandeliers and 26 Moorish-style arches. And it's refreshingly cool inside this Gothic-style monument.

Gems and precious jewelry have long been associated with Thailand, which remains an important source for both the gems themselves and for gem processing. Precious stones are now rarely found in large quantities within Thailand, but rubies, emeralds, and sapphires continue to pour into the country from Myanmar (Burma) and Cambodia. Gems are mined in the lower Cambodian hills near Chanthaburi and brought to the city for cutting and merchandising by jewelry dealers, who arrive daily in steady numbers. Chinese gem dealers can still be observed at work in their sidewalk stalls and inside modern stores just off Sukaphiban Road, near the bridge.

Visitors with extra time may want to explore the old-style houses situated along Sukaphiban Road, just behind the Kasem Sarn I hotel. Several of these atmospheric old homes, notable for their intricate woodcarvings and elaborate wooden altars, still have colonial shutters and filigree plasterwork that reflect the town's French and Vietnamese origins. ∎

Trat & Laem Ngop

Travelers heading down to beautiful Ko Chang (see pp. 160–161) must pass through Trat, a small but thriving commercial enclave, and the sleepy port village of Laem Ngop, the launching point for ferries across to the island. Neither place offers much charm, though the intricacies of transportation in this part of Thailand may necessitate an overnight stop in one or the other.

Trat has played a surprisingly important role in Thai history, most notably after 1767, when it was the launching point for a counterattack against the Burmese conquerors of Ayutthaya.

The city also figured in the French colonial conquest of Indochina, when it was ceded to France in 1894 in exchange for Chanthaburi. It returned to Thai control in the early days of the 20th century, when it was exchanged with the French for Cambodia. A treaty signed that year by King Chulalongkorn ceded the Cambodian provinces of Battambang, Sisophon, and Siem Reap in exchange for Trat, Ko Chang, and Ko Kong. France later attempted to take back Ko Chang, sparking a sea battle off the island's southern coast in 1941. Thailand lost three warships in the confrontation but retained sovereignty over it.

Trat is the only town in Thailand that celebrates an independence day. This commemorates the day in March 1906 when the town and province were "liberated" from their French colonial overlords.

Attractions are in short supply, but the stranded visitor may enjoy the bustling and reasonably clean market, with its inexpensive food stalls and an impressive fish market in the rear. The town also has a pair of night markets that provide a degree of interesting diversion.

Wat Bupharam, also known as Wat Pai Klong, is the only historical building of note. It was constructed in 1652 during King Thong's reign. This temple is 2 miles (3 km) west of town, opposite the Trat hotel.

Laem Ngop

Laem Ngop, 11.5 miles (18 km) south of Trat, functions as the departure point for ferries and fishing boats to Ko Chang and other islands toward the Cambodian border. Visitors hang around the pier's cafés, waiting for the next boat to Ko Chang. A sign in the parking lot notes the 1941 naval battle between the Thais and the French (see above). ∎

Trat

- Map p. 149
- Bus from Ekamai (Eastern) Bus Terminal, Bangkok

Visitor Information

- Tourism Authority of Thailand, 100 Mu 1, Trat-Laem Ngop Rd., Tambon Laem Ngop, Amphoe Laem Ngop, Trat
- 038-597250

The coconut industry thrives on east coast islands. Here, coconuts are unloaded at Laem Ngop's port.

Ko Chang

In 2002, the government announced plans to transform Ko Chang from a backpacker's haven into a posh resort tagged the "Phuket of the East." Since then, the number of upscale hotels has increased, paved roads have extended southward, and a mainland airport was constructed in Trang. The 197-square-mile island (492 sq km), 85 percent of which is national park, has lost some idyllic charm, but development is not any worse than that on other Thai islands.

Listing coconut palms and gleaming white sand grace Ko Chang's beaches.

Ko Chang (Elephant Island) and the numerous small islands nearby make up **Ko Chang Marine National Park.** Rain forest carpets much of Ko Chang, climbing a steep wall of hills laced with waterfalls. These hills run through the center of the island, splitting it in two. Closer to the water, mangroves proliferate, and clear water laps up on lovely, white beaches. The new beach resorts can be reached by a paved ring road that skirts the island.

Ferries regularly leave the pier at Laem Ngop (see p. 159) on the mainland and stop at a number of beaches around the island. Most people dock at Ao Sapporot, about 45 minutes away, which is the most convenient destination from Laem Ngop, at the island's northern tip. Despite development, Ko Chang remains one of the most beautiful islands in Thailand and is well worth the effort of a long overland journey from Bangkok.

The island's longest and most popular beach is **Hat Sai Khao,** or White Sand Beach, which extends from the northwestern tip of Ko Chang down the upper one-third of the island. Hat Sai Khao has the largest choice of accommodations and the best restaurants. **Hat Khlong Phrao,** just to the south over a hillock, is a golden beach with a greater degree of peace and solitude. South of here, smaller—but by no means less appealing—stretches of sand can be found at **Hat Bae** and **Hat Kruat.** At the former, the gentle drop-off is ideal for less-experienced swimmers.

Most visitors are content to

relax on the sands, but there are several natural attractions that make interesting diversions. You can hike from Khlong Phrao Beach into the rain forest to **Khlong Phlu Waterfall;** longer treks over the mountainous spine of the island require guides, who can be hired through bungalow owners. Attractions on the east coast include an almost deserted **visitor center** with a three-dimensional model of the island, the six-level **Tham Mayom Waterfall** with a small swimming pool at its base, and modest **Don Keo Waterfall** in the northeast corner of the island, past the main town of Don Mai.

Islands near Ko Chang

More than a dozen islands of the Ko Chang group that lie in the warm waters of the Gulf of Thailand between Ko Chang and Cambodia are accessible by ferries from Laem Ngop. They run frequently from December to April, the tourist high season. Ferries also island-hop at this time. During the wet season (May to November), some resorts close down and transportation is difficult.

Ko Kut, the second largest island in the archipelago, is not under the supervision of the National Parks Division and is therefore the most developed in the region. Fortunately, the mountainous island's large size and inaccessibility have preserved the environment and left most of the beaches, coves, and lagoons in almost perfect condition. Beaches with bungalows or superior resorts are located mostly on

the north and northwest coasts.

Several rivers with waterfalls snake down from the central mountain ridge and plunge into the sea along the west coast of Ko Kut. Other waterfalls, such as **Khlong Chao** and **Khlong Anamkok,** can be reached by taking a boat to Khlong Chao and then a short hike through the jungle. The island also has some striking coral beds.

Ko Mak is smaller and flatter than Ko Kut, but is still the third largest island, and one of the most developed, with some upscale resorts. It is blessed with fine beaches, coconut groves, and colorful coral reefs off its northern tip.

INSIDER TIP:

The most accessible of Chang's many beautiful waterfalls is Khlong Phlu, on the island's western side near Khlong Phrao and Kai Bae beaches. The fall plunges into a pool where you can swim.

—BARBARA A. NOE
National Geographic editor

The other, smaller islands in the Ko Chang archipelago are within the marine national park. **Ko Kradat** ("paper island") has a 4-mile (6.5 km) beach, with decent diving among the coral. This island, along with the smaller islands south of Ko Chang, is often visited on day trips. Other islands with overnight facilities are **Ko Phrao, Ko Ngam, Ko Laoya,** and **Ko Wai.** ■

Ko Chang

- Map p. 149
- Ferries from Laem Ngop (see p. 159)

Visitor Information

- Tourism Authority of Thailand, 100 Mu 1, Trat–Laem Ngop Rd., Tambon Laem Ngop, Amphoe Laem Ngop, Trat
- 038-597252 or 038-597260
- Laem Ngop tourism office: Ban Hin Ta Loy, Laem Ngop, Trat
- 039-597259 or 039-597250

The Road to Cambodia

East, and then south, of Trat, Sukhumvit Highway—under the guise of Highway 318—runs down a sliver of land hemmed between attractive beaches along the Gulf of Thailand and the Cambodian border. The area, once restricted because of Khmer Rouge activity, is now open for travel. Thais flock to a casino on the Cambodian side of the border.

Rubber being tapped at one of the numerous plantations near Trat

Road to Cambodia

 Map p. 149

Visitor Information

✉ Tourism Authority of Thailand, 100 Mu 1, Trat-Laem Ngop Rd., Tambon Laem Ngop, Amphoe Laem Ngop, Trat

☎ 038-597259 or 038-597260

Ko Kong International Casino

◪ Map p. 149
✉ Ko Kong Island
🚌 Bus to Hat Lek from Trat, then speedboat or ferry from Hat Lek

Several small towns are located along the 60-mile (100 km) road that runs south from Trat to Hat Lek, a village at the southeasternmost tip of Trat Province.

At **Hat Ban Chuen,** about 40 miles (60 km) south of Trat, is an inviting, long stretch of sand. Other beaches, including the Hat Sai Si Ngoen (Silver Sand Beach), Hat Sai Kaew (Crystal Beach), and Hat Thaptim (Sapphire Beach) are spread along the coast before Ban Chuen. These beaches, backed with casuarina (sea pine) and eucalyptus trees, are fine in their own right but do not match the quality of Ban Chuen.

At the Kilometer 70 signpost, just off the highway, a road climbs to **Jut Chom Wiw,** a lookout that offers panoramic views of the coast and Cambodia. A little farther south is **Khlong Yai,** the

last sizable town in the area; it is notable for its smuggling activities and its big border market. The beaches here are not as attractive as those farther north. At Khlong Yai you can catch boats to Ko Kut and other islands of the Ko Chang Marine National Park (see pp. 160–161).

Like Khlong Yai, **Hat Lek** enjoys the benefits of a thriving smuggling industry and a busy border market. But the village is also notable for a steady influx of Thais who are more intent on gambling than sightseeing. The village sometimes resembles little more than a parking lot as both private vehicles and tour buses unload tourists for trips to nearby **Ko Kong,** across the border in Cambodia and, in particular, to the **Ko Kong International Casino and Resort.**

The casino is one of a number along the Thai border with both Cambodia and Myanmar to circumvent Thailand's ban on casinos and encourage the Thais' love of gambling. It attracts more than a thousand visitors a day. They board boats at Hat Lek for the short trip to the island of Ko Kong. Foreign visitors can visit the casino without acquiring a Cambodian visa.

From Ko Kong, you can catch a speedboat to visit Sihanoukville in Cambodia. From here, there are buses to Phnom Penh, the country's capital. ∎

A realm full of rural charm, crisp forested mountains, ancient temples, and one of the world's great rivers

Northeast Thailand

Traditional dress made from northeastern silk

Northeast Thailand

The northeast of Thailand—known as Issan—has never been high on the international visitor's agenda. Of the nearly ten million tourists who pour into the country each year, fewer than 4 percent venture into the region. The reasons point more to the bounty of attractions all over Thailand, rather than the lack of any in Issan. In this vast and unpretentious region you will find a polite, independent people clinging to the traditional ways of Thailand with a tenacity not seen in other parts of the country.

Issan is the largest, most populated, and poorest region of Thailand, and its rural inhabitants forge a hard-earned living growing rice, tapioca, and cotton. Mulberry trees bear leaves to feed worms that spin silk, which is then woven into cloth of the highest quality. The region sprawls across 66,000 square miles (171,000 sq km) on the high sandstone Khorat Plateau, which reaches north to the Mekong River and south to the Dongrek Mountains, on the Cambodian border. It can be a harsh place. Droughts are as frequent as flooding, and hardships and deprivation have forced many to quit the land and move to the cities in search of work.

Yet this vast region holds many pockets of great beauty, especially on the heights of its mountainous national parks. Peaceful monastic retreats hide among the forests; fascinating remnants of past civilizations dot the area; and there are plenty of lively, bustling cities. Issan's detachment from tourism is more of a bonus than a hindrance, sharpening its frontier feel.

In the late 1950s, with help from the United States, the Friendship Highway was built from Bangkok to Nong Khai, on the banks of the Mekong River and bordering Laos, opening up the region. During the ensuing war with Vietnam. untold amounts of money were pumped into the region as the U.S. military set up bases. Towns like Nakhon Ratchasima and Udon Thani boomed overnight. The Friendship Highway is the arterial route into the region, and along its veins you find the riches of Issan.

Khmer Monuments

Princpal among these are the extraordinary Khmer monuments. Ruled by a succession of god-kings, the Khmer Empire (802–1431) at one stage stretched from Angkor in Camboodia, west across Thailand to Myanmar (Burma), south to the Malay Peninsula, and north to the Laotian capital of Vientiane. More than 300 sites have been located in Thailand's northeast. Some have been painstakingly restored, to reveal a culture of remarkable cosmological architecture, preserted in a symmetry of structures that are festooned inside and out with wildly imaginative and intricate sculptures and stone carvings. Either of the two best examples, Prasat Hin Phimai or Prasat Phanom Rung, alone is worth a visit to Issan.

NOT TO BE MISSED:

Mekong River

The Mekong River, which runs along much of Issan's border with Laos, is another draw. The opening up to tourism of neighboring Laos in recent years now allows travelers to cross the Mekong at several points, notably the Friendship Bridge near Nong Khai. At the end of the rainy season in October, communities celebrate their affinity with the river in colorful and hotly contested boat races, during a series of raucous festivals. ■

Area of map detail

Khao Yai National Park

Khao Yai ("big mountain") is Thailand's oldest national park, founded in 1961, and it is also one of the country's most ecologically diverse and wildlife-abundant areas. The 840 square miles (2,176 sq km) of the park straddle four provinces along the eastern Dongrek Mountains, at the southwestern edge of the vast Khorat Plateau, the dominant geological feature of Issan.

A handful of Thailand's few remaining tigers inhabit Khao Yai; sightings are rare.

Khao Yai National Park

 Map p. 165

✉ Just off the Friendship Hwy. (Hwy. 2); turn off 3 miles (5 km) before the Pak Chong.

Visitor Information

✉ National Park Division of the Royal Forestry Department, Paholyothin Rd., Bangkhen, Bangkok

☎ 02-562-0760

www.dnp.co.th

The park is a convenient wilderness, only 125 miles (200 km) northeast of Bangkok. Cn weekends and holidays, people escape the gasping capital and besiege the park, so it is best avoided at these times.

Over the years the crowds have strained the park's resources. Between 1992 and 1993 overnight stays were stopped for 12 months because rangers could not cope. Khao Yai's outstanding natural beauty is also forced to withstand the land encroachment, illegal logging, poaching, understaffing and corruption that exist within many of the country's national parks.

Khao Yai is generally mountainous, rising from near sea level at its southeast perimeter to 4,432 feet (1,351 m) at the summit of **Khao Laem.** While mountains in the north slope gently to its northern boundary, those in the south and west form a steep escarpment that drops to agricultural plains outside the park. The long wall-like mountain, Khao Kamphaeng, bounds the northeast.

Hiking in the Park

Many of the park's 13 hiking trails, from 1 mile to 6 miles (1.5 km to 9.5 km) long, take you through lush tangles of

INSIDER TIP:

Your chances of spotting a tiger in Khao Yai are slim, but look for the colorful fireback pheasant, Thailand's national bird. It has a bright red head.

—DANIEL STILES
National Geographic field researcher

monsoon forest, along numerous streams to tumbling waterfalls, past caves, and up to rain forests and spectacular viewpoints on the hillsides. High up on the ridge tops, cooler temperatures encourage stands of pine woodlands. Hikes take from about 90 minutes to seven hours, depending on the trail. Many of the numbered trails, with routes set by colored markers, radiate from the park headquarters and visitor center, or the nearby Kong Kaeo Waterfall.

Some routes (numbers 6, 7, 8, and 9) loop back to, or near, the visitor center. On others, be prepared to backtrack or organize transportation to return to the start point. Some trails are poorly marked or confusing, so a guide is needed. The visitor center can advise on this; it also has trail maps.

The 3.5-mile (6 km) Trail 6, from the visitor center to Nong Phak Chi wildlife observation tower, is relatively easy, taking about three to four hours. Easy to follow, Trail 8 is about 1 mile (1.5 km) long, takes 90 minutes, and returns you to park headquarters. Trail 9 (1.5 miles/2 km and 60 minutes) is similar. Trail 11, from the old restaurant up to Tat Ta Phu Waterfall,

is more testing. This 5-mile (8 km) trek will take all day and follows a stream to the falls, then backtracks (a guide is required).

Wildlife

Much of Khao Yai's wildlife congregates near the park headquarters. Elephants—their numbers estimated at 250 to 300—are not difficult to spot, nor are the mouse deer and barking deer that congregate in the evening at Nong Phak Chi observation tower. The park's 50 or so tigers are rarely, if ever, sighted. You are also unlikely to see the leopards, leopard cats, marbled cats, and shy Asiatic black bears.

Khao Yai has tens of thousands of white-handed and pileated gibbons. The latter often gather in a 6-mile-wide (9.5 km) contact zone around Lam Ta Klong stream. Other primates include the pig-tailed macaque; and the arboreal, nocturnal slow loris. There are also Asiatic wild dogs and giant flying squirrels. One of the park's most amazing sights is the dusk eruption of myriad wrinkle-lipped bats from a large cave at Khao Luk Chang ■

Guides

Hiring a guide is a good idea if you want to reach deeper into Khao Yai to view wildlife from observation towers in the evening or to climb higher into the mountains. There are tour companies and accommodations at Pak Chong. Wildlife Safari is recommended *(39 Pak Chong Rd., tel 044-312922).*

Nakhon Ratchasima (Khorat)

Nakhon Ratchasima—abbreviated to Khorat by dropping the first syllable of the first word and the last three of the second—is the gateway to Issan. The province is scattered with ancient Khmer monuments, including Thailand's most famous at Phimai, and is renowned for its silk industry. Khorat is the country's largest province; its burgeoning capital, the first major stop on the arterial northeast route, the Friendship Highway (Highway 2), is the region's commercial heart.

A statue of the Brave Lady, heroine of Nakhon Ratchasima

The capital (also called Nakhon Ratchasima—in Thailand provincial capitals carry the same name as the province) concerns itself with progress, but interesting remnants of its past remain. Presiding over a square in the city's center, at the tenth-century **Chumphom gate** and reconstructed town wall, there is a statue of Khunying

Mo, known as **Thao Suranari** (Brave Lady). In 1826, Prince Anuwong of Vientiane captured Khorat and threatened to enslave its residents. The feisty Khunying, wife of the deputy governor, persuaded the young women of the city to seduce the invaders and involve them in drunken revelry. That done, the women killed the soldiers while they slept. The springtime Thao Suranari Festival, Khorat's most popular, celebrates this triumph with musicians, dancers, parades, fireworks, and a beauty contest.

A curious vestige of Khorat's more recent history is found at the **VFW Café** *(167 Poklang Rd., tel 044-256522)*. The city's airfield was one of seven in northeast Thailand used by U.S. troops to launch raids on Laos and Vietnam during the 1960s and 1970s. A legacy of those turbulent times—along with the ample collection of neon-pulsing massage parlors—the VFW (Veterans of Foreign Wars) Café is a U.S. roadhouse-style restaurant locked in the 1960s. It's also the base for a close-knit band of Vietnam veterans who retired there after the Vietnam War.

South of the Thao Suranari monument on Ratchadamnoen Road, a small but edifying collection of artifacts and archaeological discoveries from surrounding Khmer ruins are housed in the **Maha Weerawong National Museum** *(closed Mon.–Tues.)*. The museum is on the grounds of Wat Suthachinda, just south of the intersection with Mahad Thai Road. Its more memorable displays include a statue of the female Hindu deity Uma, Shiva's consort, and Mahayana Buddhist images from Prasat Hin Phanom Wan.

More Khmer icons are found at Khorat's oldest monastery, **Wat Phra Narai Maharat,** west of the Thao Suranar statue on Prachak Road. The collection

While overshadowed by the bigger and more celebrated Khmer monument of Prasat Hin Phimai (see pp. 170–171), **Phanom Wan,** set in a peaceful rural area off Highway 2, about 12 miles (19.5 km) northeast of the city, is still impressive. Venerated Buddha images in saffron-colored wraps, food offerings, and glowing incense sticks remind visitors that Phanom Wan, unlike most Khmer temples, has been in use for worship since the ninth century. The best time to visit this peaceful temple is when soft morning or late-afternoon light brings out the colors and textures of the sandstone and laterite.

Nakhon Ratchasima (Khorat)

 Map p. 165

Visitor Information

✉ Tourism Authority of Thailand, 2102–2104 Mittaphap Rd., Nakhon Ratchasima

☎ 044-213666 or 044-213030

www.tat.or.th

EXPERIENCE: Dan Kwian Ceramics

Found nowhere else in the country, a rough-textured, rust-colored ceramic has long been produced in the region around Dan Kwian, Chokchai district. The clay results from a chemical composition unique to the area. It is worked into everyday implements such as bowls, dishes, utensils, and tools.

Historically, this area was a staging ground between Khorat and the Burmese border. Some bull carts leftover from those long-ago caravans are still here, turned into pottery stands. Other shops are found in simple long bungalows. Chances are, you'll haggle with an artisan who has earned every baht of his life from fired clay. You can also arrange demonstrations from artisans.

To find Dan Kwian, take Route 224 9 miles (15 km) southeast of Khorat to the Chokchai district.

---

here includes the Khorat city pillar, plus sandstone images which were taken from other nearby Khmer ruins.

The central sanctuary at **Wat Sala Loi,** built in 1973, deviates imaginatively from the typical temple style. Perhaps because of its location by the Lamtakhong River, 440 yards (402 m) past the northeastern end of the city's moat, it is shaped like a Chinese junk.

Twenty miles (32 km) south of Khorat, along Highway 304, **Pak Thong Chai** is a thriving center of silk weaving, with more than 70 silk factories around the district. A variety of silks, including the beautiful hand-dyed *mud mee,* are woven here. Weavers demonstrate their skills at the Silk Weavers Association's museum and cultural center. Local retailers are not necessarily less expensive than those in Khorat or Bangkok. ■

Prasat Hin Phimai

The restored Khmer Sandstone Sanctuary and temple of Prasat Hin Phimai is a spectacular revelation into the grandeur of one of Asia's great civilizations. The town itself sits at the Thai end of the fabled Royal Road, the major route of the Khmer Kingdom that led 140 miles (224 km) from its capital at Angkor in Cambodia.

Extensively reconstructed, this Khmer shrine conveys a sense of its original scale and majesty.

On the banks of the Mun River, some 37.5 miles (60 km) north of Khorat, Prasat Hin Phimai is probably the most significant of all Khmer buildings. It was once a vice-regal center for an empire that dominated this part of Southeast Asia for more than 600 years, until its final defeat in 1431. Buildings at Phimai date from the late 11th and the 12th centuries—the height of the empire. The last great Khmer king, Jayavarman VII (r. 1181–1220), was a fervent Buddhist, and he built on the largest scale ever known in the empire,

remodeling temples honoring Hindu gods to serve the Tantric gods of Mahayana Buddhism—a style widely seen in Phimai.

Phimai was built in the 12th century as the temple of the city of Vimayapura; its outer enclosure is in fact the old city wall. Phimai is still surrounded by a community, and its layout is believed to be based on the old city plan.

The Temple Complex

The temple complex consists of two rectangular walled enclosures, with the inner enclosure housing the dominant, cone-shaped *prang*, the central structure of all Khmer temples. The main entrance into the temple is a naga (serpent) bridge, a cross-shaped terrace with rearing naga heads symbolizing the transition from the temporal world into the domicile of the gods. The bridge leads to the heavily embellished southern *gopura*, the main entrance to the outer enclosure.

This outer enclosure spreads over 10 acres (4 ha) and contains four ponds. At the southern corner, a pond once lined with stone blocks gives a clear view to the inner enclosure, with the magnificent prang reflected in its waters. A causeway dividing the ponds leads to the inner southern gopura, its entrance dominated by a lintel with a central design of a giant holding a pair of elephants aloft, and standing over the head of the demon guardian Kala. In the central courtyard, the elaborately carved white sandstone prang lies directly ahead, flanked by two towers.

In and around the buildings of the inner enclosure, Khmer mythology unfolds in a treasury of exquisitely carved lintels and pediments. On one lintel, for example, troops build a bridge across the sea to the mythical Lanka, in a tale from the *Ramakien*. Monkey warriors carry boulders to throw into the sea, symbolized by fish and dragons. A pediment above depicts a battle scene from the same epic. Another shows the hero Rama parading home, victorious from his battles with the Lankans, and being blessed by a gathering of the gods Shiva, Brahma, Indra, and Vishnu.

Kings asserted their royal authority by building the grandest structures. Khmer mythology lies not only in these superb carved details, but in the temple compound's entire layout (see pp. 50–55). The meticulous construction of the temples reflects the Khmer belief in cosmology. Phimai stands as the Khmer Hindu/Buddhist model of the universe: Concentric mountains and seas surround a single continent, from which rises the central Mount Meru (represented by the prang), the five-peaked home of the gods. Moats, ponds, and enclosing walls all play a part in this microcosmic universe.

The **museum** *(closed Mon.– Tues.)* at the town's northern end is an essential part of a visit here. It houses more beautifully carved lintels from the monument and relics from other northeastern temples. ■

Prasat Hin Phimai

🅰 Map p. 163

✉ 35 miles (60 km) NE of Khorat

Visitor Information

✉ Tourism Authority of Thailand, 2102– 2104 Mittapap Rd., Nakhon Ratchasima

☎ 044-213666 or 044-213030

www.tat.or.th

Rocket Festivals

Rocket festivals *(bun bang fai)* are held throughout the northeast—usually in the second week of May— to celebrate the end of the dry season and appease the rain god Phaya Than. Rockets are traditionally fashioned from bamboo filled with saltpeter and charcoal. Huge timber launching pads are erected, and missiles are launched to the delight of spectators. Similar events were held during the reigns of Khmer kings. The festival is most fervently celebrated in Yasothon, northeast of Nakhon Ratchasima, near Ubon Ratchathani.

Surin & Around

Thousands flock to Surin on the third weekend of November to witness Thailand's internationally famous Elephant Roundup, when hundreds of elephants lumber into town for a festival of fun and games. While it is this festival that has put the town of Surin on the map, evocative Khmer monuments and thriving basketry and silk industries in the province—on the frontier with Cambodia—make it well worth a visit.

Surin's Elephant Roundup offers a rare opportunity to see large groups of pachyderms.

The Elephant Roundup celebrates the ethnic Suay people's affinity with the beasts. The Suay, who came mainly from neighboring Cambodia, have been hunting and training elephants since the Ayutthaya era. The festival is unabridged fun. Elephants are paraded through town with their handlers (mahouts), then herded into Surin's Sports Park. Here they entertain with soccer games, dancing, races, an elephant-versus-people tug of war, and colorful processions. The carnival attracts up to 40,000 visitors, and hotels are booked months ahead. After the show, tourists take elephant rides around town. Besides the enjoyment of it all, the roundup provides a rare opportunity to see a large number of elephants in one place.

Some of the elephants that take part in the roundup are trained at **Ta Klang Elephant Village,** 36 miles (58 km) northeast of Surin town (tel 01-999-1910). A museum and elephant educational center go some way to explain the importance of the great beasts in Thai culture and their sad plight, which has threatened their existence in modern Thailand (see Threatened Elephants, below).

Silk & Basket-Weaving

Centers of Surin's silk and basket-weaving industries are within easy reach of the capital. **Khawao Sinarin,** east of the town off Highway 226, and **Ban Chanron,** southeast on Highway 2071, both produce quality silks using traditional hand-weaving techniques. You can watch the silk being made at factories and buy the finished product. Just off Highway 226, 8 miles (12 km) east of Surin, villagers at **Butom Basket Village** make tightly woven and intricately designed baskets, and sell them to visitors at bargain prices.

evocative places, set in thick jungle. Passing an armed military checkpoint on the approach road, and posted warnings not to stray into the jungle because of land mines, add an edge to the experience. Khmer Rouge rebels occupied the area in the 1980s and pillaged many of the monuments' carvings.

Ta Muan Thom, on the Cambodia border, is the largest and earliest of the three temples, constructed during the reign of Udayaditya-varman II (r. 1050–1066). The most impressive view is from the bottom of its staircase, framed by solid laterite ramparts, which leads to the main entrance pavilion.

Ta Muan Toch, a hospital temple, and **Ta Muan,** an overnight rest house, were built a century later by Jayavarman VII, whose Buddhist beliefs necessitated a building spree of public works throughout the em-

---

Threatened Elephants

At the beginning of the 20th century, Thailand was home to 100,000 elephants. Today, there are fewer than 5,000. Half of these are domesticated, while the rest find protection inside national parks. The elephant's decline is due to the loss of its natural environment, to hunting, and to poaching.

In 1989 Thailand banned logging, and the elephants that had been used to shift logs in the forests for centuries were no longer needed for work. Many own-

ers have turned to tourism for income through popular trekking camps and shows, while others lead their beasts along the choking highways into the heart of Bangkok to beg. Tourism is a way to maintain elephant numbers until the authorities quit their lip service and make real attempts at preservation. Most operators treat their elephants well, and demands for the beasts in the industry affords them protection—something they have lacked in the past.

Khmer Ruins

Remnants of the Khmer Empire stud Surin Province. Three such sites are on the Cambodia border, 55 miles (90 km) south of town along Highway 214. These are intensely atmospheric and

pire. Arrange tours to all three sites at Pirom's Guesthouse (272 Krung Sri Rd., Surin, tel 045-515040).

The two smaller monuments near Ta Muan Thom confirm this area was part of the famed Royal Road from Angkor. ■

Prasat Phanom Rung

Sixteen years of restoration between 1972 and 1988 transformed Prasat Phanom Rung into the most spectacular Khmer site in Thailand. Its towering *prang* rises from the crest of an extinct volcano, 1,250 feet (381 m) above sea level, with views over flat farmlands extending to the Dongrek Mountains and the Cambodian border in the south.

Prasat Phanom Rung is a treasure trove of exquisitely detailed stone carvings.

Phanom Rung's elevated position realizes Hindu cosmology, symbolizing Shiva's home on Mount Meru. Located 30 miles (48 km) south of Bur Iram, off Highway 218, it was constructed between the early 10th and the late 12th centuries. Various inscriptions at the monument offer sketchy accounts of its history. A battle scene carved on one of the upper pediments above the southern entry of the central prang indicates an alliance of powerful local ruler Narendraditya with the fiercely combatant Khmer king Suryavarman II (r. 1113–1150), builder of Angkor Wat. The scene depicts war elephants, one of which is crushing an enemy soldier with its trunk.

Narendraditya's allegiances allowed him to maintain suzerainty over Phanom Rung for some time after Suryavarman claimed the throne at Angkor, a situation confirmed by more iconography devoted to the exploits of Narendraditya and his family. These carvings suggest that he gave up his warring ways after the birth of his son Hiranya and became a yogi and guru.

Visiting Phanom Rung

Phanom Rung is spread along an east-west axis in an amazing 550-yard (500 m) journey from a laterite terrace along a system of causeways and promenades, steps and terraces to the eastern *gopura* (entrance pavilion), and into the central prang. The complex has an almost intimidating, grandeur. Its dramatic stairway entrance, ornate carving, and spiritually inspired design reflect the power needed to expand and control an empire for five centuries.

INSIDER TIP:

When buying souvenirs, be aware that it is illegal to take antique Buddha images out of Thailand without proper documentation.

—MARGARET LOFTUS
*National Geographic Traveler
magazine writer*

The first significant point is the White Elephant Hall, down the slope from the visitor center in the direction of the first terrace. This large rectangular building of laterite and sandstone, with its porches, galleries, and walls, derives its name from the royal predilection for keeping rare, sacred white elephants. Just south of the hall, at the cross-shaped terrace, a 175-yard-long (160 m) laterite-paved causeway, lined with 67 lotus bud-tipped boundary stones, draws you toward a large raised stone terrace and bridge. Intricately carved five-headed *nagas* form the bridge's balustrade, symbolically transporting the visitor from the temporal world into the divine.

From the bridge, the stairs

begin their spectacular rise to the enclosure, a climb interrupted by five leveled sections. The wide, grass-covered terrace at the top holds four ponds, arranged symmetrically and probably used in some sort of ritual. A second bridge here has three more naga balustrades facing north, east, and south. Like the first bridge, the nagas are exquisitely carved from stone, although with subtle differences in design. The bridge takes the visitor up to the eastern entrance pavilion, which broadens, joins, and then wraps around the entire main temple ground.

The eastern gopura is the most important of four that cut through the middle of each side of the rectangular wall protecting the enclosure. Significantly, it faces the sunrise and is aligned with the succession of doorways that run the length of the temple's axis through to the exit at the western gopura.

The main pediment of the eastern gateway is of a Hindu yogi, surrounded by female attendants and celestial dancers representing Shiva. More iconography can be seen on the other gopuras and around the galleries that surround the complex. The lintel below the pediment shows a divinity seated over demon guardian Kala, gripping the hind legs of a pair of disconcerted lions.

Passing through the door of the gopura and crossing a third naga bridge, you come almost immediately to the antechamber to the main prang (*mandapa*), which has an extraordinary pediment and lintel, sublime examples of Khmer craftmanship. The pedi-

Prasat Phanom Rung

 Map p. 165

Visitor Information

✉ Tourism Authority of Thailand, 2102–2104 Mittapap Rd., Nakhon Ratchasima

☎ 044-213666 or 044-213000

www.tat.or.th

INSIDER TIP:

Don't miss Issan's night markets, where you'll find some of Thailand's spiciest barbecue chicken and sausage served with sticky rice.

—KAREN COATES
National Geographic writer

ment depicts the ten-armed Siva-Nantaraja enthralled in a cosmic dance. At Shiva's feet are Ganesh, the divinity's elephant-headed son, and two female disciples. Below the pediment is the famous Nara lintel (see Nara Lintel, this page) depicting Vishnu reclining on a naga. Brahma rises from the reclining Vishnu on a lotus flower, while Lakshmi, Vishnu's wife, cradles his legs. The two motifs on either side of Vishnu show Kala issuing garlands, and two elegantly carved parrots. Nagas, winged *garudas*, elephants, and monkeys crowd the lintel with amazing precision.

The Main Prang

From here you move toward the main prang. On each of its four sides are gallery entrances (each gallery is a smaller version of the main prang), which, in turn, have entrances into the prang. The galleries, along with the towering prang, represent the five peaks of Mount Meru, the center of the Khmer universe and home to the Hindu gods.

The gallery entrances are set with intriguing carvings, a number of which highlight the anguishes and triumphs of Rama, the earthly incarnation of Vishnu and hero of the romantic *Ramakien*. One scene depicts monkey warriors triumphantly swooping down on the enemy. The interior of the prang has a number of Khmer statues and an altar on which priests poured holy waters and laid offerings of garlands and fruit.

Outside, a wild conglomerate of sculptured Shivas, dancers, charging elephants, *rishis* (Hindu sages, usually hermits), and other Khmer icons climb up the sandstone walls of the prang. ∎

Nara Lintel

Sometime between 1961 and 1965 the Nara lintel disappeared from Phanom Rung, ending up in the Art Institute of Chicago. Investigations showed U.S. art benefactor James Alsdorf had donated it. It was not until December 1988, six months after the completion of Phanom Rung's restoration—and after strong protests from the Thai government and others—that the Alsdorf Institute decided to return the lintel, at a cost of $250,000 (donated by U.S. interests). Around that time, a Thai rock group, Caraboa, had a hit with a protest song that included the line: "Take back your Michael Jackson, and give us back our Phra Narai." Rumor has it that six of the seven Thais involved in the original theft have met "unnatural" deaths.

Ubon Ratchathani

Ubon Ratchathani is one of several northeast cities whose growth was spurred by the presence of the U.S. armed forces during the Vietnam War. It sits at the eastern corner of Issan, near where two major rivers, the Chi and Mun, converge before flowing about 30 miles (48 km) east to the Mekong, at the border with Laos. Ubon is the gateway to the "Emerald Triangle," a tourist-using description of the province's abundant forests and its borders with Laos and Cambodia.

Established by the Khmers, Ubon came under Ayutthayan control in the 15th century. The **Ubon National Museum** *(Kheuan Thani Rd., tel 045-255071, closed Mon.– Tues.)* gives insight into these developments. The museum, housed in a former summer palace of Rama VI, was opened in 1989, the first provincial museum in the northeast. Rooms are devoted to regional geography, geology, pre-history, and local handicrafts, with a handsome collection of art from the 6th to the 17th centuries. A highlight is the huge 4th-century ceremonial bronze drum.

The most impressive of Ubon's temple compounds is **Wat Supattanaram Worawihan,** on the banks of the Mun River. Built in 1853 by Vietnamese craftsmen, it has an appealing confusion of Thai, Western, and Khmer architectural styles.

Beyond the Upparat Road bridge and about 9.5 miles (15 km) southwest on Highway 2193, **Wat Pa Nanachat Beung Rai** ("temple of the international forest") is one of the more curious forested wats hidden among Ubon Province's thick woodlands. The North American, European, and Japanese monks here follow the strict tenets laid down by Ajaan Man (1870–1949), a monk

A group of stilt shelters on the Nam River makes a picturesque spot for relaxing.

who has inspired more than 40 forested wats in Issan, with simple teaching methods that opened the Buddhist faith to many Westerners. Lay people are welcome to stay, but it's best to contact the abbot beforehand in writing (*Wat Pa Nanachat, Ban Bung Wai, Amphur Warin, Ubon Ratchathani 34310*).

At the start of the Buddhist lent, in July, representatives of the temples construct floats holding huge candles and wax carvings, and parade through town in a two-day **Candle Festival.** ∎

Ubon Ratchathani
- Map p. 165

Visitor Information
- Tourism Authority of Thailand, 264/1 Kuang Thani Rd., Ubon Ratchathani
- 045-243770 or 045-250714
- **www.tat.ubon.org**

Silk

Silk weaving has thrived since the Khmer Empire (802–1431) and wove its way into the conventions of the Sukhothai, Ayutthaya, and Chakri dynasties. In Thailand's northeastern villages, silk production has changed little. Silkworms still feed on the leaves of hardy mulberry trees. Villagers still pluck the worms' cocoons from the tree, and spin them into smooth, glossy, and flexible threads. And ancient looms still clack with the sound of yarns, cleaned and dyed, being woven into fabulous silk fabrics.

Thailand's world-famous silk comes in a rainbow of shimmering colors and designs.

Today silk remains a valuable trading commodity, and the silk of the northeast is famous worldwide for it beauty, artistry, patterns, and colors.

But the industry has survived by the narrowest of margins. A wave of cheaper factory-produced fabrics from China and Japan flooded the markets toward the end of the 19th century, and despite attempts by King Chulalongkorn to keep the craft alive, the silk industry fell into serious decline, and almost extinction. Silk production, an intricate, time-consuming process, simply could not compete with the price and availability of mass-produced fabrics.

Jim Thompson

The revival and subsequent international acclaim for Thai silk is attributed to the most unlikely of characters: an American ex-serviceman and member of the Office of Strategic Services—OSS, the precursor to the CIA—named Jim Thompson (1906–1967).

After serving with the U.S. military in Europe during World War II, Thompson, an architect and native of Delaware, arrived in Asia as part of a force formed to liberate Thailand from potential Japanese occupation. He then joined the OSS and was stationed in Bangkok for a short time before moving to New York. But he was soon back in Thailand, where his entrepreneurial spirit and eye for the exquisite beauty of the local silk would lead to the industry's resurgence in Thailand and introduction to the rest of the world.

Thompson devoted the next 20-plus years to promoting Thai silk. He sent samples to London, Milan, New York, and Paris, gradually building up a worldwide clientele. A gifted designer and innovator, he introduced colorfast dyes that preserved the distinctive luminosity and brilliant jewel colors. He also introduced new colors and weaves for the Western market, and created a new market for heavy silks to be used for upholstery.

Thompson recognized silk weaving as an art form, a cottage industry, and part of a traditional way of life. At Pak Chong, in Nakhon Ratchasima Province, his company, Jim Thompson Thai Silk Co., built the largest hand-weaving facilities in the world. More than 70 factories are now spread around the district, making it the major silk-producing area in Thailand.

On March 27, 1967, Jim Thompson disappeared without a trace while hiking alone in Malaysia. During the 1970s Thailand Queen Sirikit, a tireless promoter of traditional Thai art and handicrafts, took up the baton, pushing Thompson's work into a new dimension. Her public appearances in updated designs of traditional Thai silk styles prompted a new popularity among fashion-conscious Thai women, ensuring the survival of this very special fabric.

EXPERIENCE: Silk Weaving

The process of harvesting silk worms and weaving Thai silk has remained relatively unchanged for centuries. Larvae of the Thai moth, a domesticated species that has lost its ability to fly, form cocoons on mulberry bushes; the cocoons are then placed in vats of boiling water, where the threads come undone.

The raw silk, which varies from yellowish gold to light green, is then washed, often in a solution of bark, banana leaves, and other natural ingredients. It's occasionally bleached and then dyed with natural products, such as indigo and krajai berry. Finally, weavers use wooden looms to handcraft their exotic creations. Thai silk has a soft, bumpy quality that is more suitable to hand weaving, and it is almost equally durable to machine-woven silk.

One of the best places to watch the entire process is along **San Kamphaeng Road** in Chiang Mai.

Surin Province is justly famous for its silk, with **Thasawang Silk Village** being the most celebrated venue. Strolling around town, you'll see women hard at work on giant wooden looms in their front yards, protected beneath thatched roofs. Under the Queen's royal patronage and celebrated for its outstanding quality, this silk is noted for its interweaving of "golden" threads.

In Khon Kaen Province, you can visit a silk museum and watch demonstrations of silk weaving using traditional methods at **Sala Mai Thai** (*17 Chaeng-Sanit Rd., Chonrabot district, Khon Kean Province, tel 043-286160, www .salamaithai.com*). Utilizing the *dong* method to make silk smooth and soft, Sala Mai practices *mud mee*, a unique dying process that is integral to the design process.

That Phanom

In 1975 the grand *chedi* at Wat Phra That Phanom collapsed after four wild days of torrential rain. Local authorities soon gathered into action: This talismanic symbol, one of the most revered in Issan, was too important to leave a crumbled waste. With the help of Thailand's Fine Arts Department, the chedi's reconstruction was completed in 1979. Pilgrims once more flocked to the small Mekong River town of That Phanom.

That Phanom

🄰 Map p. 165

Visitor Information

✉ Tourism Authority of Thailand, 184/1 Sunthon Wichit Rd., Nakhon Phanom

☎ 042-513490 or 042-490192

www.tat.or.th

Thousands of people come from all over the northeast and across the Mekong River from Laos every full moon of the third lunar month (February or March), crowding into the That Phanom for its annual fair, to pay homage at the rebuilt chedi.

Legend indicates that the construction of Wat Phra That Phanom took place 2,500 years ago, when a wandering monk, Maha Kasapa, arrived in the area with the Buddha's breastbone. The bone was subsequently placed inside the gold-tipped spire of the chedi. Archaeologists, however, say that the construction of the *wat* dates back only about 1,500 years.

Regardless of when the chedi was built, it is an imposing and beautiful structure. Its spire reaches 185 feet (57 m) into the air, dominating the town. Its sharpened tip—decorated with 240 pounds (109 kg) of gold—plays late-afternoon glinting games with the scorching sun. With the Mekong River a few hundred yards away and the clay-red harshness of the Issan terrain all around, this Lao-style chedi takes on a wondrous aspect.

That Phanom earns its stripes as a border town on Mondays and Thursdays, when hundreds of Laotians cross the Mekong and set up a lively market near the pier. Opposite the market is a collection of French-Lao buildings.

Nearby, you will find a scaled-down version of Wat Phra That Phanom in the village of **Renu Phanom,** some 10 miles (16 km) away. It's known for cotton and silk weaving; at a weekly **market,** weavers gather here to sell their wares. ∎

That Phanom's riverside market features bamboo products.

Nakhon Phanom

The Mekong River reaches its panoramic best along the landscaped promenade of its banks at Nakhon Phanom. Views here look across the busy river traffic to smoke-blue craggy mountains rising behind the small town of Tha Khaek in Laos. The U.S. armed forces launched rescue and reconnaissance missions from Nakhon Phanom's air base during the Vietnam War, but the town has long since retreated into its more familiar relaxed character.

At the end of the rainy season and Buddhist retreat, on the full moon of the 11th lunar month (usually late October), Nakhon Phanom takes to the river. The Nakhon Phanom Festival features the evening launch of thousands of *reua fai*, or fire boats. The tiny boats, crafted from banana logs or bamboo and carrying offerings of flowers, rice, and cakes, glide down the Mekong, illuminating the river with thousands of dots of light.

Nakhon Phanom's restaurants and cafés, fronting the river along **Sunthon Wichit Road,** near the clock tower and passenger pier, are a good place to try the giant Mekong catfish, or *pla buk* (great and powerful fish). The fish is the largest of its type in the world, growing up to 10 feet (3 m) long and weighing up to 660 pounds

Tobacco—one of numerous crops grown in the Mekong River area—dries in the sun.

(300 kg). It once thrived, but numbers have now diminished. The New Suan Mai (271 Sunthon Wichit Rd., tel 042-511202) is one of the best places for this local specialty.

Directly across the river, the Laotian town of **Tha Khaek** has interesting French-style architecture. Travel agents in Nakhon Phanom will arrange visas, which takes from a few hours to a day. Count on paying $50 plus, but the ferry costs less than a dollar. Before the Communists came to power in 1975, Tha Khaek's casino prospered with Thai visitors' gambled cash. ∎

INSIDER TIP:

Nick Ascot at North By Northeast Tours in Nakhon Phanom has a wealth of information on the area and specializes in meaningful ecotourism.

—PETER HOLMSHAW
*CPA Media, Chiang Mai &
National Geographic contributor*

Nakhon Phanom

🅰 Map p. 165

Visitor information

✉ Tourism Authority of Thailand, 184/1 Sunthon Wichit Rd., Nakhon Phanom

☎ 042-513490, 042-513492, or 042-490192

North By Northeast Tours

✉ 746/1 Sunthornvichit Rd.

☎ 042-513572

Udon Thani

The establishment here of a huge U.S. air base during the 1960s and 1970s was the springboard for Udon Thani's development. The base, on the outskirts of the city, was handed over to the Thai authorities in 1976 and now serves as an important civilian airport and Royal Thai Air Force facility for this bustling regional center.

Pottery unearthed at the village of Ban Chiang, which archaeologists believe thrived 3,500 years ago

Udon Thani

⛰ Map p. 165

Visitor Information

✉ Tourism Authority of Thailand, 16/5 Mukmontri Rd., Udon Thani

☎ 042-325406 or 042-325407

The American influence lingers, albeit on a much smaller scale. A number of U.S. citizens, mainly ex-military and diplomatic personnel, have retired in Udon Thani, with its U.S. consulate *(35/6 Suphakit Janya Rd.),* Veterans of Foreign Wars association, and Voice of America radio transmitter dispatching news and music throughout Asia. The city offers the urban indulgences of cinemas, restaurants, and malls.

About 30 miles (50 km) east of Udon Thani is the archaeological site of **Ban Chiang,** which was propelled onto the world stage in the 1970s with the discovery of bronze relics purportedly dating to 3600 B.C. Since this startling find

predated the earliest recognized Bronze Age civilizations in China and the Middle East, it upset accepted historical notions. Many dispute the findings, though, saying that a more accurate time span would fall between 2500 B.C. and 2000 B.C. The nearby **Ban Chiang Historical Museum** *(closed Mon.–Tues.)* displays an extensive collection of relics including bronze tools, human skeletons, and swirling red-on-buff painted pottery.

About 40 miles (64 km) northwest of Udon Thani, some elaborate Buddhist shrines mingle in and around the delightfully weird rock formations that jut from the sandstone foothills at **Phu Phrabat Historical Park.** ∎

Nong Khai

Leafy Nong Khai lounges along the banks of the Mekong River. Its proximity to the Laotian capital of Vientiane has blessed it with French-Laotian architecture and a distinctly French culinary fraternity with its formerly colonial neighbor. A few of the town's bakeries turn out baguettes, croissants, and other pastries, and restaurants serve thick, strong Lao-style coffees.

A pleasant place to take in the colorful action on the river is at the timber-decked restaurants that jut over the water on **Rimkhong Road.** The street is home to the old immigration and customs building, and a pier where small rickety boats flying Thai and Lao national flags, ferry locals and Lao people back and forth—foreigners need to cross at the nearby Friendship Bridge (see pp. 186–187). The building still serves as a departure point to Tha Deua in Laos, but business is slower since the opening of the Friendship Bridge in 1994. Also worthwhile is the sunset river cruise (Mekong sunsets amaze with stunning deep red and yellow hues) on board the floating restaurant, which departs at 5 p.m. daily from behind Wat Hai.

The floating restaurant churns past **Phra That Nong Khai,** a *chedi* that slid into the river over a span of 150 years. For those who want to explore the Mekong further, information desks at guesthouses along Rimkhong Road will arrange trips.

Just east of the immigration and customs building at the end of Rimkhong Road is a long, narrow daily **market** brimming with Laotian and Issan handicrafts, along with the usual souvenirs, inexpensive clothes, cheap electrical appliances, and kitchen utensils. The market eventually opens up to an unexpected brick-paved, unshaded river promenade.

In the late 16th century a revered Buddha image was being transported across the river from Laos when the boat sank in a storm. According to local legend, the image miraculously resurfaced some years later and was eventually placed in **Wat Pho Chai,** off Prajak Road in the eastern part of town, just past the bus terminal. Murals in the *wat* recount the tale of the icon's travels from the interior of

Nong Khai
🗺 Map p. 155

Visitor Information

✉ Tourism Authority of Thailand, 15/5 Mukmontri Rd., Udon Thani

☎ 042-4273 16, 042-325406, or 042-325407

A gate, sculpted as an open mouth, is one of the bizarre offerings at Hindu-Buddhist Wat Khaek.

Laos to its current resting place on an altar that is bedecked with elaborate carvings and mosaics.

Nong Khai's star attraction is the bizarre **Wat Khaek,** also called Sala Kaew Ku, situated about 3 miles (5 km) southeast along Highway 212. It is the masterpiece of Vietnamese monk Luang Pu Bunleua Surirat (died 1997). The wat, begun in 1978, represents a thematic merger of Hinduism and Buddhism, splashed with unfettered imagination and humor, as well as a bewildering mix of Buddhist and Hindu statues. The core theme of the wat is the life of the Buddha before he left India on his travels through Asia, over 2,500 years ago.

Where else would you see Buddha, surrounded by his disciples—scantily clad women— a coiled, seven-headed serpent. The *naga* is said to be protecting Buddha against rain and wind for seven days and seven nights as he meditates. You will find hundreds of other fantastic offerings at Wat Khaek, where it is easy to spend a few hours wandering the pathways, captivated by the inventiveness and skill of Luang Pu and his followers.

Boat Races

A good time to visit Nong Khai is during its hectic annual **boat races,** which are held toward the end of October to celebrate the end of both the Buddhist lent and the rainy season. Scores of sleek naga-headed boats are frantically powered along the river, with

EXPERIENCE: Great Balls of Fire

Nong Khai's annual boat races draw crowds from all around Thailand. Yet as the first full moon hangs over the Mekong River in late October, people rush to the riverbanks to witness another point of regional pride: Bang Fai Phaya Nak, or the Naga Fireballs.

In a strange phenomenon, hundreds of multicolored fireballs gurgle up from the murk, only to disappear as just as quickly. This uncanny sight occurs every year around the same time and is heralded as evidence of the divine. Locals believe that the fire comes from the *naga*, a fabled ser-

pent. Scientists, on the other hand, claim that this strange occurrence is caused by biodegrading river matter. Regardless of origin, a spontaneously combusting river shouldn't be missed.

Since the appearance of the Naga Fireballs is tied to the lunar calendar, be sure to verify dates before making your plans. There are many hotels in Nong Khai, but the crowds drawn by both the fireballs and the boat races make reservations essential. The epicenter of the spectacle is the bustling Rimkhong Road, which runs parallel to the Mekong.

being tempted by their gifts? The Enlightened One can also be found sitting on top of a peacock. One statue has Hindu god Vishnu atop a parrot. The most imposing statue is the 82-foot-high (25 m) image of the Buddha perched on as many as 40 oarsmen in each. People come from all over the province to enjoy the spectacle. (Many other towns along the Mekong also celebrate the end of the Buddhist lent in this fashion.) ∎

Mekong River Valley

Thailand's contact with the Mekong may be confined to its fringes, but it is still a rewarding flirtation with the world's 12th longest river. The northeast remains the most convenient place to view the Mekong along part of its 2,600-mile (4,200 km) journey, which begins in Tibet and ends with a multiveined exit into the South China Sea at the southern tip of Vietnam.

The Mekong River skirts Thailand on its route between Tibet and Vietnam.

After skirting Thailand's far northern reaches, the Mekong River turns east into Laos, before switching south to rejoin the country near Loei. From here, its middle section flows along the Thai-Laotian border, then abruptly moves back into Laos at its confluence with the Mun River, near Udon Ratchathani.

Thailand and Laos have had a volatile relationship over the years, but today the two are cozy neighbors and the river thrives. People crisscross the waterway almost at will, and international tourism, especially since Laos opened outposts along its borders, is on the rise.

About 30 miles (48 km) north of Loei, the river joins the Thai border at **Chiang Khan**. Timber homes and shops nestle in an attractive forest and river setting. The town is known for its delicious bananas.

About 3 miles (5 km) downriver at the **Kaeng Kut Khu** rapids, you can sit on decks above the river. Farther downstream, **Pak Chom** encapsulates the rural charm of Issan's river villages. During the dry season, locals pan for gold on Don Chom Island, at the confluence of the Mekong and Chom Rivers. Stark evidence of the once volatile relations between the Mekong neighbors is found at the **Ban Winai Refugee Camp.** The camp once held 30,000 Hmong tribespeople, displaced from Laos after the Communist Pathet Lao took power in 1975.

Mekong River Valley

🅰 Map p. 165

Visitor Information

✉ Tour ism Authority of Thailand, 16/5 Mukmontri Rd., Udon Thani

☎ 042-325406 or 042-325407

✉ Tourism Authority of Thailand, 184/1 Sunthon Wichit Rd., Nakhon Phanom

☎ 042-513490 or 042-490192

Highway 2186 continues along the Mekong's banks to **Si Chiangmai,** turned into one of the world's leading producers and exporters of spring-roll wrappers by a large Laotian and Vietnamese immigrant population. Wrappers can be seen drying on bamboo racks all over town. A little downstream, the market town of **Tha Bo** shows the fruits of the fertile floodplains: bananas, vegetables, and tobacco.

Continuing downstream from Nong Khai (see p. 183), the Mekong widens in places to nearly half a mile (0.8 km). Many small towns dotting the river route take on the prefix of Nong or Beung, referring to freshwater ponds fed by streams from the Mekong. Vietnamese and Thais, wearing conical straw hats,

INSIDER TIP:

The road along the Mekong between Chiang Khan and Sangkolm offers great views and little traffic—ideal for biking.

—PETER HOLMSHAW
*CPA Media, Chiang Mai &
National Geographic contributor*

tend rice and vegetables.

Beyond Nakhon Phanom (see p. 181) and the revered *chedi* of That Phanom (see p. 180), more beautiful riverside scenery reveals itself at **Mukdahan,** the last sizable Thai town on the Mekong. Opposite the Laotian city of Savannaket, Mukdahan bustles as a major trade link between the two countries. A planned second bridge over the

Mekong would open an avenue along Route 9 in Laos, stretching to the Vietnamese port of Danang.

At Mukdahan, Highway 2034 runs beside the river. About 10 miles (16 km) on, near Ban Na Kam Noi, is **Mukdahan National Park,** a 20-square-mile (52 sq km) area with bizarre rock formations and cave walls with prehistoric paintings.

At the village of **Khong Chiam,** at Mae Nam Song Si ("two-color river"), the relatively clear waters of the Mun clash with the Mekong's muddy flow. Nearby is Pha Taem, a sheer cliff with paintings of uncertain origins depicting fish, elephants, and buffalo; it dates back 2,000 to 3,000 years.

Friendship Bridge

The Thai-Lao Friendship Bridge extends over the lower reaches of the Mekong at Nong Khai. When it was completed in the mid-1990s, it linked two countries that, despite sharing strong cultural ties, had been at each other's throats for much of the previous 30 years. Its opening was a defining moment in reconciliation.

Construction began in 1991, three years after Thailand and Laos ended hostilities that had flared sporadically since the end of the Vietnam War in 1976. The two had been ideological enemies since then. Thailand was a robust capitalist economy, striding—and often stumbling—along the path to modern democracy. Laos had bolted its doors to the West and embraced socialism. By the late 1980s, relations improved after Thai prime minister Chatichai Choonhavan (1922–1988) announced his "turn battlefields into marketplaces" policy. Laos cautiously opened up to foreign investment to kick-start its moribund economy.

At the opening in April 1994, Buddhist monks performed *rote nam,* a water-blessing ceremony ensuring *mong-kon* (an auspicious future) in front of King Bhumibol, Prime Minister Chuan Leekpai, and the then Australian Prime Minister, Paul Keating (Australia provided $30 million for bridge construction).

Situated at the Bangkok–Nong Khai railhead, the Friendship Bridge was to signal a new era for Issan. A railway would be built through Laos to Vietnam, connecting Singapore to China. Foreign investors would be enticed to landlocked Laos by easier access to ports in the Gulf of Thailand, and trade would flow both ways over the bridge. Today, few of the lofty ambitions set for the 3,851-foot (1,174 m) span have been realized. The decimating 1997–1999 Asian economic crisis stalled the dream, but perhaps more pivotal is the Lao authorities' cautious stance. Laos has a population of just 4.5 million, governed by a mix of halfhearted market economics and debilitating bureaucracy. Fear of outsiders importing divergent views and exploiting natural resources is holding up bridge traffic.

Into Laos

Tourists can cross into Laos by paying about $45 for a 30-day visa at the Laos immigration point, filling out application forms, and producing two passport photos. Minibuses carry passengers over the bridge for about 20 cents; private cars are not allowed. At a traffic circle just off the bridge's Laotian end, vehicles suddenly find themselves on the right-hand side of the road (in Thailand vehicles travel on the left, in Laos on the right). From here, fixed-fare taxis leave for the capital, **Vientiane,** about 20 miles (32 km) east.

Outside of Hanoi, in Vietnam, Vientiane retains some of Southeast Asia's best examples of French colonial architecture. A plethora of

The Wai

The graceful wai—hands joined in a prayer-like posture, accompanied by the bowing of the head—is the traditional greeting in Thailand. Though it appears simple, the wai is tied up in complicated social rules involving age, community status, wealth, and power. Who wais first, whether a wai is returned, how high the hands are held, and how long they remain in that position, as well as the length and depth of the bow, depend on your status and that of the person you are greeting.

Buddhist temples testifies to the Communist government's failure to purge the state of religion after it took power in 1975. Not that it tried very hard—Laotians are devout, and any wholehearted attempts to destroy Buddhism would have alienated a significant portion of the population The country's sustained fling with the Soviet Union shows in drab, worn-out Stalinist architecture. Sidewalk cafés sell Laotian coffee and mountains of freshly baked baguettes are sold at the morning market. Add all this to a Mekong frontage and a rambunctious city center, and Vientiane makes a funky diversion. ∎

National Parks of Loei

Being sent to Loei, in the far northeast near the Laotian border, once was the Thai equivalent of being sent to Siberia. Government workers posted to Loei found inhospitable terrain, searing summers and frigid winters, few creature comforts, isolation, and troublesome Communist insurgents, plus shaky career prospects. Now the province, with its rugged mountains and fertile valleys along the Khorat Plateau's western edge, is recognized for its beautiful national parks.

More than 1,500 species of wild orchid grow in the mountains of Phu Luang National Park.

National Parks of Loei

🄰 Map p. 165

Visitor Information

✉ Tourism Authority of Thailand, 16/5 Mukmontri Rd., Udon Thani

☎ 042-325406 or 042-325407

✉ National Park Division of the Royal Forestry Department, Paholyothin Rd., Bangkhen, Bangkok

☎ 02-562-0760

Phu Kradung National Park

The prize among Loei's parks is 138-square-mile (359 sq km) Phu Kradung National Park, established in 1962 to protect its unusual and diminishing temperate fauna. The park embraces a hilly sandstone plateau atop a steep-sided mountain—peaking at 4,462 feet (1,360 m)—and the fertile surrounding lowlands. On the plateau, as you wander past azaleas and rhododendrons and through carpets of wildflowers, it is hard to believe you're in tropical Thailand.

Phu Kradung is set up for hiking, with 30 miles (48 km) of well-marked trails. The visitor center at Si Than, 50 miles (80 km) south of Loei, has maps and blankets, stores baggage, and arranges porters and guides. The park gets busy on weekends and holidays, so try to visit on weekdays.

The 4.5-mile (7 km), steep climb to Phu Kradung begins at the visitor center and takes about three hours (ladders and stairs ease the chore at more difficult points). You pass mixed deciduous, hill evergreen, and cloud forests, and tracts of bamboo, before pulling over the top of the plateau's ridge. It's another 2 miles (3 km) to the park headquarters, where you buy provisions and rent bungalows. Trails onto the plateau snake through meadows, stands of pine, patches of evergreen forest, oak and birch, and ground flora of violets, orchids, and daisies, to breathtaking views at the summit. Bring warm clothes, food, a flashlight, candles, and insect repellent. The park closes from June to September, when rains make the trails slippery and dangerous.

Phu Luang National Park

About 12.5 miles (20 km) north of Phu Kradung, near the village of Wang Saphung, Highway 2250 turns southwest for about 16 miles (25.5 km) before heading into Phu Luang National Park. The park shares many of the features of Phu Kradung but is less visited. It comprises a steep-sided sandstone plateau rising to 3,600 feet (1,100 m)—and upwards to its 5,154-foot (1571 m) summit—scattered with rocky outcrops and boulders. Mini-trucks from Loei rumble about halfway up the mountain, from where you climb a tough trail for three to four hours before reaching park headquarters. On the plateau, park rangers have blazed trails through shrubland interspersed with deciduous pine and occasional stands of bamboo. The trails lead to waterfalls, freshwater springs, and spectacular cliffs with expansive mountain and valley views.

Humid conditions promote a jungle growth packed with mosses, ferns, and more than 1,500 species

of wild orchid, the park's most treasured natural attribute. Phu Luang has an abundance of wildlife, including long-tailed deer (sambars), elephants, tigers, leopards, Asiatic black bears, and about 140 species of migratory and resident birds.

Phu Luang is not as popular as Phu Kradung, simply because access is more difficult. Tours arranged by park rangers (tel 042-801955) are recommended. The three-day, two-night tours cost about $20 per person and include transportation from Loei, food, guides, and accommodations in park bungalows.

INSIDER TIP:

For an excursion from Loei, visit Namsom, with its night market. You'll sample true small-town Thailand and be the only *farang* (foreigner) around.

—CHRISTY RIZZO
Adventure travel expert

Phu Rua National Park

This largely mountainous park is about 30 miles (48 km) west of Loei. A three-hour climb from park headquarters passes through tropical, evergreen, and pine forests to the 4,571-foot (1,375 m) summit, where a slab of cliff juts over fine mountain vistas. Although the 75-square-mile (121 sq km) Phu Rua is isolated from the much larger Phu Luang National Park, similar fauna includes sambars, Asiatic black bears, and tigers. ∎

Khon Kaen

The fourth largest city in Thailand, Khon Kaen is the gateway to Issan for travelers moving across the country from northern Thailand. Speared by both the Friendship Highway (Highway 2) and the other major Issan route, Highway 12, it could also claim to be at its crossroads. Add a modern airport and an important rail stop on the far-reaching Bangkok–Nong Khai line, and you have a city that is a convenient base from which to explore the northeast.

Khon Kaen

⬛ Map p. 165

Visitor Information

✉ Tourism Authority of Thailand, 15/5 Prachasamoson Rd., Khon Kaen

☎ 043-244498

Khon Kaen's unbridled growth over the past decade has pushed it to the regional fore in transportation, communications, finance, and education. The sprawling 2,000-acre (810 ha) Khon Kaen University is Issan's largest. Khon Kaen is not an unpleasant place, but besides the customary urban diversions of a modern Thai city, and boat rides and picnicking at the expansive **Khaen Nakhon Lake** on the city's outskirts, it has little to offer in the way of attractions.

An exception is the well-managed **Khon Kaen National Museum** (*Lungsun Rachakhan Rd., tel 043-246170, closed Mon.–Tues.*). Artifacts include superbly complex lintels from the Ku Suan Taeng temple in Buriram Province, built by the Khmer king Jayavarman VII. Jayavarman, a devout Buddhist, initiated a network of public works, including 102 hospitals. A stone stela at the museum identifies one such structure. A 12th-century conch shell laden with Mahayana Buddhist motifs and small votive deities is among the museum's more exquisitely quirky relics. There is also a collection of artifacts excavated from Ban Chiang (see p. 182).

Away from the capital, provincial Khon Kaen quickly slips into Issan's calming rural heartland. **Chonnabot** (*35 miles/57 km SW of Khon Kaen on Hwy. 229*) is known throughout Thailand for its tie-dye *mud mee* cotton and silk. The process involves dyeing individual threads of silk before weaving. Examples are displayed at Chonnabot's handicraft center on Pho Sii Sa-aat Road, opposite Wat Pho Sii Sa-aat. In the nearby streets a number of weaving houses sell similar products at better prices. ∎

EXPERIENCE:
Excavating Dinosaurs

Since 2007, visitors have come to the Sirindhorn Museum at the **Phu Kum Khao Dinosaur Excavation Site** (*Amphur Sahaat Sakaan, Karasin Province, Issan, tel 043-871014*) to get up close and personal with dinosaurs of the Paleozoic era. Here you'll find life-size skeletons of dinosaurs discovered in the immediate area— among them *Siamotyrannus isanensis*, a predecessor of the fearsome *Tyrannosaurus rex*, and the *Compsognathus*, the world's smallest dinosaur.

More than 800 fossilized bones are housed in the two-story museum, where you'll learn how these dinosaurs fit into the evolutionary scheme through multilingual and multimedia presentations. You can also examine the actual dig sites where fossils of six different dinosaurs (including the near complete skeleton of a Sauropod) were unearthed.

Home to the magnificent old capital of Sukhothai, the seat of the golden age of Thai civilization

Central Thailand

Classical Thai dancer

Central Thailand

Central Thailand, where the ancient kingdoms of Siam arose, is considered the essential source of the country's culture, pride, and religious traditions, and of traditional Thai values, including the generosity and humanity that permeates life today. The landscape is unremarkable, but rich soil and plentiful rainfall make it the breadbasket of the country, and its rice and corn crops are a vital source of national income.

The area has a complicated system of rivers and canals that have long helped the people to support themselves in the agricultural sector. Although the area is fairly prosperous and modernized, most residents still make their homes in rural villages, where life centers on family, farming, and the Buddhist faith.

Sukhothai

Central Thailand's greatest attraction is the ancient city of Sukhothai, the original capital of the first true Thai nation in a

period recognized as the golden era of Thai history. The splendid and remarkable ruins give an insight into the magnificence of Sukhothai culture during the 13th and 14th centuries. Sukhothai Historical Park is a collection of the finest and most intriguing ruins in the land.

Nearby Phitsanulok is a bustling commercial center that briefly enjoyed status as the capital of the country after the fall of Sukhothai and before the rise of Ayutthaya. It is best known today as the home of one of the most famous Buddha images in the world.

Within striking distance of Sukhothai are two more destinations of great architectural interest: Si Satchanalai, a vice-regal seat in the Sukhothai period, and Kamphaeng Phet, the final part of the Sukhothai Kingdom.

Young monks take a break at Sukhothai Historical Park.

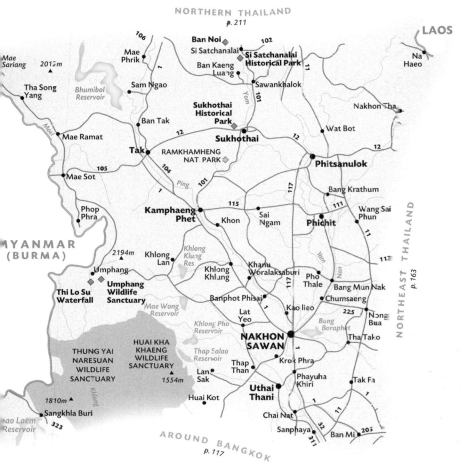

Jungles & Rivers

Visitors wanting to explore some of Thailand's remoter areas, including jungles and rivers, can head to the towns and villages along the rugged border with Myanmar (Burma). The dusty town of Mae Sot, in Tak Province, offers a mix of Thai, Chinese, Indian, and Burmese, plus Karen and other hill-tribe ethnic groups. It is the center of the gem and jade trade along the border and has a tinge of appealing frontierism. Just outside the town, right on the border, you'll find one of the most colorful markets in Thailand. To the south, isolated Umphang, well off the conventional tourist track, is a good place to organize trekking and river-rafting trips. ■

| 0 | | 100 kilometers |
| 0 | | 50 miles |

Area of map detail

Phitsanulok

Central Thailand's leading business center and regional transportation hub, Phitsanulok sits on the banks of the Nan River, 235 miles (376 km) north of Bangkok. Today the sprawling, friendly city appears to have all modern conveniences, yet it is among the oldest and most historic towns in Thailand. It was an early Khmer military outpost and, during the Sukhothai era, was a military garrison for the first Siamese kingdom. King Naresuan the Great was born here.

Traditional houses fringe the Nam River in Phitsanulok, one of Thailand's oldest towns.

Phitsanulok

 Map p. 193

Visitor Information

✉ Tourism Authority of Thailand, 209/7–8 Surasi Trade Center, Borommatrail-okanat Rd., Amphoe Muang, Phitsanulok

☎ 055-252742 or 055-252743

Phitsanulok's major attraction is the exquisite and highly revered image of the **Phra Phuttha Chinarat,** housed inside the equally impressive **Wat Phra Si Rattana Mahathat** (or Wat Yai) *(Phutthabucha Rd.),* one of the few Ayutthaya-period structures to survive a catastrophic fire that took place in 1955.

Entry is via a pair of elaborately carved doors into a stunning interior, resplendent with decorated black and gold columns, a richly colored red roof, delightful murals of courtesans and hunters, and a dramatic architectural scheme that points toward the central image.

Phra Phuttha Chinarat is one of the finest examples of Sukhothai art, with its extraordinary casting and mesmerizing beauty, and should not be missed.

An amazing collection of rural artifacts is displayed in **Sergeant Major Thawee's Folk Museum** *(Wisuth Kasat Rd., closed Mon.)* in the southeast section of town. Objects range from fish traps and musical instruments to sculpted coconut grinders and clunky elephant bells.

Opposite the folk museum, the Buddha **foundry** *(Wisuth Kasat Rd., closed Mon.)* still makes bronze Buddha images. ∎

Sukhothai Historical Park

Sukhothai is to Thailand what Angkor is to Cambodia, Tikal to Mexico, and Giza to Egypt. Lying 281 miles (450 km) north of Bangkok, Sukhothai was the center of Thailand's first independent kingdom and is probably its most impressive and popular archaeological site. In this vast national park, you will find superb artistic and architectural achievements of a kingdom that spread far west to Vientiane in Laos, east to Pegu in Myanmar, and south to Nakhon Si Thammarat.

Formerly a strategically well-placed Khmer military outpost, Sukhothai ("dawn of happiness") was established in 1238 by two Thai princes who sought independence from Khmer rule. The city flourished until it was swamped by the rise of Ayutthaya in 1378.

Over a relatively short period, Sukhothai successfully conquered many small principalities in the region to create the most powerful nation in Southeast Asia at that time. Early kings preached a philosophy of political power share rather than military might and the importance of respecting the wishes of the people—in direct contrast to the ruthless oligarchy practiced by both the Khmers and the Burmese.

The golden age of Sukhothai—a time of remarkable political, cultural, and religious freedoms—came under the leadership of King Ramkamhaeng (r. 1278–1318), famous throughout Thai history for his enlightened rule and wide-ranging accomplishments. Not only did Ramkamhaeng make his mark as a successful warrior, but he also was an economic revolutionary who introduced a free-trade economy and is credited with inventing the modern Thai alphabet. A great religious leader, too, he actively promoted the pure sect of Theravada Buddhism, the national religion of today. Unlike his predecessors and

contemporaries across Southeast Asia, who reigned from a position of godlike terror, Ramkamhaeng ruled with a surprising degree of humanity. It is said that he ruled from his throne, and citizens could seek his judgment by ringing a bell just outside the palace.

Subsequent Sukhothai kings had less impact overall than Ramkamhaeng, but some left their mark in other ways. During the reign of King Mahalithai in the mid-14th century, the art and architecture of Sukhothai reached its dizzying heights, and the city developed its role as the

Sukhothai Historical Park

- Map p. 193
- $, or $$$ for admission pass to all park sites

Visitor Information

- Tourism Authority of Thailand 209/7–8 Surasi Trade Center, Borommatrailokanat Rd., Amphoe Muang, Phitsanulok
- 055-252742 or 055-252743

A colossal Buddha dominates Wat Mahathat, Sukhothai's spiritual center.

largest center of Buddhism in the world. The kingdom continued to thrive until 1378, when it started to be subsumed by the emerging power base of Ayutthaya. Minor kings ruled the slowly declining empire until 1438, when the final king abdicated in favor of an Ayutthayan prince, and Sukhothai's fate as little more than a subservient outpost to the

In 1977 work began to restore the historical site, and 16 years later the Sukhothai National Historical Park, covering some 28 square miles (70 sq km), opened to the public. Today the splendidly restored buildings of this UNESCO World Heritage site, which top

rising Ayutthayan Empire was sealed.

Sukhothai faded into history and was largely forgotten by the Siamese people until 1782, when the Chakri dynasty became established in Bangkok. To legitimize his power through royal and religious kinship, Rama I (r. 1782–1809) collected hundreds of Sukhothai images to grace his temples and monasteries. Several of his building projects were designed to reflect Sukhothai prototypes, and the mythology of the earlier kingdom was actively promoted to inspire and unite the people.

King Mongkut promoted the memory and reverence of Sukhothai after he visited the abandoned site in 1833, returning with stone tablets that confirmed the brilliance of the ancient empire.

Remains of a large, square-based, stepped *chedi*

Wat Mahathat, Sukhothai Historical Park

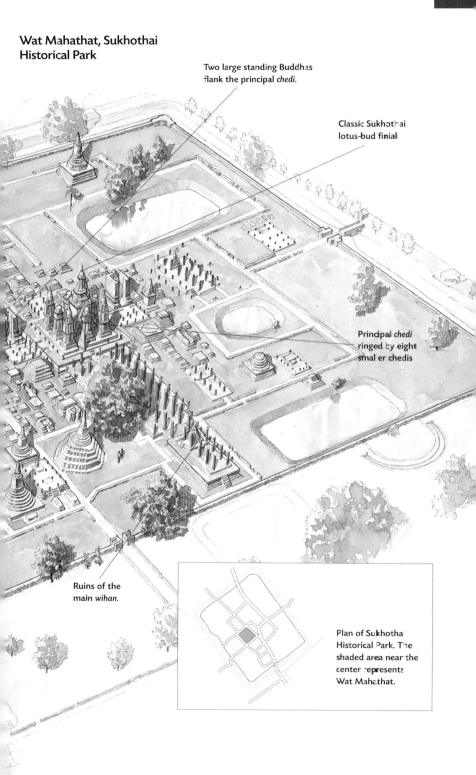

Two large standing Buddhas flank the principal *chedi*.

Classic Sukhothai lotus-bud finial

Principal *chedi* ringed by eight smaller chedis

Ruins of the main *wihan*.

Plan of Sukhotha Historical Park. The shaded area near the center represents Wat Mahathat.

most visitors' must-see lists, give a revealing insight into Sukhothai's golden past.

Ramkamhaeng National Museum

An excellent introduction to the history, arts, and crafts of Sukhothai, Si Satchanalai, and Kamphaeng Phet is given in this modern and spacious building at the entrance to the central zone of the Sukhothai Historical Park. The well-planned museum features graceful Sukhothai Buddhas, treasured Sawankalok

During Loy Krathong, which originated in Sukhothai, lotus-shaped banana-leaf boats are floated on rivers for good luck.

ceramics from Si Satchanalai, ancient Khmer statues, and other archaeological artifacts from central Thailand.

A highlight is the magnificent bronze walking Buddha that faces the front entrance. The main floor includes models of the old city and a reproduction of the four-sided pillar that claims fame as the first example of written Thai script. Household objects

and farming implements show the degree of sophistication of the common people in early Sukhothai. The second floor is largely devoted to Buddha images in the slender-waisted Sukhothai style, which emphasized simplicity and grace.

Sculpture around the grounds of the museum ranges from a rare Khmer phallic shrine to a collection of stucco temple elephants gathered from local shrines. A statue of King Ramkamhaeng, seated on a replica of the Manangasila throne, is located west of museum. The historic throne, imbued with magical properties, was discovered in 1833 by King Mongkut, and the highly revered original is now in the National Museum in Bangkok (see pp. 82–86).

Wat Mahathat

The spiritual center of old Sukhothai was the huge complex of Wat Mahathat, which was both the royal temple and the most important Buddhist monastery in Southeast Asia. Though largely in ruins as a result of the ravages of war and the effects of the elements, Wat Mahathat remains important as the religious focus of the most brilliant of all Thai kingdoms. The temple monastery was constructed by Sukhothai's first king, Si Intharathit (r. ca 1240–1270), and was expanded and remodeled by subsequent rulers, including Ramkamhaeng and King Lo Thai (r. 1298–1346).

To appreciate its former splendor, imagine the *wat* in its prime, when it boasted almost 200 *chedis* erected to protect royal remains, around a dozen *wihans* for public worship and an impressive central *bot*, surrounded by moats. Today, large Buddhas sit serene amid the crumbling masonry. The highlight is the soaring central chedi, erected by Lo Thai to house two sacred Buddha relics donated by a Sri Lankan monk. The monument has been modeled in the Sinhalese style, with a bulbous, lotus bud-shaped outline that is now considered the classic architectural motif of Sukhothai.

More Local Sights

Just west of Wat Mahathat are the rough foundations of **Ramkamhaeng's Royal Palace.** Constructed almost entirely of wood, it has not survived. Only religious structures were built of stone, and so almost all historic royal and domestic architecture has disappeared. King Mongkut discovered the famous Manangasila throne here in 1833.

One of the most interesting and evocative structures on the site is **Wat Si Sawai,** a striking Khmer-style sanctuary of three closely set, corncob *prangs* erected by King Jayavarman VII of Angkor, and completed in the 14th century. Enclosed within a deep moat, this intriguing shrine first honored Hindu Brahmanic deities favored by the Khmers but was adapted in the 15th century to suit Buddhist sensibilities. The central nave and trio of complementary brick prangs follow the classic motif found in many Khmer temples in Thailand.

Perhaps the most beautifully situated temple at Sukhothai is

Wat Traphang Ngoen ("silver lake monastery"), which rises gracefully on a small island in the center of an artificial lake. Today the wat is the focus for the festival of Loy Krathong, usually held in November. The monastery features an elegant lotus-bud chedi, modeled after the one that crowns Wat Mahathat.

Another temple in a superb watery setting is nearby **Wat Sa Si,** which overlooks a lake. The temple features a well-restored, large Buddha image, and on the temple grounds is a small black Buddha image in the famous Sukhothai walking style.

The Khmers also left behind another laterite temple of the Hindu type, **San Tapa Daeng,** with its four porticoes and Angkor Wat-style statuary that dates the monument to the early

INSIDER TIP:

Arrive at Sukhothai early or stay late to enjoy the temples and Buddha statues at sunrise or sunset.

—SIMON WILLIAMS
The Nature Conservancy

12th century. The Angkor deities have been removed and are now displayed in the Ramkamhaeng National Museum.

Wat Sorasak, constructed in 1412, is known for its base—which is made up of reconstructed elephant buttresses—and its classic Sri Lankan-style chedi. ∎

Arts of Sukhothai

Beginning in the late 13th century, Sukhothai developed into a major creative center. To assert its cultural identity as separate from the once dominant Khmer, Sukhothai eschewed Mahayana Buddhism and embraced Sri Lankan Theravada Buddhism. It fused artistic influences from other Asian cultures, principally from the Indian subcontinent and, ironically, the Khmers, to create Thailand's first indigenous art.

Despite the short duration of the Sukhothai Kingdom, its artistic endeavors were prolific and varied. Through its architecture, sculpture, ceramics, and paintings—although few examples of the latter have survived—it produced a remarkable sense of beauty and grace that has proved to be both profound and enduring.

Architecture

Sukhothai architects seemed intent on developing fresh and more delicate styles, improving on the heavy stupas from Sri Lanka and the Khmer *prangs*.

The most distinguishable forms of Sukhothai architecture can be found in the lotus-bud motifs crowning *chedis*, a style that evolved from Khmer and Burmese Bagan influences. Khmer prangs were modified and enhanced to form bell-shaped chedis. Their square bases were adorned and buttressed with elephant stucco carvings. Taking the cue from the Lanna period, stupas were designed with square redented bases. The main body of the stupa was indented with alcoves in which Buddha statues were housed. The bell-shaped stupas were crowned with ornamental rings.

The crafting of Buddha footprints in stone and bronze was popular during the reign of Li Thai (r. 1347–1368). The footprints were richly symbolic, identifying the presence of Lord Buddha. Temples where the footprints are placed became highly revered.

Sculpture

Perhaps the best example of this—indeed, some suggest it is the most notable of all Sukhothai artistic expressions—is the design of Buddha icons. Influenced by Sri Lankan style, Sukhothai Buddha sculptures were marked by a fluid, almost ethereal design; their lithe curves and cylindrical forms produced a weightless elegance. Other distinguishing characteristics were wide shoulders tapering to narrow waists, a head crowned with flame ornamentation, and the flap of the robe draped over the left shoulder and ending in a wavy pattern at the waist. Also notable were the facial expressions—elongated heads with strongly defined noses, eyes, and mouths. These expressions captured, more than any other style of Buddha iconography before and, arguably, since, an amazing degree of serenity and spirituality.

Sukhothai Buddhas typically come in four postures: seated in the half-lotus posture with right hand performing the earth-touching gesture; standing; reclining; and walking. This last posture, however, is recognized as the greatest design achievement by Sukhothai artists. Although this image had existed before, it was almost always carved in relief and was not used as a canonical type. Sukhothai artists created a sublime image frozen in a moment of movement. With one heel raised and one foot planted on the ground, Buddha appears to move forward in a supple, but essential surge. Most of the walking Buddhas from Sukhothai temples have been moved to museums in Sukhothai and Bangkok, but a few are still seen on their original monuments.

Ceramics & Other Crafts

Similar craftsmanship are found in rare woodcarvings on doors and ceilings, and

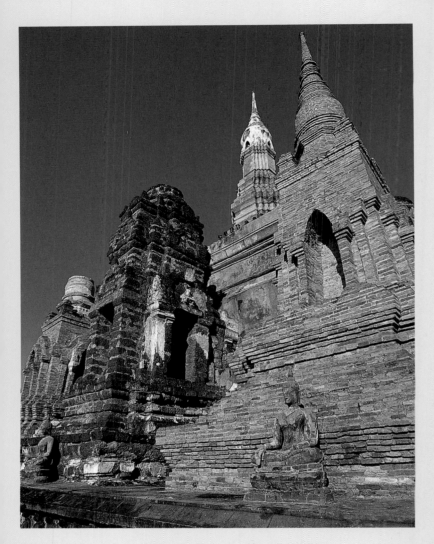

Sukhothai architects refined architectural styles developed by earlier kingdoms.

in slate engravings. Finely crafted, if faded, stucco reliefs can still be seen in some of Sukhothai's temples: the best examples are at Wat Traphang Tong Lang (see p. 203)—the southern panel shows the Buddha's descent to Earth, surrounded by angels and bodhisattvas.

The works of the kingdom's ceramicists are also notable. Craftsmen, who learned the trade from the Chinese, used Sukhothai's and Si Satchanalai's expansive kilns to make exquisite ceramics in brown, white, and celadon, or with a painted design known as Sangkhalok. These ceramics and other forms of decorative pottery, sometimes molded into animal and human shapes, were exported to Malaysia, the Philippines, Indonesia, and Japan. Artifacts recovered from shipwrecks in the Gulf of Thailand and off the coast of Indonesia and the Philippines attest to this trade.

Around Sukhothai

Some of Sukhothai's finest monuments lie outside the old city walls, north of town. Several more noteworthy temples are situated to the west, south, and east of the central zone, although few compare to those previously mentioned and the distances deter some visitors. One way to get around is to rent a bicycle near the east gate—you can then escape the beaten track to experience a simpler, less commercialized version of the old city.

Mudras, or Buddha image hand gestures, help instruct devotees.

Wat Phra Phai Luang ("temple of the great wind"), situated almost a mile (1.6 km) north of Wat Mahathat, was once a Buddhist monastery second only to Wat Mahathat in importance. Built in the 12th century by the Khmers as a Hindu religious shrine, Wat Phra Phai Luang was converted into a Buddhist monastery after the fall of the Khmer Empire. Only one of the three laterite *prangs* remains. Sadly, looters stole many valuable Hindu and Buddhist images in the 1950s.

A number of huge **pottery kilns** make a welcome change from temple touring. Believed to predate Sukhothai, they were used to produce an outstanding range of ceramics, from glazed tiles to Sangkhalok bottles.

Among the most impressive Buddhist monuments found in Sukhothai is the gigantic Buddha image inside the square *mondop* of **Wat Sri Chum.** The image, dating from the late 14th century, is seated in the attitude of subduing the evil goddess Mara and is still an active religious icon for Thai pilgrims.

To the west of the old city are several brick temples that show signs of vandalism by robbers and an ancient reservoir, which has been renovated and now serves as the main source of fresh water for modern Sukhothai.

The trek up a very steep hill to **Wat Saphan Hin** ("temple of the stone causeway mountain") is a tiring one, on a confusing landslide of stone steps, but those who reach the top are rewarded with a giant Buddha image and superb views over the entire valley. The Buddha, with its raised hand in the aspect of ensuring

stucco works, including divinity figures, standing elephants, and superb *garudas*. Most impressive of the remaining structures is **Wat Chetuphon,** which has two tall, upright stucco Buddhas; the walking image is particularly fine.

Although the distances to the eastern sector are great, and the landscape rugged and dry, most of the temples here remain blessedly free of restoration and

Around Sukhothai
 Map p. 193

Visitor Information

 Tourism
Authority
of Thailand,
209/7–8 Surasi
Trade Center,
Borommat-ail-
okanat Rd.,
Amphoe Muang,
Phitsanulok

☎ 055-252742
or 055-252743

EXPERIENCE: Ghosts

Belief in ghosts is widespread in Thailand: Spirit houses outside of buildings in Sukhothai and everywhere are the most prevalent acknowledgements of the supernatural. Thais recognize at least 25 different types of ghosts, in addition to "commonplace" spirits of the dead.

One popular ghost (she is included in a number of feature films) is **Mae Naak**— a lovelorn woman who died in childbirth. At her supposed burial place near Bangkok's On Nut BTS station *(Sukhumvit 77, Soi 7, beside Wat Mahabute)*, a likeness of her was made, some say, of the soil from seven cemeteries. Visitors can pay her respect and receive good luck, particularly with lottery numbers.

While not openly professing that it is the best place to get genuine interaction

with ghosts, the sea gypsies of **Ko Lipe** in southern Thailand believe their island to be haunted by spirits of the jungle and trees, who often wander the forests and beaches at night. A number of tourists have reported seeing them, too.

The ultimate ghost experience, however, occurs in Dan Sai district in Loei Province, where the **Boon Luang Festival** is held over three days during the eighth month of the Thai year—either June or July, depending on lunar and spiritual schedules. During the Phi Ta Khon procession, locals dress up in colorful costumes featuring specialized masks and long phallic swords and playfully interact with onlookers. For dates, contact the Tourism Authority of Thailand *(tel 042-325406, www.tourismthailand.org)*.

---

peace, seems to be blessing the valley, the city, and even the occasional Western visitor who makes the tough climb up the dusty hill.

Monuments to the south are also rather modest, chiefly renowned for their traces of rare and fine stuccoes. The remoteness of the area means that it has suffered from pillagers, who have stripped most of the ancient monuments of their priceless

display more of their original character than monuments found elsewhere in the old city. Highlights are the *chedi* of **Wat Chang Lom,** with its sculpted elephants; the beautifully proportioned chedi of **Wat Chedi Sung; Wat Traphang Tong,** with its highly revered footprint of the Buddha; and **Wat Traphang Tong Lang,** known for the superb stucco decorations on the walls of the mondop. ■

Si Satchanalai

This memorable and rarely visited set of ancient ruins provides a complementary overview of early Siamese architecture and makes for an excellent day excursion from Sukhothai, which lies some 35 miles (56 km) to the south. Si Satchanalai has fewer ruins than Sukhothai, and the site is smaller, too—about 3 square miles (7 sq km). However, the setting on the west bank of the Yom River and the sheer isolation of the old city make for a very evocative tour.

Monks wander among the ruins of Wat Chang Lom, built in 1285.

Si Satchanalai's history is inextricably linked with that of Sukhothai. Both towns were founded by the Khmers as military and administrative centers. In 1238, two Siamese princes raised a rebel force to finally drive the Khmers from the area, and their first target for release was Si Satchanalai, which would serve as a springboard for the successful attack on Sukhothai.

The princes divided their army into two contingents, one of which battled the Khmers at the midway point between the two cities, while the other marched into an unoccupied Sukhothai. This clever strategy worked as planned, and Sukhothai was transformed in a short time to become the first Siamese kingdom. One of the leaders renamed himself King Sri Indraditya and began to build both Sukhothai and Si Satchanalai.

Si Satchanalai enjoyed a steady building boom over the ensuing century, and the sheer number of temples and the grand proportions of the royal monastery demonstrate that the city enjoyed great political and religious significance. Si Satchanalai fell from favor after the rise of Ayutthaya and, after repeated attacks from Burmese forces, was

INSIDER TIP:

Just a spoken Thai word of *sawadee* (hello) or *kawp khun* (thank you), followed by *krap* or *ka* (a form of politesse used by men or women respectively), goes a long way.

—SIMON WILLIAMS
The Nature Conservancy

almost completely forgotten by the 18th century. After centuries of disuse, most of the ruins were renovated in the mid-1980s.

Visiting the Site

Si Satchanalai today has three areas of historical and architectural interest, with the vast majority of the ancient ruins found inside the central laterite walls that mark the first outlines of the township. The **museum** near the entrance has a scale model of the old city and is a useful place to get your bearings.

At Si Satchanalai's center is the Sri Lankan-style *chedi* of **Wat Chang Lom** ("temple surrounded by elephants"), constructed in 1285 by King Ramkamhaeng while his eldest son ruled the city. The handsome bell-shaped structure rises above the tier of stucco

elephants for which the structure was named. Situated on the upper terraces are what remains of almost a dozen stucco Buddhas.

Paths and grassy lawns lead to all the following attractions. Start at **Wat Khao Phnom Phloeng** ("temple of the mountain of fire"), in the northern quadrant. Climb the 114 steps to the summit for splendid views over the ancient city's scattered ruins. To the west is a smaller hill, topped by the ruins of Wat Suwan Khiri. A Sinhalese-inspired chedi known as the Temple of the Golden Mountain dominates the site. Here, too, are excellent views. You can then walk back to Wat Chang Lom and continue south to **Wat Chedi Chet Thaeo** ("seven rows of chedis"), with its impressive lotus-bud crown on the main chedi—a distinctive Sukhothai style. The smaller chedi behind the main chedi houses faded murals depicting the lives of Buddha and dignitaries of the Sukhothai period. Reproductions can be found in Sukhothai's Ramkamhaeng National Museum (see p. 198). **Wat Suan Kao Utayan Yai** dates from the mid-15th century, its crumbling chedi done in Sri Lankan style. The large **Wat Nang Phaya**, also dating from the 15th century, has an elegant bell-shaped chedi, and a south wall has some fragments of stuccowork.

South of the central ruins is the old Khmer military outpost at **Chaliang,** while to the north are impressive pottery kiln sites, **Ban Noi** and **Ban Pa Yuang,** where Sangkhalok ceramics were produced. (You need a rental bicycle or private transportation to reach the kiln sites and Chaliang.) ∎

Si Satchanalai

- Map p. 193
- On Hwy. 101, 35 miles (56 km) north of Sukhothai
- $

Visitor Information

- Tourism Authority of Thailand, 209/7–8 Surasi Trade Center, Borommatrai-okanat Rd., Amphoe Muang, Phitsanulok
- 055-252742 or 055-252743

www.tourismthailand.org

Kamphaeng Phet

Lying 53 miles (85 km) southwest of Sukhothai, Kamphaeng Phet, along with Si Satchanalai, once served as a satellite city of Sukhothai. Li Thai, the fourth king of the Sukhothai dynasty, founded it in 1347, raising the existing town's status by installing relics of the Buddha at Wat Phra Boromathat. Kamphaeng Phet saw intense construction for several decades, until it was abandoned to the dominating forces of Ayutthaya. It continued to serve as a regional capital.

Ruins at Wat Phra Boromathat. Kamphaeng Phet thrived for only a few decades before it succumbed to the forces of Ayutthaya.

Kamphaeng Phet

Map p. 193

Visitor Information

Tourism Authority of Thailand, 193 Taksin Rd., Tambon Nong Luang, Amphoe Muang, Tak

055-514341 to -3

The old city of Kamphaeng Phet is a short distance north of the uninspiring commercial district of the modern town. The site of this **historical park** comprises several notable structures inside the original walls, along with more unusual temples to the north of the walls, just off the highway to Sukhothai. Kamphaeng Phet is too distant from Sukhothai for a day trip, and most visitors prefer to stay overnight in the modern town on the banks of the Ping River.

The ideal first stop of any tour is the finely stocked **Kamphaeng Phet National Museum** (*Ratcha-damnoen Rd., closed Mon.–Tues.*), inside the old walled city. Among highlights on the ground floor are a highly regarded bronze statue of Shiva, cast in 1510, and a superb Buddha in the Uthong style. There are exhibits of prehistoric terra-cotta, iron, and stone artifacts, and tools 2,000 to 4,000 years old. Dvaravati-period (eighth– ninth centuries) coins have faces stamped in images of the moon, *naga* heads, and flowing water. The second floor has 16th-century bronze statues of Hindu deities Vishnu and Lakshmi from local excavations; more recent terra-cotta (14th–18th centuries) and ceramics of the same period are also here, including 15th-century Sangkhalok jars (see Sangkhalok Ware, below).

Near the National Museum is the **Kamphaeng Phet City National Museum** (Ratchadamnoen

Rd., closed Mon.–Tues.), often called the Golden Teakwood Museum for the abundant use of teak throughout both the exterior and interior. Opened in 1997, it focuses on the history, ethnology, and handicrafts of the province.

Two Buddhist temples situated within the old crenellated city walls are worth inspection. **Wat Phra Kaec,** the royal chapel, has largely

crumbled away, but the wonderfully eroded Buddhas elevated on brick pedestals are elegant and evocative. Opposite the National Museum, **Wat Phra Thak** has a splendid *chedi* with an octagonal base, surrounded by pillars.

The remaining religious structures are north of town and require local transportation. **Wat Phra Non** once featured a large reclining Buddha, but it has largely eroded away. However, its well-preserved chedi, behind the reclining Buddha's *vihara*, with lotus-leaf tiers and bell-shaped crown, is a fine example of Sukhothai craftsmanship. Also impressive are the huge laterite columns, among the largest ever found in Thailand. **Wat Phra Si Iriyabot** ("temple of the four postures") is notable for its fragmented statue of a walking Buddha in Sukhothai style and a particularly fine standing Buddha statue in fairly good condition. **Wat Sing,** close by, has a trio of badly weathered standing Buddhas.

A good hike northwest of **Wat Sing** is **Wat Chang Rop** ("temple surrounded by elephants"), set on a hilltop with superb views over Kamphaeng Phet. The reward for a tough climb is a huge ruined chedi supported by 68 crumbling elephants of brick and stucco, the most impressive monument in Kamphaeng Phet. Superbly crafted stucco images of demons, divinities, and other heavenly beings make this a must-see attraction.

Wat Nak Chet Sin, Wat Awat Yai, and **Wat Tuk Praman,** near the historical park's northern entrance, are under reconstruction and will be worth a visit when work is completed. ∎

Sangkhalok Ware

Sukhothai potters learned their skills from Chinese craftsmen brought to Thai and by King Ramkamhaeng. With guidance from the Chinese, potters began modeling glazed ceramic wares, of which Sangkhalok was the most famous. Sangkhalok's pale blue or off-white porcelain features floral, foliage, and fish designs. Kilns in Si Satchanalai and, later, Kamphaeng Phet also produced pieces for architectural decoration, and "Sangkhalok dolls." Sangkhalok ware was exported all over the region.

Tak & Mae Sot

These two towns, in the western borderlands of central Thailand, are rarely visited. An increasing number of young backpackers, however, are being drawn to this remote corner by the sense of adventure and a desire to enjoy the nearby national parks.

Mae Sot's Wat Maune Pai Son is one of the town's many Burmese-style temples, reflecting the influence of neighboring Myanmar (Burma).

Tak & Mae Sot

Map p. 193

Visitor Information

✉ Tourism Authority of Thailand, 193 Taksin Rd., Tambon Nong Luang, Amphoe Muang, Tak

☎ 055-514341 to -43

Tak was an outpost of the Sukhothai Kingdom; after its decline, it came under the influence of the northern Lanna Kingdom. Today, it is a busy provincial capital with little to see, apart from a handful of splendid teak houses. The town was the birthplace of the revered King Taksin, who defended Thailand against Burmese invaders.

At **Phra Chao Taksin Maharat** *(Phaholyothin Rd., between Taksin & Mahathai Bamrung Rds.),* a venerated shrine houses a seated Taksin with a sword lying in his lap.

Tak has long been a major teak distribution point, owing to its fortuitous location on the Ping River, which runs from the forests of Myanmar (Burma), via the Chao Phraya, all the way to the processing plants in Bangkok. Local citizens also construct their houses and businesses with this valuable, beautiful wood; some of the best are along **Mahathai Bamrung** and **Taksin Roads,** and in the network of alleyways just south of the town park. Enjoy these remarkable structures while you can—collectors of historic houses regularly visit Tak to buy, dismantle, and then move them to the buyers' hometowns.

The lively border town of **Mae Sot** is much more charming and colorful than the modernized commercial enclave of Tak and lies just 3 miles (5 km) east of the Myanmar border, on the Moei River. Its inhabitants are a fascinating mix of ethnic groups, including Thais, Burmese, and Chinese, plus minority tribes such as the Karen and Hmong. The best introduction to this ethnic melding is the morning **market,** where traders offer food, Burmese handicrafts, and glittering gems, from sapphires to rubies, smuggled in from Myanmar.

Several Burmese-style temples are scattered around town, most notably **Wat Chumphon Khiri,** which gleams in its covering of golden tiles. **Wat Mae Sot Luang** has a reclining Buddha, covered in small brass tiles. **Wat Maune Pai Son** is covered in little *chedis,* reminiscent of Loha Prasart in Bangkok (see p. 88). ■

Umphang

Intrepid travelers to central Thailand head to the jungles and rivers some 102 miles (164 km) south of Mae Sot, near a village called Umphang. For almost a decade, this area has been hosting increasing numbers of hardy visitors who prize the kingdom's untouched corners. The winding and sometimes treacherous Highway 1090 from Mae Sot to Umphang—once called the Death Highway because of guerrilla activity—takes in magnificent mountain scenery.

Umphang is a very simple village, situated at the confluence of the Mae Khlong and Umphang Rivers, and surrounded by some of Thailand's most pristine countryside. Some people come here just to relax on the riverbanks, while the more active join expeditions to raft down the raging waters or trek through ancient forests to visit some of the remote hill-tribe villages. The region also has magnificent roaring waterfalls—best seen during the rainy season—and isolated caves engulfed by thick jungle.

Umphang is a base camp for ecotourists, who mostly head south of town into protected reserves such as **Umphang Wildlife Sanctuary** and a nearby park that combines two wildlife sanctuaries—**Thungyai Naresuan** and **Huai Kha Khaeng.** The vast, largely untouched regions make up one of the largest protected forests left in Southeast Asia.

Rough roads suitable only for four-wheel-drive vehicles crisscross the region. While elephant trekking is a popular activity, most visitors choose to explore the jungles and waterfalls on one of the daily river-rafting expeditions. These organized adventures typically start in Umphang and proceed down the Umphang River. Where this river intersects with the Mae Khlong, it picks up volume, continuing south through tropical jungle to a series of outstanding natural wonders: waterfalls, hot springs, limestone cliffs, bloodred karsts, and caves.

The highlight of a visit to Umphang is a sight of the lofty **Thi Lo Su Waterfall,** one of the best limestone waterfalls in Southeast Asia. The falls are so remote that they were discovered only in 1987 by a low-flying helicopter, but they can be reached in two days by raft and on foot. ■

Umphang

🄼 Map p. 193

Visitor Information

✉ Tourism Authority of Thailand, 193 Taksin Rd., Tambon Nong Luang, Amphoe Muang, Tak

☎ 055-514341 to -43

It's a two-day journey on raft and by foot to reach the magnificent Thi Lo Su falls.

The Road to Mae Sariang

Adventurous travelers can head north from Mae Sot, following the road that runs parallel with the Moei River to Mae Sariang. Highway 1085 offers a rare journey through one of the remotest districts in Thailand. Buses and trucks leave Mae Sot and wind their way along this backdoor entry to northern Thailand, an unusual approach that avoids the tiresome return to Tak or Phitsanulok, and links up with connections to Mae Hong Son, Pai, and, finally, Chiang Mai.

Road to Mae Sariang

🗺 Map p. 193

Visitor Information

✉ Tourism Authority of Thailand, 193 Taksin Rd., Tambon Nong Luang, Amphoe Muang, Tak

☎ 055-514341 to -43

Along this rough and untamed section of Thailand, Highway 1085 winds alongside the Moei River before climbing into verdant hills that are clothed in stands of teak forest and dotted with hill-tribe villages clinging to their traditional lifestyles. Eventually it arrives in Mae Sariang, 141 miles (226 km) north. The largest hill-tribe group is the Karen, who continue to challenge the Myanmar (Burmese) government for control of their homelands across the Moei River. The river itself is an oddity, as it flows north—rather than south, the typical direction—until it changes course in the Dawana Range, to flow south through the interior of eastern Myanmar.

You can arrange treks into the surrounding hills at villages along the way—including Mae Ramat, Mae Sarit, Tha Song Yang, and Ban Sop Ngao—but most travelers prefer to wait until arrival in Mae Sariang and seek out treks organized by local guesthouses.

Moei River Market

Before setting out on Highway 1085, it is worth making the effort to take a side trip by *samlor* or *songthaew* to colorful markets on the Myanmar border post, 4 miles (6 km) west of Mae Sot. Visitors will find a large variety

INSIDER TIP:

During Thailand's Loi Krathong festival in November, candle wax balloons dot the night sky and flower floats illuminate waterways. Book ahead for a room along a river.

—CHRISTY RIZZO
Adventure travel expert

of goods in this dusty outpost, including gems (especially jade), an abundance of handicrafts, and foodstuffs. From the market you can walk along the Moei River and take in views of the Myanmar town of Myawaddy.

A concrete and steel bridge was completed here in 1999, much to the delight of traders in Mae Sot, who rely on business carried over these waters. Unfortunately, the sometimes shaky relations between Myanmar and Thailand often cause the closure of the bridge. The construction of the bridge was tagged as a major part of the ambitious Pan-Asian highway, known as Asia Route 1, which promises some day to link Singapore with Istanbul, providing all the countries along the way with a land crossing. ∎

A delightful corner of the kingdom, with fantastic landscapes of mountains and valleys, distinctive art, and two capital cities of the ancient Lanna Kingdom

Northern Thailand

Detail of a woodcarving, a Chiang Mai specialty

Northern Thailand

Northern Thailand has always been a world apart, physically and emotionally separate from the rest of Thailand, with a sense of grace and style uniquely its own. Historically, the north managed to remain independent of Siamese control until the early part of the 20th century and instead was ruled by a distinguished kingdom known as Lanna.

The north has famously attractive landscapes of rolling hills, soaring mountains, crashing rivers, thick jungle, and other variations of a natural environment that are not found anywhere else in the country. Among the people of the region there is a wide variety of ethnic types, whose identity is preserved in the remote corners of this mountainous region. The tribes are associated with a wide range of handicrafts and other traditional forms of artistic expression. It used to be said that the people here considered themselves superior to the lowlanders of Bangkok and the central plains—and notably for the great beauty of their women—though this attitude is no longer commonplace.

The main city is the old Lanna capital of Chiang Mai, full of cultural interest as well as good shopping and traditional dining. Chiang Mai has grown tremendously in recent years but remains the heart and soul of the north, and is the key destination for most visitors.

Just south and southeast of Chaing Mai are the historic towns of Lamphun and Lampang, where some of the most elegant examples of Mon and Burmese architecture are seen— and, as a bonus, there is the elephant training ground en route to Lampang.

West of Chiang Mai are the previously remote towns of Mae Hong Son and Pai, where trekking and river rafting remain the principal draws.

Northern farmers winnow rice. Thailand is the world's largest rice exporter.

North of Chiang Mai are Chiang Rai and the notorious region known as the Golden Triangle, once home to the world's most powerful opium smugglers. Beyond these easily accessible destinations are the smaller towns that skirt the Mekong River, such as Chiang Saen and Chiang Khong, and interior towns rarely visited by foreigners, including Phayao, Phrae, and Nan.

The north awaits those travelers who long for adventure. ■

NOT TO BE MISSED:

A walking tour of Chiang Mai's ancient temples **218–219**

Studying meditation at Wat U Mong **223**

A Thai cooking class **224–225**

Magnificent Wat Doi Suthep **226**

The handicrafts villages around Chiang Mai **227–228**

Driving the Mae Hong Son loop **231–233**

A trek to a hill-tribe village **231–233**

Visiting or volunteering at an elephant sanctuary **238**

Chiang Mai

First stop for most visitors to northern Thailand will be Chiang Mai, heart and soul of the ancient Lanna Kingdom, which flourished from 1250 to 1860. Along the banks of the Ping River and within the confines of the original city you will discover elegant religious structures, cultural emporiums for demonstrations of local dance and music, and very special forms of food and festivals.

Bargaining—here at Chang Klang market in Chiang Mai—is the norm in Thai markets.

Chiang Mai is tucked away in a lush valley surrounded by rivers and green hills. As it is set at a higher altitude than Bangkok and the cities of the south, it has a drier, cooler climate and brings welcome respite for visitors.

Yet it is the people of Chiang Mai that make this city—indeed, all of northern Thailand—such a warm and wonderful destination. Their cultured dignity and intrinsically gentle nature is often attributed to the city's association with the independent kingdom of Lanna.

Chiang Mai was officially founded in 1292 by Mengrai, a Thai-Laotian prince from Chiang Rai who absorbed the early Haripunchai Empire to establish the Lanna Kingdom. During his five-decade rule, Mengrai built a royal city resplendent with palaces and Buddhist temples. He left behind an empire that continued to rule most of northern Thailand for the next two centuries.

King Tilok's reign was the next highlight in Lanna's history, ushering in a golden age of arts, crafts, and Buddhism. Chiang Mai suffered through years of warfare with its neighbor Burma, which ruled the area from 1556 to 1774. Lanna was finally absorbed into the burgeoning empire of Bangkok. Subsequent kings of Thailand acknowledged the historic roots of the Lanna Kingdom by reviving the region's hereditary line of rulers, and most of northern Thailand—including Chiang Mai—remained a semiautonomous state until 1939.

Temples on Tha Phae Road

Several small but significant temples are situated on this busy and very narrow commercial thoroughfare, which connects the Ping River with the Tha Phae Gate. Distinct architectural treatments in the temples of Chiang Mai include the use of Burmese decoration and elegantly mounted roofs that swoop down much lower to the ground than their counterparts elsewhere. Other unique traits are the use of muted colors and flamboyant woodcarving, which is closer to Burmese than Thai styles.

Wat Saen Fang is typical, incorporating Burmese-style architecture in its *chedi* and monastery, along with more modern Thai styling in the brightly painted *wihan*, which is gilded with abstract *nagas*. Across the street stand the three wihans of **Wat Bupparam**, including a garish structure on the left that demonstrates every cliché of modern Thai architecture, and a far more refined, much older wooden wihan on the right. This 17th-century gem is worth a close look for its elegant proportions and the workmanship in its exterior stucco decorations.

Two other temples of note are

Chiang Mai

🅼 Map p. 213

Visitor Information

✉ Chiang Mai National Tourist Office, 105/1 Chiang Mai – Lamphun Rd., Chiang Mai

☎ 053-248604 or 053-248607

EXPERIENCE: Classical Thai Dancing

Thai dance, or *fawn thai*, is best described as poetry in motion (see pp. 58–59). A typical dance is a couple's dance, which tells a story and is performed in a circle with other dancers.

There are many places to observe classical Thai dancing—ask your hotel's front desk for recommendations. But why not try to learn some of these most graceful of movements yourself? Here are some venues in Chiang Mai and Bangkok:

Ban Rak Thai (14/6 Nimmanpromenade Nimmanhaemin Rd., Soi 4, Chiang Mai, tel 086-910-5822, www.banrakthai.com/eng) Designed for foreigners wishing to learn Thai dance. Classes can be extended depending on the length of your visit.

Ban Ram Thai Don Thi (Pattanakarn 72, Muang Thong Thani, Bangkok, tel 081-613-8294) Northern-, southern-, central-, and eastern-style dancing instruction is available for Thai and foreign students of all levels. **Thai Dance Institute** (53 Kohklang Rd., Chiang Mai, tel 053-801375, www.thai danceinstitute.com) Beginner courses instruct students to perform a classical Thai folk dance. Students able to perform the dance adequately may dress in traditional Thai costumes for a souvenir photo and are given a CD to practice at home.

farther west on Tha Phae Road, en route to the restored gateway. **Wat Mahawan** is a small complex that neatly combines Burmese influence in its gaily decorated wihan with later Lanna-Thai styling in its *bot* and monks' residences. Among the details are the monumental elephants encircling the chedi and wooden filigree on many exterior facades. Across the road is **Wat Chedowan,** noted for its trio of chedis donated by wealthy pilgrims and an elegant wihan that has

INSIDER TIP:

Chaing Mai has several cooking schools that offer 1- to 5-day courses. You'll begin at a local market and then cook and eat your Thai favorites. Inquire at your hotel front desk.

—RUSS BAHORSKY
National Geographic Books

outstanding woodcarvings on the gables and naga posts.

Tha Phae Road ends at a large town square, fronted by the recently restored **Tha Phae Gate,** which marks the formal entrance into the old city. Most of the original walls have collapsed over the centuries, but the rectangular network of protective moats has been excavated, and several of the ancient gateways rebuilt. This is an excellent place to take a break, at one of the several good cafés and restaurants found here.

Temples in the Walled City

The following temples are widely scattered within the walled city; it is necessary to hire a three-wheeled rickshaw *(samlor)*, motorized three-wheeler *(tuk-tuk)*, or other form of private transportation to reach them all.

Wat Cha Si Phum (*Chaiyaphum Rd.*) is worth a quick look, for its buildings include a chedi graced with highly unusual Romanesque columns. The temple complex of **Wat Pa Pao** (*Mani Noppharat Rd.*), just outside the northeastern walls, is rarely visited and somewhat difficult to find, with a richly decorated monastery and a romantic chedi set with gleaming blue tiles.

Wat Chiang Man (*Ratcha Phakhinai Rd.*), within the city walls, was the original residence of King Mengrai. Most structures were rebuilt in the 18th and 19th centuries, but the older wihan with its elaborately carved wooden gable is worth close inspection—it depicts the elephant god Erawan. The modern wihan has a pair of highly venerated Buddha statues: a crystal Buddha endowed with miraculous rainmaking powers, and a bas-relief marble Buddha from the eighth century. On the grassy grounds are a 19th-century bot filled with valuable bronzes, an elevated wood and lacquer library, and a 15th-century chedi supported by life-size elephants.

Two smaller monuments worth a quick stop are **Wat Duang Di** (*Phra Pok Klao Rd.*), for its baroque pediments, and the wihan at **Wat Pan Tao** (*Phra Pok Klao Rd.*), for its masterly Lanna woodcarving.

Next to Wat Pan Tao is the vast ruined chedi of **Wat Chedi**

Luang *(Phra Pok Klao Rd.)*, built in 1401 to a height of 299 feet (90 m) but reduced by half in an earthquake in 1545. Restoration work over the last few decades has reconstructed some of the structure and brought back the elephant buttresses and naga-lined staircase, but it looks like the restoration work will never be completed. Chiang Mai's **Lak Muang Shrine** is situated under the shade of an enormous gum tree on the grounds of the temple.

Chiang Mai's most famous building is the temple complex of **Wat Phra Sing,** or "monastery of the lion lord" *(Singharat Rd.)*. According to tradition, the site was established in 1345 to house the ashes of King Kham Fu and to mark the religious center of the Lanna Kingdom. The modern wihan at the entrance has little architectural significance, but the library next door is among the finest in the country, both for its brilliant stucco *devas* (heavenly beings) and for the flowery scrollwork around the foundation. You'll also find a Lanna-style bot constructed on an unusual perpendicular axis and a large whitewashed stupa on the grounds. **Wihan Kham** is a small chapel in the southwest corner. This striking building, which dates from 1811, is noted for its superb interior murals and its central Buddha statue, the powerful **Phra Buddha Sing.**

Two minor temples are worth a visit. **Wat Phapong** *(Singharat Rd.)*, beside Wat Phra Sing, has sensitively carved teakwood windows and doors, while the 17th-century Chinese-influenced **Wat Puak Hong** *(Samlan Rd.)* has traces of original stucco on its upper terraces.

Chiang Mai Museums

Chiang Mai's history and culture are reflected in a number of museums located throughout the city. At these places you will encounter both modest and exuberant displays. Traditional national museums, displays of contemporary art, exhibitions of hill-tribe life, and presentations of the more offbeat can be found.

Chiang Mai National Museum:

This small museum on the busy superhighway on
(continued on p. 220)

Monks dine at one of Chiang Mai's richly decorated monasteries.

A Walk Through the Heart of Chiang Mai

This walk avoids heavy traffic areas while giving you a chance to experience the different aspects of inner Chiang Mai, from the peace of the Chiang Mai First Church to the contrasting bustle of Worowat Market; the frantic pace of Tha Phae Road to the aura and quietude of the many temples along the way.

Wat Phra Sing was built in the 14th century as the religious center of the Lanna Kingdom.

Beginning at the **Chiang Mai First Church** on the eastern bank of the river, cross over the Nawarat Bridge, keeping to the northern (right-hand) side. As you reach the city side, turn right and continue along the pleasant, though usually fairly untidy riverside path, passing in front of the police station and onto the pedestrian bridge, 50 yards (45 m) upriver.

Cross over the bridge, descend to the left, and then turn right at the bottom of the steps into **Warowot Market ①.** Following this path from the bridge will take you past fresh seafood stalls, then across Wichayanon Road and through into the next section of the market, where fruit sellers have set up among the clothes, toys, and other stalls in a cheerful muddle. Feel free to wander deeper into the market on your own; provided you keep your bearings, it is easy enough to find

NOT TO BE MISSED:

Warowot Market • Wat Chedowan • Tha Phae Gate • Three Kings Monument • Wat Chedi Luang • Wat Phra Sing

your way back onto the main path.

Leave the main market building by the exit onto Kuangmane Road, and turn left. You may notice a Chinese influence here, and as you walk down Kuangmane Road you will come to the **Kuan U Shrine ②** on your right. This small Chinese temple opens at sunrise every day *(closes 5 p.m.)*, and it is worth a look to experience a change from more traditional Thai temples. Continue along Kuangmane Road, and turn right at the three-way intersection to come out at Tha Phae Road.

Busy Tha Phae Road is at the heart of Chiang Mai's commercial district. Along the road on the right side you will come to **Wat Saen Fang ❸**; be careful as you cross over Chang Moi Road, as the traffic switches over to the right side—look left first before you cross. Stay on Tha Phae Road. Farther down from Wat Saen Fang you will soon reach **Wat Chedowan ❹**. Wat Mahawan, across Tha Phae Road, is also worth seeing.

At the end of Tha Phae Road, you will find yourself in the more touristy Tha Phae Gate area. The walk continues through the rebuilt **Tha Phae Gate ❺**—you may want to climb to the top for a look, before crossing over Mun Muang Road to continue up Ratchadamnoen Road, directly opposite. After passing the American University Alumni (A.U.A.) building and Chiangmai Fellowship Church, leave the main road and turn right into Rachadamnoen Soi 5. Turn left at the red cobbled path (Mun Muang

Lane 5), then right at Ratcha Phakinai Road and left again at the traffic lights. Continue straight ahead until you arrive at the **Three Kings Monument ❻**, where Lanna kings worshiped.

Continue southward along Phra Pok Klao Road to reach **Wat Chedi Luang ❼** on the right, whose huge *chedi* is a long-term restoration project. Leave the temple by the back entrance so that you exit onto Jhaban Road. Walk just 30 yards (27 m) to your right, then turn left at the intersection, past the Chiang Mai Metropolitan Police Station and directly on to the last attraction of this walk, **Wat Phra Sing ❽**, Chiang Mai's most famous temple complex.

Ⓜ	Also see area map p. 213
►	Chiang Mai First Church
⊕	1.5 hours
⟷	2.5 miles (4 km)
►	Wat Phra Sing

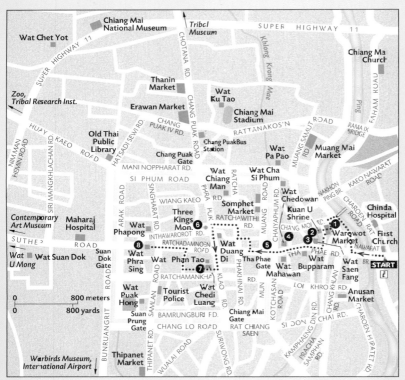

Chiang Mai National Museum

- ▲ Map p. 219
- ✉ Hwy. 11
- ☎ 053-408568
- 🕐 Closed Mon.–Tues.
- 💲 $

the town's outskirts is the main repository for the arts and crafts of Chiang Mai and northern Thailand. The Lanna-style concrete building was opened in 1973 by the King and Queen, and it was designed to be not only the guardian of regional arts but also an education center for both Thais and visitors.

The museum has been expanded to include displays on the natural and cultural history of

This terra-cotta statue is part of the Chiang Mai National Museum's fine collection.

the Lanna Kingdom, the trade and economy of recent centuries, and modern developments in banking, education, and public health. Among the more traditional themes, most of the classic Thai art movements are represented here, from early Mon sculpture

to Bangkok-era styles, with an emphasis on local Lanna art.

As with most museums in Thailand, the Chiang Mai National Museum chiefly features bronzes, sculptures, and early pottery on the ground floor, and handicrafts and household goods on the upper floor. A pair of 15th-century pottery kilns has been installed on the grounds.

Displays on the ground floor include Sangkhalok ceramics, pottery shards discovered near Kanchanaburi (see p. 124) just after World War II, an impressive collection of Chiang Saen images, and terra-cotta figurines from the Haripunchai and Srivijayan Empires. Perhaps the most striking item is a massive Buddha head, uncovered at Wat Chedi Luang, in Chiang Mai, which—to judge from its impressive dimensions—must have been part of an enormous image.

Displays on the second floor are more utilitarian, but they do an excellent job of portraying the lifestyles of the ordinary Thai. Along with a small room devoted exclusively to Burmese-Shan arts, there are intriguing (if simple) displays of betel-nut boxes, a richly carved ox cart, traditional coffin covers, a modest presentation on the hill tribes of northern Thailand, and some examples of royal regalia, including giant Dongson drums and elaborately carved beds.

Chiang Mai Contemporary Art Museum:

This historic city's most recent addition to its cultural scene is the concrete modern art museum on the grounds of Chiang Mai University. While the exterior belies the sensitivity of traditional Lanna architecture, the displays are quite impressive, as Chiang Mai is home to some of Thailand's most talented modern artists. Much of the artwork is created by local students, with contributions from local and international professional artists.

The museum also sponsors art education workshops in both Thai and English.

Warbirds Museum: Another recent addition to the local museums is the Warbirds—the collection of restored airplanes that occupies three hangars at Chiang Mai International Airport. The collection of primarily military aircraft is owned and operated by members of the Royal Thai Air Classics Association. Among the more interesting aircraft are a Douglas Dakota DC 3 and a Cessna Dragonfly A-37. Six Birddogs and T-28 Trojans make up the core of the collection.

The museum was the suggestion of Princess Chulabhorn's husband, who had admired an old Trojan, and had the derelict aircraft restored and reflown in 1991. In 1993, the association was registered as a foundation and placed under the royal patronage of the King.

Visitors register at the front gate, where they must leave some form of identification, and then tour the classic aircraft with an escort. It is best to bring a Thai-speaker or guide with you, as the military guards here speak little, if any, English. The best time to visit is around 9 a.m. on Tuesday and Friday, when the maintenance team tests the engines of several of the old airplanes.

Tribal Museum: In a beautiful location overlooking a lake, in the northern section of town, the small but fascinating Tribal Museum is a modern structure designed to resemble a Lanna-style chedi. With its displays on the major hill tribes of northern Thailand (see pp. 234–235), it is an excellent place to visit for research before participating in an organized trek.

Chiang Mai Contemporary Art Museum
- 🅜 Map p. 219
- ✉ Nim Man Hem in Rd.
- ☎ 053-944833
- 🕐 Closed Mon. & holidays

www.finearts.cmu.ac.th/cmu

Warbirds Museum
- 🅜 Map p. 219
- ✉ Opposite entrance to Chiang Mai International Airport
- ☎ 053-270222 to -33 or 053-203300 to -19
- 🕐 Closed Sat.–Sun.

Tribal Museum
- 🅜 Map p. 219
- ✉ Chang Puak Rd., Ratchamangka a Park
- ☎ 053-221933
- 🕐 Closed Sun.
- 💲 $

Wat Suan Dok

A significant site with ancient and modern relics is situated outside the old city walls, in the southwestern corner of Chiang Mai, along Suthep Road. Wat Suan Dok (tel 053-278304), the "monastery of the flowers," dates from 1383 and was constructed to honor a relic of Buddha—hair and a fragment of collarbone.

Today the largest building within the enclosure is a massive open-air wihan raised in 1932, housing a particularly fine collection of Buddhas, including the highly regarded 500-year-old Phra Chao Kao Tue. Dozens of gleaming white miniature chedis and cenotaphs adorn the neighboring garden—they entomb the remains of Chiang Mai nobles and important Buddhist leaders.

Traditional Thai massage is provided by old women in the large wihan, which was erected by the same Buddhist monk who inspired the construction of the hillside Wat Doi Suthep (see p. 226).

Chiang Mai Zoo

🅼 Map p. 219
✉ Huay Kaeo Rd.
☎ 053-221179
💲 $

The well-presented exhibits include a range of handicrafts, colorful costumes, textiles, musical instruments, and farming implements. English-language boards explain the histories and traditions of the area's major tribal groups.

The museum also has exhibits on the contributions of the king and his family concerning the health and welfare of the hill tribes, and research projects sponsored by various government and nongovernmental agencies.

Chiang Mai Zoo

Located on the western edge of town, at the base of the mountains, this is Thailand's second largest zoo. It has a reasonably good collection of local wildlife, including an abundance of monkeys and other creatures, such as crocodiles, miniature deer, and Asiatic elephants, always eager to pick up the occasional banana. The original ensemble of endangered animals was donated by a concerned Westerner,

EXPERIENCE: Shop Like a Thai

Contemporary Thai society may shop in modern shopping malls, but many rural and lower-middle-class Thais still shop at traditional markets. In most towns this includes fresh markets that sell foodstuffs from the wee hours, town markets that sell household items throughout the day, and all-inclusive night markets. The following are a few such markets, popular with locals but virtually unvisited by foreigners.

Dalat Tung Fa Bot: Southeast of Chiang Mai, about 20 minutes along route 108 to San Patong, this market occupies both sides of the road—so it's easy to spot. The market is a patchwork of makeshift tents where everything from plants to raw meat, clothes to Buddha amulets is for sale. Early in the morning, on the far northern end of the market is a cattle

and buffalo market, beside which are cockfights and the occasional "black magic" snake charmers.

Klong Toey Market *(corner of Narong & Rama IV Rds., Bangkok)*: Live chickens, whole eviscerated pigs, and squirming eels are a sampling of the sights (and smells) of this local market in one of Bangkok's poorest neighborhoods. Bring your camera and a strong stomach, as this is as "fresh" as most Thai markets come.

Lang Krasuang Market: Situated in Bangkok's Rattakosin, between the Royal Hotel and the Interior Ministry (the name literally means "behind the ministry"), this market is the Thai equivalent to a flea market, with secondhand items that include musical instruments, photography equipment, and other used or antique electronics, as well as other curios.

Those with a particular interest in the northern hill tribes may also enjoy a visit to the **Tribal Research Institute** *(Chiang Mai University, tel 053-210872, closed Sat.–Sun.)*. It has a modest display of hill-tribe culture, and a limited amount of research information is available in English.

and the Thai government has made efforts to expand the zoo in recent years. Zoo conditions may still appear substandard to some visitors, however.

Wat Chet Yot

Among all the religious structures in Chiang Mai, perhaps the most significant in regional terms is this oddly constructed, seven-spired chedi. Wat Chet Yot dates from 1455 and, according to local tradition, was modeled after the famous Mahabodhi temple in India. Its religious importance derives from a convention held here by King Tilok in 1477, which commemorated the 2,000th year of the Buddhist era. All of the wat's old gold ornamentation was stripped out during the following century by Burmese invaders, but 12 stucco figures of seated civinities—its main glory—have survived the ravages of time, making it an important stop for all visitors interested in the region's aristic heritage.

Wat Ku Tao

Although this peculiar 17th-century structure may not be the most elegant in Chiang Mai, it certainly wins awards for its unique five-orbed chedi, which combines Burmese and Chinese architectural elements to enshrine the remains of a Burmese leader who once ruled the province. The five-melon monument is in an odd location, just north of the White Elephant Gate, up a poorly marked alley, and close to the Chiang Mai stadium.

Wat U Mong

Thai monks have traditionally constructed their temples, monasteries, and religious retreats either in the city or out in the country to escape the distractions of urban life. One of Thailand's most famous forest monasteries is Wat U Mong, at the edge of Chiang Mai, and

Wat Ku Tao's *chedi* combines Burmese and Chinese architectural styles.

at the base of a magnificent mountain. Established about 1380, it is still an active retreat for Buddhist pilgrims.

This fascinating destination, rarely visited by foreigners, has a welcome hall with a map of the site and Buddhist literature. On the site are dozens of tiny wooden huts, inhabited by robed monks, and some much older caves carved into the mountainside, where the most ascetic of residents choose to make their homes. Meditation classes in English are given here by a team of Western monks. ∎

Wat Chet Yot
- Map p. 219
- Superhighway

Wat Ku Tao
- Map p. 219
- Chang Puak Rd.
- 053-211842

Wat U Mong
- Map p. 219
- Suthep Rd.
- 053-277248

EXPERIENCE: Thai Cooking

Thai cuisine is famous the world over for a reason: Its delectable balance of flavors, the freshest of ingredients, and its exquisite presentation combine to create unforgettable feasts. You can literally eat your way through Thailand, but why not pick up some practical skills, so you can re-create the experience back home? Thailand offers a plentitude of cooking schools, for both novice and professional chef.

Many cooking classes begin with a morning trip to the local market, where students learn about Thai ingredients. Most classes also provide a souvenir recipe book and apron. Some schools simply require students to mix prepre-pared ingredients and then sit down for a feast, while others require students to prepare dishes from scratch (including mashing the all-important chili paste with mortar and pestle).

Anantara Golden Triangle (229 Moo 1, Chiang Saen, tel 053-784084, www.goldentri angle.anantara.com) Anantara adds a pinch of historical flavor to its cooking classes. Following a market tour in Chiang Saen, guests are served a picnic breakfast within a centuries-old temple grounds surrounded by crumbling ruins. Back at the school, students measure ingredients by eye and pre-pare recipes in red clay pots, stirring with wooden spoons, rather than with shiny, modern cooking utensils.

Blue Elephant (233 S. Sathorn Rd, Bangkok Tel 022-659-9000, www.blueelephant. com) The cooking school is housed on the second floor of the stately Blue Elephant restaurant. After an informative market tour, students observe the instructor's preparation of each dish and sample her creations. Students then enter a modern, glass-enclosed kitchen to try their hand at preparing the meal. After completing four recipes, students are served their dishes in the elegant dining room. Morning and afternoon sessions are available, as are multiday and private, professional chef courses. Take home ingredients in designer packaging make excellent souvenirs and gifts.

Four Seasons (Mae Rim-Samoeng Old Rd., Chiang Mai, tel 053-298181, www.foursea sons.com/chiangmai/cooking_ school) Just up the hill from the resort's rice fields, cooking classes are conducted in a breezy, open-air kitchen. The market tour is optional, but the course itself should not be missed. A personable chef who enthusiastically explains how to alter dishes to suit different palates and how to tailor presentation for parties teaches morning and afternoon classes. Students create delectable creations from the hotel's menu, such as northern-style spicy salad, served in a dragon fruit.

Mandarin Oriental (48 Oriental Ave., Bangkok, tel 02-238-0265, www.mandarinori ental.com/hotel/510000001 .asp) Located in a charming wooden house across the river from the hotel, the Mandarin Oriental's cooking school is Bangkok's oldest one, and arguably its most well regarded. Morning-only classes do not include tour of the market, but instead offer a comprehensive discussion of Thai ingredients. Although the cooking stations are shared by groups of students, the instructors' demonstrations can be watched both directly and via an angled mirror that gives all students an overhead view of the chef's work station.

Samui Institute of Thai Culinary Arts (46/6 Moo 3, Chaweng Beach, Ko Samui, tel 077-413172, www.sitca. net) One-day, one-week, and comprehensive professional training courses are available at this professional culinary school. Make chili paste from scratch, a curry, and two other dishes, invite a friend to dine with you, and then relax at the beach. Multiday fruit and vegetable carving courses teach elaborate garnish-making skills; DVDs are for sale should you wish to continue your education.

Thai Farm Cooking School (203 Moo 5, Tambon

A bounty of different dishes create a typical Thai meal—the secrets of which can be learned at cooking schools throughout Thailand.

Muanglen, Chiang Mai, tel 081-288-5989., www. thaifarmcooking.com) A unique cooking experience from start to finish, Thai Farm begins with a cursory market tour, during which students select the five dishes they wish to prepare. A bumpy ride through the countryside leads to the organic farm, where ingredients are explained in greater detail, not to mention smelled and sampled. Next, students pound their own chili paste to taste, and then cook the recipes in an open-air kitchen. Unlike most schools, Thai Farm's instructor walks the group through the process step by step, and students even wash their own dishes.

Around Chiang Mai

As you would expect of one of Thailand's major tourist destinations, the area surrounding Chiang Mai is crowded with attractions, all easy to visit thanks to the city's excellent tourism infrastructure. You can choose from scenic, sometimes spectacular, drives into cool mountain areas, dozens of magnificent temples, and seemingly limitless shopping opportunities.

Gilded Wat Doi Suthep sits atop Doi Suthep mountain, promising fine aerial views of Chiang Mai.

Doi Suthep–Doi Pui National Park

 Map p. 213

Visitor Information

✉ Tourism Authority of Thailand, 105/1 Chiang Mai–Lamphun Rd., Chiang Mai

☎ 053-248604 or 053-248607

Doi Suthep–Doi Pui National Park

Several day trips are possible from Chiang Mai. The most popular leads 10 miles (16 km) northwest to a mountain named for a revered hermit who lived on the slopes and inspired the construction of the winding road up to the temple. Doi Suthep rises to a summit elevation of 5,497 feet (1,676 m), while the temple—the primary destination—clings to the mountainside

at 3,454 feet (1,053 m). Clean air and spectacular panoramic views are the big draws here, as well as a visit to the golden temple of **Wat Doi Suthep.**

The temple is reached via a monumental 304-step staircase, flanked by fantastical undulating *nagas.* Alternatively, you can make the trip via a restored tramway. Although the temple is modest by Thai standards, the site is highly venerated as it contains a sacred Buddha relic. The central stupa is the most dazzling structure in northern Thailand.

Many visitors simply make the climb up to the temple and then return to town, but Doi Suthep has several other interesting attractions, including the beautifully tended rose and orchid gardens on the grounds of the **Phuping Royal Palace,** 3 miles (5 km) beyond the temple (Doi Suthep Rd.).

Three miles (5 km) farther again is the turnoff down to the small, scruffy **Doi Pui** Hmong village. Although it is highly commercialized and mainly geared to tourists, lifestyles remain traditional; interesting attractions include a replica opium den and a small museum dedicated to the northern hill tribes (see pp. 234–235).

En route to Wat Doi Suthep is another modest attraction, **Monthathon Falls,** 8 miles (13 km) from Chiang Mai along a winding, unsealed road that leads to the foot of the falls.

Handicraft Villages

Chiang Mai is well known as the handicrafts center of Southeast Asia, rivaled only by the Indonesian island of Bali. It's a wonderful place to shop for a mind-boggling array of items, including fabulous woodcarvings, fine filigree and silverwork, glazed ceramics, top-quality Thai silks, and other crafts that have made this region so famous.

The best place to learn about these crafts—and empty your wallet—is along Highway 1006, between Chiang Mai and the silk-weaving village of **San Kamphaeng,** a 12-mile (18 km) stretch of road with more than 50 major shops and factories. Here you can watch the craftsperson at work, and then, with some sharp bargaining skills, purchase his or her products at excellent prices (or at least less than you would pay in Bangkok). Although this district is highly commercialized and tourist-oriented, it is unquestionably the best place to watch the creation of silk, learn about the skills required for pounding out silver bowls, witness ceramics creation, and watch young women paint splashy

INSIDER TIP:

Bo Sang is known for well-crafted paper umbrellas, hand-painted by artisans. Ignore hard-sell sales pitches; take your time and bargain for a good price.

—JOHN SEATON CALLAHAN
National Geographic contributor

flowers on bamboo umbrellas.

San Kamphaeng marks the end of the "handicraft highway." It's an excellent place to eat lunch and observe the local silk-weaving industry—and perhaps visit one of the large silk factories. A few miles before San Kamphaeng is the umbrella village of **Bo Sang,** so called because of its numerous umbrella makers. As well as thousands of painted umbrellas, shops here sell fans, straw handicrafts, silverware, bamboo and teak products, celadon, and lacquerware. Standards vary from tacky to excellent.

Several other villages near Chiang Mai produce handicrafts,

Mae Sa Valley

 Map p. 213

Visitor Information

 Tourism Authority of Thailand, 105/1 Chiang Mai–Lamphun Rd., Chiang Mai

 053-248604 or 053-248607

including **Muang Kung,** 6 miles (10 km) south of Chiang Mai. The small village—just off Highway 108—has a reputation for the quality of its pottery, especially the giant water jugs *(nam ton).* Take a walk around, and you will notice potters shaping clay with wheels under their stilted homes. At **Hang Dong,** 8 miles

elephants. Ban Tawai also has several large factories that churn out impressive imitation antiques, which have fooled many a shopper.

Mae Sa Valley

A wonderful day trip, easily arranged at your hotel, can be made to the Mae Sa Valley, 17 miles (27 km) north of Chiang

---

Traveling Like a Thai

Outside of Bangkok, taxis are rare and every region has its own forms of transportation. The most efficient way to travel, local transportation is the least expensive and the best way to get an authentic-Thai experience.

Three-wheeled *samlors* consist of bicycle-powered pedicabs, found almost exclusively near Chiang Mai's Warowot Market, or motorized *tuk-tuks.* Tuk-tuks range in styles different from the typical Bangkok variety: In Ayutthaya they look like beetles, with rounded nose cones and colorful, monotone paint. Issan-style "skylabs" are motorcycles with carriages attached to the back, while in Krabi mopeds have benches on covered sidecars.

More popular with locals are *songtaews,* literally "two rows," pickup trucks with benches on their covered flatbeds. Songtaews have established routes and

make pickups and drop-offs wherever passengers wish. Prices are fixed, but should be agreed upon beforehand. These are the best option for getting around Phuket, Chiang Mai, Samui, Sukhothai, and smaller towns.

Beaches and islands, particularly on the Andaman coast, have long-tail boats that can be hired as water taxis or for half- and full-day adventures. Even in Bangkok, local boats act as buses, ferrying passengers along the rivers and *khlongs* (canals). Bangkok's khlong boats are a speedy way to get from the historic old quarter (near the Golden Mount) to the Sukhumvit area during rush hour.

In Lampang, horse-drawn carriages still exist for sightseeing the town, but once were widely used. Today they are celebrated in an annual festival occurring each April.

Queen Sirikit Botanical Gardens

 Old Sameong Rd., Mae Sa Valley

 053-299753

 $

(13 km) down Highway 108 from Chiang Mai, wickerware and, to a lesser degree, woodcarvings are for sale in its many stores and stalls. **Ban Tawai** and a clutch of nearby villages are famed for their woodcarvings, which are exported worldwide. Here, hundreds of houses and shops carve, chip, and sand wood into an incredible range of products—everything from delicate spoons to near life-size

Mai, which features a number of attractions. A short way into the valley, you can learn about orchid cultivation at orchid farms. The biggest and most famous is the **Queen Sirikit Botanical Gardens,** which displays a variety of orchids and other flora common to northern Thailand. Several orchid farms have creatively added small butterfly enclosures, thereby attracting both the fauna and the flora crowds.

The Mae Sa Valley also has a small snake farm, with several shows scheduled daily. But the most popular stop is the **Mae Sa Elephant Camp,** situated in the middle of the beautiful valley, by a river and under the cool shade of a towering forest. Twice-daily shows take the elephants gently through their paces, with a display of training and bathing games in the river. The shows are followed by optional rides for the tourists. Elephants once hauled teak in Thailand, but now that logging has been sharply curtailed, tourism is the only form of employment left to them.

Shortly before the elephant camp, **Mae Sa Waterfall** tumbles down through the trees in eight steps, past a visitor center. The road continues through the valley in a counterclockwise direction to reconnect with Chiang Mai. This is a full day of driving through remote countryside, past more orchid gardens, a waterfall, a Meo tribal village, another village with a café and gas station, and a half dozen mid-range resorts chiefly geared to local travelers. Eventually, the road comes out at the back of **Doi Suthep** (see p. 226), joining Highway 108 near Hang Dong

Along the Chiang Mai–Lamphun Road

Several worthwhile attractions lie southeast of Chiang Mai on the road to Lamphun, the ancient Haripunchai capital. The old Chiang Mai–Lamphun Road is far more attractive than the trunk line, which provides faster access but misses most of the sights.

History enthusiasts may enjoy a visit to the diggings at **Wiang Kum Kam,** an ancient village 6 miles (10 km) outside of Chiang Mai. Founded by King Mengrai and long forgotten after centuries of neglect, the lost town has been excavated and partly restored, to reveal extensive building foundations and significant religious structures, including early stupas

and elegant Lanna-style chedis.

Just past the remains of the village is the **McKean Leper Institute,** established in 1908 by Presbyterian missionaries to treat what was then a fairly common disease. The grounds are spacious and magnificent trees soar over the small cottages where the patients

Mae Sa Elephant Camp
- ✉ Mae Sa Valley
- ☎ 053-206247 or 053-206248
- 💲 $$

The many organized tours out of Chiang Mai include river rafting.

Mae Sariang

Map p. 213

Visitor Information

Tourist Police Office, Singhanat Bamrung Rd., Mae Hong Son

053-612983 or 053-612982

live. Visitors are welcome to tour the patient facilities, the medical clinics, and the historic church on a small island in the Ping River.

To the Southwest

Travelers heading southwest from Chiang Mai to Doi Inthanon National Park or onward to Mae Sariang or Mae Hong Son can also make some interesting stops. Just past the town of **San Pa Tong,** 15 miles (24 km) south of Chiang Mai, is a collection of wooden pens where northern Thailand's largest cattle market is held every Saturday morning. This traditional event has expanded in recent years into a gigantic flea market, selling Japanese electronic goods and the latest Hollywood DVDs alongside the livestock.

The turnoff to Doi Inthanon National Park is marked by the small town of **Chom Thong**— 36 miles (58 km) south of Chiang

Mai—and its well-maintained and magnificent **Wat Phra That Si Chom Tong.** The gilded Burmese chedi was built in 1451 and its *bot* was built about 55 years later. The Burmese-style bot is one of the most beautiful in northern Thailand, with masterfully crafted woodcarvings along the eaves and inside the ceiling, which is supported by massive painted teak columns. The Lanna-style altar resembles a miniature *prasat.* Finely carved statues of Buddha rest in front of the altar. Antique Thai weaponry and more Buddha images are displayed in the room behind the altar.

Mae Sariang

One of the most popular driving routes from Chiang Mai heads southwest, past the turnoff for Doi Inthanon National Park, to the sleepy little town of Mae Sariang. It then turns north up to popular Mae Hong Son, before completing the loop by returning

Temperate fruits such as tomatoes can be grown in the north's cooler climes. Here, a family of Karen sell their crop.

to Chiang Mai via the lovely, rarely visited town of Pai. Most of this excursion passes through Mae Hong Son Province, one of the most mountainous regions in the country. This is also one of Thailand's most ethnically diverse districts, with a dozen major hill tribes scattered among the hills and mountains, notably the Karen, Hmong, Lisu, and Lahu.

INSIDER TIP:

Join a tour into the hills near Chiang Mai to visit hill tribes and obtain insight into traditional cultures [see information this page].

—SIMON WILLIAMS
The Nature Conservancy

Mae Sariang, 117 miles (188 km) southwest of Chiang Mai, is a typical one-horse town with a handful of guesthouses and small cafés, many of which face the scenic Yuam River. There is not a lot to see, but it is a pleasant base from which to explore the area.

A quick stroll around town reveals several noteworthy temples, mostly constructed in Burmese-Shan style. Among them, both **Wat Sri Bunruang** *(Mae Sariang Rd.)* and the adjacent **Wat Chong Sung** *(Mae Sariang Rd.)* are the work of Burmese laborers, who composed the majority population here before the influx of Thais arrived in the early 20th century.

Mae Sariang's best example of Burmese monastic architecture is at the sprawling **Wat Chong Kham** *(Wai Wueksa Rd.)* by the bridge. The

original wooden roof was replaced with tin several decades ago.

Mae Sariang is a departure point for hikes to the hill-tribe villages (see pp. 234–235). Treks are organized by guesthouses in town and chiefly head north to visit the villages around **Mae La Noi** and **Khun Yuam,** roughly midway to Mae Hong Son. This district also has several large waterfalls and is famed for its profusion of yellow sunflowers in the spring.

The town is also a base for river-rafting journeys down the nearby **Salween, Thanlwin,** and **Yuam Rivers.** Most excursions start with a dusty truck ride down to a nearby waterway, from where rafts and noisy long-tail boats head up and down the rivers, passing simple Myanmar (Burmese) villages, remote waterfalls, and logging camps with working elephants (despite the ban on logging imposed in 1989).

Mae Hong Son

A thriving commercial enclave tucked in the mountains near the Myanmar (Burma) border, Mae Hong Son has recently become a major tourist destination, largely due to a government-sponsored campaign to portray the area as Thailand's mystical, hidden Shangri-la. While the reality may not match the hype, Mae Hong Son, 230 miles (369 km) northwest of Chiang Mai, is an ideal center from which to explore the mountains and rivers, trek to hill-tribe villages, and visit waterfalls and caves. It's well supplied with guesthouses and hotels, cafés, and souvenir shops.

Mae Hong Son started as an

Mae Hong Son

 Map p. 213

Visitor Information

✉ Tourist Police Office, Singhanat Bamrung Rd., Mae Hong Son

☎ 053-612983 or 053-612982

elephant herding camp in 1831, and it wasn't until the completion of the tortuous road south from Chiang Mai in 1965 that either Thai or Western tourists made the long journey to this isolated spot. In fact, the village had long been a place of exile for disgraced government officials, who dubbed it the "Siberia of Thailand." Today, the city is jammed with backpackers, vacationers, travel agencies, and local entrepreneurs offering trekking and anything else they can dream up to part visitors from their cash.

Royal Handicrafts

In an effort to relieve poverty throughout the kingdom, Queen Sirikit created jobs by training people to make handicrafts— silk weaving, wicker and bamboo-furniture weaving, gold- and silverwork—that could be sold. Under her auspices, the Royal Folk Arts and Crafts Training Center at Mae Hong Son was established in 2005, a place for handicraft training and public exposure. Her efforts have resulted not only in helping people make a living, but in preserving age-old traditions that might have otherwise died.

Most of the attractions can easily be seen in a full day of walking, starting with the striking **Chong Kham Lake,** just two blocks off the main road. This placid lake was originally the elephants' bathing pool, but today is mostly the focus of a local fitness park, and a number of budget guesthouses now surround it.

On the far side of Chong Kham Lake stands a pair of striking temples constructed in classic Burmese style, with multitiered roofs, elaborate filigree woodwork on the facades and lintels, and gilded images of Burmese spirit gods. The 19th-century **Wat Chong Klang** is notable for its array of 35 *Jataka*-inspired wooden figures, which were carved in Burma and brought to Mae Hong Son in 1857. The images range from Buddhas to galloping horses. The temple just to the east is **Wat Chong Kham,** built by the Shan people about 200 years ago. This large monastery features a huge, 16-foot-high (5 m) seated Buddha, a tiered roof, and flamboyant woodwork.

Dramatic views over the valley can be enjoyed from the hilltop of **Doi Kong Mu,** at the western end of town, where two chedis were constructed in the mid-19th century to mark the town's admission into the Thai Kingdom. **Wat Doi Kong Mu** reveals its Burmese origins in its exterior construction and immaculately carved, white alabaster Buddha, which is placed on a gilded palanquin. The hike up the steps of the hill is exhausting, but the views over the misty valley in the morning are unforgettable.

It's well worth visiting the two temples at the base of Doi Kong Mu for their unusual construction and their highly venerated Buddhas. **Wat Moytu** is well known for its magnificent bronze Buddha and four highly stylized chedis that are covered from top to bottom with small chambers. These would once have held Buddhist amulets. Just a few steps down the road is

Wat Phra Nan, a 19th-century Burmese-style temple complex constructed by a Shan ruler to house a massive reclining Buddha. The statue is quite different from its Thai counterparts, with its realistic, heavily painted face. The temple also has a small museum, and a pair of fierce Burmese stone lions stand at the base of an old footpath leading up the mountain.

Across the road from Wat Phra Nan is **Wat Kham Khor,** another delightful treasure trove of Burmese religious architecture and curiosities. Usually missed by visitors, this fascinating, strange place has countless Shan-style Buddhas, old paintings badly in need of restoration, black-and-white photographs from the early days of Mae Hong Son, and a carved peacock throne that is thought to be over a hundred years old.

In the middle of Mae Hong Son, the collapsing, multiroofed wooden **Wat Hua Wiang** is important for its highly venerated brass Buddha, which was made in Burma and hauled here across the mountains in the 19th century. The nearby market is a good place to buy local produce, including the cigars known as cheroots.

Around Mae Hong Son

Trekking to the remote hill-tribe villages is particularly popular around Mae Hong Son. The local population is made up mainly of Shans, with other minority tribes including Karen, Lawa, Lahu, Lisu, and Meo. Most guesthouses, hotels, and tour agencies can arrange treks to these villages, which are far less commercialized than those near Chiang Mai and Chiang Rai.

Forested hills, rivers, and hill-tribe villagers make Mae Hong Son a popular trekking destination.

There are some commercialized attractions south of Mae Hong Son, including the **Pha Pang Hot Springs,** where visitors can bathe in the naturally hot water and eat at one of the small cafés. Several river-rafting companies operate from the resorts along the banks of the lazy **Pai River.** Two-hour trips are the standard, but longer odysseys are sometimes offered all the way to the Myanmar (Burma) border and beyond.

Most of the following destinations are off the main Mae Hong Son–Pai road and are best reached on an escorted tour or with private transportation such as a rented motorcycle or chartered mini-truck. The Shan village of **Na Soi** has been converted into a questionable tourist stop for the exploitation of Paduang women, whose necks are elongated by brass rings and who cheerfully pose for photographs after you've paid an admission fee. This barbaric practice had died out, *(continued on p. 236)*

Northern Hill Tribes

For many visitors, the highlight of a tour of Northern Thailand is trekking to spend time with the seminomadic hill tribes, the ethnic groups that inhabit the remote mountains. Hill-tribe trekking is well established in centers such as Chiang Mai.

Thailand's hill-tribe people, including the Akha, number between 500,000 and 800,000.

Called *chao khao*, or mountain people, by the lowland Thais, the tribes are not a homogenous group, but a series of separate cultural entities with distinct languages, religious beliefs, forms of dress, historical traditions, and even styles of architecture. Estimates of their total population vary—figures range from 500,000 to 800,000. The Thai government recognizes six major groups (Akha, Hmong, Karen, Lahu, Lisu, and Mien), while the Tribal Research Institute in Chiang Mai goes with ten, plus ten smaller subtribes.

Whatever term is attached to these people—hill tribes, mountain people, ethnic minorities—all are believed to have migrated south from Tibet, Myanmar (Burma), and China since the late 19th century, to escape famine, warfare, and the discrimination that has plagued these various groups since time immemorial. Despised by the lowland Thais, these displaced groups moved into the mountains of the north, living a nomadic existence of slash-and-burn farming and often supporting themselves through the cultivation of opium, a practice that has largely been eliminated since the early 1980s. Most are now agriculturists and settled in remote villages, still with remarkably little communication with the outside world.

Akha (Ekaw)

The Akha are distinguished by the dazzling costumes still worn by the women. Dark, long-sleeved jacket, skirt, and leggings are adorned with brilliant stitching and beadwork, with a sash of silver coins and a headdress of silver baubles and colored ribbon. Like most hill tribes, the Akha are animists who believe in the power of ghosts, nature, and departed ancestors, and so perform rituals, including the sacrifice of animals. Their relatively low level of education and refusal to integrate into Thai society have made them the poorest tribe, most discriminated against by the others.

Hmong (Meo)

The second largest group is the Hmong, who live largely around Chiang Mai and Tak Provinces and are often seen in the local night markets, selling their handicrafts, exquisite needlework, and tribal clothing. The women are notable for their bulky hairstyles, enhanced by hairpieces. Hmong, often seen on treks, divide themselves into the White and Blue subdivisions, based on the favored colors of their traditional costumes.

Karen (Yang or Kariang)

The largest hill tribe is the Karen, who are subdivided into smaller groups, including the Sgaw near Mae Hong Son, the Pwo south of Mae Sariang, and the Kayah in Myanmar.

Trekkers will probably notice the more obvious divisions based on the color of their clothing—White Karen, Black Karen, and Red Karen. The women are noted for their skillfully woven garments, the men for their tattoos. The Karen are a sophisticated group, which generally lives in the lowlands and practices crop rotation.

Lahu (Musser)

The Lahu are among the most assimilated of northern hill tribes, allowing them to move into the Thai mainstream and gain a degree of economic independence. A majority of these either animist or Christian peoples belong to the Black Lahu or Red Lahu linguistic groups, with a minority speaking variations on the Yellow Lahu dialect. Traditional costumes are black, with brilliant embroidery.

Lisu (Lisa)

The most prosperous hill tribe, as reflected by the conditions in their villages, is the Lisu, who are recognized for their business acumen and enterprising spirit. Their wealth is also evident in their beautiful clothing—blue skirts, red blouses, and turbans decorated with strands of beads and multicolored yarn, complemented by profuse silver decorations covering almost the entire neck and chest.

Mien (Yao)

The Mien closely follow their origins in their use of Chinese script, obedience to the Taoist religion, and creation of Chinese-inspired scrolls that function as portable icons (similar to Tibetan *tankas*). Mien women dress in bulbous black turbans, red boas, and richly embroidered baggy pants.

EXPERIENCE: Hill-Tribe Homestays

Supported by the Thai Tourism Authority, homestays—literally staying within the home of a Thai family—are encouraged to provide a balance of safety, comfort, and authentic experiences regarding village lifestyles, including participating in local activities and experiencing Thai hospitality. Here are some programs to consider:

Ban Muang Pon *(Mae Hong Son Province, tel 036-189-8812)* Nestled in the rugged northern peaks of Mae Hong Son, Ban Muang Pon has nearby hot springs, interesting temples, and community activities relating to hill-tribe life.

Ban Na Ta Pho Community Center *(Utaithanee Province, Issan, tel 081-971-0521)* Visitors can either stay with villagers in rudimentary Thai homes or in similar private houses, all of which rest on a sloping country hillside. Learn how villagers prepare and weave cotton cloth or practice agriculture, and watch traditional Thai boxing performances.

Homestay Bang Sai *(47 Moo 3, Bang Phli, Bang Sai, Ayutthaya, tel 081-684-3186)* Three rooms in Ayutthaya provide basic lodging (no hot water or air-conditioning) in a wood home beside the Chao Phraya river. Guests can give morning alms to monks, learn to make local handicrafts, cook Thai food on a fire-heated stove, or take leisurely bike or boat rides.

Koh Yao Homestay *(5/3 Kalankul Rd., Ko Yao Noi, Phangnga, tel 07-659-7423, www.kohyaotravel. com)* An eco-friendly, culturally sensitive homestay project initiated by local fishing villages on an island in Phangnga Bay to protect their way of life from encroaching tourism. Visitors learn about fishing, take boat trips to watch birds or net crabs, learn to make jewelry or tiger balm, and participate in other ecotourism activities.

Tham Lot National Park

 Map p. 213

$ $$

Visitor Information

✉ Tourism Authority of Thailand, 105/1 Chiang Mai–Lamphun Rd., Chiang Mai

☎ 053-248604 or 053-248607

but has now been revived for the tourist market.

Pha Sua Waterfalls provide a fine escape on a hot day but are at their best in the rainy season. Beyond the falls is the busy Hmong-Chinese village of **Mae Aw,** where opium production and trafficking were once the primary occupations. Caution should be exercised in this notoriously unstable region, which is just opposite the former army camp of opium king Khun Sa.

Tham Lot National Park

The stupendous caves of Tham Lot National Park attract an increasing number of visitors on the journey between Mae Hong Son and Pai. Most come to explore the park's most famous cave, Tham Lot, a breathtaking cavern wonderland of stalactites and stalagmites, originally cut by the Nam Lang River.

A labyrinth of auxiliary river canyons snakes off in all directions from the main chamber of Tham Lot, increasing the fascination of exploration. The intriguing journey through this cave is negotiated by boat—boatmen wait inside the cave—but with some wading involved. Guides are necessary for tours of Tham Lot and the dozen or so other caves in the park. You will find guides at the park's entrance, or they can be hired at nearby guesthouses or in the town of Soppong, 5 miles (8 km) away. Soppong is also where you arrange transportation to the caves.

The caves are also famous for the teakwood coffins discovered here, believed to have been carved thousands of years ago by Lawa tribespeople, who inhabited the region long before the arrival of the Thais. For many years, locals believed that the mysterious coffins had been carved by spirits who left behind these ungainly monuments, which seem to resemble rough dugout canoes. However, the spirit theory was thrown out after the archaeological work of American historian and archaeologist Chester Gorman, who excavated a small coffin cave near

Tham Nam Lang

With a professional guide, serious spelunkers can delve into the wonders of Tham Nam Lang, a 12-mile-long (19 km) cave in Tham Lot National Park that is one of the longest in Southeast Asia. Some years ago, four Australian spelunkers climbed down into the cave, which runs almost half a mile (1 km) below the surface, exploring chambers larger than football fields. They were lost in the subterranean darkness for several days but managed to retrace their steps to safety. Their experience should serve as a warning to all.

the Myanmar (Burma) border in the 1960s and found evidence of ancient human habitation.

Digging through layers of earth to the bedrock floor of the cave, Gorman discovered carbonized plant and animal remains, pottery shards, and stone tools. These were carbon-dated to show the slow evolution from basic hunting and gathering to the beginnings of agriculture, ceramics, and advanced stone production. What makes this spirit cave so important is the antiquity of the plant and seed remains, which were almost certainly cultivated. If Gorman's theories are correct, what is now northern Thailand may have been

INSIDER TIP:

Visit the downstream end of the Tham Lot cave just before sunset. Thousands of bats exit as the birds return for the night.

—PETER HOLMSHAW
CPA Media, Chiang Mai &
National Geographic contributor

home to the earliest agriculturalists in Asia, more than 10,000 years ago.

It is very exciting to be at Tham Lot at dusk: hundreds of thousands of Himalayan swiftlets swirl into the river cave's exit chamber to roost, while thousands of bats fly out for their night's hunting. Large bat-eating hawks soar above, hoping for a kill, while the sounds of the jungle mix with the incessant squeaks of the birds.

Another challenging cave is the **Spirit Well,** named for its shape and intimidating dimensions. Nearly 300 feet (91 m) across and more than 600 feet (182 m) deep, it is the largest known natural hole in Thailand.

Pai & Around

This unexciting little town is set in a stunning location in a broad valley flanked by green mountains. Pai is one of the best places in the country to escape the tourist crowds and relax with a most nothing to do—probably the three sweetest words to any traveler who has spent too much time rushing from temple to temple, trying to absorb all the culture and sights. The Thais are firm believers in the merits of *sanuk* (fun) and *mai pen rai* (never mind), and you'd be hard pressed to find a town that better exemplifies these traits than Pai, where you can unwind in a setting of extraordinary natural beauty.

Most visitors to this small town, almost midway between Mae Hong Son and Chiang Mai, spend their days sitting on the porch of their guesthouse contemplating nature or deciding where to try a bowl of spicy chicken soup that evening. Those with more motivation might wander over to the local market and inspect the chickens, or head down to the river and see if the fish are jumping.

Pai has just three streets and a few alleys to connect them. There's a bridge over the slow-flowing Pai River, as well as the necessary facilities such as a bus stop and post office, plus a handful of small travel agencies that can arrange local treks to hill-tribe villages and afternoon elephant rides.

A half-hour stroll west of town (*take Rajadamrung Rd. over the river and continue along the adjoining road*) is the modern **Wat Phra That Mae Yen,** situated on top of a hill, with fine views over the Pai Valley on a clear morning. Late sleepers can climb the 350-step staircase at dusk to enjoy a spectacular sunset over the distant mountains.

A welcome soak can be enjoyed in the evening at the **Tha**

EXPERIENCE: Elephants

Most domesticated Thai elephants perform shows at camps, carry trekkers through the jungle, or "beg" for bananas in Bangkok. These may provide interesting snapshots, but often do not give priority to the elephants' physical or mental well-being. The following organizations take the needs of the elephants into account, while providing educational or entertaining experiences.

Anantara Golden Triangle *(229 Moo 1, Chiang Saen, tel 053-784084, www.golden triangle.anantara.com/ Elephant-Camp)* Each morning, guests lead the elephants down to the river to bathe, ride them back to the camp, and then attend a one-hour training session, where they learn how to mount their elephants and steer them. After lunch and a visit to the baby elephant compound, guests ride their elephants through the jungle to the river for a swim. Timid guests can ride on a chair mounted on the elephants' backs and observe, rather than participate in, the river dip. Annual elephant polo events at the hotel (which guests may also participate in) raise funds to liberate more urban elephants.

Elephant Life Experience *(337 Wangsingkham Rd., Patan, Chiang Mai, tel 081-724-4211, www.elelife.com)* ELE is an intimate, luxurious experience. Arriving guests have tea and snacks in the spa-like open-air lobby. Catering to small, private groups, ELE allows guests to choose their experiences, from picnic lunches or candlelight dinners, during which guests watch the elephants relaxing or bathing in the river, to mahout training,

where they learn to ride and command elephants. Paint with the elephants to create a unique souvenir or take a bamboo raft down the Mae Tang River; these exclusive experiences are meant to be enjoyed at a leisurely pace.

Elephant Nature Park *(1 Ratmakka Soi 1, Chiang Mai, tel 053-208246 or 053-272855, www.elephant naturefoundation.org)* Elephant Nature Park turns the typical elephant experience on its head: People work for the elephants, rather than the other way around! No tricks or shows, just 30 formerly captive elephants given sanctuary on an expansive property where they roam freely, a luxury that few Thai elephants enjoy anymore. Visitors can either make day trips or volunteer for one to four weeks. Day-trip visitors watch documentary videos, feed the elephants, and bathe them in the river. Volunteers participate in a variety of activities, from planting corn to digging mud baths to mending fences. Volunteers also join occasional Jumbo Express field trips to hill-tribe villages or traditional elephant camps, where elephant-friendly practices are taught to camp operators.

Thai Elephant Conservation Center *(Km 28–29 Lampang-Chiang Mai Hwy., tel 054-228108, www. thailandelephant.org)* The government sanctioned TECC is Thailand's oldest center for elephant training, nursing, and conservation, founded in 1972 as a training facility for elephants engaged in logging. Since that time, it has undergone a series of name changes and simultaneously diversified its focus. In addition to an elephant hospital and mobile clinic, stables for the King's "white" elephants, and a rehabilitation/retirement home for aged or injured pachyderms, TECC has a number of different experiences. At the homestay/mahout training school, visitors live in rudimentary bungalows beside those of the mahouts and experience their lifestyle: fetching the elephant from the jungle, bathing it in the river, and getting it to obey voice commands. In the evening, guests dine on homemade food with the mahouts' families. Drop-in visitors can learn how elephant dung paper is made, watch bathing, and attend an elephant show, all a short distance from the informative visitor center. Shows consist of demonstrations of logging skills, elephant painting, and a musical performance.

Pai Hot Springs, in a pleasant park along the same road as Wat Phra That Mae Yen, and about 5 miles (8 km) southeast of Pai.

Around Pai: After a few days of relaxation, some visitors elect to explore the surrounding countryside. River rafting and trekking are the most popular activities; all the necessary arrangements can be made locally.

Hiking near Pai is delightful as the region is less "trekked out" than Chiang Mai and Chiang Rai. Without an airport to shuttle in visitors, the area remains a quieter trekking destination than even Mae Hong Son (see pp. 231–233).

Treks typically leave in the early morning and head north, with overnight stops in Shan, Black Lahu, and Lisu villages. Some treks include either a short rafting trip down the **Pai River** or two hours' ride on the back of an elephant. However, if such tourism does not appeal, it is easy enough to avoid any trek that includes these activities. Serious hiking enthusiasts can join a seven-day trek from Pai all the way down to Mae Hong Son, cutting through an interior district rarely seen by foreign visitors.

Rafting down the Pai River is perhaps the most popular diversion here, especially during the rainy months from July to December, when the river picks up some speed and produces some fairly exciting rapids. The rafting companies that operate from Pai are still in their early stages and generally use primitive bamboo contraptions rather than rubber boats. Unfortunately the bamboo sometimes disintegrates in the rapids, leaving

A ride from Pai's elephant camps provides an excellent opportunity to appreciate the area's spectacular landscape.

passengers floating down the river. Fortunately, a few companies are starting to use rubber rafts as it is becoming more difficult and expensive to find bamboo in the jungles of northern Thailand.

One of the best rafting adventures is a three-day excursion on rubber boats from Pai to Mae Hong Son, including stops at several waterfalls, caves, and a hot springs near the central camp, which is managed by the rafting company Thai Adventure Rafting *(tel 053-277178).* The trip passes through remote canyons and races at times down Class III rapids.

Several elephant camps are located around the town, offering rides through the jungle. The most popular operation is to the southeast of Pai, near the hot springs. ∎

Pai

🗺 Map p. 213

Visitor Information

✉ Tourism Authority of Thailand, 105/1 Chiang Mai– Lamphun Rd., Chiang Mai

☎ 053-248604 or 053-248607

North of Chiang Mai

Many visitors heading north from Chiang Mai take a bus or private taxi directly to Chiang Rai. The adventurous traveler, however, may favor the more exotic route to Tha Ton, followed by a riverboat trip down to Chiang Rai, or even a motorcycle journey through the heart of the Golden Triangle (see p. 244) to Chiang Rai via Mae Salong.

The Kok River winds past the town of Tha Ton.

Tham Chiang Dao

Chiang Dao is a small but active trading town, with the standard collection of shops and services. A narrow road leads west toward an immense limestone mountain called **Doi Chiang Dao,** at 7,500 feet (2,285 m) the third largest peak in the country. Tucked away at the mountain's base is Tham Chiang Dao, several caves that— while they may not compare with those at Tham Lot National Park (see pp. 236–237)—are worth a quick look if you have private transportation.

You enter the caves from the lower parking lot, which is itself of some interest for its massive tamarind tree, old Burmese-style *chedi*, and small pool filled with giant carp. A covered stairway leads to a series of caves filled with dozens of sacred Buddha statues, including several donated by Shan pilgrims who migrated from their home in Myanmar (Burma) to new residences in northern Thailand.

Tham Chiang Dao has two major caverns and several smaller openings, best explored with the guides—and their lanterns—who wait near the entrance. **Tham Num** features several impressive Buddhas Illuminated by floodlights and some natural sunlight, while **Tham Ma** is a completely darkened cave set with stalactites and stalagmites, imaginatively named after their odd shapes.

Tha Ton

The road north from Chiang Ma reaches Tha Ton at a bend in the **Kok River,** a medium-size body of slow-moving water that demarcates the southern boundary of the infamous Golden Triangle (see p. 244). Most travelers leave Chiang Mai in the morning, visit some of the natural attractions along the route, and overnight in Tha Ton, then depart the next morning for the river journey down the Kok to Chiang Rai.

Tha Ton is a very small, sleepy village set in a marvelous riverbank location, with soaring mountains to the north and west. Cafés and guesthouses are located on the road that faces the river, while more luxurious appointments are across the bridge on the northern bank of the river. Looming over the town from a northern hillside are an immense white Buddha on the grounds of **Wat Tha Ton** and another gigantic golden Buddha farther up the hill. It's a long and tiring hike to reach them, but you will be rewarded with wonderful

views over Tha Ton, the river, and the Golden Triangle.

It is possible to trek from here, without the need for a guide, to plenty of the lower elevation hill-tribe villages, though walkers should exercise some caution as this region remains popular with opium smugglers. Few travelers are bothered by the local entrepreneurs, but avoid asking too many questions or photographing heavily laden mini-trucks.

Kok River Journey

For more than 30 years, travelers have stopped off at Tha Ton to join tours on the large bamboo rafts that make their way north

INSIDER TIP:

Malee's guesthouse in Chiang Dao arranges hiking tours to the summit of Doi Chiang Dao. A long but rewarding day trip.

—PETER HOLMSHAW
CPA Medic, Chiang Mai &
National Geographic contributor

to Chiang Rai on the Kok River, past small settlements in a region once strongly associated with the Golden Triangle.

Commercialization has perhaps reduced the romance factor on this river experience—and noisy long-tails have largely replaced the old bamboo rafts—but this still remains one of the best little river trips in Thailand and certainly beats the mundane bus ride. One passenger boat

Malee's
Nature Lover's
Bungalows

✉ 144/2 Moo 5, A, Chiang Dao

☎ 053-456426 or 053-456508

www.maleenature
.com

**Hill-tribe
Education Center**
✉ 620 Thanalai Rd.
☎ 053-740088

leaves Tha Ton daily, but you can also charter boats for a reasonable price. Such boats give you more deck space and some flexibility when stopping at villages along the way.

Chiang Rai & Around

Established in 1262 by King Mengrai as the centerpiece of the first independent kingdom in the country, and heart of the Lanna Kingdom, Chiang Rai is one of the oldest cities in Thailand. Yet, after just 34 years of glory, Mengrai moved his capital south to Lamphun and then finally to Chiang Mai. Chiang Rai largely fell into disuse and was fought over by the Siamese and Burmese until 1786, when it was finally incorporated into the Siamese Kingdom.

Lying 112 miles (180 km) northeast of Chiang Mai, Chiang Rai

is a medium-size city with plentiful guesthouses, hotels, and cafés, nondescript urban architecture, and a handful of more interesting sights in the historic quarter on the banks of the Kok River. The town is reasonably compact and can be toured in a single day, perhaps before heading off for a trekking adventure (see opposite).

Most visitors start at **Wat Phra Kaeo** (*Trirat Rd.*), a locally venerated temple once home to the Emerald Buddha, now housed in the identically named temple in Bangkok (see pp. 69–73). A model of the sacred image formerly displayed here has been moved to its own **Ha Phra Kaeo** (Jewel Buddha Hall), but the distinguished old wooden *bot* is worth a close inspection. The structure dates from 1890 and displays a large early Lanna-style Buddha statue.

Several other minor temples are worth a look, including **Wat Phra Sing** (*Singhakhrai Rd.*), with its reproduction of the Phra Sing Buddha image from Chiang Mai; the seven-spired chedi at **Wat Chet Yot** (*Chet Yot Rd.*), and a modern hilltop temple called **Wat Doi Chom Thong** (*Winitchaikul Rd.*), which has particularly good views over the Kok River.

Probably more intriguing than these modest temples is the Population and Community Development Association (P.C.D.A.) **Hill-tribe Education Center,** where volunteers from a nongovernmental organization discuss political and economic conditions of the hill tribes. The center has an informative museum, a bookstore, and a small handicraft showroom selling tribal craftwork.

Betel Nuts

Betel nuts come from the areca palm, widely grown in Southeast Asia. A small piece of the areca palm's fruit is wrapped in a leaf of the betel pepper, along with lime, to cause salivation and release stimulating alkaloids. Cardamom or turmeric may be added for flavor and stimulation. Chewing betel nut produces a slight narcotic effect. Users carry their betel chew in boxes made of worked silver or brass, sometimes highly decorated. Antique betel-nut boxes are much prized collector's items.

Trekking Around Chiang
Rai: Most travelers use Chiang Rai as a base for visiting the hill-tribe villages in the vicinity (see pp. 234–235). Over 20 agencies and guesthouses provide escorted trekking, which takes place chiefly in the rolling hills around **Doi Tung, Mae Salong,** and **Chiang Khong,** near the Mekong River.

You can take a self-guided trek ing history. After their defeat in China by Mao Zedong's (1893–1976) Communists in 1949, members of the Chinese Nationalist Army—also called the Kuomintang (KMT)—isolated in Yunnan Province, headed across the border to Myanmar (Burma) and Thailand, many settling in Mae Salong. In the early 1950s the KMT received financial support and military equipment

Chiang Rai
Map p. 212

Visitor Information

Tourism Authority of Thailand, 448/16 Singhaklai Rd., Amphoe Muang, Chiang Rai

053-717433

A modern temple high up in Mae Salong provides spectacular views of forested mountains.

to hill-tribe villages with minimal planning, as the hills around here have been walked for years, and everyone in the area is familiar with independent trekkers. Route options include a river journey up the **Kok**—trekkers can follow well-marked paths from villages such as **Ban Ruammit.** Another option is to start from any of the popular hillside guesthouses west of **Mae Chan** or in Mae Salong.

Mae Salong: This remote village, about two hours northwest of Chiang Rai, has an intrigu-

from the CIA to stem the Communist threat. The group began taking over the Golden Triangle opium trade and by 1967 controlled 90 percent of the market in Thailand. A number of battles between rival groups loosened the KMT's control.

When opium warlord Khun Sa was driven into exile across the border into Myanmar in the 1980s, the town took on a new name, Santikhiree ("hill of peace") and a fresh identity.

Nowadays Mae Salong is no longer the lawless, opium-

The Golden Triangle, once famous as an opium-growing area, is now a major tourist destination.

Golden Triangle & Sop Ruak

🅰 Map p. 213

Visitor Information

✉ Tourism Authority of Thailand, 448/16 Singhaklai Rd., Chiang Rai

☎ 053-717433

smuggling capital of Thailand that it once was. But it still looks like a pretty bamboo village somewhere in China's Yunnan, and there is a Chinese feel to the place rather than anything remotely Thai.

Signs of Chinese influence include the continued use of the Mandarin language by many residents and architectural features such as Chinese talismans and yin-yang mirrors. Tea, cabbages, and herbal medicines have replaced the opium crops.

Golden Triangle & Sop Ruak

Describing the expanse of hills and mountains of north Thailand where it borders on Laos and Myanmar, the name Golden Tri-

angle conjures an air of mystery and excitement, long serving as a buzzword for spy novels, drug movies, and lurid magazine articles about opium warlords and renegade armies.

The Golden Triangle's traditional apex is a small village called Sop Ruak, but the actual area spreads over hundreds of miles, covering a vast region that for years was the world's center of the opium and heroin trade. Most of the opium cultivation has moved across the border into Myanmar (Burma) and Laos, where small-scale farmers continue to produce much of the world's illegal opiates, which are then smuggled down to Chiang Mai and Bangkok, and from there on to the West.

Unfortunately, recent growth in mass tourism has largely destroyed whatever aesthetic or romantic appeal Sop Ruak once possessed. Those lonely nights in some simple wooden hut, gazing out over the Triangle under a full moon, are but a distant memory. Luxury hotels are now the norm, and most visitors to Sop Ruak are brought here on tour buses, with just enough time to take a few photos and purchase a few trinkets from the local vendors. Fake hill-tribe children in snappy new costumes pose for the tourists, while the owners of the luxury accommodations desperately put out signs advertising huge discounts on their largely empty white-elephant hotels.

A stake was driven through the town's heart a few years ago when, just over the border in Myanmar, on the spit of land that marks the exact tip of the Golden Triangle, Thai investors opened a massive hotel and casino complex geared to Thai and Chinese gamblers.

After decades of romance and intrigue, the Golden Triangle's reputation should be laid to rest.

Mae Sai

The Golden Triangle as typified by Sop Ruak may rank low in the authenticity stakes, but several other places nearby are worth exploring, including Mae Sai, the northernmost town in Thailand. Mae Sai is a large commercial enclave with concrete hotels and modern shopping complexes, yet it has far more mystery and romance than Sop Ruak, thanks to its location at the bridge crossing to Myanmar (Burma).

Mae Sai's focal point is the **bridge,** which crosses the Sai River to the Burmese town of **Tachilek.** The bridge buzzes constantly with traffic and traders bearing the exotic products of Myanmar, such as antiques, fake jade Buddhas, marionettes, mouse-ear mushrooms, sweet orange wine, peacock tails, stuffed armadillos, and Mandalay cheroots. Some want to tell your fortune, others to provide foot reflexology treatments. Beggars plead for baht. Masses of Burmese move across into Thailand, while Thais and foreign visitors can cross with little difficulty into Myanmar. Foreigners, after leaving their passports at Burmese immigration, receive permits and can pass into Tachilek. This is a great place to spend some time, even if you don't make the crossing.

Doi Tung: Visitors with private transportation may enjoy a scenic drive along the winding road that leads from Mae Sai up into the mountains to the west. About midway between Mae Sai and Mae Chan, a road heads west to Doi Tung, passing several Shan, Akha, and Lahu villages before reaching the tenth-century monastery of **Wat Phra That Doi Tung,** restored in the early 20th century. The shrine, with its fat Chinese Buddha statue, is not overly impressive, but the 11-mile (18 km) drive from the main highway is an amazing journey, with wonderful views when visibility is good.

A short distance away from the monastery is **Doi Tung Royal Villa,** a summer palace constructed in 1988 for the King's mother. Up to her death in 1995, she was very active in reforesta-

INSIDER TIP:

For the ultimate elephant experience, try the *mahout* school at the Anantara hotel, which sits right on the Golden Triangle. You'll learn to pilot your own elephant.

—KRIS LEBOUTILLIER
National Geographic photographer

tion projects and in encouraging local hill-tribe farmers to raise alternative crops to opium. It was hoped that the presence of the royal family would move the opium fields back into Myanmar, away from the public (continued on p. 248)

Mae Sai
- Map p. 213

Visitor Information
- Tourism Authority of Thailand, 448/16 Singhaklai Rd., Chiang Rai
- ☎ 053-717433

Anantara Resort & Spa Golden Triangle
☒ See p. 375

Orchids

Thailand is a land of sensual beauty, personified by its most famous flower, the orchid. Thailand's orchid industry is dominated today by a handful of large corporations near Bangkok, such as the Bangkok Flower Center, and by the many smaller operations in the Mae Rim Valley, just north of Chiang Mai. These smaller farms are excellent places to see the cultivation process and pick up some sprays to take back home.

Cut at dawn, orchid flowers (such as these purple orchids) are on sale the next day in San Francisco, London, and Tokyo.

Orchid refers to any member of the family Orchidaceae from the order Orchidales, a range of flowering plants that includes up to 800 genera of orchids and at least 35,000 documented species. Along with the obviously erotic shapes of the flower, the word orchid also has a male sexual connotation, for it is derived from the Greek word *orchis*, for "testicle," after the shape of the root tubers of some species. Orchids in Thailand are incredibly resilient and can be found from sea level up to 3,300 feet (1,000 m). Some grow on the floors of rain forests hidden from the sun, while others thrive in the arid plateau of northeastern Thailand. They may sprout from the ground, attach themselves to trees, or even grow out of crevices in mountain rocks.

The export of refrigerated orchids started in the 1950s and now brings in more than $100 million annually, with the primary markets in Europe, Japan, and the United States. Despite the fact that orchids are abundant in tropical countries such as Thailand, the industry remained largely unexploited until the mid-1980s, when local horticulturists decided to challenge Singapore's dominance in this field. They soon discovered that the drier climate of Thailand was superior for orchid cultivation, and orchid farms boomed.

The major genus of the orchid family is the *Epidendrum*. These are mainly wild orchids with more than 1,000 species. The next largest genus is the *Dendrobium*, which can be found as far north as the Himalaya and as far south as Australia; this group contains 900 species. Most species in the strikingly colorful *Cattleya* genus are hybrids, ranging in hue from violet and yellow to cream colored. The species of the *Cymbidium* group—of which there are about 40—are prized for multiple blooms found on one stem and their longevity. The *Brassavola* genus flowers are generally white and fragrant, and feature heavily fringed lips on the edge of the blossom.

Choosing *Dendrobium*

Thai orchid growers concentrated on the production of *Dendrobium*, one of the few genus of orchids that can produce flowers within a single year and up to 30 orchid sprays within that time. (Most orchids produce only three sprays per year, leading to lower production and higher costs.) Another great advantage to *Dendrobium* sprays is their ability to live without water for up to a month, and the fact that the plants continue to blossom year-round. Within a decade, Thailand had become the largest exporter of tropical orchids in the world.

Orchids can last for several weeks with proper care and refrigeration, but the finest flowers are those cut in the early morning hours inside vast cultivation sheds, packed in cardboard boxes with moisturizing agents, and then trucked to the Bangkok International Airport at Don Muang for immediate export.

Adapting to Survive

To remain successful in the face of fierce competition from Japan and other countries, Thai orchid growers must not only run their export operations with military precision, but also be prepared to change their planting, cultivation, and export styles according to international trends. Throughout the 1990s, many of the more common orchid types declined in price as worldwide markets were flooded with an oversupply of classic favorites, such as the purple "Madame Pompadour" *Dendrobium*. Faced with falling prices,

cultivators shifted to more exotic species to maintain profit margins, including the *Mokkara*, *Alando*, *Vanda*, and *Cattleya* genera.

Orchid Cloning

Always seeking to maintain and perhaps improve profit margins in the highly competitive orchid industry, orchid farmers have recently moved into the world of controversial technology—the cloning of orchids into perfectly identical plantlets. Less complicated and headline grabbing than cloning sheep or dinosaurs, orchid cloning was quickly recognized as superior to seed reproduction, as it halved the time needed for maturation and ensured perfect production of disease-resistant plants. Cloning also provides the mechanism to produce exact replicas of the most attractive—and hence most profitable—species of the plants.

Knowledge gained in orchid cloning has spilled over into other important areas of cultivation, notably growing and exporting asparagus, decorative ferns, and exotic fruits. An industry that started with the exotic orchid has now expanded to include almost every fruit and vegetable in the kingdom.

EXPERIENCE: Orchids

Thailand showcases its abundance of orchids at the annual **Chiang Mai Flower Festival** *(first weekend in Feb.)*. If you miss the festival, opt to visit one of the orchid farms in the Mae Sai Valley, just 8 miles (13 km) north of Chiang Mai city.

The **Sai Nam Phung Orchid and Butterfly Garden** *(60-61 Moo 6, Mae Rime-Samoeng Rd., Chiang Mai, tel 053-297152, $)* is the area's largest orchid garden, home to some of the rarest orchid species. Nearby **Mae Rime Orchid and Butterfly Farm** *(tel 053-298801, $)* and **Suan Bua Mae Sa Orchid Farm** *(tel 053-298564, $)* offer further feasts for the eyes.

EXPERIENCE: Fortune-tellers

Mor doo, or "doctors who see," are taken more seriously in Thailand than are their counterparts in the West. Utilizing astrology, card reading, palmistry, and the features of the face, Thai fortune-tellers are consulted by a large percentage of Thais for advice on business, health, or love.

Many Thai marriages occur on the auspicious dates predicted by mor doo, and business ventures are launched or delayed depending on astrological readings. Even Wat Pho in Bangkok, Thailand's first university, taught astrology, and at nearby Wat Rachanada, they continue to do so.

You can find mor doo in nearly any city or village; ask a Thai friend if they know a good one. The most respected mor doo have of-fices, much as private prac-tice medical doctors do. Be sure to know the time of your birth for the most "accurate" predictions.

In **Chiang Mai,** temples and fortune-tellers scatter amid the shops and aging buildings in the back alleys between Tha Phae and Loi Kroh. At the **Ayutthaya** ruins, you'll find mor doo at Wat Phra Mahatha and Wat Yai Chi Mongkhon.

In **Bangkok,** Tha Phra Chan (the boat pier next to Thammasat University in Rattanakosin) hosts a concentration of mor doo, lined up in shops and on tables along its north-ernmost alleyway. The sidewalk along Sukhuvmit Road is a popular venue for late-night fortune-tellers, who specialize in using tarot cards.

Prices and quality are variable (a mor doo's quali-fications and experience are factors in their ability to divine accurately), as is English ability, though many speak well.

---

eye. Still, visitors are advised to keep to main roads and trek only with a local guide.

Chiang Saen

Chiang Saen is a quiet, charming little town in a pastoral setting on the banks of the Mekong River. Its attractions include in-triguing historic ruins. The town consists of a handful of almost deserted streets, with a few shops for essentials and s mple guesthouses that welcome a steady trickle of backpackers. It is a lovely place, overflowing with shady trees, with a relaxed atmosphere that is all toc rare in this bustling part of the world. Chiang Saen may lack major monuments, and the accom-modation scene is basic, but the peace and quiet make an ideal escape for the unhurried traveler.

The town dates from the tenth century, when local chieftains constructed a palace and a few temples. After a brief run, this set-tlement disappeared, and Chiang Saen lay abandoned until 1328, when a grandson of King Mengrai, named Saenphu, reestablished the city as a military post.

Saenphu hoped to prove himself a devout Buddhist by constructing a large number of temples, the remains of which bear witness to the former glory of this isolated town. Chiang Saen was later absorbed into the Lanna Kingdom, subsequently invaded and conquered by the Burmese in 1558, and then finally restored to Siamese control in 1804.

The **Chiang Saen National Museum** (*Chiang Saen Rd., closed Sun.–Mon.*) and the nearby tourist office are useful places to pick up maps and to get your bearings before you explore the ruins inside the ancient city walls.

Among the highlights of the museum are a small but excellent collection of elegant Lanna-period Buddhas and some demon heads and *garudas* discovered in the ruins of Wat Pa Sak (see below). The Lanna bronzes and a large stone Buddha head are also excellent examples of local craftsmanship. Utilitarian objects such as gongs and bronze kettledrums are

the town. The 190-foot (58 m) structure has partially collapsed, as has the nearby *wihan*, which houses a highly revered Buddha image. Despite its dilapidated condition, and the weeds that are eating their way up the walls, this is a monument of great power and grace.

The importance held by Chiang Saen before the rise of Chiang Mai and the Lanna Kingdom is demonstrated at **Wat Pa Sak** (*Chiang Saen Rd.*), outside the old walls. This is the city's oldest surviving structure, with a construction date estimated at 1295. Many of the Buddhas now displayed in the local museum and the National

Chiang Saen

✉ Map p. 213

Visitor Information

✉ Tourism Authority of Thailand, 448/16 Singhaklai Rd., Chiang Rai

☎ 053-717433

✉ Chiang Saen local tourist office, Hwy. 1016, Chiang Saen

Villagers along the Mekong River construct rafts from bamboo.

displayed in the back rooms, while collections on the second floor concentrate on lacquerware, works of rattan, and Lanna-era swords.

One of Chiang Saen's most impressive monuments is the immense octagonal chedi behind the museum, **Wat Chedi Luang** (*Chiang Saen Rd.*), built in 1331 by Saenphu and reconstructed shortly before the Burmese conquest of

Museum in Bangkok (see pp. 82–86) were discovered here, and the extremely rare stepped pyramidal design makes this monument particularly important in Thai history. All of the Buddhas that once occupied the wall niches have been removed or stolen, and some of the restoration work has been shoddy. Nevertheless, the remaining stuccowork on the upper levels remains remarkable in terms of its execution and sensitivity.

Two other monuments that predate the founding of Lanna-era Chiang Saen are located northwest of town, on a small hill overlooking the Mekong River. **Wat Phra That Cham Kitti** and the smaller **Wat Cham Chang** have lost most of their original statuary and stucco-work, but four remaining standing Buddhas are in excellent condition and make the trek worthwhile.

Back in town, near the banks of the river, stands **Wat Phra Khao Pan,** its four restored Buddhas standing in hollowed niches on the upper levels of the temple.

Several other minor monuments are worth visiting on foot or with a rented bicycle. **Wat Phra Buat,** the unusually shaped temple opposite Wat Chedi Luang, has

a gateway with a splendid stucco Buddha torso. **Wat Mung Muang** dates from the reign of the second Lanna king of Chiang Saen. **Wat Prachao Lanthong,** the "temple of a million golden weights," is now little more than an immense brick base that once supported a gigantic chedi. **Wat Sao Kien** is a scattered ruin, but it has a seated, completely headless Buddha.

Chiang Khong

Another sleepy town on the Mekong's south bank, Chiang Khong, is chiefly used by travelers as an exit point to Laos. The town actually comprises three villages strung together, which have maintained their individual monasteries as their commercial districts blended together.

Despite its remote location, Chiang Khong's economic base has expanded recently, owing to increased trade between the town and Huay Sai—chiefly agricultural goods and livestock imported from Laos, in exchange for consumer goods and luxury items from Thailand. Most trade is conducted in town on Soi 5 and at the larger pier of Tha Rua Bak, at the far north end of town.

For many years, Western visitors were confined to the Thai side of the border and could only gaze across the river into Laos, wondering about mysteries the landlocked country might hold. This situation has changed, and now travelers with a visa for Laos are permitted to take a small ferry across to **Huay Sai** and continue on into the country. Visas should be obtained in advance from the Lao Embassy in Bangkok, though guesthouses in

A hill-tribe villager carries produce to market.

Chiang Khong can quickly obtain them for a premium service fee.

Chiang Khong lacks much in the way of historical buildings, despite a long and somewhat remarkable history. The city began as a minor fiefdom in the early days of the eighth century and later played a subservient role to stronger empires in Chiang Rai and Chiang

original chedi once contained two hairs of the Buddha. A few blocks north is **Wat Phra Kaeo,** with lions guarding the entrance, *nagas* crawling up the wihan, and rickety wooden monks' quarters to the rear of the temple compound.

A far more interesting place to visit is the old **Kuomintang Cemetery,** where around 200 soldiers

Chiang Khong

✉ Map p. 213

Visitor Information

✉ Tourism
    Authority
    of Thailand,
    448/16
    Singhaklai Rd.,
    Chiang Rai

☎ 053-717433

Making Merit

Theravada Buddhists believe that one's actions in this life determine the outcome of the next. Merit is the collection of good deeds (karma) committed in one's lifetime, and can be earned through giving, meditating, and right thinking.

A common form of merit making *(tam bun)* is to give alms to monks. Arriving at a market or neighborhood near a Buddhist

temple between 6 a.m. and 7 a.m. with fruit or individually wrapped packages of food, you may present these to monks as they stop and open their alms bowls, making sure to maintain a respectful air while doing so. Monks are typically barefoot and it is respectful to remove your shoes. Women should be particularly careful not to hand things directly to monks.

Saen. After a period of decline, Chiang Khong joined the Lanna Kingdom and served as a major military stronghold, until it fell to Burmese forces three centuries later. Returned to Siamese control in 1880, it was then ceded to the French in 1893, as French colonial forces seized most of the left bank of the Mekong River in their creation of Indochina.

Chiang Khong is a town long on views but short on sights. Among the small number of minor attractions is **Wat Luang,** a classic Lanna-style temple complex in the center of town. Dating from the 13th century, the *wat* was reconstructed in 1881 after Chiang Khong returned to Thai control. Local folklore alleges that a stupa has existed on this site since the early eighth century and that the

of Chiang Kai-shek's (1888–1975) Chinese Nationalist Army (KMT) are laid to rest.

As KMT forces lost their battle against the Communist uprising of Mao Zedong in the southern Chinese province of Yunnan, thousands of soldiers fled south, finding refuge in Thailand. Most of the soldiers and their families elected to establish outposts in remote districts such as Mae Salong (see pp. 243–244) in the hills west of Chiang Rai, and here in Chiang Khong, where they served as a cultural and military buffer zone to hostile forces to the north.

Following the Chinese custom, the grave mounds and tombstones are elevated on a hill to ensure good feng shui and to provide eternal views in the direction of their homeland.

Phayao
✉ Map p. 213

Visitor Information
✉ Tourism
   Authority
   of Thailand,
   448/16
   Singhaklai Rd.,
   Chiang Rai
☎ 053-717433

Nan
☎ Map p. 213

Visitor Information
◪ Tourist
   Information
   Center, District
   Offices,
   Suriyaphong
   Rd., Nan
☎ 054-751029
   or 054-773047

Another peculiarity of Chiang Khong is the *pla buk* (great and powerful fish), a monstrous species of catfish, possibly the largest of its kind in the world and increasingly rare. At the south end of town, in the village of **Ban Hat Krai,** fishermen occasionally snag one of these "monsters of the Mekong," which is then sold to local cafés and served up as a highly prized delicacy—the flesh is white and tasty. The fish can grow to 8 feet and weigh 650 pounds (2.5 m/300 kg), but the record is held by a fisherman who pulled in a 6-foot, 480-pounder (1.8 m/218 kg).

Phayao

Phayao is a quiet, rarely visited town. Set in a wonderful location on the edge of an immense lake, it has a majestic view to the mountains on the far shore. Most visitors whiz past the town in a fast-moving bus, but Phayao is a pleasant place to pause, and it features several impressive temples down at the lakeside.

Phayao gains great benefit from its large freshwater **Lake Phayao,** which covers almost 15 square miles (39 sq km) and provides a wide range of fishing, sporting, and economic opportunities, including numerous fish farms that can easily be spotted from the municipal pier. Behind the placid lake looms **Doi Bussacarun,** a 6,088-foot-high (1,826 m) mountain that gives Phayao the air of a Swiss mountain village. Over the mountain range is the **Wang River Valley,** which continues south, down to the rivers and valleys of Chiang Mai.

The lakeside has been well developed, with a promenade, several popular seafood restaurants, a public park with fitness games, and a boat launch that rents paddleboats and larger craft for a day of leisure. The few visitors who stop in this town are likely to be approached by groups of friendly young Thai students, anxious to practice their English and show you around the modest collection of temples in the center of town.

Phayao's great religious attraction is **Wat Si Komkan,** about 2 miles (3 km) north of the city center on the banks of Lake Phayao. This is one of the most important religious sites in northern Thailand, as the central wihan holds a highly revered, 400-year-old Buddha called

INSIDER TIP:

Roses, orchids, and other flowers are ridiculously cheap at local flower markets. A few bundles can add an extra touch to any hotel room.

—BRAD SCRIBER
National Geographic magazine researcher

Phra Chao Ton Luang. This vast 52-foot (16 m) statue of brick and stucco is one of the biggest icons in Thailand and is worth the effort to reach, despite a poor-quality restoration job by local monks.

Striking a humorous note, the temple grounds have been converted into a wonderland of kitschy statues that are intended to provide life lessons to visiting pilgrims. Among the silly images are those of dinosaurs and the

Sukhothai-style Buddhas are a feature of the *wihan* in Nan's Wat Phumin.

title character from the movie *E.T.*, along with evildoers being tortured by devils to teach devotees that life is transitory and the ways of the flesh impermanent.

The modern wihan has exquisite murals painted by one of Thailand's most famous contemporary artists, Angkarn Kalyanaponsga.

Nan

This is an exquisitely remote and rarely visited town and province near the border with Laos, with enough rustic charm and character to keep some travelers happy for weeks. Some say it resembles the Chiang Mai of several decades ago, while others simply describe it as a world apart and would rather see the region kept a secret from visitors. The prosperous little town is surrounded by misty mountains and lush valleys filled with rice fields.

Nan today is a fairly modernized town, with a great deal of history preserved in its temples and other remains. The town was established in 1368 as an independent northern kingdom with close ties to Sukhothai (see pp. 195–199). After the demise of Sukhothai, Nan aligned itself with the Lanna Kingdom at Chiang Mai, with periods of control by the Burmese. In 1788 it was absorbed by the Chakri dynasty in Bangkok. Nan was allowed to remain a semi-autonomous kingdom until 1931, when it was integrated into the modern Thai nation.

Much of Nan's long and rich history can be navigated inside the confines of the **Nan National Museum** *(Phakwang Rd., closed Mon.–Tues.)*, in the center of town. The building itself is a renovated former palace, dating from 1903, and final home to the last two princes of a semi-independent Nan regency. Unlike many other regional museums in Thailand, this one has well-arranged exhibits, with explanations provided in both Thai and English. It has an outstanding collection of local ceramics, Buddhas, dioramas explaining provincial history, displays of northern Thai textiles (including contemporary examples from local hill tribes), and a highly revered black elephant tusk on the second floor. This magical talisman was brought to Nan some 300 years ago; it was the prized possession of the Nan rulers until they surrendered their authority to Bangkok.

Several venerable temples near the National Museum provide a historical context for the town, showing the wide variety of local architectural styles. **Wat Phra That Chang Kham** (Phakwang Rd.), across from the museum, dates from 1547. The primary wihan is supported by stucco elephants, in a manner similar to temples in Sukhothai, Si Satchanalai, and Kamphaeng Phet. The Buddha images here include a pure-gold statue 4.75 feet (145 cm) high, discovered by American archaeologist Alexander

Nine teakwood houses compose Phrae's Ban Prathup Chai.

Griswold in 1955, when a plaster covering broke away to reveal the treasure hidden inside.

The highlight of Nan is **Wat Phumin** (Phakwang Rd.), a national treasure that dates from 1596, with extensive restorations in the 19th and 20th centuries. The wihan is designed in a cruciform shape to accommodate the quartet of identical, gilded Sukhothai-style Buddhas, who sit back to back around a central column, facing the cardinal points. The interior is adorned with carved and painted pillars and coffered ceilings, but Wat Phumin's most famous attributes are its murals. Painted by unknown artists about 1893, the murals depict the *Jataka* tale of the Buddha's reincarnation as Khatta Kumara and scenes from life in Nan in the late 19th century. Enchanting portraits show local people hunting, fishing, planting rice, playing musical instruments, and riding elephants. Just as fascinating are the depictions of the Buddhist hell, comical portraits of Western visitors and French diplomats, starving holy men, Catholic priests, and a famous scene of a young tattooed man courting an elegantly dressed woman.

Several other temples in Nan are worth a quick visit. **Wat Praya Phu** (Suriyaphong Rd.) has a pair of rare Sukhothai-style walking Buddhas dated 1426. **Wat Suan Tan** (Mahayat Rd.) has a soaring Khmer-style *prang* (unusual in this region) and a 15th-century wihan.

Just outside town, the 1862 Thai-Lue **Wat Nong Bua** is known for its murals, believed to be by the same artists who worked at Wat Phumin. The Thai Lue are an ethnic group famed for their distinctive woven textiles.

Energetic visitors can climb the royal staircase, just southeast of town, to the top of Mount Phubhiang, to admire the 14th-century **Wat Phra That Chae Haeng.**

Phrae

The provincial capital of Phrae is

National Parks of the North

Northern Thailand's national parks are cool, mountainous retreats from the tropical heat at lower altitudes. The best are easily accessible from Chiang Mai, including the most renowned park, Doi Inthanon, located 36 miles (58 km) southwest of the city.

The park, on the road to Mae Sariang, was created to protect four of the Mae Ping's main tributaries and Thailand's highest mountain, a granite massif named after Chiang Mai's last ruling prince, which soars to 8,415 feet (2,565 m). Doi Inthanon offers vast evergreen montane forests, acres of spring wildflowers, impressive waterfalls, great views from the summit, and interesting wildlife.

Doi Inthanon is the only place in Thailand with notable montane forests thick with oaks, chestnuts, and magnolias—vegetation usually associated with temperate climates. The range of flora is extended by varieties that thrive in the fog-enshrouded mountain's cool, damp climate, such as epiphytes, lichens, mosses, and orchids.

This protected area is also rich in birdlife, including blue-winged minlas, red-headed trogons, and green-tailed sunbirds, which congregate at the summit in a sphagnum bog, the only one in Thailand. Naturalists and bird-lovers come in droves to observe nearly 400 bird species. The park is also home to the Assamese macaque, monkeys, and gibbons, plus endangered mammals such as the Szechuan burrowing shrew and Asiatic black bear.

Inside the entrance gate, near the base of the road to the summit, visitors first encounter **Mae Klang Falls,** then the spectacular **Vachiratarn Waterfall** on the Mae Klang River. The road winds up the mountain, following the Mae Klang River through deciduous and evergreen forests, to reach **Sriphum Falls** at the midway point. From here, the road continues past several Karen and Hmong villages, where the inhabitants operate an experimental farm, until it reaches the summit. About 3 miles (4 km) before the summit is Phra Mahathat Naphamethanidon, built to commemorate the King's 60th birthday. The two marble *chedis* feature terra-cotta reliefs. Views are spectacular.

Monks view Vachiratarn Waterfall.

Doi Suthep–Doi Pui National Park, covering some 100 square miles (261 sq km), is the pride of Chiang Mai. It includes two high mountains—Doi Pui and Doi Suthep—which rise majestically from the floor of Chiang Mai Valley to 5,527 feet and 5,497 feet (1,685 m and 1,676 m), respectively.

Ten miles (16 km) from the historic capital, Doi Pui is swathed with deciduous and evergreen trees, with semi-evergreen cover in the waterways at lower elevations. The park supports more than 2,000 species of flowering plants. Among the fauna are small mammals, some of the world's largest moths, and a profusion of exotic birds, including the audacious blue magpie.

The park is well organized—you can pick up a map at the headquarters (where you can stay in dormitories or bungalows); hikes include a challenging trail that leads past remote Hmong villages to Doi Pui's summit. A funicular railway leads to the *wat* atop Doi Suthep (see p. 226).

Phrae

 Map p. 213

Visitor Information

Tourism
Authority
of Thailand,
448/16
Singhaklai Rd.,
Chiang Rai

053-717433

Siamese Twins

The most famous Siamese twins, Chang and Eng, were born in 1811 on the outskirts of Bangkok. An opportunist British trader, Robert Hunter, took them to the United States in 1829. The twins earned a fortune making public appearances, then became farmers in North Carolina, married sisters, and fathered numerous children. The pair had very different personalities and fought constantly toward the end of their lives. Chang, a heavy drinker, died from a cerebral blood clot in January 1874. Eng, who was not ill, died a few hours later from what doctors determined to be panic.

a busy commercial town on the Yom River, long made prosperous from the exploitation of its natural resources, notably coal and timber. Although teak has largely disappeared, Phrae thrives on its rattan industry, as well as on the production of homespun blue farmers' shirts, worn all over Thailand as a symbol of the rural roots of most citizens.

Like most towns in central and northern Thailand, Phrae spent time under Burmese control and later welcomed large numbers of Burmese immigrants. Their influence is reflected in temples such as the early 20th-century **Wat Chom Sawan** (*Ban Mai Rd.*), with its multi-tiered roofs and ceilings gilded in Burmese designs. Laotian influence is seen at the 18th-century bot at

Wat Phra Bat (*Charoen Muang Rd.*), where the modern wihan contains the most important Buddha image in the province. Laotian design styles are also obvious at **Wat Phra Non** (*Wichairacha Rd.*), known for its reclining Buddha image.

For a change of pace, visit the **Ban Prathup Chai teakwood house** just west of the city center, where a wealthy merchant created one residence out of nine old houses. It lacks unity, but you will almost certainly never see so much teakwood in one place again.

A highlight is **Wat Phra That Chaw Hae** (*Chaw Hae Rd.*), a hilltop temple complex several miles east of Phrae. You can hike up the path past undulating nagas to visit an impressive chedi sheathed with gilded copper plates and often wrapped in heavy satin (*chaw hae*) by pilgrims. A smaller shrine holds the image of **Phra Chao Than Chai,** believed to grant wishes.

Phrae Muang Phi, 12 miles (18 km) from Phrae off a side road on Highway 101, just before the Kilometer 143 marker, is an eerie wonderland of rock pinnacles.

Lampang

The historic town of Lampang, distinctive for its Burmese-style temples, horse-drawn carriages, and nearby Wat Phra That Lampang Luang, is an easy day trip from Chiang Mai. It has grown dramatically in recent years and is now the second largest city in northern Thailand. Lampang was originally founded in the seventh century, and traces of its long heritage can be seen in the old city's core, near the Wang River.

The city owes its early prosperity to British merchants in the 19th century, who developed the district as the center of Thailand's teak industry. They employed thousands of Burmese workers, who left many of the temples and monasteries that still grace the old town.

Among the Burmese-style gems is **Wat Phra Kaeo Don Tao** (*Suchada Rd.*), in a residential neighborhood on the east bank of the Wang River. This is one of the finest examples of Burmese architecture in Thailand, as exempli-

Further significant temples in the Burmese style include **Wat Pa Fang** (*Prabhat Rd.*), known for its alabaster Mandalay-style Buddhas, and **Wat Si Rong Muang** (*Takranoi Rd.*), a Burmese monastery with a dazzling multicolored exterior of carved wood, home to sacred images presented by wealthy patrons. **Wat Chedi Sao** (*Khong Rd.*) is a simple temple in a peaceful location outside the city limits, with 20 whitewashed chedis crafted in a composite Burmese-Thai style.

Lampang

🗺 Map p. 213

Visitor Information

✉ Lampang Tourist Office, 2nd Floor, District Office Bldg. Rawp Riang Rd., Lampang

☎ 053-248604 or 053-248607 or 053-241466

Ban Sao Nak

✉ Phra Kaeo Rd., Lampang

☎ 054-227653

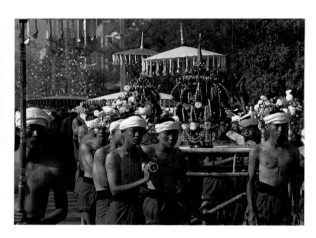

A procession carries Buddha images through the streets of Lampang during its Luang Wiang Lakon festival in February.

fied by its elaborately carved and ornamented *mondop* topped off by a nine-tier roof. In the same compound are several gilded wihans, a brightly painted Burmese-style reclining Buddha, and an extensive museum filled with local artifacts.

A few blocks south, also on the river's east bank, is **Ban Sao Nak,** a huge ancestral mansion of teak, known as the "many pillars house" for its 116 square teak supporting pillars. Furnished with Burmese and Thai antiques, it is now a museum.

Wat Phra That Lampang Luang:
Lampang's greatest claim to fame is this 11th-century walled temple complex, 16 miles (25 km) south of town in a region of hot dry plains and scattered rice fields. Wat Phra That Lampang Luang is considered a masterpiece of Thai art for its wealth of decoration and purity of architectural style.

Originally part of an eighth-century fortressed city, the temple as seen today dates from the

Lamphun

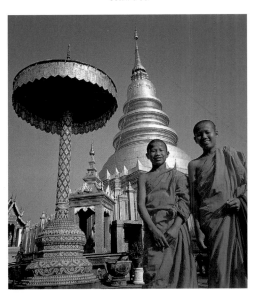 Map p. 213

Visitor Information

✉ Tourism
Authority of
Thailand, 105/1
Chiang Mai–
Lamphun Rd.,
Chiang Mai

☎ 053-248604
or 053-248607

15th–19th centuries. A staircase flanked by naga serpents leads to a striking 15th-century monumental gateway lavishly decorated with stuccowork and gilded in brilliant hues of gold. The centerpiece of the courtyard is the huge open-sided wihan, its pillars lacquered and inlaid with gold, its main Buddha image enclosed in a Lao-style gilded prang.

A vast chedi looms behind it, and the temple grounds include more structures of great artistic interest: the 16th-century **Wihan Nam Tam** is perhaps the oldest wooden building in Thailand, and the beautifully carved Lanna-style **Wihan Phra Phut** is a treasure house of priceless Lanna-era Buddhas. Several more chedis, bots, and wihans are set around the walled compound, along with a dusty old museum, and a huge *bodhi* tree.

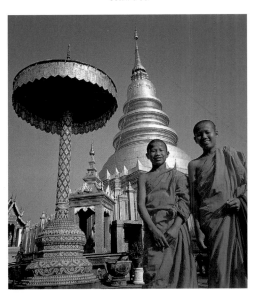

Lamphun's Wat Phra That Haripunchai, dating back to A.D. 897, contains a dazzling array of religious structures.

Lamphun

The ancient and almost deserted town of Lamphun lies 16 miles (26 km) south of Chiang Mai. The original capital of the Haripunchai Empire is a quiet river town of wood houses, with a handful of remarkable temples that predate the Lanna Kingdom.

Lamphun is believed to have been founded in the eighth century by a wandering monk, Suthep Reussi, who invited a Lop Buri princess named Chama Thewi to be its first queen. The town, initially called Haripunchai, formed the northernmost extremity of the old Dvaravati Kingdom of central Thailand. Within a few years, a moat, ramparts, and several Mon-inspired temples were built on the Kuang River. Over the next six centuries Haripunchai held sway over vast portions of northern Thailand in its role as an independent Dvaravati kingdom. The city fell to King Mengrai and his Lanna Kingdom in 1281 but revived the following century when it was transformed into the heart of Theravada Buddhism in northern Thailand.

Lamphun National Museum: Lamphun's rich history and the artistic traditions of Haripunchai are revealed in this small but well-organized museum in the center of town, just opposite Wat Phra That Haripunchai. Exhibits include examples of early Haripunchai stucco figurines and relics from the final rulers of Lamphun.

Wat Kukut: Lamphun's oldest monument, Wat Kukut (also known as Wat Chama Thewi, after the legendary queen), is the final surviving example in Thailand of original Dvaravati architecture. Quite unlike the style of Sukhothai or Ayutthaya temples, the pyramidal chedi dates from 1218 and is thought

Wat Phra Yun

Constructed as a forest monastery for local monks, this temple in Lamphun is notable for its Burmese-style square *chedi* built on the original site of a *mondop* dating back to 1370. Steps climb to a terrace framed by four smaller chedis. The larger chedi has four standing Buddha icons in alcoves. To get to the temple, head east first across the moat from Wat Phra That Haripunchai, then across Kuang River for half a mile (1 km).

to have been modeled after a similar structure in Polonarawa, Sri Lanka, or perhaps the Maha-bodhi temple in Bodgaya, India. No matter the design inspiration, Wat Kukut provides a direct link between the architecture of India and the Siamese mainland.

Wat Phra That Haripunchai:

This temple complex in the town center provides an intriguing range of religious structures. Siamese chronicles date the walled compound's founding to A.D. 897, when an early Mon king ordered its construction to house a sacred relic of the Buddha—believed to be either a fragment of the sage's skull

or a hair from his head. The complex has been expanded and renovated several times; it now consists of almost a dozen Burmese-style buildings.

The main feature of the spacious temple courtyard is a massive, bulbous chedi covered with gleaming copper plates. Older structures are believed to exist underneath, but the present monument dates from the early 20th century. The summit is capped with a solid gold, nine-tiered umbrella to signify the supremacy of the Buddhist order.

Many of the original Lanna- and Haripunchai-style Buddhas once mounted around the temple buildings are displayed inside the dusty but fascinating **temple museum,** in the complex's southwest corner. Hidden away in the northwest corner is a classic Mon-style chedi that closely resembles Wat Kukut with its stepped pyramidal outline and arched niches, which would once have held standing Buddhas. The 1925 wihan behind the golden chedi is an excellent example of modern temple architecture, with its gracious proportions, colorful interior murals, and well-crafted Lanna-style bronze Buddha image displayed on the central altar.

Several other minor structures add to the overall appeal, including the 19th-century library, which has been raised on a steep platform to prevent destruction of the manuscripts by ants and termites. There is a Burmese-style bell tower, a bronze gong purported to be the largest of its type in the world, and a modern bot with a pair of impressive bronze Buddhas. ■

Lamphun National Museum

✉ Inthayongyot Rd., opposite Wat Phra That Haripunchai

🕐 Closed Mon.–Tues.

💲 $

More Places to Visit in Northern Thailand

Mrabi Hill Tribe (Phi Thong Luang)

One of northern Thailand's most reclusive minority groups is the Mrabi tribe. These nomadic hunters, believed to number only in the hundreds, were discovered several decades ago and have since been heavily proselytized by United States missionaries. The Mrabi—also known as "spirits of the yellow leaves," after the pale color of their temporary leaf huts—can be visited on excursions from Phrae and Nan. Local tourist offices or your hotel will arrange a guide. Map p. 213

Nong Bua

A short ride north of Nan is a small village inhabited by migrants from Yunnan Province in southern China, known as Lue, who have maintained their traditions in weaving, domestic architecture, and religious shrines, as highlighted by their famous temple, **Wat Nong Bua.** The temple features lintels and carved porticoes of rare design, as well as murals that were probably painted by the artists of Wat Phumin (see p. 254). Traditional Thai-Lue handwoven fabrics are sold locally. Map p. 213

Pa Sang

This small town to the south of Lamphun is the center of the traditional cotton-weaving industry. The cotton, woven with distinctive designs, is made into clothing—mainly shirts and sarongs—which is sold along the town's main street. A guide can be arranged by your hotel or local tourist office. Map p. 213

Tobacco Kilns

The rich soil and climatic conditions of northern Thailand near the Mekong River make it an ideal environment for growing temperate vegetables such as cabbages and tomatoes, and also for the production and processing of Virginia tobacco, used in local cigarettes such as Krung Thep. Several large and unmistakable tobacco kilns and factories can be spotted near smaller towns such as Fang and Chiang Saen, and in the countryside near Phrae and Phayao. Although there are no organized tours of the factories, visitors are welcome to wander through the storage yards and inspect the primitive kilns. Arrange a guide through your accommodations or local tourist office.

Tobacco for Thailand's homegrown cigarette brands is dried in kilns such as these.

An enchanting realm of quiet beaches, lively resorts, secluded islands with psychedelic underwater worlds of coral, and mountains blanketed by tropical rain forests

Southern Thailand

Houseboats on Chieo Lan Reservoir

Southern Thailand

South of Bangkok, the country undulates between the Gulf of Thailand and the wild mountains of the Myanmar (Burma) frontier. In places barely 7.5 miles (12 km) of land separates the gulf from Myanmar. Farther south, the Isthmus of Kra marks the narrowest point between the Indian and Pacific Oceans. From there, Thailand widens—not by much—to form the Malay Peninsula, eventually exposing its east and west coasts.

Monks' robes drying at a *wat* in Ranong catch the early morning light.

Three centuries ago, when the southern Burmese port of Mergui was part of Siam, towns along this narrow strip of land enjoyed great importance. On the route between Ayutthaya and India, the eastern trade center was Prachuap Khiri Khan, where markets brimmed with perfumed woods, rare porcelain, and fine silks. Khmer dynasty temples prove that Phetchaburi once lay at the southern extremities of the mighty Khmer Empire. Farther south, people have found evidence showing that Chaiya was a significant city during the Srivijaya Empire (8th–13th centuries), which ruled much of what are today Indonesia, Malaysia, and southern Thailand.

Throughout the 19th and 20th centuries,

and up to the present day, the area enjoyed the patronage of Thai royalty. Kings and princes built magnificent palaces as retreats from the pressures of their regal duties. It was at the Royal Hua Hin Golf Course in 1932 that King Prajadhiphok (Rama VII) was informed he had been overthrown in a bloodless coup, ending the 165 years of absolute monarchy of the Chakri dynasty. The current monarch, King Bhumibol, vacations in the royal palace in Hua Hin, where he used to sail a dinghy he personally built. Three kings (Ramas V, VII, and IX) even made it to isolated Ko Phangan, in the Ko Samui archipelago, to carve their insignia on a rock beside Than Sadet Falls.

Foreign visitors rarely explore the first section of southern Thailand, the finger of land between Phetchaburi (about 100 miles / 160 km south of Bangkok) and Chumphon, yet it has a richness of attractions that belies its limited area. The string of low-key beach resorts and a surprisingly rugged and verdant interior are mainly the domain of Thai tourists. One exception is Hua Hin, now a nascent international resort steadily gaining in popularity.

At the appropriately named Chumphon (derived from the Thai *chumnumphon,* or meeting place), visitors are faced with a choice. They can follow the arterial Highway 4 as it cuts through the scenic mountains to Ranong and the beautiful—but hardly investigated—west coast and pristine islands. Or they can continue south along the east coast on Highway 401 to Surat Thani, the launching pad for journeys to the tropical splendor of the Ko Samui islands. ∎

Phetchaburi & Around

Thailand is well known for the variety of transliterations of its place-names into English, and Phetchaburi is an example of this at its quirky best. The town is known variously as Phetchaburi, Phetchburi, Petchburi, Petchaburi, Phetburi, and Petburi—certainly a record. But whatever you care to call it, Phetchaburi has a plethora of cultural, historical, and natural attractions.

King Mongkut built the Phra Nakhon Khiri palace in Petchaburi as a summer retreat in the mid-19th century.

Phetchaburi

 Map p. 263

Visitor Information

✉ Tourism Authority of Thailand, 500/51 Phetkasem Rd., Cha-am

☎ 032-471005 or 032-471006 (fax)

Like other locations on this thin neck of land, Phetchaburi won favor with Chakri dynasty kings in the late 19th and early 20th centuries as a royal hideaway. King Mongkut built the dominant symbol of this patronage in 1859, **Phra Nakhon Khiri.** Crowning the 302-foot (92 m) hill, Maha Samana, the grand complex— now a historical park—includes a temple (Wat Phra Kaeo), a *chedi*, and a neoclassical mansion. An observatory (you can climb the spiral staircase to the glass-domed roof) let King Mongkut, an avid astronomer, indulge in one of his favorite pastimes.

Other buildings, including throne halls, a theater, stables, and guardhouses, are all done in a jumble of architectural styles that blend together delightfully. The views over the town and lush landscape are outstanding. You can get to the palace by negotiating a strenuous cobblestone path and dodging gangs of rowdy monkeys, or by riding a cable car.

On the palace grounds, **Phra Nakhon Khiri National Museum** *(closed Mon.–Tues.)* houses memorabilia, bronze and brass sculptures, ceramics, and furnishings of royal households. The weeklong Phra Nakhon Khiri Fair, featuring a sound and light show at the palace, is held in early February.

Beyond Town

The vast main cavern at the cave complex of **Tham Khao Luang,** about 3 miles (5 km) north of town on Highway 3173, is dramatic. Shafts of light pour through sinkholes, bathing Buddha images, miniature chedis, and the magnificent arrangement of stalactites in an ethereal glow. Buddha images are placed there by pilgrims, including one from King Chulalongkorn, dedicated to his father, King Mongkut.

Tham Khao Yoi, 14 miles (22 km) north, off Highway 4, is another sensational fusion of nature and spirituality. Large caves are enshrined with Buddha images, and spectacular stalactites drop from vaulted ceilings. In the main cavern, soft light gently pours over an enormous reclining Buddha.

Thailand's biggest national park, **Kaeng Krachan,** is well worth the day trip from Phetchaburi. The park, 44 miles (70 km) southwest of town, encompasses 1,120 square miles (2,900 sq km) of wild and spectacular scenery as it runs to the Tenasserim Mountains, which separate Thailand from Myanmar (Burma). Dense rain forests, waterfalls, limestone peaks, and numerous caves, enlivened by screeching wildlife, offer good trekking. The huge Kaeng Krachan Dam has created a vast reservoir here, a popular stopover for migrating birds.

A few beaches intersperse the fishing villages along the 25-mile (40 km) route south from Phetchaburi along the coast road to **Cha-am,** but they lack the quality of beaches farther south. Few foreign visitors venture here, but the area is popular with Thai vacationers.

Faded **Hat Chao Samran,** 7.5 miles (12 km) north of Cha-am, was once a seaside resort for the Thai elite. Now it is passed over for nearby **Laem Luang Beach,** 4 miles (7 km) south.

Hat Puk Tian is a sandy strip of coast lined with casuarina trees. Locals flock here on the weekends, enjoying the water and the food that is dished up by swarms of vendors. Offshore a sizable statue of Phi Seua Samut, a watery female deity from the epic poem *Phra Aphaimani,* is an interesting aberration from an otherwise totally normal local beach scene.

INSIDER TIP:

Taste authentic cuisine and meet villagers in traditional costumes at the Song Dam festival held in April in tribal villages throughout Petchaburi's Khao Yoi district.

—SOLANGE HANDO
National Geographic writer

The long beach that fronts **Cha-am** is popular among Thais. The city fathers promote the resort as a quiet alternative to busy Hua Hin (see pp. 268–271). Cha-am's southern end has a number of luxury resorts; it is part of a green belt of quality golf courses stretching between the two towns. ∎

Phetchaburi Walk

A walking tour of Phetchaburi's temple complexes gives visitors an insight into the pervasive role that Buddhism played, and still plays, in everyday Thai life. It also provides a good introduction to the religious and historical importance of this charming town.

Inside the Ayutthaya-period Wat Ko Kaew Sutharam

Begin at the eastern end of Chomrut Bridge, in the northern part of the town, and walk away from the bridge along Pongsuriya Road. **Wat Yai Suwannaram ❶** is on the right. Built during the 17th century, this outstanding *wat* is best known for its large *bot*, with intricately carved wooden doors, octagonal pillars, murals featuring Hindu deities paying homage to Buddha, and flowing decorative art with vivid flora and fauna. The murals date from the end of the Ayutthaya period. The bot is surrounded by a cloister with gilded Buddha images. A splendidly ornate *hor trai,* or library, sits in the middle of a pond next to the bot.

Opposite Wat Yai Suwannaram are the neighboring **Wat Borom ❷** and **Wat Trailok ❸**. Both appear a little untidy and are overrun with dogs. (People dump their unwanted pets at temple complexes rather than have them

NOT TO BE MISSED:

Wat Yai Suwannaram • Wat Kamphaeng Laeng • Wat Ko Kaew Sutharam • Wat Mahathat

put down.) Long, fragile-looking wooden dormitories on stilts contrast with the heavy mortared, ornate Ayutthaya-period buildings in the center of the grounds.

Turn right off Pongsuriya Road and head south along Pokarong Road, opposite Wat Trailok. After about ten minutes, **Wat Kamphaeng Laeng 4**, Phetchaburi's oldest temple, appears behind some buildings on the right. The wat houses a 13th-century Khmer monument consisting of a central *prang* framed by three smaller prangs and a *gopura*. The prang nearest the wat entrance contains a Buddha footprint, while the central prang—once dedicated to Hindu deities—now holds a Buddha image. The other two prangs provide refuge for the numerous chickens that roam the grounds of the wat.

Walk west along Phra Song Road, fronting Wat Kamphaeng Laeng, and turn left at Matayawong Road. Walk south for about 15 minutes to the town's clock tower. Turn right just before a small bridge, and follow the road for a minute or so to **Wat Ko Kaew Sutharam 5**. The wat is difficult to see from the road, so look for the *sois* (side streets) Wat Ko Kaew I and Wat Ko Kaew II on the left.

Wat Ko Kaew Sutharam is one of Phetchaburi's best temples. The bot and its adjacent building are both fine timber buildings raised on stilts that were constructed during the Ayutthaya period. The bot has a pillared porch whose gables and pediments are decorated with stucco floral art and deity motifs. If the bot is locked, ask a monk to open it. Inside, some of Thailand's finest, oldest, and most originally conceived murals fill the walls. Dating to the mid-18th century, these murals are a delightful depiction of Phetchaburi life 300 years ago.

One of the walls shows foreigners converting to Buddhism, while another depicts a Jesuit priest in the robes of a Buddhist monk. Another superb mural is a sea of intricately connected scenes depicting Buddha's victory over evil.

Follow the road in front of Wat Ko Kaew Sutharam until it merges with Phanit Jeroen Road. Turn right and head north for ten minutes back to Phra Song Road, and turn left over the bridge. **Wat Mahathat 6** is easy to spot, with its huge, white, Ayutthaya-period prang rising from the middle of the temple grounds; you can climb it for some great views. Wat Mahathat is the town's most popular wat and buzzes with activity.

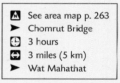

🅼	See area map p. 263
➤	Chomrut Bridge
🕒	3 hours
⬌	3 miles (5 km)
➤	Wat Mahathat

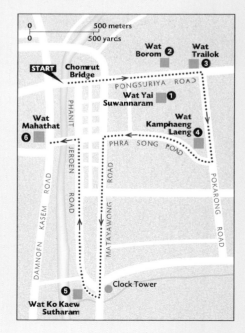

Hua Hin & Around

Thailand's first beach resort originally attracted the leisure class from Bangkok in the early 20th century. Its popularity among foreign visitors has been more incipient, but vacationers are drawn to the beach town for its amiable, wholesome atmosphere. With this salubrious feel, Hua Hin adds another dimension to Thailand's wonderful and varied beach resorts. Unfortunately, ill-conceived 1990s development has sucked some of the charm out of the town.

A royal seaside resort since 1926, Hua Hin has developed into one of Thailand's favorite beach getaways. The King makes his home here for most of the year.

Hua Hin

🅰 Map p. 263

Visitor information

✉ Hua Hin Municipal Office, corner of Phetkasem Rd. & Damnoen Kasem Rd., Hua Hin

☎ 032-511047

The resort has long enjoyed the favor of Thai royalty, which has contributed to its status and growth as a premier resort among Thais. The country's revered King Bhumibol now makes Hua Hin his home, returning to Bangkok only for special events. Partially as a mark of respect to the resident King, Hua Hin has avoided the excesses of other beach resorts. Although the number of tourists—mainly from Europe—has increased markedly

over the past few years, Hua Hin remains quiet and relaxing.

Yet city fathers need to be more judicious in town planning if Hua Hin's sanguine sobriquet, Queen of Tranquility, is not to end up a sad irony. Foreign visitors, a rare sight just a few years ago, are now well cared for with first-class facilities, including international brand hotels.

In 1910, Rama VI's brother, Prince Chulachakrabongse, visited Hua Hin on a hunting trip. The prince was so delighted with his success and the location that he built **Klai Kangwon** ("far from worries"), a palace at the northern end of town on Naret-damri Road, one street from the waterfront. It is still used by the royal family.

Rama VI followed him in the early 1920s. Also enamored with the surroundings, he ordered the construction of a beachfront summer palace in 1924. **Marek Khantayawan Palace,** the "palace of love and hope," was the king's idyllic royal retreat. The renovated palace is a harmonious collection of teak and marble buildings linked by elevated corridors that lead to *salas* on the beach, all rendered in elegant Thai-Victorian architecture. The center of the palace provided the royal family's living quarters. Further opulence is found in the throne room and theater. The palace, 9 miles (15 km) north of Hua Hin, is well worth a visit.

King Bhumibol maintains a palace in Hua Hin and occasionally visits to sail his dinghies, adding a century-old continuity to the resort's relationship with royalty.

Prompted by visiting royalty, a railway from Bangkok was completed in 1922. Two stations were built within a hundred yards of each other—one for royalty and one for commoners. The smaller **Royal Train Station** is a flamboyant

EXPERIENCE: Hit a Hole in One

Beautiful weather and a variety of courses contribute to Thailand's reputation as a top golfing destination. Reasonable prices and the relative ease of tee times are further reasons many visit Thailand specifically to golf. Here are some popular courses:

Alpine Golf Club (*99 Moo 9 Bangkhan–Sathaneevitayu Rd., Pathum Thani, tel 02-577-3333, www.alpine golfclub.com*) Built on reclaimed rice fields, Alpine uses the waterways that once irrigated them to create beautiful landscaping and a number of hazards, including two virtual island greens. A short drive from downtown Bangkok, it's conveniently located, but tee times are only available through select Thailand golf tour operators.

Royal Hua Hin (*Damnoen Kasem Rd., Hua Hin, tel*

032-512475, www .golfhuahin.com/royal huahin.htm) The first golf course in the kingdom is still one of the most popular. Founded in 1924, this par-72, international championship course spans 240 acres (97 ha) of forest and hillsides; it's a distance from the beach.

Santiburi Samui Country Club (*12/15 Moo 4, Baan Donsai, Ko Samui, tel 077-421700, www.santiburi .com*) One of the kingdom's most scenic—and trickiest—courses, Santiburi CC is situated on the rolling hills of Ko Samui.

Nearly every hole has a spectacular sea view, as well as a test or two, from blind drives to challenging greens.

Sheraton Grande Laguna Phuket (*10 Moo 4, Srisoonthorn Rd., Talang, Phuket, tel 076-324101, www.starwoodhotels.com*) Winner of "Thailand's leading golf resort" at the 2007 Annual World Travel Awards, the Sheraton Phuket is a beachside resort with a host of activities in addition to its spectacular 18-hole course featuring an island green.

Hua Hin Hills Vineyard

✉ 25 miles (40 km) from Hua Hin, at 204 Moo 9, Baan Khork Chang Patana, Nong Plup

☎ 081-701-8874

www.huahinhills vineyard.com

Thai-temple gem with a staggered, steeply pitched, four-cornered tiled roof, angled windows, timber slats, and carved timber poles and gables supporting the roof overhangs. The luxurious Eastern & Oriental Express train, which runs from Singapore to Bangkok and on to Chiang Mai, stops here.

A year after the railway line reached town, the **Sofitel Centara Grand Resort and Villa Hua Hin** (Damneon Kasem Rd., tel 032-

INSIDER TIP:

Hua Hin Hills Vineyard makes some very tasty white wines. The tour of the vines on an elephant (take a bottle along) will make the experience unforgettable.

—KRIS LEBOUTILLIER
National Geographic photographer

512021) was built, as Hua Hin's popularity was growing among the Thai elite. Once known as the Hua Hin Railway Hotel, renovations in 1986 returned it to its former colonial glory. With its breezy open-fronted lobby, leisurely rotating ceiling fans, forests of potted palms, timber paneling, shiny brass fittings, and imaginative gardens of animal topiary, it is now a trademark Southeast Asian colonial hotel. Before the lavish restoration, it was used as the setting for Phnom Penh's Hotel Le Phnom in the 1984 movie *The Killing Fields*.

Hua Hin still retains a little of its fishing village character. The fishing pier, **Tha Thiap Reua Pramong,**

along the town's north waterfront, livens up in the late afternoon and early evening, when fisherfolk return with their daily catch piled in plastic baskets. Judging by location, nearby restaurants should have the freshest seafood. As you might expect, Hua Hin has a plethora of seafood restaurants, from the upscale selections in four- and five-star hotels, to folding-table rudimentary on the beach, along the footpaths, and in the markets. Be aware that price does not always reflect freshness or quality.

Wedged between the Sofitel resort and Tha Thiap Reua Pramong is the main tourist area, with restaurants, cafés, and bars lining the maze of narrow streets. This is the oldest part of Hua Hin, and a large number of lovely teak buildings and houses (many renovated) have survived. The gentrification gives the area a degree of charm rarely found in entertainment and tourist districts in Thailand.

The Sofitel resort opens graciously to **Hua Hin Beach,** a wide, impressive stretch of white sand that runs south uninterrupted along the Gulf of Thailand for about 3 miles (5 km) before its rocky conclusion at Khao Takiap. Rounded boulders stick out from the shallows, while the water—although clean—has the cloudy appearance typical of the gulf coast.

An almost iconic feature of the beach are its horses, most of which are no bigger than ponies. They can be rented for gallops on the beach—an especially popular pursuit at sunset.

To the south, the beach edges onto a rocky bluff called **Khao Takiap,** or "chopsticks hill," because of its twin peaks. A golden 66-foot (20 m) Buddha image abuts the cliff face with appropriate prominence at **Wat Khao Lad.** Watch for the army of precocious monkeys roaming the temple's lower grounds; they like to steal eyeglasses and handbags. A staircase leads to the top of the *wat*, from where there are wide views of the coast and mountains, forest-shaded beaches, and high-rise resort development.

Khao Takiap frames the northern end of a slightly curving bay before meeting Khao Tao about 3 miles (5 km) south. In between are the resort beaches of **Hat Takiap, Hat Suan Son,** and **Hat Tao.** The turnoff to Khao Takiap is 2.5 miles (4 km) along the coast road south from Hua Hin, or you can walk along the beach.

Farther south, the road cuts in from the coast to Pran Buri. Head through forests to the busy fishing village of **Ban Pak Nam Pran,** which has secluded beaches nearby.

In 1932, Rama VII was playing golf at the **Royal Hua Hin Golf Course** *(tel 032-512475)* at the western edge of town when he was told he had been overthrown in a bloodless coup. The course was designed by Scottish railway engineer A. O. Robins in 1924, which accounts for its "British" layout. Yet this Anglo-centric feel is belied by views of hilltop *chedis* and monkeys that make off with golf balls at the fairway's jungle fringes.

Nowadays, golf courses are more refined. The **Springfields Royal Country Club of Cha-am,** was designed by top U.S. golfer Jack Nicklaus and is one of the finest golf resorts in Thailand.

Eight quality courses in Hua Hin and nearby Cha-am make this area one of Asia's premier golf destinations. Fees are reasonable, and you can rent clubs and golf carts. Caddies are provided, and tips are expected. Because of the debilitating tropical heat, the courses all have plenty of refreshment stops. Hua Hin Golf Tours *(tel 032-530479)* can help with suggestions and arrangements.

About 18 miles (29 km) west of Hua Hin, near the village of **Ban Nong Phlab,** interesting caves are found hidden in the forests that carpet the mountains of Hua Hin's scenic backdrop. Dao, Lablae, and Kailon are caves a few miles apart, near the village of Ban Nong Phlab. They are notable for their profusion of unusually wide, snell-shaped stalactites and contorted stalagmites. The best way to get to the caves is with a half-day tour, booked at your hotel. ■

Springfield's Royal Country Club of Cha-am

✉ 193 Huay-Sai Nua, Petchkasem Rd., Cha-am

☎ 032-471324

In addition to meditation and learning, a monk's duties include the maintenance of the temple grounds.

Khao Sam Roi Yot National Park

Khao Sam Roi Yot ("mountain of three hundred peaks") was Thailand's first coastal national park. Its 38 square miles (98 sq km) of land and small offshore area were mapped in 1966. Steep limestone hills harbor deep caves, above coastal marshes, lagoons, and secluded beaches. Inland, wooded valleys give way to precipitous cliffs, and extensive marshland shelters rich bird life. The visitor center at Ban Khao Daeng (off Highway 4) has information on all the sites below.

Extensive wetlands and 300 species of birds make Khao Sam Roi Yot National Park a popular bird-watching area.

Khao Sam Roi Yot National Park

🔺 Map p. 263

A royal pavilion, bathed in streams of light from sinkholes (best viewed at 10:30 a.m.), was built in one of the magnificent caverns at **Tham Phraya Nakhon** in 1890, in honor of a visit by King Chulalongkorn. In 1868 King Mongkut had visited, along with a huge entourage of Thai and European dignitaries, to observe a total solar eclipse that he had predicted.

The cave sits high above **Laem Sala Beach,** a deep circular cove hemmed by bare limestone hills

on three sides, with bungalows and a restaurant shaded by groves of casuarina (Australian pine) trees. A boat brings visitors from the nearby village of Ban Bang Pu for a few dollars, or walkers can take the steep cliff trail, with views of a chain of limestone bluffs rising at the sea's edge and scrolling along the coast. From the beach, a well-maintained trail leads up to the cave and takes about 20 minutes.

A couple more caves here are worth exploring. At **Tham Kaeo,** about a mile from Ban Bang Pu, you climb down a ladder to chambers connected to passageways, passing giant limestone formations, including spectacular petrified waterfalls. Many of the formations are encrusted with calcite crystals, and glitter in the dull light.

To get to **Sai Cave,** take a 1.5-mile (2.5 km) trail from the coastal hamlet of Ban Khung Tanot to the start of the hike. The trail climbs 920 feet (276 m) up a hillside to the mouth of the cavern, which has all sorts of weird rock formations and unusually shaped stalactites and stalagmites. Ask for a guide at park headquarters.

Ban Khung Tanot overlooks **Sam Phraya Beach,** with its wide, long sands and fringe of trees along the base of a string of hills.

INSIDER TIP:

Hire a guide if you plan to see the holy Phraya Nakhon cave at Khao Sam Roi Yot; it's jungle and you never know what you might meet.

—SOLANGE HANDO
National Geographic writer

At Ban Khao Daeng, **Khlong Daeng** winds past mangrove swamps rich with bird life. Monkeys hide in the tangles of branches, and the occasional monitor lizard can be seen basking on the muddy banks. Hire boats for the 90-minute canal trip in the early morning or late afternoon, when wildlife is more active.

A steep, rocky climb starting near the park headquarters leads to the 523-foot (157 m) summit of **Khao Daeng.** From here, there are dramatic mountain vistas.

The 12,350 acres (5,000 ha) of freshwater marshes at **Rong Yai Marsh,** combined with an abundance of tidal marshland, offer one of the largest wetlands in Southeast Asia for migratory birds making their way along the Asia-Australia flyway. About 300 species have been identified, of which about 180 are migratory. Thousands of bird-watchers visit the park during the peak viewing time between September and November.

Shrimp farmers have encroached on the park and, at one stage, threatened to destroy the wetlands. Belated action by the authorities finally abated this menacing advance (see p. 151).

Visitors can pick up a bird-watching guide at park headquarters. You can also take boat rides with rangers through the marshes and get closer views of the limestone cliffs. Rong Yai Marsh is reached from Highway 4, near the town of Ban Rai Mai. Cross the railway tracks into the park, and drive on for about 4 miles (7 km) ∎

National Parks Division

✉ Royal Forestry Department, 61 Phahonyothin Rd., Bangkhen, Bangkok
☎ 02-562-0750
www.dnt.go.th

Visitor Information

✉ Tourism Authority of Thailand, 500/51 Phetkasem Rd., Cha-am
☎ 032-471005 or 032-471006 (fax)

EXPERIENCE: Bird-watching

The diversity of Thailand's natural terrain consists of various forests, including bamboo, pine, and mangrove, all of which are home to a wide array of native and migrant birds.

More than 900 species of bird have been seen in Thailand, with Khao Sam Roi Yot, Chiang Mai, Krabi, Phuket, Khao Sok, and Khao Luang being popular spots. Here are two organizations offering birding tours:

Nature and Bird Site Exploration Co. *(Baan Tha Khao, Ko Yao Noi, Phangnga, tel 089-868-8639,*

www.thailandbird watching. com) Birding day trips take in the mountains around Chiang Mai, Krabi's mangrove forests, and Phuket's forests and marshlands. Customized, multiday excursions include trips to Khao Sok, Khao Luang National Park, and the lakes of Thale Noi-Patthalung and Thale Ban. Overnight adventures are also offered.

Thailand Birding *(9/71 Moo 3 Thanon Rasdanusorn, Ban Kuku, Phuket, tel 076-240952, www.thailandbird ing.com)* Kayaking tours visit Khao Sok, home to six species of hornbill, and Phangnga Bay. Tours are led by Thai and American guides. Overnight trips include stays in basic, floating bamboo or beach bungalows.

Prachuap Khiri Khan

This peaceful town is viewed with passing interest rather than as a place to explore. Its location, on the slender neck of land attaching Bangkok and the central plains to the Malay Peninsula, has a lot to do with it; tourists tend to ignore Prachuap as they dash along arterial Highway 4. But Prachuap is a relaxing fishing town at the edge of a curving bay on the Gulf of Thailand.

A fishing boat at anchor in Prachuap Khiri Khan's attractive bay. The town is famed for its seafood.

Prachuap Khiri Khan

 Map p. 263

Visitor Information

✉ Tourism Authority of Thailand, 500/51 Phetkasem Rd., Cha-am

☎ 032-471005

Buttressing the bay's northern end is **Khao Chong Gra Jok** ("mirror tunnel mountain"), a limestone cliff named for an arch worn through its side that appears to reflect the sky. From its base, stairs climb to sweeping views. The cliff is crowned by a small temple, **Wat Thammikaram,** surrounded by fragrant frangipani trees and inhabited by pickpocketing macaques.

The shores below buzz with the activity of fishing boats. Prachuap Khiri Khan is famous for its seafood; a meal at one of the two night markets *(by the seawall on Cha Thelah Rd., next to the municipal offices in the town's center)* is a lively, tasty way to while away an evening.

Prachuap's best beaches are found along the scenic road that runs past the rocky headland of Khao Mong Lai, which frames the southern end of the bay. **Ao Manao,** a lovely white-sand bay 3 miles (5 km) from town, is fringed where invading Japanese troops landed in 1941. At **Hat Wa Ko,** 5.5 miles (9 km) farther south, there is another fine beach with a museum and monument paying tribute to King Mongkut, who predicted a full solar eclipse in the area in 1868.

About 5 miles (8 km) north of Prachuap, on the road that rings Khao Chong Gra Jok, is Ban Ao Noi. Follow the path from the small town's hillside temple to a limestone peak and the temple cave **Tham Khao Khan Kradai** to view the impressive 53-foot (16 m) reclining Buddha. ∎

Chumphon & Beyond

The town of Chumphon sits on the eastern side of the Isthmus of Kra. From here, the major route south divides, with Highway 4 slicing through the mountains of the Malay Peninsula to Ranong and the Andaman coast, while Highway 41 skirts the Gulf of Thailand to Surat Thani and beyond. A string of good beaches lines the coast, with coral-fringed islands offshore.

Forty limestone islands off Chumphon's coast have recently been incorporated into the **Mu Ko Chumphon Marine National Park.** The diving here is excellent but not yet fully explored. About 7.5 miles (12 km) north of town, **Thung Wua Laen Beach** is set in a picturesque bay, backed by forested mountains. Here, dive trips can be organized through Chumpon Cabana Resort (tel 077-550245 to -47) to the outlying islands of the archipelago.

The colorful reef at **Ko Ngam Yai,** about 75 minutes by boat from Thung Wua Laen, sits just 6 feet (1.8 m) beneath the surface in some places, making it ideal for snorkeling. Good snorkeling can also be found off the northern point of nearby **Ko Ngam Noi,** but the island itself, an accumulation of impossibly balanced boulders and precarious bamboo dwellings, is off-limits. The dwellings belong to gatherers of swiftlets' nests, part of a lucrative bird's-nest concession. An undersea ledge at **Ko Lak Ngam,** south of Ko Ngam Noi, has platform gardens of sea anemones leading to a wall clustered with clams, oysters, and multicolored sponges.

About 17 miles (28 km) southeast of Chumphon on Highway 4001, you pass several stretches of sand and sea before reaching **Hat Sai Ri,** where a torpedo boat

War Blessings

An enemy target since Ayutthaya days, this area has long been a popular prewar congregation point for armies to pray for victory. Hence the town's original name: Chum Num Phon ("chum" means "to assemble, "phon" means "blessing").

rests forever on a bed of concrete. At Pak Nam and nearby beaches, charter boats are available to reach more islands close to the coast. The diving is not so good, but there are accommodations, good beaches, and great snorkeling. ∎

Chumphon

 Map p. 263

Visitor Information

✉ Tourism Authority of Thailand, 5 Talat Ma Rd., Surat Thani

☎ 077-288818

Mu Ko Chumphon Marine National Park

✉ National Parks Division, Royal Forestry Department, 61 Phahonyothin Rd., Bangkhen, Bangkok

☎ 02-562-0760

A puppet master displays the tools of his trade in Chumphon.

Ranong & Around

This border town was established in the late 18th century as a tin-mining center, settled by Hokkien Chinese. Today, their lingering influence is seen in pockets of architecture and in an industrious spirit among the people. Ranong's proximity to the funky Myanmar (Burmese) trading town of Victoria Point, just across the murky Pak Chan Estuary, and its role as a major regional fishing port give it a bustling feel that belies its relatively small population.

Long-tail boats at Ranong's port of Saphan Pla wait for passengers traveling to Victoria Point in Myanmar (Burma).

Ranong & Around

🗺 Map p. 263

Visitor Information

✉ Tourism Authority of Thailand, 5 Talat Mai Rd., Surat Thani

☎ 077-288818

A monument at the former residence of Koh Su Chiang—a 19th-century tin-mining boss, tax collector, and, under Rama V, Ranong's first governor—is found at **Nai Kai Ranong,** off Ruangrat Road on the northern edge of town. In the compound's ornate Hokkien-style buildings, mementoes trace his ancestral history.

Long-tail boats jostling at the town's large diesel-stained fishing port of **Saphan Pla,** 5 miles (8 km) west of town on Tha Muang Road, take passengers across the estuary to **Victoria Point** (Kawthung). The trip offers

a fleeting, if deceptive, glimpse of neighboring Myanmar (Burma). Victoria Point feeds off the prosperity of southern Thailand and throngs with marketers, along with an unexpected mix of Buddhist and Muslim inhabitants. A more comfortable way to get to the town is by taking day excursions with Jansom Travel (tel 077-835317) at the Jansom Thara Spa Resort hotel.

A modern casino resort and 18-hole golf course sprawl over a small island only a few minutes from Victoria Point on the Burmese side of the border, attracting a large Thai clientele.

Ko Chang, with bungalows, good beaches, and snorkeling, can be reached by chartered boat from Saphan Pla, or tours can be arranged from Ranong.

Laem Son Marine National Park

This important protected area slides down Ranong's southern coastline and into neighboring Phang-Nga province, collecting a string of white-sand beaches and swaths of mangrove forests along the way. The park encompasses 62 miles (100 km) of coastline, one of Thailand's longest stretches of protected seaboard. Its jurisdiction also extends offshore to 20 sparsely populated and deserted islands, pushing out to the edges of the Myanmar maritime border.

A 7.5-mile (12 km) road off scenic Highway 4, 30 miles (50 km) south of Ranong town, snakes its way through mangroves before arriving at park headquarters on **Bang Ben Beach** (National Park Co-operation Center, Ranong, tel 077-823255). Edged with casuarina trees, Bang Ben is wide, long, and sandy, and offers views across the water to the islands. One of the park's most popular beaches, it can get crowded and litter-strewn on weekends.

For more seclusion, walk 2.5 miles (4 km) north along the coast, past more twisted stands of mangroves teeming with bird life, deer, and monkeys, through shallow streams that have carved weird designs into the rocks, to **Laem Son Beach,** a superior and usually deserted stretch of sparkling sand (accessible only on foot).

During the area's dry season from November to April, park rangers can arrange trips to some of the offshore islands (monsoons whip the coast for the rest of the year, closing the park.) Sister islands **Ko Kam Yai** and **Ko Kam Noi,** southwest of Bang Ben, a little over an hour away, share the familiar features of secluded beaches—clear waters and good coral close to the shore for snorkeling.

Ko Kam Noi and the smaller **Ko Kam Tok** have freshwater springs. No accommodations are available on these two islands, and while you can camp, park rangers discourage this because they are not patrolled.

The larger **Ko Phayam,** 11 miles (18 km) northwest of Bang Ben, has private accommodations backing some of its beaches. Silt from the mouth of the Pak Chan River can cloud its waters.

There are no other options for accommodations on any of the islands in the group. ∎

Laem Son Marine National Park

 National Parks Division, Royal Forestry Department, 61 Phahonyothin Rd., Bangkhen, Bangkok

📞 02-562-0760

📅 Closed Dec.–March

Hot Springs

On Highway 4005, about half a mile (1 km) east of Ranong beside the small Wat Tapotaram, pools in a tropical garden are fed with steaming water from nearby hot springs. There are also rooms set aside for bathing in the spring water. At the Jansom Thara Spa Resort hotel (Phetkasem & Kamlangsap Rds., tel 077-821511), a giant Jacuzzi is kept well supplied with water from the springs.

Surat Thani & Around

This businesslike port receives plenty of visitors, but unfortunately most arrive with the intention of leaving as soon as possible. The role of the city as the major transportation hub for the alluring Ko Samui archipelago, Phuket, and Thailand's far south has determined its fate. But it is also a busy and prosperous commercial center, with enough attractions in its own right to keep visitors entertained while they wait to catch the next ferry, train, or bus out of town.

One of Ko Surin's glorious beaches

Surat Thani
🏔 Map p. 263
Visitor Information
✉ Tourism Authority of Thailand, 5 Talat Mai Rd., Surat Thani
☎ 077-288818

The local tourist office can arrange boat trips along the **Ta Pi River Estuary,** which winds in from the Gulf of Thailand to form the city's waterfront. The cruise takes you past areas of mangroves interspersed with rickety fishing docks and shipbuilding and repair yards. It also provides opportunities of viewing surprising populations of bird life. On the north banks of the river, *khlongs* (canals) lead off into the verdant landscape.

At the cleaner southeast Tha Thong estuary, Surat Thani's famously succulent giant *tilam*

oysters are farmed. Taste them for yourself at the restaurants along the bustling waterfront.

About 5.5 miles (9 km) southwest of the city on Highway 401, at the **Surat Thani Monkey Training School** *(tel 077-227351),* pig-tailed macaque monkeys are taught to scamper up trees and fetch coconuts. Macaques are traditionally used by plantation owners for coconut harvesting, and it is a delight to watch them work.

Surat Thani is Thailand's most famous monkey school, established in 1985 by Somphon

Saekaew under royal patronage. Visitors are welcome to watch daily training for free or pay a fee to watch a demonstration, performed upon request.

About half a mile (1 km) west of the monkey training school, on the Highway 4009 turnoff, the tall white and gold stupa of **Si Surat** rises from a hilltop above the forests. The stupa houses Buddhist relics that were donated by the Indian government. It also offers good views down to the meandering Ta Fi River.

Continue along Highway 41 to Highway 4142. The road runs to the coast and **Wat Khao Suwan Pradit**, a tremendous 150-foot (45 m) pagoda commanding a hilltop with a broad sweep of coastal views.

Chaiya & Wat Suan Mok

Historians suggest that until the tenth century Chaiya was the capital of the Hindu Srivijaya Empire that ruled over much of Indonesia, Malaysia, and southern Thailand. They contend its name is derived from Srivichai, the Thai rendering of the Javanese Srivijaya. Others disagree, sticking to the established belief that Srivijaya was ruled from Sumatra.

Even so, the surfeit of artifacts unearthed at Chaiya, one of Thailand's oldest cities, is more than enough to prove that the city played a significant role in the Srivijaya Empire. Most of the artifacts excavated from Chaiya, now a nondescript town 34 miles (54 km) north of Surat Thani on Highway 4, are in the care of the National Museum in Bangkok (see pp. 82–86).

Phra Boromathat Chaiya, about a mile (1.5 km) southeast of Chaiya on Highway 4191, was abandoned at the end of the Srivijaya Empire. The restored 1,300-year-old stupa is a fine example of Srivijayan art, with its ornate stacked-box architecture reflecting a style similar to the *candis* of Java. The museum on the grounds of the *wat* contains models of artifacts removed to Bangkok's National Museum. At **Wat Kaew,** a worn Srivijaya-period monument with five brick chambers rises from a square terrace.

INSIDER TIP:

In Chaiya, once the regional capital of the ancient Srivijaya Empire, don't miss Phra Boromathat and the ruin of Wat Kaew.

—KELLY FELTAULT
National Geographic contributor

Wat Suan Mok ("temple of the garden of liberation") is a modern forest monastery on Highway 41 southwest of Chaiya that shines with the unconventional style characterizing its founder, Thailand's most famous monk, Buddhadhasa Bhikkhu (1906–1993). His no-frills approach to Buddhism cut through ritual and superstition, earning him the wrath of the religious hierarchy and adoration among the people.

Wat Suan is Thailand's most popular Buddhist meditation retreat for Westerners, fusing Zen,

Chaiya
🗺 Map p. 263
Visitor Information
✉ Tourism Authority of Thailand, 5 Talat Mai Rd., Surat Thani
☎ 077-288818

Mu Ko Surin Marine National Park

⚑ Map p. 263

Marine National Parks Division

✉ Royal Forestry Department, 61 Phahonyothin Rd., Bangkhen, Bangkok

☎ 02-562-0760

Visitor Information

✉ Tourism Authority of Thailand, 5 Talat Mai Rd., Amphur Muang, Surat Thani

☎ 077-288818

Taoist, and Christian elements into an unconventional whole. Monks at the wat give meditation lessons (these are conducted in English) during the first ten days of each month. Meditation cells dotted around this beautiful forested setting are perfect for peace and solitude. Reservations for cells should be made at the wat a few days in advance.

INSIDER TIP:

From Chaiya, head east through Phumriang town, until you get to two seafood restaurants at the end of the road. Go to the one on the right.

—KELLY FELTAULT
National Geographic contributor

Mu Ko Surin Marine National Park

This spectacular protected area of marine park presents an ideal opportunity to explore some of Thailand's most pristine environments, both above and below the water, in agreeable isolation. While this group of five islands in the Andaman Sea, 62 miles (100 km) north of the Similan Islands and 37 miles (60 km) from the mainland, is known for its diving, the archipelago has dimensions that also make it appealing to non-divers.

Some excellent hiking trails cut across the two major islands of **Ko Surin Nua** and **Ko Surin Tai**, separated by a narrow channel

that can be crossed on foot at low tide. These trails climb through rain forest, with quantities of wildlife (monkeys, lemurs, mouse deer, squirrels, and birds) sheltering in a canopy of green that averages 106 feet (32 m) in height. The islands are indented with shimmering white-sand bays, protected by rocky headlands.

Easily accessible reefs just off the coast and in shallow waters around the islands, together with vivid coral and teeming marine life, make the five Surin islands Thailand's premier snorkeling location. The park headquarters near **Ao Mae Yai**, a deep, tranquil bay on the southeast side of Ko Surin Nua, rents snorkeling gear, although the quality is variable. They also run long-tail boat charters to snorkeling sites and beaches, and operate a restaurant and small bar.

Inexpensive, basic dormitory-style bungalows on Ko Surin Nua are available but must be reserved at the park's mainland office in Ban Hin Lat (*tel 076-472145*), north of Kura Buri, which is 100 miles (160 km) north of Phuket. They can also be booked at the Marine National Park Division of the Royal Forestry Department in Bangkok.

Distance from the mainland, deep water, and strong north–south ocean currents keep the waters clean around the islands, stimulating the growth of coral, especially in the sheltered bays on the eastern seaboard.

Visibility of up to 66 feet (20 m) is not uncommon during the dry season, from November to April. The best site for snorkeling is Ao Mae Yai, where shallow, clear waters drop into abundant and beautiful corals, with colorfully attendant parrot fish, clownfish, lionfish, and angelfish.

Ko Chi, a large rocky outcrop north of Ko Surin Nua, is also suitable for snorkeling. It is notable for its large visiting pelagics, and it is one of the best places on the islands to see sea turtles, including the occasional giant leatherback. **Turtle Ledge,** a shallow platform off the east side of Ko Surin Tai, is also a good place to spot turtles swimming around the sloping reef. Thick schools of darting batfish are also found among the staghorn and spiny acropora corals.

Just east of Turtle Ledge, **Hin Kong** is a spectacular undersea muddle of boulders, cliffs, caves, and arches.

The premier dive site is **Richelieu Rock,** southeast of Ko Surin Nua and Ko Surin Tai. The reef here is covered with a profusion of purple and pink gorgonian coral. Divers are presented with a rare pleasure—the chance to swim with magnificent whale sharks, the largest fish in the world. Richelieu Rock is one of the few dive sites in the world where these creatures are seen regularly.

At **Ko Torinla,** half a mile from Ko Surin Tai, a sloping reef takes you past vivid gardens of sea anemones. Grouper and red coral trout hide in the corals. A shallow section is a carpet of staghorns. There are many shelves along the reef; the shallower ones harbor hermit crabs, urchins, and shrimp.

A community of sea gypsies (*chao lae;* see pp. 284–285) lives on a beach in Ko Surin Tai. Visit their village for an insight into the subsistence lifestyle of these mostly nomadic people. The chao lae on Ko Surin are paid to collect turtle eggs for a hatchery on Ko Surin Nua. In April, Surin's chao lae honor their ancestors by launching colorfully decorated miniature boats from the beach. The boats represent the fortunes of their clans, and if they return to the same beach, the tradition holds the community must move to a new location.

Trips from the mainland aboard marine park boats run daily, from mid-November to April from **Ban Hit Lit** (the park is closed other times). Rangers also help arrange private charters. Dive boats take non-diving visitors (see Ko Similan, pp. 286–288). Several companies also offer excursions from Phuket. ∎

A pig-tailed macaque gets a lesson in gathering coconuts. Farmers in the south still use monkeys to collect coconuts.

Khao Sok National Park

The park, with the adjoining Kaeng Krung and Khlong Nakha wildlife sanctuaries, and Sri Phang-Nga National Park, forms the largest area of protected land on the Malay Peninsula, some 1,550 square miles (4,000 sq km). Khao Sok is characterized by precipitous limestone outcrops and mountains carpeted in rain forest.

Jungle-laden limestone cliffs dominate much of Khao Sok National Park's scenery.

The major attraction of Khao Sok is the **Chieo Lan Reservoir,** a lake created on the Pasaeng River in 1982, situated some 40 miles (64 km) from the park's entrance and accessible by road from park headquarters, just off Highway 401. More than a hundred craggy limestone monoliths protrude from the immense lake, creating an awesome, primordial wonderland. Visit in the early morning, when these limestone islands are shrouded in a light mist.

The limestone peaks around the reservoir are pockmarked with caves. Subterranean streams, fantastic rock formations, and stalactites and stalagmites make up the **Tham Nam Thalu** cave complex. In the 1970s, Communist rebels used the confusing passageways of **Tham Si Ru,** a cave with four converging passageways, as a hideout. The entrance to **Tham Khang**

Dao, a haunt for thousands of bats, is high on a cliff.

Maps of the park, marked with a number of trails, can be picked up at the visitor center at park headquarters. Tracks running along the park's major watercourse, the **Khlong Sok,** wind past enormous stands of bamboo and tangled tropical rain forests. About 1.5 miles (2.5 km) from the headquarters, the falls at **Wing Hin** ("running rock waterfall") tumble 65 feet (20 m) onto huge rocks worn smooth by the incessant wash. Another 2 miles (3 km) farther along is **Tang Nam,** where the Khlong Sok has worn a dramatic gorge through the mountains. At the gorge is a deep pool of crystal-clear water, perfect for swimming.

Some 2 miles (3 km) beyond Tang Nam is one of the park's most beautiful waterfalls, **Ton Gloy.** Water tumbles into a clear pool fringed by thick jungle. On top of the falls, flat rocks make platforms for panoramic views over the park.

A track behind the park's restaurant leads 2.5 miles (4 km) past tall bamboo forests, criss-crossing the Bang Laen River six times, to the base of **Sip Et Chan waterfall.** Here, waters cascade over 11 tiers before crashing into a wide pool.

Trails and river crossings are safer and more manageable during the dry season, from December through April. However, to see waterfalls at their surging best, and to have a better chance of spotting the monkeys, gibbons, gaurs and bantengs (both species of ox), langurs, wild boars, elephants, and Malayan sun bears that live in the park, go toward the end of the wet season—August to October.

Longer excursions into the park, including elephant and pony trekking and river rafting, can be arranged at the guesthouses just outside the park's entrance or with rangers. Park-administered accommodations are available, but most visitors opt for the nearby private guesthouses. Tree Tops Jungle Guesthouse *(contact Vieng Travel in Bangkok, tel 02-280-3537 or 02-280-3538; or Greenwood Travel Phuket, tel 076-331018)* has tree houses, cave lodges, and raft houses. ∎

Wild Lotus

Khao Sok is home to one of the world's rarest and largest flowers, the bua poot, or wild lotus (Rafflesia kerri meijer). The parasitic flower spends most of the year as microscopic threads drawing nutrients from inside the roots of lianas, a common jungle vine. Buds develop inside the bark of the roots, bursting through and swelling to the size of a chicken. When they bloom, in January and February, the reddish brown flowers grow to an astonishing 32 inches (82 cm) in diameter. The scent is most unpleasant to humans, but insects love it. The flower can be seen along some of the park's trails. Ask the rangers for directions.

Khao Sok National Park

🅰 Map p. 263

National Park Division

✉ Royal Forestry Department, 61 Phahonyothin Rd., Bangkhen, Bangkok

☎ 02-561-4292

Visitor Information

✉ Tourism Authority of Thailand, 5 Talat Mai Rd., Amphur Muang, Surat Thani

☎ 02-562-0760

People of the Sea

Thailand's sea gypsies come in three groups—Moken, Urak Lawoi, and Moklen—but are collectively called *chao lae* (people of the sea) by the Thais. Their dusky complexions, thick mops of black hair, and small but sturdy frames distinguish them from Thais.

Because of the sea gypsies' poverty and their transitory way of life, their dwellings are frequently ramshackle.

Their beliefs are strongly rooted in animist ritual, and they have no interest in becoming either Buddhist or Muslim. The chao lae forsake material possessions. They are shy, coy, and vulnerable, and avoid confrontation. They are egalitarian; any central authority is anathema, and they cannot countenance officialdom. The chao lae, therefore, present all the credentials needed to push them beyond the margins of mainstream society: They look different, they think differently, and they worship different gods.

Thailand's estimated 4,000 chao lae mostly live as ocean itinerants, sailing, fishing, diving for oysters, and camping from island to island. Others are packed into ramshackle villages of corrugated iron and cardboard on Andaman Sea islands to fish in ever decreasing areas or to sell trinkets to tourists.

Thailand accepts the chao lae as long-term guests, not citizens. They have no political rights and no security of tenure. This, and their refusal to deal with anything outside their own belief systems, has made the sea gypsies outcasts.

The chao lae have a hidden history. There is no written language, and the eschewing of material possessions has left them with few heirlooms with which to trace their past. A nomadic existence has left no monumental legacies, and their taciturn nature precludes an oral history. Colonial tales cast them as pirates who terrorized maritime traffic in the Strait of Malacca.

The chao lae choose to live within confined geographical boundaries, from the islands in Myanmar to Langkawi, just south of the Thai-Malaysia sea border.

The Different Groups

The 400 Moken most exemplify the romantic notion of the sea gypsy: Families live aboard boats and fish, with no terrestrial roots. The thousand or so Moklen live in beach shacks on islands from the Surins to the northern tip of Phuket, using long-tail boats for fishing. The Urak Lawoi are the largest group and the most settled, numbering about 2,500. They are mainly found n Phuket, in villages on Ko Sirey near Phuket town, and at the northern end of Rawai Beach. Other settlements are found on the Phi Phi islands, Ko Lanta, and the Tarutao archipelago The three groups have different but not dissimilar languages. They intermarry and share the same strong sense of community and solidarity.

An Untenable Future

The chao lae continue to fish to survive, but they can't compete with the huge trawlers that have depleted their traditional fishing grounds. Large areas of these have been taken away from them in the cynical and uncompromising name of environmentalism. In frustration they have resorted to explosives and poisons to increase their catch, and end up in jail. They are now—again because of depletion—prohibited from collecting the shells and corals they used to sell to visitors. Their future is bleak.

Many sea gypsies earn a meager living selling fish at small markets.

Mu Ko Similan Marine National Park

The nine islands of the Mu Ko Similan Marine National Park present a combination of beauty above and below the sea that few places can match. The archipelago, basking in the Andaman Sea about 25 miles (40 km) from Thailand's southwest coast, is rated as one of Asia's top dive sites. Similan is derived from the Malay word for "nine," *sembilan*—a prosaic name for such a stunning place.

Visitors to isolated Mu Ko Similan need to bring their own supplies.

Mu Ko Similan Marine National Park

🔺 Map p. 263

The huge granite boulders that form the Similan Islands slide into crystalline waters to create an underwater theme park of extreme and bizarre beauty. Under the water, the boulders form canyons, caves, tunnels, and twisted overhangs garnished with vivid coral. Reef walls slope steeply downward for 133 feet (40 m) to the seabed, with huge bommies (coral heads), riotously colored soft corals, and sea fans waving in the surging current.

Above the water's surface the beauty continues. Sweeps of brilliant white sand touch azure

Long-tail Boats

Originally used as fishing and trading vessels, these sleek, speedy, but noisy boats are now more likely to be found ferrying tourists and locals across rivers and lakes and to and from islands. They were designed as sailboats but now come with 10-foot (3 m) rods attached to a huge diesel motor at the stern. The rod or "tail" has a propellor affixed to it and works as a rudder. One crew member has the arduous task of steering the boat by pushing and pulling the end of the tail.

Fantasy Reef, on the west coast of Ko Similan (Island #8), is one of the most popular dives. Rock formations cover a huge expanse, delivering an imagination-stretching array of caves, arches, boulders, and nooks flush with iridescent corals and giant fans, in depths ranging from 45 to 133 feet (15 to 40 m). **Beacon Reef (South),** at the southern end of Ko Similan, has a steep drop-off with a remarkable diversity of hard corals from near the surface to the seabed, 116 feet (35 m) below.

Three giant rocks rear from the sea at **Elephant Head,** between Ko Similan and Ko Payu (Island #7), and fall 100 feet (30 m) to the seabed to form a natural amphitheater that gives the

Marine National Parks Division

✉ Royal Forestry Department, 61 Phahonyothin Rd., Bangkhen, Bangkok

☎ 02-561-0777

Visitor Information

✉ Tourism Authority of Thailand, 5 Ta at Mai Rd., Surat Thani

🖷 077-283813

waters, while inland, thick green foliage creeps over steep, craggy hills and hangs from the cliffs.

On the west coast, which takes the brunt of the southwesterly monsoons from May to October, are rugged coastlines where weathered boulders on the shoreline roll down into the sea.

Around Ko Similan's nine islands—each of which carries a number as well as a name—are 19 recognized dive sites, all claiming special characteristics. On the northern edge of the group, **Christmas Point,** at Ko Bangru (Island #9), has a drift taking you through a maze of giant arches. Abundant radiant soft coral growth mingles with huge sea fans and hordes of small fish. **Breakfast Bend,** also on Ko Bangru, is best tackled in the early morning, when light filters through the water, enhancing multicolored coral gardens.

INSIDER TIP:

In the Ko Similan islands, you'll scuba dive with a kaleidoscope of underwater tropical life; book a multiday live-aboard trip to best experience this top-rated dive destination.

—SIMON WILLIAMS
The Nature Conservancy

impression of swimming in a giant aquarium. Yellowtails, snapper, lionfish, coral trout, yellowed and black Moorish idols, and angelfish are found in abundance.

And so it goes on, from the inquisitive batfish escorting divers at **BatFish Bend** near Ko Miang Sang (Island #6), to the sheer 130-foot (40 m) coral

Low tide exposes some of Mu Ko Similan's rich variety of corals.

wall and leopard sharks at **Ko Miang** (Island #4). There are more incredible dive sites at **Ko Payan** and **Ko Payang**. At **Ko Huyong** (Island #1), at the southern end of the island group, boulders create a deranged jumble of underwater ledges, caves, and archways.

Visiting the Islands

National park offices are on Ko Miang and Ko Similan. Ko Miang has a camping area and bungalows. Reservations for the bungalows must be made at least a month in advance through the Marine National Parks Division of the Royal Forestry Department in Bangkok, or at its office in Thap Lamu (*tel 077-411914*). Long-tail boats can be hired at Ko Similan or Ko Miang for trips to other islands. A good beach on Ko Similan is Campbell's Bay; climb the huge boulder at the north end for wide views.

Most visitors arrive on live-aboard dive boats from Phuket, 62 miles (100 km) south (see pp. 323–328), for three- to five-day diving expeditions. Others come via Thap Lamu, 25 miles (40 km) east, near the resort town of Khao Lak, in Ranong. Reputable operators in Phuket include: Fantasea Divers (*tel 076-281387*), Siam Diving Center (*tel 076-330936*), Marina Divers (*tel 076-330272*), Scuba Cat Diving (*tel 076-345246*), and Dive Asia (*tel 076-330598*). ∎

Getting Away From It All

Still one of the south's best kept secrets is the 15-mile (25 km) string of beaches paralleling Highway 4 between Takua Pa and the sleepy village of Khao Lak, north of Phuket.

There are numerous understated resorts along this stretch, a favorite place for European visitors. Khao Lak's long golden-sand beach is the most popular, but hardly crowded, even during the November to March peak season. You can charter long-tail boats at the resorts, for snorkeling trips to a large coral reef about 45 minutes offshore, or speedboats, for trips to the Similan Islands.

Khao Lak's beach runs nearly as far as Hat Ban Sak, 8.5 miles (14 km) north, a beach fringed with casuarina trees on a wide, scenic bay that is a great spot for picnics on weekends.

EXPERIENCE: Massage

Thailand is celebrated for its massage, an art that is taken seriously around the country. Believed to have been invented in India 2,500 years ago, it gradually made its way to Thailand, where its Ayurvedic techniques and principles intermingled with traditional Chinese medicine. Known in Thailand as *nuat phaen boran* (ancient-manner technique), Thai massage involves stretching and deep massage. Here are some popular places to study this ancient and revered art, ranging from Ko Samui to Bangkok to Chiang Mai:

International Training Massage School (ITM) *(17/6-7 Morakot Rd., Chiang Mai, tel 053-218632, www.itmthai massage.com)* Social butterflies may enjoy ITM, one of Chiang Mai's most popular massage schools. Five levels of study, from beginner to teacher training, provide instruction on northern-style massage, which incorporates medium pressure and rhythmic stretching, reflecting the slower lifestyle of the north and yoga-inspired techniques while focusing on fluid movement and tailor-made treatment. Traditional techniques meet modern amenities at the nearby Mantra spa training facility. Thai herbal hot compress, aroma massage, hot stone healing massage, and *tok sen*—using a wooden hammer and wedge to stimulate acupressure points—are provided in a luxurious Lanna-style spa environment.

Tamarind Massage Academy *(205/3 Thong Takian, Ko Samui, tel 077-424221, www .tamarindsprings.com)* Amid the rolling hills and tropical jungle of southeastern Ko Samui, Tamarind Massage Academy has the most ideal setting in which to study (or receive) massage. Set on the grounds of the Tamarind Springs, the academy

teaches traditional Thai yoga massage, which follows the principles of *sib sen* influenced by aspects of yoga. Beginners and professional massage therapists learn the history and techniques of massage, as well as Buddhist principles of mindfulness, from expert instructors in between morning yoga classes and afternoon steam baths at the Tamarind Springs Spa. Manual lymphatic drainage and Ingham method reflexology can also be studied here. Students may stay on the spa's grounds in exotic bungalows that incorporate trees and boulders in their walls.

Thai Massage School of Chiang Mai *(203/7 Mae Jo Rd., Chiang Mai, tel 053-854330, www.tmcschool.com)* A harmonious balance of professionalism and relaxation characterizes the TMC school, where classrooms feature human skeletons and charts of the muscular system, and lunch is eaten on the patio beside a small, tree-lined stream. Students are given comfortable gowns akin to medical scrubs, and classes are smaller and more intimate than at some of the busier schools. Several levels of instruction from highly ex-

perienced teachers cater to both beginners and certified massage therapists looking to earn credit hours. Morning meditation and yoga, philanthropic field trips to practice massage on the elderly or teach troubled youths, and dancing during the graduation ceremony round out the TMC experience.

Wat Pho *(Ta-Sahakon Bldg., 392/25-28 Soi Pen Phat 1, Maharaj Rd., Bangkok, tel 02-622-3533, www.watpo massage.com)* Thailand's oldest university began massage instruction in 1962, although the marble tablets illustrating the principles of anatomy and sib sen, which are located on the temple grounds, are centuries old. Today, around the corner from the 16th-century *wat*, both Thai and foreign students take courses in traditional massage (Wat Pho style), foot massage, and oil massage. All students must attend the general class before moving on to the advanced program, during which theory and practice of the tablet inscriptions are taught. Classes are available at branches in Chiang Mai, Nonthaburi, and Chetawan, where professional spa classes, based on traditional principles, are offered.

Ko Samui Archipelago

Off the coast of Surat Thani, in the Gulf of Thailand, is a tousled array of 80 islands—only five of them populated—with myriad shapes, sizes, and persuasions. The Ko Samui archipelago has a swashbuckling history of seafarers, shipwrecks, pioneers, and trailblazers. The archetypal tropical island of Ko Samui, the group's largest, is one of Southeast Asia's favorite getaways.

Casuarina trees typically edge the beaches of the Ko Samui archipelago.

These days visitors are also attracted to the "Big Island's" idyllic satellites. About 150 years ago, Hainanese explorers sailed south from China to settle on Ko Samui and began harvesting coconuts. Though it earned a reputation as a prolific coconut exporter, the island was known for little else. Ko Samui and its people—the independent *chao Samui* (people of Samui), industrious Hainanese, and a scattering of Muslim Thai-Malay settlers—basked rather anonymously under the Gulf of Thailand sun for 125 years. As backpacker legend has it, the second major wave of international travelers began arriving in the mid-1970s and were instantly overwhelmed by the island's deserted, palm-packed beaches and friendly, unaffected people.

Those idyllic times are long gone. Samui now bursts at the seams with a million visitors a year. More than 400 hotels and bungalow "resorts" line the beaches, ranging from mosquito-net basic to five-star cabana. Nightlife covers the gamut, from rowdy down-to-earth to nascent sophistication. The tourist infrastructure is first class, and access to water sports and other activities is unhindered. Nonetheless, after all these years and all these changes, Ko Samui, with its unshakable carefree nature and honest island feel, is still a great place to visit.

Ko Samui's popularity has awoken its neighboring islands. People wanting to escape the crowds have sometimes found other, more tranquil gems. Frequent interisland boat services, organized day trips, and diving and snorkeling tours to islands around the archipelago smooth the rough edges of adventure. Ko Phangan, the second largest island of the group, best known for its raucous full moon parties, has dozens of isolated, tranquil coves with shimmering sands

hiding along its rugged coastline. Lonely Ko Tao, on the outskirts of the archipelago, has become a scuba diver's paradise, with a plethora of excellent dive sites just off its coastline.

And there is the magnificent Ang Thong group. Wrapped in a blanket of national park protection, this beautiful group of more than 40 islands is swamped with idyllic bays, indented hills

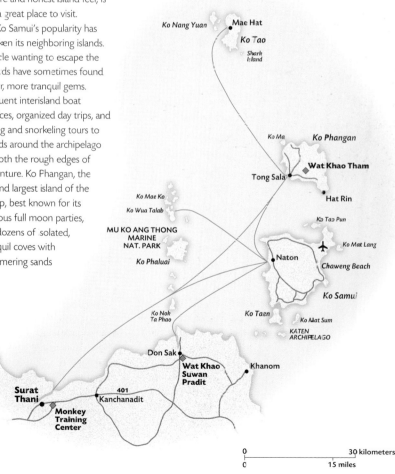

Ko Samui

 Map pp. 263, 291, & 293

Visitor Information

 Tourism Authority of Thailand, 5 Talat Mai Rd., Amphur Muang, Surat Thani

 077-288818

 Tourism Authority of Thailand, northern end of Naton, Ko Samui

 077-420720 or 077-420722

of deep green jungle, and clear waters. Add to this the dozens of other uninhabited islands, and the archipelago becomes a tropical paradise.

The archipelago is best visited during the dry season, from January to June. Rains begin in early July and continue to build until the end of the year. Torrential rains often lash the islands in November and December.

Ko Samui

No matter what their budget, inclination, or pleasure, visitors to 95-square-mile (247 sq km) Ko Samui usually find what they are looking for. Ko Samui is that sort of place—easy-going and

INSIDER TIP:

Avoid crowded Chaweng and its tour groups; head for less congested areas like charming Bophut village, where many expatriates have settled.

—JOHN SEATON CALLAHAN
National Geographic contributor

hedonistic. Rustic bungalows occupy remote enclaves hidden away from luxurious five-star resorts. Crowded, lively beaches lie a rocky headland away from sweeping, near-deserted bays. Luxury resorts in secluded coves front modest jungle-spa hideaways. The nightlife disappoints few. And all this is built on the

solid foundation of excellent tourist facilities and services.

Only a few minutes from Samui's airport (one of the most delightful anywhere in the world, with open-sided palm-thatched halls and landscaped gardens blazing with tropical flowers) is **Chaweng Beach,** the island's most popular and longest beach. A 4.5-mile-long (7 km) sweep of fine white sand on the east coast of the island gently inclines to clear waters. Generous groves of coconut palms edge the beach, and a backdrop of Samui's green and rugged interior completes the tropical island scene. Despite a concentration of development, Chaweng Beach manages to maintain its tropical charm and is an agreeable place to spend some time.

Along the shore, a few bungalow-style mid-range hotels sit beside grandiose luxury resorts. More representative of Samui's earlier years, when bamboo huts dominated the shores, these boutique bungalows and the remaining open, timber-decked restaurants add to the beach's tropical appeal.

The crowded middle reaches of the beach are the most attractive and the best sector for water sports. Windsurfers, Jet Skis, and catamarans (instructors are available) can be rented. Parasailers towed by speedboats float high above the coconut palms.

The shallow waters at the northern end of Ko Samui are sheltered inside a coral reef running parallel to the beach. The reef creates a lagoon here at low tide. The southern end of Chaweng is more open to the ocean and less crowded.

The laid-back tropical ambience of Chaweng Beach dissipates about 100 yards (90 m) back from the shore. A road parallel to the beach runs nearly its entire length, lined with bars, restaurants, mini-marts, tailor shops, video parlors, tour agencies, banks, and dive shops. Midway along this route is Chaweng's entertainment epicenter: a chaotic, thumping collection of bars, nightclubs, and discos blasting away into the night and reverberating onto the nearby sands.

South of Chaweng, just off Samui's ring road, Highway 4169 is **Lamai Beach,** the island's second most popular beach. It's about half the length of Chaweng but shares many of its characteristics—a long, wide, fabulous stretch of white sand and clean water, fringed by bending coconut palms under which sit bungalows and hotels. However, the water here is deeper,

there are fewer visitors, and the beach has fewer pretensions than its neighbor. A less frenetic, although in some places seedier, nightlife erupts along the road on the far side of the coconut palms. Lamai has a more down-market feel, escaping—for better or worse—much of the newer resort development found on Chaweng.

At the rocky outcrop that defines Lamai's southern end are a pair of conspicuous formations known as **Hin Yai** and **Hin Ta,** or "grandfather rock" and "grandmother rock," weathered into the suggestive shapes of male and female genitalia. Legend has it that the bodies of an elderly couple were washed up on the shore after a shipwreck to create the rocks.

Heading north from Lamai, past Chaweng Beach, Highway 4171, the secondary route, skirts a headland through rugged terrain, past isolated coves to the

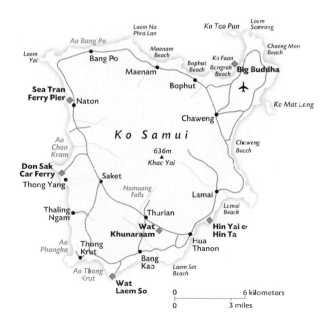

quiet and curving **Choeng Mon Beach.** Here, abandoned rice barges have been converted into upscale accommodations, adding an idiosyncratic touch to one of the island's most attractive bays. Toward the tip of the headland, off a dirt road, is **Laem Samrong,** a cape indented with rocky coves and patches of brilliant white sand at the end of narrow paths.

From Laem Samrong, the road continues, passing the landmark golden **Big Buddha** statue, which is set on an islet attached to a

---

EXPERIENCE:
Full Moon Party

For more than 20 years, Ko Phangan, the island just north of Ko Samui, has hosted an all-night full moon beach party attended by up to 10,000—mostly foreign—revelers. The party commences at dusk, as the full moon rises over the sea, and consists of DJs blasting electronic music from a strip of beachfront clubs, fire shows, and copious alcohol (and drug) consumption. While hardly a "Thai" festival, the party has an international reputation, and accommodation around Hat Rin Beach is typically booked a week in advance of the event, which falls on each full moon other than those coinciding with Buddhist holidays. Boats from Samui shuttle night-trippers to the event and back. For more information, visit *www.fullmoonparty-thailand.com.*

---

short causeway, at the top of a brightly painted *naga* staircase. The 38-foot (12 m) image dominates **Bangrak,** or "big Buddha beach," a narrow 2-mile (3 km) strip of coarse brownish sand with shallow and cloudy water.

Beyond the headland Bangrak gives way to **Bophut Beach,** more notable for its charming, unaffected village (believed to be Samui's first settlement) than the quality of its sand or sea. Thickets of leaning coconut palms and a verdant hilly backdrop add to its character and appeal. The beach is favored by visitors who seek peace and quiet, and a friendly community feel. Quaint timber buildings at Bophut village—a short walk from the beach—have been dressed up as European restaurants.

From Bophut and Bangrak, speedboats can be chartered to Ko Phangan, Ko Tao, and other islands.

To the west of Bophut, past a jutting cape, a right turn at the village of Maenam leads to **Maenam Beach,** an isolated, 3-mile (5 km) gentle curve of narrow white sand and clear water. The water offers good conditions for renting catamarans and windsurfers, and there are clear views of Ko Phangan from restaurants along the beach.

Scenic Highway 4169 follows the island's rocky northern coastline, passing villages and coral-fringed bays, before turning down to Ko Samui's bustling port and commercial center, **Naton.** The majority of visitors arrive here by ferry from Surat Thani. (There is also a car-ferry port south of Ataon at Thong Yang.) Naton offers little reason to stay around, but the Tourism Authority of Thailand's office *(tel 077-420504)* at the town's northern end is worth a visit.

Ko Samui's western and southern coastlines are more noted for their solitude than their sandy bays. Highway 4169 cuts a hilly course inland from Naton, through coconut palm plantations, then joins the east coast at the Muslim village of **Hua Thanon,** near Lamai.

To visit the south coast, take Highway 4170 just before the village of Ban Saket. A handful of luxury resorts nestle along the rocky shoreline. On the tip of a cape at one end of Ao Thong Khao Yai near the center of the island. Trails crisscross the island, climbing through thick jungle, past streams and waterfalls. You can hike to overlooks offering fabulous panoramas or take elephant treks to tumbling waterfalls. One of the best of these, **Namuang,** pours

Rocks frame Lamai Beach. After Chaweng, this is Ko Samui's second most popular stretch of sand.

Krut, waves wash the striking **Wat Laem So,** a Srivijaya-style *chedi* embellished with hundreds of bright yellow tiles. Towering coconut palms just yards from clear waters set an idyllic scene at **Laem Set Beach,** which can be found on the southeastern corner of the island.

Just a mile (1.5 km) north of the junction where Highway 4169 meets the ring road is **Wat Khunaraam,** famous for the macabre sight of Luang Pordeang, a monk who died while meditating 25 years ago and was "mysteriously" mummified. The venerated monk still sits in the lotus position.

Samui's rugged hinterland rises to a peak of 2,087 feet (636 m) at

250 feet (80 m) over a sheer cliff and thunders into a cool emerald pool. The falls are at their best toward the end of the rainy season, in November and December.

The best way to travel around the island is by car or motorbike, both of which can be rented from operators in Naton, Chaweng, Lamai, and other beaches.

Ko Phangan

This, the Samui archipelago's second largest island, is hardly a convenient paradise. A rugged coastline and mountainous interior put up intimidating barriers against infrastructure, so that much of the island *(continued on p. 298)*

Ko Phangan

🖼 Maps pp. 263 & 291

Visitor Information

✉ Tourism Authority of Thailand, 5 Talad Mai Rd., Surat Thani

☎ 077-288818

✉ Tourism Authority of Thailand, Naton, Ko Samui

☎ 077-420504

Marine National Parks of the South

Only about 5 percent of visitors to Thailand's 80 national parks are foreigners, and most of those crowd into only a few of the 17 marine national parks in the south.

Aerial view of Ang Thong National Marine Park, Ko Samui

The country's ongoing environmental abuse and the delays in starting to preserve its coastal and marine heritage have taken their toll, but the marine national parks still offer some of the most gorgeous scenery and pristine environments in Thailand—both above and below the water.

The first marine national park, Khao Sam Roi Yot, was not set up until 1966, and the second, Mu Ko Tarutao, an archipelago spreading down the southwest coast to the Malaysian border, was not declared until 1974.

Many more marine national parks have been added to the list since then, but much of the environment had already been badly damaged through carelessness and greed: overfishing,

dynamite fishing, and anchor drag have depleted marine life and destroyed coral reefs. Wetlands and mangrove forests have been turned into shrimp farms, destroying the habitats of wildlife. Unfortunately, all of this is still happening.

The advent of mass tourism in southern Thailand in the early 1990s has compounded the problem, as pressure increases to develop tourist resorts inside marine national parks. This is especially evident in the Phi Phi–Hat Nopparat Thara Marine National Park, where some of the beaches and islands have been burdened with ill-considered (and frequently illegal) development.

While legislation is in place to protect the national parks, at times it is flagrantly abused, often by high-ranking politicians and prominent businessmen. However, a small, vocal environmental lobby and a sympathetic media are slowly turning the tide. Growing numbers of people are speaking out against encroachment and other abuses.

Despite these difficulties, southern Thailand's marine national parks, in general, are well managed and still have plenty to offer. Some of the more isolated parks are sparkling, untouched gems rarely visited by foreigners. Here you find the special solitude that gives tropical islands their enchanting edge. Such islands are not very difficult or prohibitively expensive to get to—try Ko Surin, Ko Tarutao, Ko Phetra, or Hat Chao Mai.

On most marine park islands, rangers operate clean and comfortable bungalows (mainly dormitory style), which can be rented as complete units. Many parks also have privately run accommodations. Rangers hand out maps, offer advice, help visitors arrange boat trips to other islands or coral reefs, and often act as guides. At the more isolated islands, there are park-run restaurants and small provision stores.

Southern Thailand's marine parks can get irritatingly busy on weekends, public holidays, and school vacations, but at other times they remain almost deserted. It is safest to book accommodations in advance at the Marine National Parks Division of the Forestry Depart-ment head office in Bangkok (61 Phahonyothin Rd., Bangkhen, Bangkok 10900, tel 02-562-0760). The Tourism Authority of Thailand (www.tourismthailand.org) offices in provincial capitals or tourist centers also book accommodations.

For scuba divers, marine national parks offer some of the best dive sites in Asia. Like many other tourism sectors in Thailand, the diving infrastructure is first class. There are numerous dive shops in southern Thailand that supply training, equipment, and transportation—and they are inexpensive.

EXPERIENCE: Diving for a Cause

Thailand is a diver's paradise for both beginners, who benefit from inexpensive courses and shallow waters at Ko Tao, and experienced divers, who enjoy live-aboards in the Andaman Sea. However, Thailand's underwater ecosystem is under threat from an increasing number of divers. Here are some diving organizations that will allow you to help:

Green Fins Thailand (www.greenfins-thailand.org) is working to protect Thailand's reefs through environmentally friendly guidelines provided to over 80 dive operators. Participating companies include Phuket's **Dive Asia** (www.diveasia.com) and Ko Samui's **Easy Divers** (www.easydivers-thailand.com).

Marine Conservation Ko Tao (New Heaven Dive Shop, Chalok Baan Khao, Ko Tao, tel 077-457045, http://marineconservationkohtao.com) Aiming to preserve and restore Ko Tao's fragile ecosystem, MCKT allows certified divers to perform reef checks, work on reef regeneration and coral nursery projects, or partake in a sea turtle release program. Certification courses incorporate ecological education and underwater cleanups.

Sustainable Marine Adventure and Responsible Tourism (56/73-74 Pechakacem Rd., Takuapa, Phangnga, www.etcth.org) This eco-friendly dive operator runs day trips and live-aboard diving off the Similan Islands. SMART is affiliated with the Ecotourism Training Center, which is involved in preserving the local marine environment. ETC trained, Thai student interns work aboard the luxury dive boat, providing underwater videography and gaining hands-on experience, while divers enjoy the most beautiful underwater conditions in Thailand in comfort and directly aid the local community.

remains undeveloped and, apart from the riotous full moon bashes, tranquil and laid-back. For many, Ko Phangan is a pleasing throwback to the Samui and Phuket of the 1970s. Ferries from Naton, Surat Thani, and Ko Tao arrive at **Tong Sala,** Phangan's jumbled port town and service center. Speedboats and long-tail boats from Ko Samui's Bophut and Bangrak Beaches deposit visitors at the beach of Hat Rin, in the south of the island.

The roads are poor, and transportation around the island can be treacherous. Motorbikes may be rented but are not recommended unless you are an experienced rider. The best option for visiting the glorious string of east coast beaches is chartering long-tail boats.

Hat Rin, Phangan's most popular beach, runs along a stubby tail of land on the island's southern tip. It can be reached from Tong Sala by boat or along a winding and very hilly road with spectacular coastal views. There are beaches on both sides of this wide verdant cape, although **Hat Rin Nok** on the eastward side, with its fringe of palm trees, wider stretches of sand, and cleaner and deeper water, is

EXPERIENCE: Destination Spas

Beyond exquisite decor, obsequious service, and signature soundtracks, Thai spas go the extra length to make sure guests feel both pampered and healthy, following holistic practices designed to bring the body into harmony. Here are some of the most celebrated spas:

Amanpuri Resort (Pansea Beach, Phuket, tel 800/477-9180, www .amanresorts.com/ amanpuri/home.aspx) Tailor-made holistic treatments amid lush vegetation.

Banyan Tree Spa (21st fl., Thai Wah Tower, II Sathorn Rd., Bangkok, tel 02-679-1042, www.ban yantreespa .com) Sixty-three floors above the city, this urban escape offers the epitome of pampering with an assortment of spa packages. After treatment, dine a the Vertigo Grill, high above the city.

Chiva Som (73/4 Petch-kasen Rd., Hua Hin, tel 032-536536, www

.chivasom.com) This luxurious beach resort, situated just south of Hua Hin, organizes personalized wellness programs based on the holistic approach of treating the mind, body, and spirit.

Dheva Spa (51/4 Chiang Mai-Sankampaeng Rd., Chiang Mai, tel 053-888888, www.manda rinoriental.com/chiangmai) Housed in a replica of Myanmar's Mandalay Palace, the spa is a feast for the eyes, while the suites within the "palace" grounds exude luxury. Treatments based on Ayurveda, the "science of life," balance spiritual and mental guidance with

physical therapies. Wellness programs include rejuvenation and weight-management programs.

Oriental Spa (48 Oriental Ave., Bangkok, www .manda rinoriental.com) An urban sanctuary offering massages, water-based treatments, and Ayurveda treatments in the Ayurveda penthouse.

The Sanctuary (Hat Tien beach, Ko Phangan, tel 081-271-3614, www .thesanctuarythailand.com) The Sanctuary epitomizes Ko Phangan's "hippie" reputation, offering communal vegetarian dinners, yoga courses, meditation, and natural healing therapies.

the preferable side of the cape. On the full moon each month, up to 10,000 people descend on Hat Rin for the full moon party, a recent tradition that has quickly become an institution, attracting international attention. It is a wild, dusk-till-dawn, cacophonous affair of blasting music and frantic, wide-eyed mob dancing.

Pretentious "backpacker chic" can pervade the atmosphere along Hat Rin's beaches, and a messy collection of bungalows, restaurants, souvenir shops, and bars have grown up along parts of the cape. Visitors who prefer peace and quiet to attitude and posturing would do better to look elsewhere.

Boats or chartered long-tails from Hat Rin (between February and November) travel up the east coast past beautiful beaches with palms, jungle-clad cliff ridges, and milk-white sand following the contours of coves and bays. Some of these remote beaches have a few modest bungalows for hire.

Hiking near Hat Rin: A two-hour hike to the north along a well-marked trail from Hat Rin leads to the first beach—deserted, beautiful **Hat Yuan.** Farther along the trail is **Hat Tien,** tucked in a crescent-shaped bay, with bungalows shaded by coconut palms. North of Hat Sadet is magnificent **Ao Tong Nai Pan,** a twin-horseshoe bay chiseled out of the rugged coast. Here, basic bungalows face the beaches.

It is possible to follow the coastal trail all the way from Hat Rin to Ao Tong Nai Pan, staying at bungalows or camping along the way—it's about 9 miles (15 km),

and guides, who can be arranged for at the bungalows or through travel agents, are required.

Other hiking trails offer chances to explore the island's interior. With an experienced guide, you can climb rug-

Uncrowded Ko Phangan reminds many people of Ko Samui and Phuket in the 1970s.

ged limestone slopes through luxuriant jungle, past streams to tumbling waterfalls.

From Ao Tong Nai Pan, a rough dirt road tapering into a trail leads to Hat Khuat, or **Bottle Beach**—one of the most attractive on the northeastern corner of island. Continuing west, around the imposing cliffs of Laem Kung Yai, you come to **Hat Khom,** yet another splendid beach, curving at the edge of rugged, forested hills. Both Hat Khuat and Hat Khom

Ko Tao

Maps pp. 263 & 291

Visitor Information

✉ Tourism
Authority of
Thailand, 5
Talad Mai Rd.,
Surat Thani

☎ 077-288818

beaches have basic accommodations, and are joined by a steep trail over the ridge. You can also get there, and to Ao Tong Nai Pan (depending on the weather), by chartering a long-tail boat from the pleasant fishing village of **Ban Chaloklam,** set on a deep bay. To get to Ban Chaloklam, an adventurous *songthaew* ride from Tong Sala is required.

marine life have made it a hot spot for scuba divers.

Sandy bays defined by rocky headlands dot the south and west coasts of Ko Tao. On the north and east coasts, huge smooth granite boulders run from the shore, and rest on jungled hills in a quirky display. The island's lush, hilly hinterland squeezes into an area of just 8 square miles

Steep cliffs edge Chalok Ban Kao Bay, providing glorious views all around.

On the road from Tong Sala to Hat Rin, just before the village of Ban Tai, a dirt road leads to **Wat Khao Tham,** a Buddhist retreat atop a forested peak. The *wat* holds meditation classes for foreigners, but is strictly regimented.

Ko Tao

Named Turtle Island for its mountainous hump-backed, turtle-shell shape, Ko Tao is a green and white speck of an island lolling in the Gulf of Thailand, 26 miles (45 km) north of Ko Samui and 25 miles (40 km) from the mainland, and is easily missed. Its lucid waters, abundant coral, and swarming

(21 sq km), peaking at 1,027 feet (313 m). Although the island has plenty of beaches, shallow waters preclude serious swimming.

Ko Tao's exceptionally clear waters, and those of nearby islets— removed from coastal runoffs—allow coral to thrive. The abundance of coral has lured large numbers of reef fish, creating the best dive sites in the Gulf of Thailand.

Despite its relative isolation, Ko Tao is easy to reach. Regular ferries and charter boats ply from Ko Samui, Ko Phangan, and Chumphon to Ban Mae Hat, the island's service town, where there are a number of dive shops. Expect to be accosted by touts offering dive trips; head to your resort before committing to dive excursions or day trips around the island.

Dive Destination: One of the great advantages of diving around Ko Tao is the dive sites' proximity to the island and to each other. Virtually all are within 30 to 45 minutes of the island, allowing for several dives per day. Dive tours can be booked from Ko Samui or from dozens of dive shops on Ko Tao. Competition and convenience have kept prices down, and made the island the least expensive place in Thailand to earn or improve scuba-diving certification.

About a half mile (1 km) south lies Hin Khao, or **White Rock,** so called because the sunlight refracting through the water makes the two coral-dressed submerged pinnacles appear ghostly white. The dive drops about 65 feet (20 m) among varied coral and marine life, including feisty trigger-fish. It's popular for night dives, when the abundant small marine life attracts turtles and barracuda.

Eastward, the four **Chumphon Pinnacles** rise high above the sea, the tallest reaching 52 feet (16 m) above the surface. The dive averages 65 feet (20 m) and features ledges, overhangs, and gorges. This is a favorite haunt for pelagics, including schools of barracuda, tuna, mackerel, and giant trevally.

At dorsal-shaped **Shark Island,** just off Ko Tao's southeastern tip, gorgonian fans wave in the tidal surges. An underwater tunnel and cruising pelagics add drama here.

Closer to shore, coral reefs growing in shallow waters off the headlands and beaches are ideal

for snorkeling. The best spot is off the beach at **Ao Leuk,** on Ko Tao's southeast coast.

Sai Ree Beach dominates the west coast with its long stretch of palm-backed sand. It is just north of Ban Mae Hat and easily accessible by songthaew or on foot. A mile (1.5 km) southeast of Ban Mae Hat, arching **Chalok Ban Kao Bay** sits beneath steep cliffs.

Ko Tao's popularity with both divers and young partiers moving on from Phangan's full moon party has spoiled much of its quiet, tropical getaway atmosphere. During peak season, many resorts on primarily dive-oriented Sai Ree and Chalok Ban Kao will not rent to non-divers, and music from late-night beach parties carries to nearby bungalows. Furthermore, dive sites around the island are so crowded that it seems divers outnumber the fish. Yet quieter, isolated beaches still exist, and a snorkeling day trip via long-tail boat remains a magical experience.

Mu Ko Ang Thong Marine National Park

The 42 island wonders of the Mu Ko Ang Thong Marine National Park line up on a north-

Mu Ko Ang Thong Marine National Park

Maps pp. 263 & 291

Marine National Parks Division

Royal Forestry Department, 61 Phahonyothin Rd., Bangkhen, Bangkok

02-562-0760

Visitor Information

Mu Ko Ang Thong Marine National Park Office, 26/1 Mu 5 Talad Lang Rd., Surat Thani

077-286025

south axis between the mainland and Ko Samui, reaching as far north as Ko Phangan and south to within 6 miles (10 km) of Surat Thani Province. They come in a multitude of shapes and sizes, but all share one attribute—remarkable natural beauty.

Mu Ko Ang Thong was declared a national park in 1980. Previously it had been under the administration of the Royal Thai Navy, which used its maze of sea corridors, channels, and bays for training. As a result, the islands remained safe from encroachment.

This unspoiled environment meets all the preconceptions of a tropical paradise. The rocky limestone islands are carpeted with thick, deep-green forest. Brilliant

Bird's Nest Soup

Swiftlets build their nests in crevices high in the caves that pockmark the limestone crags found in southern Thailand's coastal areas. Their handicraft, once softened and separated into vermicelli-like threads, ends up on the tables of Chinese restaurants around the world as the expensive delicacy bird's nest soup. Sea gypsies (chao lae) scamper up rickety scaffolding to dislodge the nests from the rocks. The government awards much sought-after concessions to local groups to harvest the nests. So lucrative is the trade that armed guards are often found in front of caves.

white sands hide in idyllic coves and spread generously along bays that slope gently to the water's calm edge. When outlined against a deep-blue sky and the sparkling waters of the Gulf of Thailand, they present a majestic spectacle.

Ang Thong Islands: The varied shapes of the islands have inspired whimsical appellations: Rhinoceros Island, Sleeping Cow Island, Camera Head Island, and Tree Sorrow Island.

The Ang Thong islands vary in size, from craggy cliffs towering above ribbons of white sand on the biggest island, Ko Wua Talab, to small, understated mounds no bigger than a tennis court. On the larger islands, beaches are wider and shaded by forest, while mangroves thrive in sheltered areas where sandbars and mudflats have developed. Lush evergreens are dominant inland; limestone forest clings tenaciously to exposed cliffs.

Each of these 42 islands could stand proudly against the beauty of most other tropical islands, but the effect of having so many jewels encrusted into one crown in an area of just 39 square miles (102 sq km) is almost overwhelming. Ang Thong is reminiscent of the limestone islands and monoliths that crowd into Phangnga Bay near Phuket (see pp. 331–334), although it lacks the haunting drama of that place.

Nevertheless, you should not miss the experiences of kayaking or sailing among these lovely islands, exploring the caves, lagoons, and beaches, or climbing to breathtaking panoramas.

Excursions to Ang Thong are

made from Ko Samui. Many operators run daily trips to the islands,
which lie about 19 miles (30 km)
east. Boats depart at 8:30 a.m. and
return at 5 p.m. Ask your hotel or
TAT office to recommend a reputable operator. Other organized
tours can be arranged with travel
agents on Samui or your hotel's
travel desk; these, however, tend
to ply a well-worn route to the
islands' attractions and haul mobs
of other visitors along. If you can, it
is better to take a private or small
group charter organized through
the larger hotels and resorts. At
least one company, Blue Stars Kay-
aks *(tel 077-413231),* on Chaweng
Beach, offers kayaking trips around
Ang Thong, a recommended way
to explore the islands. (Also see
Sea Kayaking, pp. 332–334)

Though dive trips around Ang
Thong are available, they are not
recommended because of generally poor visibility, caused by the
sediment washed out from the Ta
Pi River Estuary. However, there is
good snorkeling at **Hin Nippon**
and **Ko Wao,** at the northern
outreaches of the archipelago, well
away from the estuary

Staying on the Islands: The
national park administers accommodations, which must be booked
and paid in person at the office
in Surat Thani on the mainland.
Camping is allowed on certain
islands, but permission must be
obtained from park rangers.

The accommodations on **Ko
Wua Talab,** where the ranger
station is located, are basic but
comfortable dormitories, and can
be rented as complete units. It is
worth staying over for the unri-

The shapes of Ang Thong's islands have inspired quirky names
with meanings like Rhinoceros Island and Tree Sorrow Island.

valed panoramas and the unusual
opportunity to catch sunrise and
sunset from the same viewpoint,
atop a 1,300-foot (400 m) peak.

Bird-watching can be rewarding
around the park headquarters, as
kingfishers, Brahminy kites, white-
bellied sea eagles, and sandpipers
frequent the area. Swiftlets, whose
nests form the basis for the Chinese
delicacy bird's nest soup (see sidebar
opposite), also inhabit caves here.

From the park headquarters,
a tough 656-foot (200 m) climb
brings you to **Tham Bua Bok,** or
"waving lotus cave," a name that
describes the unusually shaped
rock formations that fill the cavern.

The abiding beauty of **Thale
Nai** waits at the top of **Ko Mae
Ko,** a 790-foot (240 m) climb from

the shoreline. Here, towering limestone peaks encircle an emerald lake, fed from a stream that cuts through the mountains. From the lake's rim, magnificent views take in the archipelago. The site gives the islands their name—Ang Thong means "golden bowl."

Nearby **Ko Thai Phlao** and **Ko Wua Kan Tang** are noted for their particularly dazzling beaches.

Hiking on most islands is limited by a lack of trails, but the bigger islands of Ko Wua Talab and Sam Sap have some tracks.

Katen Archipelago

The seven islands of the Mu Katen archipelago are scattered across the strait between the port of Don Sak, in Surat Thani, and Ko Samui. The islands are popular day-trip destinations from Ko Samui; book your trip through your hotel or a travel agent on the island. Minibuses pick visitors up from their hotels and deliver them to the small fishing village of Ban Throng Kruk. Tours pass a fleet of colorful fishing boats before heading to the islands.

The 3-square-mile (7.5 sq km) Ko Katen is the largest island in the group and the only one that is populated (pop. 70). Good nature trails cut through the island's forested interior.

Ko Katen is unusual in that no dogs—domesticated or stray—live there. Mostly docile, stray dogs are found throughout Thailand. Buddhism dictates that all life is sacred, and dogs seem to be the major beneficiary of this precept. On Ko Katen, locals say dogs cannot survive because of the supernatural powers of the island's thriving cat population: The cats place a curse on any canine that has the misfortune to be washed up on the island. Ill fortune also befalls people who might bring dogs onto the island—or so legend has it.

A coral reef offers good snorkeling at **Laem Hua Sai** on the northern tip of Ko Katen. The Katen archipelago lacks good beaches, but the best are on the attractive island of **Ko Mat Sum,** where white stretches of sand incline to crystal-clear water. **Ko Daeng** is also worth a visit for its clear waters, white beaches, coral, and lack of inhabitants. Basic—in some cases

The islands at the northern end of Ang Thong are the best for snorkeling.

EXPERIENCE: The Underwater World

With some 1,355 miles (2,170 km) of coastline on the Gulf of Thailand and the Andaman Sea, Thailand offers a wide variety of dive possibilities among some of the world's richest marine fauna. There's something here for everyone, from quick, offshore dives to all-day excursions to overnights on a live-aboard boat.

Go between December and May. For most scuba trips, you must have open water diver certification; almost all dive shops offer courses. Most trips are under 3,000 baht ($100). See pp. 387–388 for further information.

Southwest Thailand
Phuket Probably the best place to start a dive trip. Thailand's largest island has dive opportunities ranging from easy day trips to longer multiday excursions to the Similan and Surin islands. Several dive companies also offer escorted dive trips beyond the Surin Islands into Myanmar waters around the so-called Burmese Banks.

Ko Lanta & Trang South of Phuket and Krabi, several islands and beach towns with promising dive sites are just making their impact on the scuba scene. Dive companies on Phuket can help with details.
Ko Phi Phi Islands south of Phuket are often limestone karsts that drop into the sea and provide unique underwater vistas for divers. Ko Phi Phi Don and Ko Bida Nok are the favored dive sites.
Similan Islands This nine-island archipelago is one of the premier dive sites in Southeast Asia for its varied topography and rich sea life. Four hours from Phuket, they are best visited with a live-aboard vessel.

Surin Islands North of the Similans is the final dive archipelago before you enter Myanmar's waters. The Surin islands are known for their superb corals, inhabited by sailfish and large pelagics.

Southeast Thailand
Chumphon Bustling Chumphon marks the point where corals and fringe reefs make their appearance in Thailand.
Ko Samui & Ko Tao Samui may be the country's second most popular resort, but divers head two hours north to the tiny Ko Tao, which has the best diving in the Gulf of Thailand. Dive shops on Samui organize multiday dive excursions.

primitive—accommodations are available on Ko Katen, Ko Mat Sum, and Ko Rab.

Ko Nang Yuan
If you are looking for a dose of upscale isolation in an incredible setting, then Ko Nang Yuan is highly recommended. Just off the northwest tip of Ko Tao, this trio of small islands is strung together by wide, crescent-shaped, white sandbars that form two shallow, clear bays filled with coral. The middle island, a squat jumble of boulders and jungle, has a solitary upscale resort *(Ko Nang Yuan Dive Resort, tel 077-456088 to -93)*. The two larger islands are giant mounds of granite covered with thick foliage and strewn with huge boulders, both at the shoreline and on the steep hills.

The bays are perfect for diving and snorkeling courses. For experienced divers there are a number of small wall dives and swim-arounds. Fish, in places, are prolific. Day trippers arriving on long-tail boats from Ko Tao cover the island's beaches. The resort charges 100 baht per person for such visits. ∎

More Places to Visit in Southern Thailand

Burma Banks

About 81 miles (130 km) off the coast, past the Surin Islands, is one of the world's fabled diving sites, the Burma Banks, with riotous underwater fields of colored coral. Farther north, the **Meguri Islands,** an archipelago laced with hundreds of uninhabited islands and multitudinous coral reefs running for hundreds of miles off the coast of Myanmar (Burma), are yet another Andaman Sea diving wonderland.

Diving tours to the Burma Banks, and diving and ecotours to the Meguris, can be arranged through the numerous dive shops in Phuket.

Map p. 263

Isthmus of Kra

From Chumphon on the Gulf of Thailand, Highway 4 slices through the luxuriant mountainous spine of the Malay Penin-sula before edging the Myanmar (Burma) border and swinging south to Ranong. From there it rolls down the scenic Andaman Sea coast toward Phuket. The narrowest point of the peninsula, the Isthmus of Kra, is signposted north of Ranong, near the town of Kra Buri. Here, a scant 14 miles (22 km) of land separate the Pacific Ocean from the Pak Chan Estuary, which opens into the Indian Ocean.

Plans to carve a canal across the isthmus are pulled off the shelf every now and again. Such a waterway would allow shipping a short cut between the Andaman and South China Seas, cutting days off the journey from Europe and the Middle East, via the Strait of Malacca and Singapore, to East Asia.

Map p. 263

Ko Ma

About 550 yards (500 m) to the northwest off Ko Phangan, hilly and verdant Ko Ma ("dog island") is an excellent snorkeling site. Here, you'll find a wealth of marine life (an-gelfish, cuttlefish, red snapper, parrot fish, and wrasse) cruising and darting around the anemones and sponges that encrust the reef just offshore. A long sandy beach edges the steep, heavily forested hills.

To reach Ko Ma, charter a long-tail boat from Phangan's port town of Tong Sala or from the popular Hat Rin. Boats can also be hired from the remote village of Hat Mae, op-posite Ko Ma. Accommodations are available on the island.

Ko Matalang

Just off the northern end of Chaweng Beach (see p. 292), easily accessible Ko Matalang is rated as the best snorkeling site in the area. Sunlight penetrates the shallow reef that fringes the southern coastline of the island, accentuating the kaleido-scopic colors of the coral. Gardens of sea anemones, staghorns, gorgonians, and foliaceous coral are found here, along with the occasional cruising blacktip reef shark. You may see people wade out and swim to the island, but chartering a long-tail boat is safer as currents can be unpredictable.

Wat Tham Prakayang

About 7.5 miles (12 km) south of Kra Buri, turn left at the Kilometer 504 road marker to the cave temple of Wat Tham Prakayang. Borrow a flashlight from the monks to explore this deep cave, which leads to an image-filled cavern. The highlight is an unusual jet-black Buddha image, with eyes fixed in mother-of-pearl.

Farther south on Highway 4, **Punya Ban Falls** can be seen tumbling from a high cliff to the left of the road, about 10 miles (16 km) north of Ranong. A little farther south, the road opens up expansive views of the Pak Chan Estuary—the border with Myanmar (Burma)—and the islands dotting the Anda-man Sea beyond.

Map p. 263

Home to some of Asia's best beaches, islands, and international resorts, with the bonus of quaint villages, bustling towns, and an intriguing mix of Buddhist and Muslim ways

Far South

Tourists relax on Phuket's Patong Beach.

Far South

Thailand's southern provinces down the Malay Peninsula have a distinctive, appealing topography. Rugged, forested hinterlands are laced with waterfalls. Limestone monoliths, pocked with sanctified grottoes, jut from land and sea. Rubber and coconut plantations buffer quaint villages and bustling tourist towns. Along the coast, glorious beaches shimmer and, offshore, coral-ringed islands captivate with tropical beauty.

Most of Thailand's three million Muslims live in the far south.

Distinctive, too, are the people, known as *khon pak tai*. The far south's long and colorful history has forged a hardy, polyglot race. Thai, Chinese, and Muslim-Malay cultures and traditions coexist and sometimes intermingle. Customs, dialects, festivals, cuisine, architecture, and entertainment are often co-opted.

The far south is linked with the Sumatra-based Srivijaya Empire, which dominated much of what is today Indonesia, Malaysia, and southern Thailand between the 7th and 13th centuries. With the disintegration of Srivijaya, the region, pinned to the authority of Nakhon Si Thammarat, fell under the respective rule of the Sukhothai and Ayutthaya Kingdoms, but still retained a high degree of autonomy. When

Ayutthaya fell in 1767, the southern provinces were controlled by the Bangkok government but remained semi-independent before being gradually absorbed into the Thai nation.

Throughout these centuries the far south played host—often a reluctant one—to streams of foreigners intent on trade, exploitation, and colonization. Early settlers arrived from the Indian subcontinent and from across the loosely defined southern borders of the Malay states. Trang and Phuket, with their strategic positions along the Strait of Malacca, became Thai centers of world trade and entry points for foreign merchants moving farther into Thailand. The influence of seafaring Portuguese

NOT TO BE MISSED:

and Chinese immigrants (many of whom arrived in the 19th century to work the tin mines) is seen in the ornate Sino-Portuguese architecture still standing in some towns. The British, who controlled Malaysia and, at various times, parts of southernmost Thailand, were a constant presence.

This centuries-long cultural mixture exerts itself in engaging ways. Malaysian-Islamic domed mosques share the landscape with elaborate Buddhist *wats*; seminomadic sea gypsies sail from island to island eking out a livelihood from fishing; attractive fishing villages and towns dot the coast; and vibrant commercial centers testify to the region's continued prosperity. ∎

Nakhon Si Thammarat

Nakhon Si Thammarat is busily shaking off its rough and ready reputation as the breeding place of some of Thailand's most notorious gangsters. These days it is being promoted heavily by tourism officials for its many historic and cultural attractions. The city, one of the oldest in the country, proudly hangs on to its past through its revered temples, excellent museum, and thriving, high-quality handicraft industry.

Buddhas at Nakhon's Wat Mahathat: The 1,000-year-old temple is one of Thailand's most important.

At the beginning of the Christian era, Nakhon (then known as Ligor) was the capital of the Tambralinga Empire, one of a number of kingdoms in Southeast Asia that were set up by Hindu colonists from India. Sometime in the seventh century, Nakhon fell under control of the Srivijaya Empire, the dominant force in Malaysia and Indonesia, and was renamed Nagara Sri Dhammaraja.

After 200 years of Srivijaya power, the Tambralinga won back Ligor, first conquering the Mon Kingdom of Lop Buri and placing Prince Suryavarman I (r. 1011–1050) on the Khmer throne at Angkor. The city remained part of the Khmer Empire until the rise of the then-ruling Sukhothai Kingdom in 1292.

Under Sukhothai rule, Nakhon thrived as an economic power and influential spiritual center. Its enduring legacy of this period is the promotion of the Sri Lankan-based Hinayana (Theravada) Buddhism, which was to become Thailand's major religion.

Wat Mahathat & Around

Nakhon's central role in helping define religion in Thailand presents itself at Wat Mahathat (*Ratchadamnoen Rd., about a mile/1.5 km S of the city center*). Also called Wat Phra Boromothat, the temple is Nakhon's founding monument. It was built about a thousand years ago by King Sri Thammaso-karaj when he moved his capital south from Chaiya.

Wat Mahathat, or "temple of the great relic," is one the oldest and most important places of worship for Buddhists in Thailand. Its centerpiece, an imposing 255-foot (77 m) *chedi* with a spire topped with 600 pounds (272 kg) of solid gold, towers over an expansive cloister teeming with Buddha icons and elephant-head statues. South of the chedi in the Wihan Luang, the prominent Buddha image smiles below a fantastically ornate red ceiling that is propped up by inward-angled pillars, the mainstays of Ayut-thayan architecture.

A short distance beyond Wat Mahathat, also on Ratchadam-noen Road, is the city's prestigious **National Museum** (*closed Mon.– Tues., tel 075-341075*). It traces the history of the region from prehistoric times through art, archaeological, and ethnological objects, including Buddha, Vishnu, and Shiva images, ceramics, and handicrafts such as basketry, textiles, and the province's famed shadow puppets (see Shadow Puppetry, p. 312).

Shadow puppetry (*nang thalung*), which was introduced to Thailand during the Ayutthaya period, was once tremendously popular in Nakhon and nearby Phatthalung (see pp. 314–315). Sadly, master practitioners are thin on the ground these days,

INSIDER TIP:

It is a traditional Thai custom to take off your shoes before entering a house or temple.

—SUCHANA A. CHAVANICH
National Geographic field scientist

and shows are rare. One such master and living treasure is Suchart Subsin. "Uncle" Suchart, who has received accolades from the King for his work, keeps the spirit of nang thalung alive at his small workshop, **Suchart House** (*110/18 Si Thammasok Rd., Soi 3. tel 075-346394*). Suchart handcrafts leather puppets to sell, shows how puppets are made, offers information on upcoming shows, and puts on private performances—involving voice characterizations, singing, and live music—and occasional impromptu demonstrations for customers.

Nakhon Si Thammarat

 Map p. 309

Visitor Information

 Tourism Authority of Thailand, Sanam Na Muang, Ratchadamncen Rd., Nakhon Si Thammarat

☎ 075-346515

Local Handicrafts

After its leather shadow puppets, Nakhon is best known throughout Thailand for its intricate nielloware *(krueang tom)* and colorful baskets woven from superfine grass *(yan lipao).* A number of centers selling these and other handicrafts have well-presented handicraft shops edging Tha Chang Road, near the local tourism office and the sports field.

Close to Bovorn Bazaar is **The Book Garden** *(1116 Ratchadamnoen Rd.),* an attractive, southern Thai-style wooden house containing a nonprofit

Shadow Puppetry

Shadow-puppet theater found its way to Southeast Asia about 500 years ago, introduced by traders from the Middle East. It slowly made its way up the Malay Peninsula, where it was modified to suit Thai legend and tradition. During the Ayutthaya period, shadow puppetry was an important form of entertainment. Shows would begin at midnight and last until dawn, when the puppets' silhouettes could no longer be seen through the screen. Today, shadow puppetry is mainly found in the southern provinces of Nakhon Si Thammarat, Songkhla, and Phatthalung. Performances are rare, usually given only for the benefit of privileged tour groups or visiting dignitaries from Bangkok.

Thailand has two forms of shadow puppetry: *nang thalung* and *nang yai,* the difference being in the size of the puppets. In both forms, puppets are viewed by the audience through a screen that is illuminated from behind. Only the silhouette, or shadow, of the puppet is visible. Dramatic effects are achieved by varying the puppets' distance from the screen. Nang thalung figures, cut in intricate, sometimes lacy, patterns from buffalo hide, are similar in size to the shadow puppets of Malaysia and Indonesia. Nang yai, however, is unique to Thailand. This form uses much larger, almost life-size, buffalo hide cutouts. In nang yai, each figure is bound to two wooden poles held by a puppet master. Several masters may participate in a single performance because of the puppets' size. In nang thalung, buffalo horns may be used as the handles for the puppets.

Nang yai is rarely performed nowadays because of the lack of trained masters and the expense involved in making the shadow puppets. Most nang yai made today are sold as decorations. Shadow puppets represent an array of characters from classical and folk drama, principally the *Ramakien.*

sprung up in town in recent years as part of the Tourism Authority of Thailand's campaign to promote the province. The central **Bovorn Bazaar** *(1106 Ratchadamnoen Rd.,)* has a grand collection of handicraft stalls and appealing cafés.

If you're seeking to shop in style, however, there are more bookstore that specializes in volumes on local history, national politics, fine arts, and religion. Like so much of Nakhon, the bookstore can boast of a long and colorful past. Since the building was constructed in 1888, it has successively served as a Chinese medical clinic, an opium den, and a brothel. ■

Khao Luang National Park

Lying at the heart of Nakhon Si Thammarat Province, this park covers 220 square miles (571 sq km) and encompasses numerous splendid waterfalls lacing the slopes of Khao Luang, the far south's highest mountain. The arduous climb to the mountain's 6,020-foot (1,835 m) summit is a challenge taken on by avid trekkers every year.

The village of **Khiriwong,** 17.5 miles (28 km) west of Nakhon Si Thammarat off Highway 4015, is the starting point for treks to the summit. The Nature Education Center there can provide guides and porters. The Tourism Authority of Thailand office in Nakhon Si Thammarat also can help with arrangements.

The first stage of the 14-hour climb rises to 1,968 feet (600 m), passing rocks, streams, and waterfalls. Villagers have planted fruit trees amid the lowlands and hill forests. At one set of falls, **Wang Ai Yang Bon,** vibrant orchids grow near the rocks. After a six-hour climb, the first night is spent in a simple hut hidden by thick jungle at **Kratom Suan** rest stop.

The next morning, continue up a steep trail through virgin rain forest to **Laan Sai.** Tree ferns and an incredible variety of orchids grow beside a watercourse. The trail then becomes extremely steep, passing through tangles of jungle dangling with beautifully colored orchids. At Laan Hor, a side trail leads to **Hubpha Sadan,** an amazing valley thick with ancient tree ferns.

Back on the main trail, the steep climb continues as the forest grows thick with rattan and blossoming begonia. During the final stage of the climb (three hours), from Laan Dr Chavalit to the summit, the incline eases slightly as it passes

Spectacular Krung Ching, "waterfall of a hundred thousand raindrops"

through thick montane forests.

A less time-consuming 2.5-mile (4 km) trek leads to the magnificent **Krung Ching waterfall.** Beginning at the Krung Ching Park Office at the park's northwestern end *(off Hwy. 4016, 53 miles/85 km from Nakhon Si Thammarat),* the trail climbs past ancient ferns and extensive stands of palms, to a difficult final ascent over rocks and boulders. Seven-tiered Krung Ching falls is a justifiable reward for the climb. Its waters eventually settle in a pool so clear you can see the granite bedrock far below ∎

Khao Luang National Park

🅰 Map p. 309

National Parks Division

✉ Royal Forestry Department, 1 Phahonyothin Rd., Bangkhen, Bangkok

☎ 02-5620760

Visitor Information

✉ Tourism Authority of Thailand, Sanam Na Muang, Ratchadamnoen Rd., Nakhon Si Thammarat

☎ 075-397218

Phatthalung & Around

Patchworks of rice fields shaded by giant limestone cliffs, temple grottoes, and teeming bird life along the shore of the vast Thale Luang lake distinguish the peaceful province of Phatthalung. It is a region rarely visited by foreign tourists but makes a fascinating diversion from the well-established attractions of the far south, especially if you are interested in observing the birds that make their home in the marshy Thale Noi reserve.

Up to 187 bird species flourish among the vibrant flowering plants at Thale Noi Waterfowl Park.

Other than the lively **Morning Market** north of the Hoa Fah hotel on Kuha Sawan Road, there is not much to see in Phatthalung's capital, but there are interesting attractions nearby. **Wat Kuha Sawan** is sheltered inside a limestone cliff, just to the west of town on Kuha Sawan Road. In the lower, vaulted cave of this Ayutthaya-period grotto are dozens of highly stylized (some say ugly) statues of monks and Buddhas.

A steep trail leads to another cave filled with more Buddha statues, giving excellent views over Phatthalung, rice fields, and mountains to the west.

The province's two famous limestone peaks, Broken Chest Mountain and Broken Head Mountain, flank the main grotto of **Tham Malai,** 2 miles (3 km) north of town on Nivas Road, or you can catch a boat (about a 15-minute ride) from behind the railway station. Legend has it that these mountains represent two jealous women, turned to stone after fighting over a man. The cave is illuminated and filled with stalagmites and stalactites.

Phatthalung's oldest temple is **Wat Wang,** 5 miles (8 km) northeast of town following Ramat Road. Built to celebrate the establishment of Phatthalung during the reign of Rama III (r. 1824–1851), its major feature is a refurbished chapel with murals dating from the 18th century. Along the same road, another 2.5 miles (4 km) beyond Wat Wang, is the fishing village of **Lam Pam,** on the banks of Thale Luang lake. This lagoon forms the northern end of Thale Sap (Songkhla Lake). The village beach, Hat Sansuk, is pleasant enough, especially for sitting in the shade and tucking into the local seafood. If the urge for activity takes hold, hire a boat for short trips to the limestone islands of Ko Si and Ko Ha. Here, in crevices on the cliff faces, swiftlets build nests that make the main ingredient in bird's nest soup.

Thale Noi Waterfowl Park

About 20 miles (32 km) northeast of Phatthalung's capital on Highway 4048 is Thailand's version of the Everglades—without the alligators. Declared a protected area in 1975, Thale Noi Waterfowl Park, the most in and part of Thale Sap, is the country's largest water bird sanctuary, encompassing 130 square miles (450 sq km) of rice paddies, peat swamp forest, grassland, tropical evergreen forest, and wetlands. Park of-

ficials estimate 187 species of birds, both native and migratory, shelter at the sanctuary, including various species of herons, ducks and geese, rails, jacanas, cormorants, and stilts.

From October to March, when migratory birds come to escape the winter in Siberia, numbers swell to nearly 50,000, and the park becomes a thunderous celebration of wildlife. Birds hiding among the lake's multitudinous purple lilies and thick grasses erupt at dawn in a cacophony of song and color. The purple swamp hens are masters at utilizing the grasses that grow in this shallow lake, pulling off shoots to construct platforms on the water, where

Khao Chong Center of Wildlife and Nature Study

This area of natural rain forest has a small conservation and botany museum. Hiking trails leading to mountains and waterfalls start from park headquarters. Scientists come from the world over to study the ecosystem here.

they can perch and walk during feeding. The grasses are also used by locals, who weave them into mats, hats, and bags. Boat tours stop at a village where you can see items being woven.

There are four large shelters around the park for visitors and an observation platform in the middle of the lake. A guided loop of the park by boat takes 90 minutes. ∎

Phatthalung
🄰 Map p. 309

Visitor Information
✉ Tourism Authority of Thailand, Sanam Na Muang, Ratchadamnoen Rd., Nakhon Si Thammarat
☎ 075-346515

Khao Chong Center of Wildlife and Nature Study
✉ 13 miles (21 km) E of Phatthalung via Trang-Phattalung Rd.

Songkhla & Beyond

This breezy and affable seaside town lies on the spit of land that divides the Gulf of Thailand from the huge area of Thale Sap (Songkhla Lake). It is a picturesque place, all but ignored on foreign tourist maps. Instead, it remains a favorite holiday spot among southern Thais, who come to enjoy its beaches, lake, and seafood, as well as cultural displays housed in two of the far south's best museums.

On the town's seaward shore is the lively 5-mile-long (8 km) **Samila Beach,** lined with all the essentials of Thai beach life: seafood restaurants, food vendors dishing up everything from watermelon to spicy

Fish farms are a familiar sight on enormous Songkhla Lake.

noodles, and plenty of shady casuarina trees. Samila may not match the quality of beaches on Samui and the southwest coast, but it is still an agreeable stretch of sand.

To the south of Samila, the small Muslim fishing village of **Kao Seng** stands on a headland. This is a good place to photograph the fleets of *kolae,* brilliantly colored and patterned traditional boats, and enjoy tasty seafood from waterside restaurants.

The centrally located **Songkhla National Museum** *(Rong Muang & Jana Rds., tel 074-311728, closed Mon.–Tues.)* houses some interesting and quirky treasures of Thailand's southern provinces. The museum is in an elegant 19th-century Sino-Portuguese mansion, once the grand home of a wealthy Chinese merchant. Highlights of the collection include Thai and Chinese ceramics, Ayutthaya-period Buddhas, Chinese furniture, Thai furnishings, and shadow puppets. There are also aerial photographs of the province and a useful topographical map. Farther south on Saiburi Road rises **Wat Machimawat,** a 17th-century temple with intriguing murals of 19th-century life.

The lake waterfront at

Thale Sap, on the opposite side of town to Samila Beach, is another colorful place. Walk along **Nakhon Noak Road** for an authentic encounter with the sights, sounds, and (at times overpowering) smells of the province's bountiful fishing

INSIDER TIP:

When in the far south, look for the best of Muslim food: *khao mok kai* (spicy chicken and rice), *roti* (pan fried bread), fried fish and tofu balls on sticks, and black sticky rice.

—KELLY FELTAULT
National Geographic contributor

industry. Part of Songkhla's old town, this area by the water contains remnants of Sino-Portuguese architecture.

Ko Yo

In the middle of the channel that connects Thale Sap to the Gulf of Thailand is the thickly wooded island of Ko Yo, noted for its seafood restaurants, traditional cotton weaving, and **Folklore Museum** at the Institute of Southern Thai Studies *(Ban Ao Sai, tel 077-311728)*. It can be reached from Highway 4146, about 8 miles (13 km) from downtown Songkhla.

This is the largest museum in southern Thailand, boasting an impressive collection of regional artifacts displayed in 17 traditional pavilion houses overlooking the lake and the island's forests. Exhibits are grouped into pottery, beads, shadow puppets, basketry, textiles, musical instruments, boats, religious arts, and weapons, with further displays of household, fishing, and agricultural implements. In addition, the museum grounds contain a cultural park, an outdoor performance area, and an audiovisual center.

Ko Yo is also home to a thriving cotton-weaving industry. Excellent deals on quality fabrics and clothes can be picked up from the weaving center to the south along Highway 4146. The clattering sound of cotton being woven on hand looms emanates from houses behind the market. A meal at the famous Porntip II seafood restaurant *(at the southern end of the island on Hwy. 4146)* is another of Ko Yo's popular attractions.

Thale Sap (Songkhla Lake)

On Thale Sap's eastern shores, about 34 miles (55 km) north of Songkhla town on Highway 4083, is the wetlands reserve of **Khu Khut Bird Sanctuary** *(Tambon Khukhut, Amphur Satning Phra, tel 074-397042)*. There are more than 200 resident and migratory species, including egrets, herons, storks, kites, sandpipers, and kingfishers. The best times to view the birds are in the morning and late afternoon from December to early January. Park rangers organize inexpensive boat trips for keen bird-watchers. ■

Songkhla

⬛ Map p. 309

Visitor Information

✉ Tourism Authority of Thailand, 1/1 Soi 2 Niphat Uthit 3 Rd., Hat Yai, Songkhla

☎ 074-231055

Hat Yai & Environs

This brash city of 200,000 inhabitants—mainly Chinese—is the closest thing to a metropolis in southern Thailand. One of Thailand's largest cities, it is the region's thriving transportation hub and its commercial, shopping, and entertainment center. The Malaysian border is just 34 miles (55 km) to the south, making this a favorite holiday spot for Malaysians.

Powerful Ton Nga Chang: The falls are best viewed after the monsoon season from October to December, when water levels are at their highest.

After sundown, vendors erect stalls along the already narrow footpaths of **Niphat Uthit No. 2 and 3 Roads,** in the middle of the city, and **Sanehanuson Road** and the **Plaza Market**, stacking them with everything from canned food to boom boxes. Good buys at these lively night markets include ready-made leisure and sportswear, preserved Thai fruits, imported Asian foodstuffs, batiks, cheap electrical goods, watches, and Thai handicrafts. This is a good city for shopping generally, and there are a number of department stores, including Diana, Ocean, and Expo on Niphat Uthit No. 3 Road, and World and Robinson on Thamnoon-vithi Road, where the shopping experience is calmer.

With its Chinese, Muslim, and Thai culinary influences, Hat Yai offers many good dining opportunities, but none so bizarre as the fare served along **Thanon Ngu** ("snake street"), on Chaniwat Road Soi 2. Along this bustling side street, the term "dining experience" takes on a whole new

INSIDER TIP:

You will find many snack foods and chocolates around Hat Yai that are imported from Malaysia and sold at good prices.

—SUCHANA A. CHAVANICH
National Geographic field scientist

meaning. Snakes are taken from cages, strangled with wire, and sliced open. Visiting Singaporean and Malaysian Chinese drink the snake's blood (mixed with rice wine) and eat the gallbladder, before settling down to a more substantial meal of snake soup cooked with herbs and spices. The snake handlers like to show off the reptiles before killing them, so it is best to keep your distance.

Hat Yai's nightlife is engineered to please Malaysian male clientele escaping the strict moral Muslim codes of their country, so there are plenty of massage parlors and seedy nightclubs. More tempered nightspots are found mainly in the hotels and include the Diana Club *(Lee Gardens Hotel, 1 Lee Pattana Rd., tel 074-234422)* and the Metropolis Club *(JB Hotel, 99 Chuti Anuson Rd., tel 074-234300).*

The city holds monthly bullfights—rowdy spectacles unique to the far south—at **Nurn Khun Thong** arena, or Highway 4 near the airport. Check venues and dates with the local tourist office.

Several attractions close to Hat Yai can be included in day excursions. About 15 miles (24 km) west of the city along Highway 4 is **Ton Nga Chang** ("elephant tusk falls"), where water cascades spectacularly over seven tiers and splits into two streams in a formation resembling elephant tusks. At **Tham Khao Rup Chang** ("cave of the elephant fountain"), some 6 miles (10 km) from the large border town of Padang Besar, three large grottoes are garnished with stalagmite and stalactite formations, and with Buddha images.

A visit to **Chana** is well worth the effort between January and June to experience the delightful dove-cooing contests (see below). ■

Hat Yai

🅰 Map p. 309

Visitor Information

✉ Tourism Authority of Thailand, 1/12 Soi Niphat Uthit 3 Rd., Hat Yai, Songkhla

☎ 074-231055

Dove Cooing

Dove-cooing contests are a popular pastime among southern Muslim Thais, notably in Narathiwat, Yala, Pattani, Satun, and Songkhla. Farms in Chana, about 25 miles (40 km) southeast from Hat Yai on Highway 407, breed the most sought-after birds. The town hosts contests on weekends from January to June. Hundreds of caged doves are raised on tall poles in open fields and begin choruses of cooing. Their songs are judged on pitch, melody, and volume. It's all taken very seriously, with champion doves valued at as much as $12,000.

Muslim South

The provinces that border Malaysia in Thailand's deep south—Pattani, Narathiwat, Yala, and Satun—are where the nation's predominant Buddhist beliefs meet and merge with the Islamic faith of Malaysia. The provinces were part of the Malay states until the early part of the 20th century. They had a culture distinct from the rest of the country, manifest in architecture, clothing, way of life, and language: the Malaysian dialect of Yawi.

Pattani

Nearly 80 percent of Pattani's population is Muslim, and as one of the centers of Islamic studies in the 17th century, the province accommodates some of the most impressive and

The imposing minaret at Pattani Mosque reflects the town's strong commitment to Islam.

important mosques in Thailand. The oldest of the mosques is **Masajid Kru Se,** located 4.5 miles (7 km) east of the provincial capital on Highway 42. Chinese immigrant Lim To Khieng began constructing the mosque in 1578, after he married a Pattani woman and converted to Islam. His sister, Lim Ko Niaw, who was upset about Lim To Khieng's change of faith, traveled from China to try to change her brother's mind. When he refused, Lim Ko Niaw placed a curse on the mosque and hanged herself from a nearby cashew tree. A replica of the tree is enshrined at **Leng Chu Khiang** temple, on Arnoaru Road.

The striking **Matsayit Klang,** or Pattani Mosque, is one of the most beautiful mosques in Thailand. This grand building has twin minarets, arched stained-glass windows, orange-hued facade, and domes inlaid with green stone. It dates from the early 1960s and is located on Yarang Road.

For a relaxing taste of southern Thai beach life, head to **Toloh Kapo,** about 10 miles (16 km) south of the capital off Highway 42. Locals come here in droves on weekends.

The Restive South

Thailand's south has been at odds with the country's central government ever since it was incorporated into the country early in the 20th century. The government's continued neglect of the region and callous disregard for the culture has led to calls for more autonomy and even independence. These calls have risen and fallen over the years, and efforts to fight for these aims have been sporadic. But since January 2004, there has been fighting. At first, the government dismissed it as the work of gangsters. But officials had to acknowledge that an organized insurgency is operating in the provinces of Narathiwat, Yala, and Pattani. Thousands of innocent people have been killed, while the government switches from peaceful to forceful methods to try to end the violence.

Narathiwat

Though Narathiwat carries the responsibilities of a provincial capital, "the residence of good people" maintains its charm as a laid-back fishing village. Hugging the curves of the Bang Nara River that flows into the Gulf of Thailand, the town is a delightful escape from the more rambunctious concrete provincial capitals and resorts of the far south.

Thailand's royal family also considers this a relaxing place; they make their way to Narathiwat for about two months a year from August to October and stay at Taskin Palace, 7.5 miles (12 km) south of town. The summer palace is open to the public at other times during the rest of the year.

About 9.5 miles (15 km) north of Narathiwat is **Wadin Husen.** Built in 1769, this timber mosque is one of the oldest in Thailand. In an intriguing deviation from the norm, it abandons traditional mosque styles for a mix of Thai, Chinese, and Malay elements.

Yala

The town's Pillar Shrine sits on a steep-roofed Thai pavilion in the center of a well-tended park on Phiphitphakdi Road in front of City Hall. The 20-inch (50 cm) pillar with a four-faced Buddha image and flame is more significant than its size suggests; it was a gift from the King to the people of Yala in 1962.

The immense reclining Buddha image at the wonderful **Wat Khu Ha Phi Muk,** about 5 miles (8 km) from the center of town, is one of the three most revered places in the south for Buddhists. A stream runs through the picturesque temple grounds, while the 81-foot (24.7 m) Buddha—believed to have been cast in A.D. 757—resides in a cave guarded by the statue of an aggressive-looking giant. Sunlight pours onto the image from a hole in the roof of the cave, creating a stunning reflective effect on the golden statue.

Satun

This province does not have a lot to offer international tourists, with the exception of its Ko Tarutao Islands (see pp. 344–345). These islands in this archipelago form a marine national park. ■

Pattani
🗺 Map p. 309
Visitor Information
✉ Tourism Authority of Thailand, 102/3 Mu 3 Narathiwat-Takbai Rd., Narathiwat
☎ 073-522411

Narathiwat
🗺 Map p. 309
Visitor Information
✉ Tourism Authority of Thailand, 102/3 Mu 3 Narathiwat-Takbai Rd., Narathiwat
☎ 073-522411

Islands of the Southwest

If you can't find your own version of tropical paradise in the generous sprinkle of islands off Thailand's southwest coast, then you are probably not looking hard enough. From Phuket— Thailand's largest island and favorite beach resort—and the limestone outcrops crowded into Phangnga Bay, down to the deserted coral-fringed gems near the Malaysian border, the beauty of the hundreds of islands that sparkle in the Andaman Sea is astounding.

The islands, many of which enjoy some degree of sanctuary within marine national parks, throw up a wealth of recreational activities, made easy by a solid tourist infra-

Built on stilts in Phangnga Bay and sheltered by a limestone monolith, the striking Muslim village of Ko Panyi is a popular stopover for day-trippers.

structure. Visitors can enjoy diving, snorkeling, hiking, beachcombing, mountain biking, water sports, camping, sea kayaking, rock climbing, golf, island hopping, and the more somnolent pursuit of sunbathing—all with minimum fuss. It generally takes no more than a stroll to the tour operator's desk at your hotel to organize an itinerary. As in most of Thailand, public transportation is plentiful, and rental cars and drivers are relatively inexpensive. The best time to visit is between November and April, when the monsoons abate.

Phuket, dubbed the Pearl of the Andaman, was "discovered" by backpackers in the early 1970s and has since developed into one of Asia's premier resorts, parading a nascent sophistication with its luxury resorts, world-famous spas, and first-class restaurants, both Thai and international. Because of its size, Phuket has been able to absorb and isolate the ugly excesses of tourist development, and today developers tend to take a long-term view.

Sadly, the same cannot be said for the miraculous island of Ko Phi Phi Don, whose na-

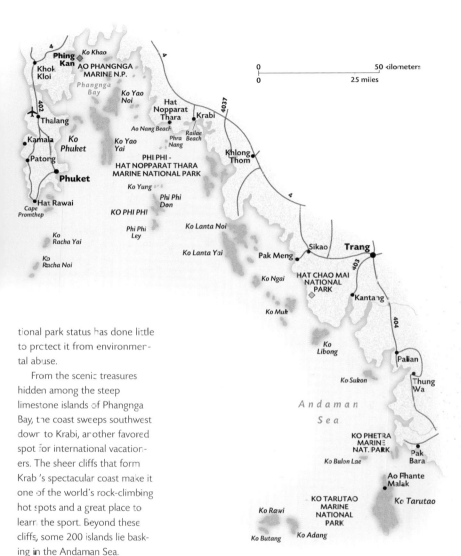

Ko Khao
Phing Kan
Khok Kloi
AO PHANGNGA MARINE N.P.
Phangnga Bay
Thalang
Kamala
Ko Phuket
Patong
Phuket
Hat Rawai
Cape Promthep
Ko Racha Yai
Ko Racha Noi
Ko Yao Noi
Ko Yao Yai
Hat Nopparat Thara
Ao Nang Beach
Phra Nang
Krabi
Railae Beach
Khlong Thom
PHI PHI - HAT NOPPARAT THARA MARINE NATIONAL PARK
Ko Yung
KO PHI PHI
Phi Phi Don
Phi Phi Ley
Ko Lanta Noi
Ko Lanta Yai
Pak Meng
Ko Ngai
Ko Muk
Sikao
Trang
HAT CHAO MAI NATIONAL PARK
Kantang
Ko Libong
Ko Sukon
Palian
Thung Wa
Andaman Sea
KO PHETRA MARINE NAT. PARK
Ko Bulon Lae
Pak Bara
Ao Phante Malak
Ko Rawi
KO TARUTAO MARINE NATIONAL PARK
Ko Tarutao
Ko Butang
Ko Adang

0   50 kilometers
0   25 miles

tional park status has done little to protect it from environmental abuse.

From the scenic treasures hidden among the steep limestone islands of Phangnga Bay, the coast sweeps southwest down to Krabi, another favored spot for international vacationers. The sheer cliffs that form Krabi's spectacular coast make it one of the world's rock-climbing hot spots and a great place to learn the sport. Beyond these cliffs, some 200 islands lie basking in the Andaman Sea.

Past Krabi, in the provinces of Trang and Satun, there are very few foreign visitors. The pristine islands that make up the Hat Chao Mai National Park and Tarutao Marine National Park revel in their isolation. It is a place where perceptions of tropical paradise sharpen into focus.

Ko Phuket

Phuket plays host to about three million foreign tourists each year, making it one of Asia's favorite holiday resorts. Tourists returned gradually following the tsunami that struck the region in December 2004, and

Ko Phuket

 Maps pp. 309, 323, &329

Visitor Information

✉ Tourism Authority of Thailand, 73–75 Phuket Rd., Amphur Muang, Phuket

☎ 076-211036, 076-212213, or 076-217138

now Phuket is back and, some would say, better than ever. Newer and, in most cases, more upscale facilities replaced older ones, and an early warning system to allay tourists' fears of another devastation has been established along the entire coast. Today, one would be hard pressed to realize that such a disaster had occurred at all.

be found in the compact capital town of **Phuket.** It has some of the best remaining examples of Sino-Portuguese architecture in the south—mainly long, narrow Chinese shop-houses with splendid 19th-century European ornamentation. The 19th-century colonial mansions of Chinese tin-mine bosses (some of which are now used as government buildings) skirt

---

Tin Mining

In 1518 the Portuguese won a concession to set up a tin-trading station in Phuket. The tin ore was mined from pits, smelted in crude furnaces, and fashioned into spear tips, swords, body armor, muskets, and bullets. As mining and smelting procedures improved, so did the quality of the tin. Bangkok needed it for coins and roof tiles, and it was also in demand in Europe.

Droves of Chinese migrated to Phuket in the mid-1800s to work the industry. Huge areas of land were stripped in the search for the ore. The first offshore dredger arrived in 1906, and hydraulic pumps, excavators, and vast furnaces were introduced. But demand for tin started to decline in the following decades, and today tin mining in Phuket has all but ceased.

The growth of tourism since the mid-1970s, along with tin mining and rubber production, has made Phuket Thailand's second richest province, after Bangkok. At 324 square miles (810 sq km), the island is Thailand's largest and most geographically diverse. Beaches vary from broad sweeps of white sand fringed by casuarina and palm trees, to rocky, isolated bays. The interior is a mixture of forested hills, limestone cliffs, tropical vegetation, and rubber, coconut, and cashew plantations. This appealing landscape is dotted with quiet Muslim hamlets, laid-back towns, and raucous tourist centers.

Capital City: Snippets of the island's multicultural past can

INSIDER TIP:

Walk down Phuket's Thalang Road, where restored mansions built in the distinctive Sino-Portuguese style of 100 years ago give a glimpse into the town before tourism.

—JOHN SEATON CALLAHAN
National Geographic contributor

the town center. Good examples of Sino-Portuguese architecture include the **Standard Chartered Bank Building** on Phangnga Road, the **Thai Airways office** on Ranong Road, and the **Provincial Hall** on Damrong Road. More can be found among the buildings on Yaowarat, Thalang, Dubik, and Krabi Roads.

Chinese heritage is also evident in the dozen or so shrines that punctuate the town with splashes of red and gold. The shrines are the focal points for the annual nine-day **Vegetarian Festival,** held in October, when young men pierce themselves with spears and swords in rituals of atonement and purification.

Tin mining has brought Phuket much of its wealth and a fair share of conflict. In 1876 the Chinese mine laborers *(angyee)* went on a bloody rampage across the island, first battling with each other, then turning on the locals. Many people sought shelter at the Buddhist compound of **Wat Chalong,** 5 miles (8 km) south of Phuket Town, on Highway 4022. Here, inspired by a monk named Luang Por Chaem, they fought off the Chinese. Luang Por Chaem's statue holds an honored place in the ornate *wat.*

Phuket Attractions: At the southern end of Highway 4129, at Cape Phanwa, is **Phuket Aquarium** *(tel 076-391126, www .phuketaquarium.org),* part of the Marine Research Center. The aquarium aids in the program to repopulate the island's depleted turtles. With the help of the Royal Thai Navy, staff collect turtle eggs from nesting sites on Phuket and nearby islands. The eggs—including those of the giant leatherback turtle—are hatched, and the young nurtured here and later released.

The privately run **Phuket Sea Shell Museum** *(tel 076-613789),*

at the southern end of the island on Highway 4024, has one the world's most valuable collections of seashells; some are for sale. Its gigantic golden pearl, weighing 140 carats, is a world-beater. A massive shell that tips the scales at 550 pounds (250 kg) is one of the museum's weightier exhibits.

Phuket Beaches: A few hundred yards beyond the Sea Shell

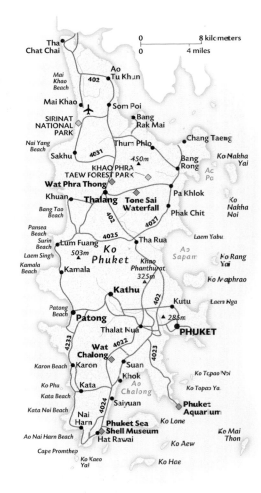

Museum, **Rawai Beach,** in Hat Rawai is a good place to begin a tour of Phuket's west coast. Rawai was, in fact, Phuket's first beach resort. This had nothing to do with its beauty; it is drab and rocky. This was the first beach to be connected by paved road to Phuket town, 10.5 miles (17 km) north. A host of inexpensive seafood restaurants line Rawai's foreshore, and you can hire long-tail boats or speedboats to the nearby islands of Ko Lone, Ko Hae, and Ko Aew for swimming, snorkeling, and sunbathing.

At the beach's northern end is a sad-looking *chao lae* (sea gypsy) village, only worth a stop if you enjoy watching tourists haggle for souvenirs from one of Thailand's marginalized minorities (see pp. 284–285). Follow Rawai's beachfront south to **Cape Promthep,** a headland at the very south of the island, to join the crowds watching the sunset.

More than a dozen main beaches, and many coves and small bays, line the island's west coast. A good coastal road, Highway 4233, makes access easy and traverses some of Phuket's most attractive countryside, climbing and winding in and out of forests, and coconut and rubber plantations, up to ridges with stunning panoramas of the Andaman Sea. The route also passes a number of elephant-trekking camps, where handlers take visitors on hour-long rides into the jungle. This has

INSIDER TIP:

Visit Phuket Island in mid-October during the annual Vegetarian Festival. Other than a lot of vegetables, you'll find a spectacle of firewalking, fireworks, trance dances, and self-mutilation.

—KAREN COATES
National Geographic writer

EXPERIENCE: Sailing

Both of Thailand's coasts provide navigable waters, but Phangnga Bay is Thailand's top sailing attraction, with most boats launching from Phuket harbor. Here are two operators that provide sailing excursions:

Asian Oasis *(7th fl., Nai Lert Tower, 2/4 Wireless Rd., Bangkok, tel 076-376192 [Phuket], www.asian-oasis.com)* Visit floating villages and Phangnga Bay's James Bond Island aboard the *June Bahtra,* a restored, traditional junk-rigged schooner.

For overnight adventures, the *Suwan Macha,* a junk-rigged luxury schooner that sleeps ten, explores beaches and islands around the bay.

Yachtpro *(adjacent to Yacht Haven Marina, Phuket, tel 076-348117, www.sailing-thailand.com)*

Yachtpro has internationally certified sailing instructors and offers sailing lessons, sailboat charters, and three- to nine-day adventure cruises from Phuket to Phi Phi, Krabi, or Ko Tarutao. They also offer sailing instruction services out of Pattaya.

proved so popular that Phuket suffers from overpopulation of the beasts, and food and water have to be trucked in.

At the southern tip of the island, near Cape Promthep and about 12.5 miles (20 km) from Phuket Town, is **Nai Harn,** an attractive beach locked between high, verdant headlands and bordered by casuarina trees. It is popular during the high season but has escaped major development because the beachfront is owned by a monastic group that prefers peace and quiet to crowds and high-rises.

Some 6 miles (10 km) north of Nai Harn is **Kata.** Its beach is on the lip of the island's third largest tourist center, a jumble of guesthouses, souvenir shops, tour operators, and restaurants, which tends to add to rather than detract from the holiday village character. Like Nai Harn, it is a pleasant sweep of beach, trapped between green headlands and backed by hills. A small island close by, Ko Phu, completes the picture; you can hire a long-tail boat from Kata Beach to take you there for snorkeling.

Just north of Kata is the long beach of **Karon.** A busy road separates sand and water from hotels. With its lack of trees and a backdrop of isolated high-rise hotels and condos, shoddily built restaurants, and disused rice paddies, the town's search for an identity continues. The town center is an uninspiring avenue of hotels, shops, bars, and restaurants at the northern end of the beach.

North of bustling Patong (see p. 329), beach life gets a bit quieter. **Kamala,** 5 miles (8 km) from Patong and 15 miles (24 km) from Phuket town, is a Muslim fishing village with a long sandy beach. The best spot is its northern end, where you can enjoy the shade of casuarina trees, if you don't mind laying down your towel over an old

Tourists rarely visit expansive Mai Khao Beach in Sirinat National Park, on Phuket's northwest coast.

Muslim graveyard. Kamala's most famous sight is the parade of water buffalo wandering down to the beach each afternoon to cool off. FantaSea is a sprawling entertainment complex at Kamala, with nightly glitzy, Las Vegas–style Thai cultural shows (complete with disappearing elephants), and

A rock climber clings to the roof of a cave high above the Andaman Sea.

Patong

🄰 Maps pp. 309, 323, & 325

Visitor Information

✉ Tourism Authority of Thailand, 73–75 Phuket Rd., Amphur Muang, Phuket

☎ 076-211036, 076-212213, or 076-217138

a buffet dinner that can accommodate up to 2,000 people.

Surin Beach, below the hills to the north of Kamala, is a favorite weekend picnic spot for locals. Just south of Surin, **Laem Singh** is a gem—a small, curving bay with rocky headlands at the foot of sheer, forest-fringed cliffs. Look for signs to a path that goes down to the beach.

North of Surin, around a small headland, is **Pansea Beach,** backed by steep hills and luxury resorts. These give the impression that this is a private beach. It is not; all beaches in Phuket are public.

Surin, Pansea, and **Bang Tao** are all beaches within walking distance of the attractive Muslim village of **Sope Sali.** Bang Tao is a large open bay, with one of Phuket's longest beaches. Its hinterland was all but destroyed by tin mining, but in the late

1980s and early 1990s it was transformed into the island's largest resort, the surprisingly unobtrusive Laguna Phuket.

Parks & Wildlife: Set next to Phuket International Airport, **Sirinat National Park** covers 36 square miles (90 sq km) of the island's northern coast with tropical evergreens, casuarina-dominated forests, and isolated beaches—perfect for dedicated beachcombers. Here, too, are Phuket's only mangrove forests.

The island's other national park is **Khao Phra Taew Forest Park,** a rain forest taking in 9 square miles (22 sq km) of the island's northern interior. The vegetation here is striking—majestic trees buttressed with tangles of undergrowth.

At the entrance to the park, off Highway 4027, is the **Gibbon Rehabilitation Center** *(tel 076-*

260492). Volunteers from around the world nurture gibbons that have been held illegally as pets, then eventually reintroduce them into the wild.

Patong: Patong is Phuket's boisterous tourist center, although somewhat muted these days as tourists have been slow to return after the Asian tsunami hit on December 26, 2004. Those returning will find the place little changed. In normal times, Patong is an energetic jumble of high-rise hotels and condos, restaurants, guesthouses, souvenir shops, beer halls, and discos. During the high season of November to March, people from all over the world crowd the sidewalks and sun themselves along Patong.

Patong sits behind the 2-mile (3 km) stretch of expansive and surprisingly attractive **Patong Beach,** its white sand curving between verdant hills. Hundreds upon hundreds of deck chairs shaded by beach umbrellas follow the contour of the beach. The chairs are inhabited by tourists relaxing and ordering coconuts, snacks, and beers from vendors who spend their days trudging along the sand.

Off the white sand and into the beach's clear waters, there are plenty of opportunities for action, including snorkeling, boogie boarding, riding personal watercrafts such as Jet Skis, windsurfing, water-skiing, and sailing. Paragliding is a pulse-quickening way to get great views of the beach and the town of Patong. Strapped to a parachute on the beach, you are launched into the sky and towed

along the beach by a speedboat.

Most of Patong's other amenities—restaurants and shops—lie along **Thawiwong Road,** or Beach Road, the town's animated thoroughfare that runs north to south. Side streets off Beach Road have more of the same, along with numerous bars and pubs. So Bangna, a street that should be approached with an open mind, is the epicenter of the action.

Ko Phi Phi

It's a credit to the resilience of the Phi Phi island group that it has absorbed some of the worst excesses of tourist development in Thailand and an immense natural disaster, yet still manages to stun even the most jaded traveler with its

INSIDER TIP:

The dozens of gibbons that hoot at visitors from cages just inside the Khao Phra Taew entrance have all been rescued from zoos, bars, and shops.

—KAREN COATES
National Geographic writer

extraordinary beauty. Up until the tsunami, the largest of the six islands, Phi Phi Don, was sinking under the weight of 500,000 tourists a year.

That has all changed. If there is anything to be salvaged from that terrible point in December 2004, Phi Phi Don is it. The waters around the island, which

Ko Phi Phi

🅰 Maps pp. 309 & 323

Visitor Information

✉ Tourism Authority of Thailand, Uttarakit Rd., Krabi

☎ 075-622163

✉ Tourism Authority of Thailand, 73–75 Phuket Rd., Amphur Muang, Phuket

☎ 076-211036, 076-212213, or 076-217138

have been cleared of both pre- and post-tsunami debris, are possibly the cleanest they have been since the advent of tourism. The authorities, who often ignored or benefitted from the illegal development of land, are now considering limiting the amount of rebuilding that should take place; the tsunami flattened or ruined just about every structure on the island. Although the authority's good

has accommodations (reserve rooms in advance).

Typically, packaged day trips include visits to other islands in the group, with lunch and an afternoon of snorkeling. To tailor your trip, buy return fares without the frills, and ask tour agents in Ton Sai to organize full-day tours around the island or overnight camping on the deserted beaches of **Ko Phai** (Bamboo Island) and **Ko Yung** (Mosquito Island).

The Beach

Ko Ang Thong was the setting for the cult novel by the English author Alex Garland, *The Beach* (1996). The book was made into the Hollywood blockbuster movie of the same name, released in 2000, produced by and starring Leonardo DiCaprio. The main protagonist in both the book and the movie finds a map in the room of a junkie who commits suicide in a flophouse in Bangkok. The map

eventually leads him to a small community of foreigners who are living in secrecy on an island of profound majesty. However, while Garland settled for a backdrop of Ang Thong for his novel, Hollywood, for its version, moved across the Malaysia Peninsula to the Andaman Sea and the stunning Maya Bay on Phi Phi Ley (see below), which is another marine national park.

intentions remain to be seen, there is little doubt that it will take many years, if ever, for the place to attract the same number of visitors it had before the tsunami. Perhaps now things will look more in tune with the island's status as part of the Ko Phi Phi–Hat Nopparat Thara Marine National Park.

Ko Phi Phi is easy to reach, from Phuket or from Krabi's Ao Nang, Phra Nang, and Ko Lanta. From Phuket, ferries take less than two hours to reach the islands (during the monsoon season, from May to October, the passage can sometimes get rough and scary). Phi Phi Don

Boat Tours: Trips can begin with snorkeling over coral beds to the east of Phi Phi Don, followed by a stop at Ko Phai. The boat then sweeps down to **Phi Phi Ley,** the second largest island of the group. The first stop here is **Viking Cave,** a vast cavern with a series of paintings of ships generously described as pictographs of Viking longboats. They are more likely to be images of Chinese junks.

Like so many places in this island group, **Maya Bay,** the next stop, is blessed with beauty. It became Hollywood's version of tropical paradise in 1999,

INSIDER TIP:

Take an early morning long-tail boat from Phi Phi Don to Maya Bay to experience the beauty of *The Beach* before the crowds block your view.

—LINDA JOHANSSON
National Geographic designer

when scenes from the movie *The Beach* were filmed here. Just when you think that it couldn't get much better, the boat channels into **Lo Samah,** bitten out of the cliffs at the southern end of the island. This finger of seawater is hemmed in by imposing cliffs.

Most tours provide snorkeling gear, or you can rent it from dive shops in Ton Sai. Tailor day trips to include snorkeling at Hin Pae on Phi Phi Don's east coast or in Phi Phi Ley's bays of clear water. Ask to visit the beautiful, relatively isolated beaches, capes, and bays around Phi Phi Don, such as Lo Bakao Hat Laem Thong, Hat Pak Nam, Hat Runtee, and Lo Loma. **Ko Bida Nok,** a small island half a mile (1 km) south of Phi Phi Ley, is the best dive site.

Phangnga Bay

An unforgettable place, with hundreds of craggy little islands jutting out of emerald-green waters, Phangnga Bay is one of the great natural wonders of Southeast Asia. The main prize of this remarkable spot is hidden inside those imposing craggy sea cliffs: It is the *hongs*, or sea caves, that provide many

visitors with the most abiding memories of the area.

The hongs (the Thai word for "rooms") are ancient caves of limestone inside large coral formations. They were formed underwater some 130 million years ago and forced upward above sea level as the Earth's continental plates shifted. The subsequent millions of years of erosion by rain, wind, and sea have opened the tops of some of these caves.

The stunning result of nature's handiwork is a bay full of rocky, foliage-laden islets,

Phangnga Bay

 Maps pp. 309 & 323

Visitor Information

✉ Tourism Authority of Thailand, Uttarakit Rd., Krabi

☎ 075-622153

Phangnga Bay, with its hundreds of soaring limestone crags, is one of the wonders of Southeast Asia.

Ao Phangnga Marine National Park

- Map p. 323
- Royal Forestry Department, 61 Phahonyothin Rd., Bangkhen, Bangkok
- 02-562-0760

SeaCanoe International

- 367/4 Yaowarat Rd., Phuket
- 076-528840

with enclosed lagoons and sandy beaches, as well as self-contained ecosystems, multichambered grottoes, and giant rock archways and passageways, a paradise that can be explored by canoe.

INSIDER TIP:

Many tour operators offer all-day long-tail-boat tours of Phangnga Bay, with its limestone pinnacles and Muslim villages on floating rafts. Bring earplugs; the engines are deafening.

—JOHN SEATON CALLAHAN
National Geographic contributor

Sea Kayaking: Some 20 companies in nearby Phuket offer sea-canoeing trips in and around the islands, lasting from one to six days; the trips can generally be booked from your hotel tour desk. The trips include pickup and drop-off at the hotels. Canoeing is made easy by the accompanying "mother" ships, which anchor near the hongs to off-load canoes.

The popularity of the tours has given rise to logjams at many of the cave entrances, and too many people can spoil the experience. SeaCanoe International was the first company to lead people into the hongs in the early 1990s, and the company tries to avoid the crowds by offering overnight trips and tours of the caves at less popular times. It also limits the number of its tours, and its guides enliven the

Gap eroded to form a cave

Water enters through fissures and erodes the limestone, forming internal passageways and caves, or *hongs.*

trip with lessons in the natural history of the bay.

Most of the hongs can be entered only at low tide, when the ebb reveals the narrow, craggy entrances. The dark tunnels are illuminated by streams of light pouring down giant shafts in the limestone. The hongs vary in size, but not in impact, with the smallest just 65.5 feet (20 m) in diameter. Some of the caverns are linked by tunnels in the rock.

The bay is part of the **Ao Phangnga Marine National**

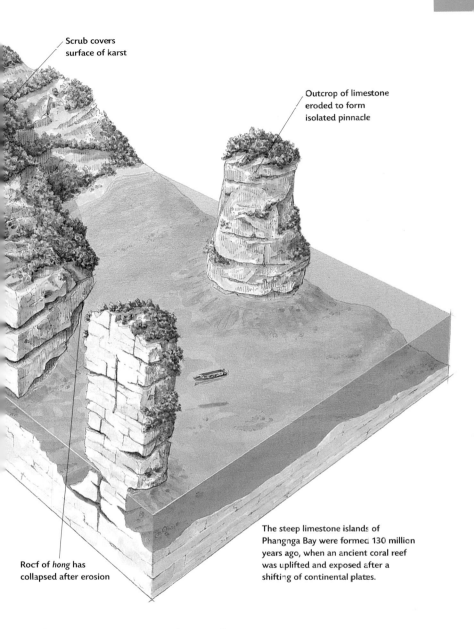

Scrub covers surface of karst

Outcrop of limestone eroded to form isolated pinnacle

The steep limestone islands of Phangnga Bay were formed 130 million years ago, when an ancient coral reef was uplifted and exposed after a shifting of continental plates.

Roof of *hong* has collapsed after erosion

Park, but some areas are given away as lucrative government concessions to companies collecting the nests of swiftlets that are used in the Chinese delicacy bird's nest soup. In the past, concessionaires have had disputes with sea-canoe operators, claiming that visitors were scaring off the birds. Concessionaires now collect a percentage of the canoe companies' earnings, as "entrance fees" to what they claim as their caves. The disagreements

Laid-back Krabi offers plenty of solitude despite its growing popularity.

reached a head in 1998, when the concessionaires barred entry to canoe companies that had not paid entrance fees, but the situation now seems to have settled down.

James Bond Island: One of the focal attractions of Phangnga Bay is James Bond Island, or Ko Khao Phing Kan ("leaning island"), the much visited rocky cleft that served as an imposing setting for the 1974 James Bond movie, *The Man with the Golden Gun,* starring Roger Moore. (James Bond returned to Phangnga Bay in 1997, this time in the guise of Pierce Brosnan, for *Tomorrow Never Dies.*) Avoid the hawkers and touristy souvenir stalls around the beach, and hike up the network of trails that leads to spectacu-

lar viewpoints overlooking this hauntingly beautiful bay.

Ko Panyi: Built on mangrove stilts over the water and tailing out from a huge hunk of limestone, this is a self-contained Muslim fishing village connected by a labyrinth of walkways. Ko Panyi is hostage to tourism during the day, but when the last of the visitors flee in late afternoon it resumes its own delightful character. It is possible, and worthwhile, to stay overnight. Cruise tours that incorporate James Bond Island, Ko Panyi, and a number of other incredible islands that dot the bay can be taken from Phuket, but it is quicker and less expensive from Phangnga town. Sayan Tours *(tel 076-430348)* at the Phangnga bus station is the best.

Krabi

When compared with Phuket and Ko Samui, Krabi Province seems relatively undeveloped, but an efficient tourism service here allows visitors to get the most out of its attractions. And there is no shortage of things to see and do when you get to Krabi. The province is famed for its coastline of limestone cliffs and an overabundance of perfect deserted islands.

Krabi town, the small, affable provincial capital on the Krabi River, has very little in the way of attractions, functioning instead as a conduit for getting visitors out to the beaches and islands. It is full of tour agents that organize camping, snorkeling, diving, and sea-canoeing trips.

Mangrove Swamps: Most new arrivals head straight for the beaches, but a trip to the Krabi River mangrove swamps opposite the town makes an interesting diversion. Long-tail boats leave Chao Fa pier (also the departure point to the province's beaches and islands) to explore the numerous channels winding through the mangroves, which harbor a wealth of wildlife. Birds include brown-winged longer kingfishers, Pacific reef egrets, Asian dowitchers, and white-bellied sea eagles. You may also spot otters, mudskippers, fiddler crabs, and formicable monitor lizards basking on the muddy banks.

Ko Phi Phi–Hat Nopparat Thara Marine National Park:

A large slice of Krabi's coast and islands comes under the jurisdiction of the 156-square-mile (390 sq km) park. At the southeastern edge of the park, near the mouth of the Krabi River, is a most curious attraction, the **Su San Hoi Shell Cemetery.** This geological oddity consists of fossil beds formed from petrified seashells. The beds, which resemble giant concrete slabs, date back 40 million years.

The park also includes a jagged coastline running southwest from the mouth of the Krabi River and a profusion of Andaman Sea islands. Park headquarters are at the southern end of **Nopparat Thara Beach,** 11.5 miles (18 km) west of Krabi town on Highway

INSIDER TIP:

Krabi town has good shopping and a great night market for Thai and Muslim food. Don't leave without trying the *roti kluay* (round flat wheat bread stuffed with banana).

—KELLY FELTAULT
National Geographic contributor

4202. Nopparat Thara is a broad sandy beach lined with casuarina trees and food stalls. Quieter and more conservative than other beaches in Krabi, it draws local families on weekends, but at other times offers fine solitude. The national park's visitor center, next to the parking lot at the end of the road, has photographs, display maps, and samples of local marine fossils. Rangers rent out basic and

Krabi

 Maps pp. 309 & 323

Visitor Information

 Tourism Authority of Thailand, Uttarakit Rd., Krabi

☎ 075-622163

EXPERIENCE: Rock Climbing

The stunning cliffs of Phra Nang, whose towering rock faces isolate Phra Nang beaches from the rest of Krabi, are a mecca for international rock climbers. With more than 500 established routes, the region features all levels of difficulty, from 33-foot (10 m) beachside walls to vertigo inducing spires.

There are a number of rock-climbing schools in Krabi. Beginners can attend half-day, one-day, or three-day climbing courses, while serious climbers scale the more challenging routes. Equipment and guides can be hired at a reasonable cost. For a place to start, visit www.railey.com for all kinds of information related to climbing at fabled Railey Beach. See pp. 341–342 for additional information.

For something different, Chiang Mai features quieter, and nearly as beautiful, peaks, such as Crazy Horse Buttress, which offers 150 routes of varying degrees of difficulty. **Chiang Mai Rock Climbing Adventures** (55/3 Ratchapakhinai Rd., Chiang Mai, tel 086-911-1470, www.thailandclimbing.com) is a good place to take a course: Introductory, intermediate, and advanced classes are available, as are caving classes, cultural student programs, and rental equipment. Day trips include a local market visit and a post-climb, hot-spring dip.

Phra Nang

 Maps pp. 309 & 323

Visitor Information

⊠ Tourism Authority of Thailand, Uttarakit Rd., Krabi

☎ 075-622163

inexpensive bungalows. Several rocky islets lying just offshore can be reached on foot at low tide.

To the south of Nopparat Thara, past sheer cliffs dropping into the sea, is **Ao Nang Beach,** which can be reached by either road or boat from Krabi town. The beach's inferior tract of sand and cloudy water is made up for by a spectacular bay setting. Developers have built huddles of bungalows, restaurants, and bars along the front and behind the beach. Consequently, Ao Nang has become a boisterous beach center and the best place to organize activities such as sea canoeing, diving, cycling, and island-hopping.

Island Jaunts: Trips to the islands can be organized via tour operators at Ao Nang or by negotiating with the long-tail boat owners on the beach. Take water and some food when

INSIDER TIP:

Unlike nearby Phuket, the island of Ko Yao Noi, in Phangnga Bay, retains its fishing villages and mangrove forests. Gibbons haunt the islands here, and eagles soar in the skies.

—ROLF POTTS
Writer, National Geographic Traveler magazine

visiting these idyllic and deserted places. The best and most convenient islands to explore are **Ko Hong, Ko Dang, Ko Lading, Ko Pakbia,** and **Ko Rai.** Camping is permitted for those who want to stay on for a day or two. Rather than just hire a boat for a two-way trip, opt for a guided tour that takes you to a number of the islands. Many of the guides are sea gypsies, with a good knowledge of the islands and their secret coves and bays.

Phra Nang

The majestic cape of Phra Nang takes your breath away. Like Ko Phi Phi and Phangnga, the cape's overwhelming grandeur lies in its towering limestone cliffs, flush with vegetation and looming above sandy beaches and crystal-clear waters. Phra Nang exists amid a cluster of other beaches and scenic wonders in Krabi Province, but is outstanding for its beauty. The cape is part of the 150-square-mile (390 sq km) Ko Phi Phi–Hat Nopparat Thara Marine National Park, west of Krabi town.

Phra Nang can be reached in 45 minutes by long-tail boat from Krabi town's Chao Fa pier, or 15 minutes from Ao Nang Beach.

Phra Nang Beach is the cape's best—a fine, bright sweep of sand offset by sparkling blue waters and awesome green cliffs. It is also the most upscale. While Phra Nang's other two beaches—Railae Beach East and Railae Beach West (the longest and most popular)—swarm with cheap guesthouses and restaurants, Phra Nang itself remains the almost exclusive domain of an unobtrusive luxury resort. A dominating limestone headland reaches out to the tip of the cape at the southern end of Phra Nang Beach. At the bottom is **Tham Phra Nang Nok** ("outer princess cave"), legendary home of a sea princess who bore a

child who was later to become her lover. Wooden phalluses, carved by local fishermen, are placed inside the cave to guarantee successful fishing and protect against bad weather.

A steep, rope-aided cave trail from behind Tham Phra Nang Nok leads up to some stunning

Streamlined long-tail boats are the major means of transportation around Phra Nang and nearby islands.

views over the cape, before dropping down to an immense seawater lagoon, **Sa Phra Nang** ("princess lake"). You'll need a guide, easily hired from the

(continued on p. 341)

Tsunami 2004

On December 26, 2004, an underwater earthquake off the western tip of Indonesia, a magnitude 9 tremor, rocked the Earth. Dozens of aftershocks with magnitudes of 5 or higher followed.

Little remained of Khao Lak's vacation bungalows in January 2005.

But the most devastating aftermath was the monster tsunami that struck 13 countries around the Indian Ocean and Andaman Sea, leaving a trail of death. In a matter of minutes, more than 200,000 people lost their lives while hundreds of thousands went missing—many never to be found. Hundreds of thousands more were instantly homeless, left vulnerable to disease and starvation.

While the worst devastation occurred in Indonesia, where more than 128,000 people were killed, and Sri Lanka, Thailand was not spared. A wall of water 30 feet high (10 m) hit Thailand's west coast, including outlying islands and the tourist resorts near Phuket. More than 5,300 people were confirmed dead, half of whom were foreign tourists from 36 countries.

Unsubstantiated reports put the death toll far higher than that. According to UNICEF, 1,221 children lost one or both parents. A staggering 12,017 households were affected. And 7,446 fishing boats were lost or damaged, leaving many fishing villages without an income source.

Khao Lak, in Phangnga Province, bore the tsunami's brunt in Thailand. Recently built five-star hotels—along with countless guests and hotel workers—were swept away. The tiny island of Phi Phi Don, between Phuket and Krabi in Krabi Province, was devastated, especially Ao Ton Sai and Ao Lao Dalam. On Phuket, the official death toll was 200, mainly in the resort area of Patong and nearby Kamala Beach and village.

Tales of extraordinary courage emerged after the tsunami, along with an endless flow of tributes heaped on the people of southern Thailand for their selflessness and generosity to aid the victims. Courage was no more demonstrable than the sight of a small Thai man clinging to a power pole in Khao Lak and finding unbelievable strength to pluck people from tumult as they swept near him. Sheer luck saved the life of a German man who was having a massage on a Khao Lak beach when the wave hit. Five minutes later he was half a mile (1 km) inland, being hauled onto a second-floor balcony by a group of survivors.

But along with these stories of the human spirit at its best, came those stories that define the worst. There was looting of not only homes and buildings, but also of bodies. Mercenary *tuk-tuk* drivers in Phuket charged $50 for rides that would normally cost $3. Widespread corruption arose in the disbursement of relief funds for the victims. Land developers forced people out of the beachfront homes their families had lived in for generations.

The Thai government refused international financial aid, accepting only technical assistance—a fact that caused much uproar throughout the country.

And then there was the bizarre side of the tsunami's aftermath, including a plan by the Tourism Authority of Thailand to operate "tsunami disaster tours" in which gawking tourists would be bused from one disaster area to another. The idea was greeted with a mixture of incredulity and disgust by the Thai people and it was shelved. Another bizarre twist was the vending of tsunami souvenirs—photos of the destruction, DVDs, CDs, and T-shirts. Many locals stated that this was their creative way to earn a living, since the government was not recompensing their losses.

Rebuilding

In many areas, initial rebuilding was slow while the government and developers debated how to proceed. By 2006, development in all areas but Ko Phi Phi was in full swing, and new visitors to Phuket or Khao Lak were hard pressed to find signs that

such devastation had even occurred. Most hotels, shops, and restaurants were repaired or replaced, and even Ko Phi Phi has now completely redeveloped. Today, infrastructure and transportation exceed pre-tsunami levels, and tourist arrivals are as high as Thai spirits. While there are still shadows of fear regarding future disasters, the coast's sheer beauty continues to draw tourists and economic promise has brought back most Thais.

It is important to note that Phuket and its offshore islands' outstanding coral reefs sustained minimal, if any, damage from the tsunami. Despite initial concerns, diving and snorkeling conditions remain superb. In all of the affected areas the beaches are fine and the water is clean (many say cleaner than ever).

Many people hope that the disaster's silver lining may be Thailand's ability to rethink tourism development in coastal Thailand and its impact on local communities and the environment. Fortunately, many tsunami relief agencies continue to work with local communities to reach such ends.

Harbor Waves

Tsunamis are ocean waves produced by underwater earthquakes or landslides. The Japanese called the phenomenon tsunami, or "harbor wave," for the devastating effect they have on coastal communities. Tsunamis are not a single wave, rather a series of long waves that can travel at speeds averaging 450 (and up to 600) miles an hour (724–966 kph) in the open ocean. Since the waves are only a couple of feet high, they generally go unnoticed—boats do not feel their movement, nor can they be spotted from the air. Nearing the coastline, however, the speed of the waves decreases and the amplitude increases. As they rush against the shore, the relentless walls of rushing water can cause widespread destruction and many deaths or injuries.

EXPERIENCE: Responsible Tourism

Responsible tourism occurs when visitors make a difference (either actively or passively) while vacationing in developing countries. Following the 2004 tsunami, Thailand became a focal point not only for relief organizations and volunteers but also for organizations promoting responsible tourism, including community development programs and ecotourism training centers. Here are some organizations that offer different opportunities to practice responsible tourism:

Andaman Discoveries *(292/1, Moo 1, Kura, Kuraburi, Phangnga, tel 081-243-3848, www.northandamantsunamirelief.com)* Andaman Discoveries helps villages develop environmentally and culturally sustainable tourism. Several hours north of Phuket, it provides cultural immersion in traditional fishing communities. Guests stay in homes or nearby resorts and participate in locally guided jungle treks or Thai cooking classes, or volunteer in community development projects, such as vocational training or mangrove forest conservation. Proceeds directly help the communities.

Habitat for Humanity (Thailand) *(253 Bldg., 12th fl., Sukhumvit 21 [Asoke], Klongtan Nua, Wattana, Bangkok 10110, tel 02-664-0644, www.habitatthailand.org)* The Thailand branch of this international organization coordinated 60 teams of volunteers to build homes at 20 projects throughout the kingdom in 2007; more than 2,000 homes were slated for construction in 2008. Volunteers work side by side with homeowners to build affordable houses, allowing visitors to get firsthand cultural experiences with communities.

Track of the Tiger *(121, Moo 14, Ban Thaton, Amphur Mae Ai, Chiang Mai, tel 081-764-9950, www.track-of-the-tiger .com)* Track of the Tiger and its nonprofit affiliate Voluntourists Without Borders (VWB) combine ecotourism and community development to provide eco-friendly, culturally sensitive activities to visitors, while assisting remote villages in economic development without sacrificing their cultural identities. Visitors may stay at the Pang Soon Lodge & Outdoor Education Center, one hour north of Chiang Mai, or the more remote Mae Kok Village River Resort in Chiang Rai, where accommodation ranges from dorms to VIP tented houses. Activities include teaching English and working on a biodiversity improvement program.

Openmind Projects *(1039/3 Keawworawut Rd., Tumbol Naimuang, Amphor Muang, Nong Khai, tel 042-413578 or 087-2335734, www.openmindprojects.org)* Following the success of its volunteer teaching program, Openmind organizes ecotourism volunteering in national parks and wildlife refuges. Volunteers stay in the parks or nearby villages, where they participate in environmental education, develop ecotourism, and evaluate training needs to help the community earn revenue. Locations in southern Thailand include Kui Buri National Park, where elephants roam the mountainous border with Myanmar (Burma), and Tai Muang Marine National Park, where there's a sea turtle hatchery.

Smiling Albino Ltd. *(2098/414 Ramkamhang Rd., Huamark, Bangkapi, Bangkok, tel 1-877-THAIWAY [U.S. toll-free], 02-718-9560 [Thailand], www.smilingalbino.com)* In addition to their informative, entertaining trips, Smiling Albino runs a biannual, 17-day Volunteer Adventure that incorporates their Bangkok, Ayutthaya, and Chiang Rai experiences with multiple outreach programs: mentoring mentally challenged persons at a Bangkok girls' home, teaching at a suburban Bangkok elementary school, and working at Highland Farm Gibbon Sanctuary in Mae Sot.

Dragonfly *(1719 Soi 13 Mookamontri, Nakorn Ratchasima, tel 0815-477-047, www.thai-dragonfly.com)* Although its headquarters is in Khorat, Dragonfly's projects are located in rural areas throughout Thailand, where they provide support to needy communities and give authentic cultural experiences to visitors. Volunteer opportunities include wildlife conservation, orphanage care work, construction projects, and even soccer coaching.

plethora of guesthouses on Railae Beach West and Railae Beach East. Experienced rock climbers can reach the top of the cliff and enjoy magnificent sweeping views over the entire cape, and to the islands of Ko Poda and Ko Hua Khwan.

Up a hill behind the disappointing Railae Beach East (mudflats and mangroves) is **Tham Phra Nang Nai** ("inner princess cave"). This beautiful cavern, acclaimed as the best in southern Thailand, has three main chambers with some wondrous and weird stone formations.

destination for rock climbers (see sidebar p. 336). The sport's popularity has spawned numerous rock-climbing schools around the cape, making it an ideal (and inexpensive) place to learn the sport. Courses range from half-day basic introductions to three-day certificate courses. The latter, designed to teach techniques and theory, includes self-rescue, rappelling, and lead and multi-pitch climbing.

Climbers have identified more than 160 routes, most at the mid-to-high difficulty level, as

Often buffalo will be your only company on Ko Lanta's deserted beaches.

Tham Phra Nang Nai was the "grand palace" of the legendary sea princess, while Sa Phra Nang was her summer palace.

Rock Climbing: The cliffs around Tham Phra Nang Nai, and all along the giant headland that dominates Phra Nang, have made the area an international

well as a few ranked as extremely difficult. Any hotel or guesthouse will put you touch with a school, and experienced climbers can rent gear from these places.

Just off Phra Nang Beach lies **Ko Rang Nok** ("bird's-nest island"), easily accessible by longtail boat, and an excellent spot for swimming and sunbathing. Snor-

Ko Lanta Yai

🗺 Maps pp. 309 & 323

Visitor Information

✉ Tourism Authority of Thailand, Uttarakit Rd., Krabi

☎ 075-622163

The Narima Bungalow Resort

✉ 98 Moo 5, Klong Nin Beach, Ko Lanta

☎ 075-662668 or 075-662670

www. narimalanta .com

kelers can explore an underwater cave and a sunken boat on the south side of the island.

Farther afield, but still accessible by long-tail boats from Phra Nang, **Ko Hua Khwan** is known also as Chicken Island because of its strange rock formations at the northern end. Aside from occasional sea gypsies camping on the beach for a night or two, the island is deserted. It has some splendid beaches, coves, and coral reefs, ideal for sunbathing, swimming, and snorkeling.

Escape the crowds in a more comfortable way at picturesque **Ko Poda,** just south of Ko Hua Khwan, by renting a bungalow.

Ko Lanta

The extensive island group of Ko Lanta dishes up a lovely spread of deserted beaches and verdant hinterlands, spiced with a tinge of isolation, bred from the popularity of other beaches rather than inaccessibility. Regular ferry services from Ao Nang and Ko Phi Phi ply to Ko Lanta, and the main islands are some of the very few in the far south

INSIDER TIP:

If you want to stay at an eco-friendly resort, try Narima resort in Ko Lanta. They serve excellent Thai food and have the most fun and reliable diving and snorkeling team!

—KELLY FELTAULT
National Geographic contributor

Dugongs

These delightful sea mammals have sad faces, hairless plump bodies, and long forelimbs ending with hands and fingers. A scallop-shaped tail works as a rudder. Sexual organs similar in appearance to those of humans is thought to have given rise to the mermaid myth. Dugongs, in Thailand found only near Trang, have diminished greatly in number since trawling began to destroy much of the sea grasses on which they feed. Conservation programs have now been instituted.

that can be reached by car.

The Ko Lanta archipelago consists of 52 islands, but only banana-shaped **Ko Lanta Yai, Ko Lanta Noi,** and a few of the smaller islands have accommodations. Ko Lanta Yai and Ko Lanta Noi can be reached by a slow and spluttering car ferry from the town of Hua Hin, at the end of Highway 406 in Krabi Province.

A 12.5-mile (20 km) road runs the length of Ko Lanta Yai's west coast. Here, wide white beaches, views of offshore islands, and fabulous sunsets prevail. From **Sala Dan,** at the northern tip of the island, beaches come into view almost immediately. (Motorbikes to use for exploring can be hired here.)

Beyond the main resort area of Khlong Dao is the beautiful 2.5-mile (4 km) stretch of sand at **Palm Beach.** Set amid palm trees, **Khlong Kong Beach,** 5.5 miles (9 km) from Sala Dan has plenty of coral just offshore. Farther south is the long and deserted **Khlong Nin Beach.** From there, the road winds around cliffs and over hills down to the isolated **Khlong Chak Beach.**

Just before Khlong Nin, a road cuts across the center of the island toward the east coast village of Jeh Lee. Midway, a sign marks a track through the forest to **Tham Mai Keio** cave. The seven connecting chambers here can be explored with the aid of fitted ropes and ladders.

Diving trips (including overnight packages) and instruction can be organized in Ban Sala Dan. Off the five islets of **Ko Ha** are sea caves, walls, and a variety of corals. The two islands of **Ko Rok** have sparkling beaches, clear waters, and plenty of interesting marine life. At **Hin Daeng,** a rock wall plunges 148 feet (45 m) to the seabed, home to barracudas and manta rays.

Trang & Around

Trang is an uncrowded place that greets visitors with a bounty of natural attractions, including lofty limestone cliffs, pristine beaches, and exquisite tropical islands. Many of the best sights are found within **Hat Chao Mai National Park,** a protected area that stretches for 75 miles (120 km) along the coast and encompasses nine of the province's 47 shimmering Andaman Sea islands.

To reach the park, take Highway 403 from Trang town to nearby Katang. A turnoff to the

west winds along the coast. The road then splits: The northern arm leads to Pak Meng Beach, 24 miles (38 km) from Trang, and park headquarters at Ao Chang Lang. **Chao Mai Beach,** on the southern road, is a long stretch of white sand backed by pine trees and cliffs with caves.

Pak Meng and Kantang are the ferry points for the park's islands. The tours organized by agents in Trang town are recommended. (Accommodations can be booked on some islands.) Trang Scuba Dive Center *(59 Hauy Yot Rd., tel 075-222192)* provides entry-level courses for divers, as well as tours for

Trang & Around
 Maps pp. 305 & 323

Visitor Information
✉ Tourism Authority of Thailand, Sanam Na Muang, Ratchadamnoen Rd., Nakhon Si Thammarat
☎ 075-346515

Hat Chao Mai National Park
 Map p. 323
✉ Ao Chang Lang, Amphur Sikao, Trang
☎ 075-215367

Huge limestone cliffs are a prominent feature of Trang's beaches and islands.

Isolated and beautiful, Ko Tarutao plays host to fewer than 20,000 tourists a year—mostly Thais.

certified divers. Day trips go to the islands, while dive and camp tours take in the wrecks of two Japanese World War II ships sunk off **Ko Kradan.** At **Ko Muk,** 35 minutes south of Pak Merg, is **Emerald Cave** (Tham Morakot). Enter at low tide and follow a long, dark, silent passage to reach a lagoon enclosed by towering, jungle-dressed limestone walls.

Ko Tarutao

Ko Tarutao and the surrounding islands form one of the far south's last backwoods bastions, greeting fewer than 20,000 tourists each year. This stunning archipelago off the southwest coast of Thailand delivers everything you could wish for in a tropical paradise. The deserted beaches, multicolored coral, roaring waterfalls, deep limestone caves, and thick jungles are delightful.

Covering 60 square miles (151 sq km), Ko Tarutao is the largest island in this marine national park. Tourist boats run daily from Pak Bara, in Satun Province, from November to April (a 90-minute trip). After this, battering monsoons dissuade people from visiting.

Boats arrive at **Ao Phante Malak,** on the northwest tip of the island, where the visitor center provides insights into local geography and history. Most of the island's basic accommodations are at Phante and are best booked ahead from Pak Bara.

Due to Ko Tarutao's isolation, the government made it a dumping ground for political dissidents and criminals during World War II. Evidence of the penal colony (concrete fermentation tanks, charcoal furnaces, and graveyards) is seen at **Talo Udan Bay,** at the southern end of the island, and at windswept **Talo Wao Bay** on the east coast. A narrow convict-built road between the two now serves as an 8-mile (12 km) hiking trail. The trail continues from Talo Wao another 8 miles

INSIDER TIP:

A great way to visit the Tarutao Islands is on a live-aboard boat out of Phuket; you camp at night on the beaches. But if you're in a rush, the Pak Bara ferry will get you there quicker and more cheaply.

—DANIEL STILES
National Geographic field researcher

(12 km) back to Phante.

Ko Tarutao's west coast is lined with sweeping bays and isolated coves that harbor glorious beaches, reached by more well-maintained hiking trails from Phante. A 30-minute walk from Phante leads you to **Ao Chak,** a beautiful twin-arced bay with powdery sands and swaying palms. The trail then snakes through a thick rain forest past a number of waterfalls to **Ao San,** a four-hour hike from Phante. This bay is a long sweep of glistening sand, with excellent coral for snorkeling just offshore.

Long-tail boats can be hired at park headquarters to drop you at the beaches, from where you can hike back to Ao Phante. ∎

Ko Tarutao

🗺 Maps pp. 309 & 323

Visitor Information

✉ Tourism Authority of Thailand, 1/1 Soi 2 Nipnat Utnit 3 Rd., Yai, Songkhla

☎ 074-231055 or 074-238518

Ko Tarutao Marine National Park Office

✉ Pak Bara, Ko Tarutao

☎ 074-711333

EXPERIENCE: Do Absolutely Nothing

Except when its gates are closed by the monsoon season from May to November, Ko Tarutao entices travelers looking for a quiet, slowly paced time. The island's name is derived from the Malay word for "old," and the environs of Ko Tarutao is a historical mélange. For now, the area is often empty, but the tourist numbers continue to grow.

The mangrove forests on Ko Tarutao are timeless (some of the standing trees have long been dead, in fact). While the beaches here are beautiful, the waters are too thick to allow any good snorkeling. Amid all this unspoiled natural beauty, however, the island also still bears the concrete scars of political prisons.

There's hardly anything to "do" on Ko Tarutao, and that is the point of coming to the island. The area's isolation, once a

curse shared by an unlucky few, now welcomes those looking for a few moments of tranquility. On the infrequent occasions when Ko Tarutao's silence is broken, it's usually the fault of one of the park's innumerable wildlife, many of which are actually quite loud. You may see monitor lizards, langurs, crab-eating macaques, and other monkeys here.

Since Ko Tarutao is a national park, lodging and amenities are in the hands of the rangers. You

choose between sleeping in a modest bungalow for 500 baht (can house up to four adults) or renting a tent (sleeps two) for 150 baht per night. One warning about the tents: They are small and are waterproof only when it's not raining. If you have your own equipment, a tent site right on the beach is 30 baht. After a few restorative days, hiking along the beach, you can hire boats to take you to more populated spots like Ko Lipe.

More Places to Visit in the Far South

Hat Nai Phlao & Hat Sichon

The small beach resort of Hat Nai Phlao, about 44 miles (70 km) north of Nakhon Si Thammarat, commands a prime position on a string of beaches along one of the Gulf of Thailand's most attractive coastal stretches. Masses of coconut palms along the white-sand bay give it an island feel. The bay sweeps 3 miles (5 km) north to **Khanom Beach** and south to a tall rocky headland. From there, the coastline weaves past the deserted twin bays of **Thong Yee** and **Thong Yang,** where patches of white sand are interspersed with rocky coves. About 3 miles (5 km) farther south, another low-key resort, **Hat Sichon,** has beach vendors and coconut palms.

Map p. 309

More Islands off Tarutao

A number of other beautiful and isolated islands west of the alluring island of Tarutao are part of the marine national park. On the forested **Ko Adang** and its smaller neighbors, you'll find some of the most pristine environment in Thailand. The rugged rain forest hills here—laced with freshwater streams—give way to narrow beaches on the south coast.

Ko Lipe, by comparison, is flat and clad with coconut plantations. It is home to a large community of chao lae (sea gypsies), who settled here for the freshwater springs. Long-tail boats can be chartered for trips to nearby islets.

About 12 miles (20 km) off Pak Bara is **Ko Bulon Lae,** part of the Ko Phetra Marine National Park. It is a laid-back island with a few small villages, excellent beaches, and shallow coral reefs offshore that are ideal for snorkeling.

While waiting at Pak Bara for boats to take you to the islands mentioned above, a visit to **Ko Kebang** is an interesting diversion. Catch a water taxi for the 15-minute ride past the towering cliffs of Laem Tanyong Du Ri, north of the port, and along the jungle-fringed channel, Pi Yai Klong, to the main village of Ban Bor Jet Lok. Here, negotiate with the boatmen at the pier for a 30-minute trip up the mangrove-choked channel, **Langu Khlong,** where you will have close-up views of the bird life.

Maps pp. 309 & 323

Piya Mit Tunnel

Hidden in the jungle in Khao Nam Khang National Park on the Thai-Malaysian border, off Highway 4113, is the amazing Piya Mit Tunnel. Malaysian Communists, in their long struggle to overthrow the Malaysian government, used this hillside bunker as a guerrilla base between the 1940s and 1980s.

The immense tunnel, which could hold up to 200 rebels at any one time, has more than a hundred rooms. There are sleeping quarters, kitchens, meeting rooms, a medical center, communication rooms—and even a shooting range and a motorcycle training area!

The rebels were granted citizenship and given land nearby as part of a peace deal brokered with the Thai government in 1990. What makes the visit to this remarkable place most memorable are the firsthand accounts of the ex-guerrillas who now act as guides.

Map p. 309

Temple Caves at Trang

A number of important temple caves hide among Trang's limestone cliffs. Head north of Trang town to Huai Yot, and continue west on Highway 4 to **Tham Khao Pina,** an expansive limestone cave on six levels. Images of Buddha fill the caverns.

North of Huai Yot on Highway 403, turn right just before the town of Khlong Pang to **Wat Tham Phra Phut.** When archaeologists discovered this cave in the early 20th century, a large Ayutthaya-period Buddha reclined over a collection of royal regalia and upper-class household items, including talismans, fine pottery, silverware, and lacquerware. The collection is thought to have been stashed in the cavern at some time before the fall of Ayutthaya.

Map p. 309

Travelwise

One of Bangkok's ubiquitous three-wheeled *tuk-tuks*

TRAVELWISE

PLANNING YOUR TRIP

When to Go

Most visitors head to Thailand during the relatively cool and dry season from December to February, when rainfall is scarce and the temperature around a tolerable 84–90°F (28–32°C). (If you're traveling in the hills, temperatures can drop sharply in the evenings, so take a sweater.) The drawback is that popular destinations are crowded and hotel rooms can be in short supply. Prices tend to be higher during the tourist season and internal transportation can be difficult to secure. March to May or June is the hottest time to visit—temperatures may reach 100°F (38°C), particularly in the plains of the northeast, and the high level of humidity (around 80 percent) can make travel uncomfortable and oppressive.

The wet season runs from June to November, and this may be the finest period to enjoy the charms of the country without the hordes of tourists. These months constitute the "rainy" season, when a dose of precipitation is almost guaranteed most afternoons. The remainder of the day will generally be dry, if overcast. Major monsoons, which can last several days, are relatively rare. Another advantage of travel at this time of year is that the countryside is vibrantly green with flooded rice fields and blooming trees. Vacancy rates are high at most hotels, and it is easier to make reservations with local transportation.

Climate

Thailand has three seasons, although the differences between them are barely distinguishable. The classic divisions are as follows: the dry and relatively cool months run from December to February; the extremely hot summer months run from March to June; and the rainy season runs from June to November.

Even in the coolest months, Thailand remains a scorching country with a brutal equatorial climate that punishes even the hardiest of international travelers. Maximum temperatures throughout the year in Bangkok generally reach 90°F (32°C), and humidity rarely drops below 50 percent. While the temperature drops slightly over the Christmas holiday season, humidity remains at sky-high levels to the point where most visitors feel compelled to take several showers daily. During the so-called rainy season it might be bone-dry for several weeks, while the supposedly dry Christmas season may be flooded out with an unexpected monsoon.

The climate is dominated by seasonal monsoons that sweep across the country. Monsoons are somewhat predictable throughout most of Thailand, although they do vary when you move south down the Thai peninsula toward Malaysia. Ko Samui and the southeast coast can be hit by monsoon winds and rain in November and December, but this area is usually drier than elsewhere during the rainy season.

What to Take

Thailand is a modern country where almost every conceivable item can be purchased—often at lower costs than you would find back home. Shopping emporiums are located in almost every urban center and smaller town throughout the kingdom.

Thailand is a perpetually hot country where jackets and sweaters are rarely needed. Coats, ties, and formal dresses may be necessary in a few exclusive restaurants in Bangkok but are otherwise little more than an additional packing burden.

Clothes should be a light cotton or other natural fiber rather than synthetics or heavy materials. Bring the fewest possible items of clothing and expand your wardrobe in Thailand, where the clothing selection is excellent and of international quality. Comfortable walking shoes are essential, and sandals are useful when visiting temples, where shoes must be removed prior to entry. Also, bare shoulders and exposed knees are unacceptable at temples; however, this rule of attire should be followed in embassies, museums, other official institutions, and while dining with Thais. Other than at the beach, bare skin is frowned upon.

Other items to consider are a small medical kit, sewing kit, mini-umbrella, insect repellent, drug prescriptions, an extra pair of glasses, spare passport photos, and photocopies of essential documents.

Electricity in Thailand is 220V, 50Hz, and plugs are generally the flat, two-prong type. If you bring electrical equipment you will need a plug adaptor plus a transformer for U.S. appliances.

Insurance

Make sure you have adequate travel and medical coverage for treatment and expenses, including repatriation and baggage and money loss. Keep all receipts for expenses. Report loss or thefts to the tourist police (see pp. 353–354), and obtain a signed statement for insurance claims.

Further Reading

Thailand has inspired a surprisingly large amount of literature, from casual adventures to serious works on art and culture. The following works are widely available.

David Wyatt's academic work, *Thailand: A Short History* (Yale University Press, 1984), is without question the finest history available on the country. A lighter, more entertaining read is *The Legendary American*, by William Warren (Houghton Mifflin, 1970), which relates the fascinating story of Jim Thompson's revival of the silk-weaving industry and of his mysterious disappearance. *Travelers' Tales Thailand* (O'Reilly & Associates, 1993) gathers descriptive writings from 46 talents and provides valuable insight into the culture, people, and eccentricities of Thailand.

Arts of Thailand, by Steve Van Beek (Thames and Hudson, 1991), is a beautiful coffee-table book with superb photographs; William Warren's *Legendary Thailand* and *Thai Style* (both Asia Books, 1988) are also recommended.

Thai cooking is well served by the popular *Thai Cooking*, by Jennifer Brennan (Futura Publications, 1984), and *The Food of Thailand*, by Wendy Hutton (Periplus, 1995).

Humor and adventure are the themes of Jarne's Eckhardt's *Way aid by the Bimbos* (Post Publishing, 1991), and Harold Stephens' *Asian Portraits* (Travel Publishing Asia, 1983). Carol Hollinger's *Mai Pen Rai* (Houghton Mifflin, 1965), is perhaps the single best book to read prior to departure to learn something about the essential nature of the Thai personality.

The best written account and photographic coverage of the colorful hill tribes of northern Thailand is the lavishly illustrated *Peoples of the Golden Triangle*, by Paul and Elaine Lewis (Thames and Hudson, 1984). A sensitive explanation of Buddhism is given in *Three Ways of Asian Wisdom*, by Nancy Ross (Simon and Schuster, 1966). Novels set in and around Thailand include *Lord Jim*, by Joseph Conrad (Penguin, 1900); *The Gentleman in the Parlour*, W. Somerset Maugham (Heinemann, 1930); and more contemporary titles such as *Crossing the Shadow Line*, Andrew Eames (Hodder and Stoughton, 1986), and *In Search of Conrad*, Gavin Young (Hutchinson, 1991).

HOW TO GET TO THAILAND

Entry Formalities

All visitors must have a passport that is valid for a minimum of six months from the day of entry. Upon arrival, nationals from 56 favored nations, including the U.S. and most European countries, receive a 30-day permit; it can easily be extended for another 10 days at immigration offices throughout the country. Take a passport photograph and photocopies of the inside page of your passport and the page on which the entry permit is stamped.

Visitors who intend to stay longer than 30 days should obtain in advance a visa from a Thai embassy or consulate. This 60-day tourist visa can be extended once for an additional 30 days. Longer visas for qualified individuals are also available at Thai diplomatic offices.

Airlines

Bangkok, a major regional air hub, is served by nearly 100 airlines, representing almost every major carrier in the world. Most flights arrive at Suvarnabhumi (su-wanna-poom) Airport. The older Don Muang Airport, located 16 miles (25 km) north of the city, has been converted into a domestic airport (coded DMK) servicing flights by One-two-go, Phoenix, Thai Airways, and Nok airlines. Suvanarbhumi (BKK) also handles domestic flights, so if you plan to transfer to a domestic flight immediately after arriving in Thailand, make sure your connection departs from BKK or allows you adequate time to arrange your own transfer to DMK.

International flights also serve Phuket, Ko Samui, and Chiang Mai, although these flights generally depart from neighboring Southeast Asian countries.

Travel times to Bangkok, including layovers and a necessary stop to refuel, are 16–20 hours from Seattle, San Francisco, and Los Angeles; 20–24 hours from Chicago; and 22–26 from hours New York via the U.S.'s West Coast. To reach Bangkok from most European cities takes 12–16 hours on a direct flight.

Arriving

Suvarnabhumi Airport lies 13 miles (30 km) southeast of downtown Bangkok. After arrival at the enormous single terminal airport you must walk along a series of moving walkways to Concourse D, in the center of the terminal. Along the way you will pass an information booth with maps of the airport and city, and a CAT telecom booth with internet and long distance calling booths (10 baht/minute to the U.S.). Both immediately before and after immigration there are duty-free shops and foreign exchange kiosks. In the baggage claim area prior to customs clearance there are booths for major car rental companies and official AOT limousine services (approximately $65 for a BMW, $40 for a Toyota or a private mini-van.)

After departing customs, you will enter the chaotic arrivals area (2nd floor). You will immediately be accosted by touts offering hotels and transportation. If you need accommodation there are several hotel and tour desks directly in front of the customs exit. Booths here provide rental phone services, and sell SIM cards with prepaid phone minutes. Friendly and informative information booth hosts are located on the 2nd and 4th floors, tourist police (and left baggage service) on the 2nd floor opposite gate 4, medical services on the 3rd floor opposite gate 3, where there are also a number of mini-marts, coffee snops, and restaurants.

Ignore the touts offering taxi and limousine service, as you have a variety of options for getting into the city, or to the greater Bangkok area, including Pattaya. Public taxi stands are between gates 3–4 and gates 8–9. Look for the official taxi stands, where you will be asked your destination, that information will be marked on a coupon, and you will be directed to a driver. Once in the taxi, confirm your destination and make sure the driver starts the meter. The fare to the hotel will be the sum of the meter, plus and airport surcharge (about $1.75), plus tolls collected along the highway into town. In most cases, to hotels along Sukhumvit Road, the Silom area, and near the river (such as the Oriental), two or three tolls will be paid, totaling around $2–3. All told, the fare will be $7–10. It takes from 25–45 minutes to reach hotels in town, depending on the traffic.

Solo travelers or those simply watching their baht may want to use bus services from the airport to their hotel. Shuttle bus service from gate 5 will take you to the public bus terminal. Buses follow various routes, including major city centers and obscure or remote destinations. Public buses to Don Muang domestic airport cost $1, run 24 hours, and take approximately 45 minutes. Other public buses cost $1–2.

Four Airport Express buses service various tourist areas: AE1 services the Silom area, AE2 the Khao San area, AE3 along Sukhumvit Road, and AE4 the Hua Lum Phong railway station. Buses depart regularly, cost about $5 and run from 6 a.m. to 11:30 p.m./midnight.

Finally, scheduled for completion in early 2009, the airport train is an electric rail service connecting the Suvarnabhumi Airport with downtown Bangkok, near the Phaya Thai BTS station, just north of Siam Square. Trains are either nonstop or eight-stop voyages, hold up to 745 passengers, and run the 17-mile stretch at speeds up to 100 mph (160 kph). Entrances are located at the lowest level beneath the airport.

Travelers departing Thailand on international flights will use the Suvarnabhumi Airport. Arrive at least two hours prior to departure, as the airport can have horrendously long lines at immigration. Prior to checking in you may be tempted to have a meal at the Sky Loft above the check-in terminal, but be aware that customs lines often exceed 30-minute waits. There are many fine restaurants (but no ATMs) inside the terminal beyond customs. Airport flight inquiries, tel 02-132-000.

GETTING AROUND
Traveling in Thailand
By Airplane
Within Thailand, airlines serve more than 20 domestic airports. In addition to Thai Airways International and Bangkok Airways, several budget air carriers, including Nok Air (Thai Airways' budget carrier), One-two-go, and Thai Air Asia, have Bangkok as their hubs. Bangkok Airways, which uses Sukhothai as its hub (though it offers direct flights out of Bangkok), owns the Sukhothai, Trat (Koh Chang), and Ko Samui airports. It is the exclusive carrier to these locations, though recently it has allowed Thai Airways to fly to Samui. Bangkok Airways also flies various routes between Thailand's beaches, notably between Samui, Phuket, and Pattaya.

Thai Air Asia has become a major player in regional air service, providing low-cost–in many cases "free" (no fare, only tax) flights to many places in Thailand, including major tourist destinations and rural destinations such as the northeastern provinces. Travel can only be booked via www.airasia.com, not through travel agents; the best fares are available when booked considerably in advance.

From Bangkok, both Thai Air Asia and Bangkok Airways use Suvarnabhumi Airport exclusively. Other domestic carriers, including Thai Airways, use both Suvarnabhumi and Don Muang Airports. It is important to check which airport you are flying out of before leaving for the airport.

Thai Airways flies from Bangkok to Chiang Mai several times daily, although the night train is a very comfortable alternative and preferred by many experienced travelers. A sensible daily flight from Chiang Mai down to Phuket with a stop in Bangkok saves a great deal of time. Another useful service is the shuttle from Bangkok down to Phuket (several daily), chiefly since Phuket lacks a direct train service and the bus journey is a marathon affair best left to hardy backpackers.

By Train
Trains provide the most comfortable, enjoyable method of traveling around the country, with limited destinations more than compensated for with reasonable fares. There are three carriage classes. Third class has seats only and is crowded and uncomfortable—best avoided. Second class has air-conditioned and non-air-conditioned sleepers, the latter slightly cheaper. First class is about 40 percent more expensive than second class but is still excellent value and provides you with your own two-berth cabin.

The State Railway of Thailand (S.R.T., www.railway.co.th) operates four main train routes in the country and a handful of auxiliary spurs that serve smaller towns. The northern line starts at Hua Lamphong train station in Bangkok and heads north to Chiang Mai, passing through Ayutthaya, Lop Buri, Nakhon Sawan, Phitsanulok, Uttaradit, and Lampang. Plans have been announced to construct a spur from Den Chai to Chiang Rai, although economic problems seem to have put train route expansion on hold.

The northeastern line also starts at Hua Lamphong and heads north to Ayutthaya and then northeast to Nakhon Ratchasima (Khorat), where it splits into two lines. The route most commonly used by visitors goes almost due north through Khon Kaen and Udon Thani to Nong Khai on the Mekong River, just opposite Laos. The Bangkok–Nong Khai overnight sleeper express is recommended for travelers to Laos. The other northeastern line heads east from Khorat to Ubon Ratchathani, passing through Buriram, Surin, and Sisaket.

A rarely used train route heads east from Bangkok to Chachoengsao and Prachin Buri, near the Cambodian border. The opening of Cambodia and the increasing popularity of Angkor Wat have raised the profile of this obscure route. You can now travel overland from Bangkok to Siem Reap (Angkor) in one day.

Trains also run southward to the beaches and islands. The southern train departs Hua Lamphong and ambles down the tracks to Phetchaburi, Hua Hin, Prachuap Khiri Khan, Chumphon, Surat Thani, Phatthalung, and Hat Yai before continuing across the border into Malaysia. The train track splits at Hat Yai: One spur goes southeast across the Malaysian border to Kota Baru (Bharu), and the other southwest to Penang and Kuala Lumpur.

The chief disadvantage to the southern line is that trains do not go directly to Ko Samui, Phuket, Krabi, and other beach towns. S.R.T. offers package deals to the more popular resorts and islands, however, such as Phuket and Samui. The packages are similar: Purchase your ticket several days in advance, and catch one of the early evening departures south. The ticket includes a comfortable sleeper; in the morning, you arrive at a connection from where buses and, when necessary, boats continue to Phuket and Samui. These packages are reasonably priced and perhaps just as convenient as making your way out to the airport.

Complimentary train schedules for the four major routes can be picked up at the information counter in Hua Lamphong train station. The red train brochure has abbreviated schedules for the southern line, while the green brochure provides schedules for the north, northeastern, and eastern routes. These immensely useful brochures include tips on refunds, fees for classes and upgrades, and other details.

By Bus

Most small towns can only be reached by bus. Buses are quick and relatively comfortable for short journeys, but longer trips are best accomplished, whenever possible, by either train or plane. Thailand has a government bus service known as Bor Kor Sor (B.K.S.), and dozens of private bus companies provide competitive services on identical routes.

B.K.S. buses come in several classes, including ordinary non-air-conditioned buses for shorter trips and comfortable air-conditioned buses for longer journeys. Ordinary buses are often the only means of reaching smaller towns, but travel this way tends to be very crowded and time-consuming as many stops are made en route to the final destination. Superior buses range from the simple air-conditioned option to top-of-the-line "tour buses" with reclining seats and hostesses who serve drinks. The superior B.K.S. buses are comfortable and priced substantially lower than similar ones operated by private companies.

B.K.S. has steadily introduced new superior bus classes over the years, removing seats to increase leg room and provide enough space for reclining seats. Many of the buses now include toilets and have a refreshment station for cold drinks and snacks. Prices are higher on these upgraded lines, but they are excellent for overnight journeys as the seats can be reclined to near horizontal positions.

B.K.S. bus terminals in very small towns are often situated right in the center near the market, while terminals in larger towns are almost always outside city limits to minimize traffic jams in the urban core. Some form of public transportation, a local bus or three-wheeler, will be necessary to reach terminals on the outskirts of town. Larger towns generally have separate terminals for ordinary and air-conditioned buses, but these terminals are usually next to each other. Ordinary bus tickets are sold directly on the bus, while tickets for superior services can be purchased on the same day or in advance at ticket counters at the terminal. Ordinary buses tend to leave throughout the day at unfixed schedules, while superior buses for longer journeys generally depart in the early morning or early evening.

Private bus companies operate between major tourist destinations, serving Chiang Mai, Phuket, and Ko Samui from Bangkok, with smaller minivans used for newer tourist destinations such as Ko Si Chang and Krabi. Private companies provide several superior options, reducing the number of seats per vehicle. Prices, of course, rise as the number of seats falls.

Most private bus companies schedule departures from their own terminals, next to the B.K.S. stations on the outskirts of town. The chief advantage to private bus companies at first appears to be complimentary transportation from your hotel to the bus terminal, but this is frustratingly time-consuming as passengers are picked up from widely scattered hotels. The best strategy is to take a taxi or other form of transportation out to the bus terminal, where you can then choose between a B.K.S. or a private bus service.

A final matter to consider is that of bus safety. In Thailand, the accident rate is very high. Choose a seat near the rear of the bus to avoid danger in case of a head-on collision. B.K.S. buses tend to be driven with more care than private buses, whose drivers seem to speed with little concern for their passengers' safety.

Do not accept food or drink from strangers and be wary of food or drink offered by seemingly official bus representatives. There have been rare cases in which the food or drink has been spiked by thieves with sleep-inducing drugs.

By Car or Motorcycle

With the exception of chaotic Bangkok and to a lesser degree, Chiang Mai, Thailand is an excellent country to tour with a rented car or motorcycle. Outside the major urban centers the traffic tends to very light, roads are in excellent condition, and signs are often in English. Exploring with a private vehicle allows you to get off the beaten track and escape the tourist hordes.

International car rental agencies such as Avis and Hertz are represented in all major tourist destinations such as Bangkok, Chiang Mai, Phuket, and Ko Samui. Local car rental agencies tend to be substantially less expensive and often rent cars for extended periods at large discounts to the daily rate. Daily rental rates are lowest for open-air jeeps and compacts and increase for mid-size sedans and larger cars. Vans suitable for larger groups are also available at reasonable rates. The majority of visitors have few problems driving around most places, but Thai drivers can be hired at very modest rates, and this service may be appropriate for those who wish to relax.

If you rent a motorcycle, check it very carefully for signs of wear and damage, particularly to brakes, lights, and tires, and make sure you wear a helmet and protective clothing. Driving or riding on a motorcycle can be a harrowing experience in Thailand. To prepare yourself, travel with an experienced rider until you get a feel for the local traffic.

An international driver's license is needed to rent a car in Thailand. You can pick one up at any local office of the American Automobile Association (AAA) or the Canadian Automobile Association (CAA).

Insurance is highly recommended whenever you rent a vehicle, and foreigners are always assumed to be the responsible party in the event of an accident. Insurance is sometimes provided with your car insurance policy back home or with the use of a major credit card for the vehicle rental, though this should be confirmed prior to your departure. Major car rental agencies include comprehensive insurance with each rental, but this may not be the case with small, locally owned rental firms, which sometimes rent cars without adequate insurance. Be sure to inspect all contracts to determine that adequate insurance is included with your rental.

Drive on the left. The city speed limit is 35 mph (60 kph), unless signed otherwise. Outside the cities, the limit is 50 mph (80 kph). Be warned—although traffic rules and regulations do exist, they are often ignored by local drivers. Gas stations are commonplace on all main roads.

Transportation in Towns & Cities

By Taxi

Taxis operate in major tourist destinations such as Bangkok, Chiang Mai, and Phuket, but are rarely found elsewhere. Taxis are legally required to be metered in Bangkok. However, taxis waiting outside superior hotels may insist on fixed prices, which tend to be about double the metered rate. Avoid these illegal fixed-rate taxis by walking down to the street and hailing an ordinary taxi.

Taxis in Chiang Mai, Phuket, and Ko Samui do not use meters but quote fixed rates for all destinations. It's best to ask for advice at your hotel front desk or check with several taxi drivers before committing to any lengthy taxi ride.

Make sure you agree on the price in advance. Taxis are also available for hire on an hourly or full-day basis.

By Local Transportation

Bangkok is the only city in Thailand with a fully developed bus system, although Chiang Mai and Phuket have public buses on a very limited number of routes. The local bus system is so confusing that most visitors take taxis or another form of private transportation to reach their destination. Minivans may double as shared taxis on popular tourist routes—such as from the local airport to city center—but the most common local conveyances are three-wheeled vehicles known as *tuk-tuks* if powered with a gasoline engine, or *samlors* if pedaled by a person. Samlors are disappearing from most towns.

Noisy tuk-tuks race around at frightening speeds but provide easy transportation at reasonable cost. Tuk-tuks are hardly necessary in Bangkok, which has an abundance of metered taxis, but they are useful in places such as Chiang Mai, Ayutthaya, and Sukhothai. Tuk-tuks are unmetered, and the drivers are quite happy to overcharge unwary visitors, so bargaining is in order before all journeys.

Another mode of local transportation are minibuses known as *songthaews*—small trucks with hard benches at the back—that can be very crowded

By BTS Skytrain & MRT Subway

Bangkok opened its elevated Skytrain service several years ago to great acclaim. The two lines reach a surprising number of hotels, sights, and shopping districts in the city. Skytrain maps are available all over town. The main routes and destinations are the river, hotels along Silom Road, the Patpong entertainment district, hotels along Sukhumvit Road, shopping centers near Siam Square, and the Chatuchat Weekend Market. You can either buy stored-value tickets (minimum 200 baht) or purchase a per-ride ticket from vending machines. Stored-value tickets and change for the machines are available at the station booths. Plans are now in place to extend the Skytrain service in future years.

The MRT subway operates between 5 a.m. and midnight every day. The subway, which requires separate tickets has "interchange" stations with BTS at Asoke (BTS)-Sukhumvit (MRT), Sala Daeng (BTS)-Silom (MRT) and Mo Chit (BTS)-Chatuchak Park (MRT).

All the subway stations are air-conditioned and equipped with elevators, escalators, shops, ATM machines, public telephone kiosks, and ticket vending machines.

PRACTICAL ADVICE
Communications
Post Offices
Thailand has an improving postal service with post offices in almost every town. Most visitors find it convenient to leave postcards and letters with the front desk at their hotel. Airmail to the U.S. takes about 7–10 days. Only nonessential items such as postcards should be sent with ordinary mail service, while important letters and packages should always be sent registered mail—a small percentage of packages seem to disappear on their way into and out of Thailand.

Letters can be mailed to any post office in Thailand, where they will be held for customer pickup for at least 30 days. Letters and packages sent should be clearly marked as "poste restante" (general delivery), and family names should be printed in capitals and underlined. If you are expecting a package and it has not been filed under your last name, be sure to check the folder for your first name.

The Bangkok G.P.O. on Charoen Krung Road near the Royal Orchid Sheraton hotel is open weekdays until 6 p.m. and weekends and holidays until 1 p.m. Post offices elsewhere close on weekdays at 4 p.m. and Saturdays at noon. All packages sent from Thailand must first be inspected at the post office prior to boxing. The procedure is to bring all unboxed items to the post office for inspection, after which you may purchase a box and wrapping materials for your package. Private mailing firms such as Mailboxes Inc. provide an alternative to the rather lengthy mailing procedure required by public post offices. DHL and Federal Express have offices in most tourist destinations in the country.

Telephones
The telephone system in Thailand is modern and efficient for both local and international calls, which can be made from hotels, public phone kiosks, and international phone offices in G.P.O.s in most provincial capitals. To call the U.S. or Canada from Thailand, dial the international access code (00), the country code (1), the area code, and finally the local telephone number. For the U.K., dial 00 144, followed by the area code (without the initial 0) and local number. The international access code for Australia is 00 61. To call Thailand from the U.S., dial 00 66, the area code for the particular city, then the local phone number.

Domestic phone calls can be tricky as all telephone area codes within the country begin with a zero. International calls do not require the use of this zero in the local area code, but you must add a zero to domestic calls. For example, to call Bangkok from the U.S. you just use 2 as the area code, but to call Bangkok from Chiang Mai you must use 02 as the area code. Many local phone lines use a variety of final digits to handle incoming calls. A phone number such as 344-9901-09 means you may use 01 through 09 to reach the central operator.

E-mail & Internet
Internet cafés are now found in almost every town and city in Thailand, providing excellent service at very low prices. Internet cafés in Bangkok are concentrated in the backpacker's enclave around Khao San Road but are also found in major shopping centers and near the tourist hotels along Silom and Sukhumvit Roads. Internet cafés are also abundant in other tourist destinations, such as Chiang Mai, Ko Samui, and Phuket. Many Internet cafés have Skype headsets that allow you to make low-cost telephone calls.

EMERGENCIES
Embassies in Bangkok
Australian Embassy 37 Sathorn Tai Rd., Bangkok, tel 02-344-6300
Canadian Embassy Abdulrahim Bldg., 15th fl., 990 Rama IV Rd., Bangkok, tel 02-636-0540
United Kingdom Embassy 1031 Witthayu Rd., Bangkok, tel 02-305-8333
United States Embassy 120–122 Witthayu Rd., Bangkok, tel 02-205-4000

Emergency Phone Numbers
Tourist police te 1155
Ambulance/English-speaking doctors (Bangkok) Bangkok Mission Hospital, 430 Phitsanulok Rd., Bangkok, tel 02-282-1100 or 02-281-1422
Immigration tel 02-287-3101 to -10
International calls tel 100

Police
Brown-uniformed police are commonly seen, and many speak a little English. However, try to contact the tourist police as they

all speak English and are better trained to deal with any problems tourists may face. They may also provide guidance and escort in remote or dangerous areas. The tourist police have offices in all major tourist areas in Thailand, as well as a hotline (tel 1155) that connects you with them directly from any pay phone.

OTHER INFORMATION
Alcohol/Drinking
The legal drinking age is 18. Alcohol cannot be bought on days celebrating the King's or Queen's birthdays, special religious holidays, election days, or from 2–5 p.m. daily.

Conversions
1 kilo = 2.2 pounds
1 liter = 0.2 U.S. gallons
1 kilometer = 0.6 miles
1 meter = 1.1 yards

Health
Thailand is a surprisingly healthy country for foreigners, with generally high standards of hygiene. It has excellent medical facilities, from pharmacies in most towns to state-of-the-art hospitals in Bangkok, Chiang Mai, and other cities.

Full health insurance should be purchased prior to travel. Visitors should be sure their vaccinations are current and should check with their doctor regarding any special precautions. Prescriptions can be filled at local pharmacies, but bring along your prescription from home or you'll need to make an appointment with a doctor. Malaria is a threat only in isolated regions such as the border districts with Myanmar (Burma) and Cambodia. Therefore, malaria pills are no longer recommended for most casual visitors.

The most common medical complaints are stomach upsets and heat exhaustion; simple precautions will help. Avoid eating raw,

unwashed vegetables and peel all fruit. Don't overdo in the first few days; allow time to acclimatize to the temperature and humidity. Drink plenty of fluids, use a high-SPF sunblock, and wear a hat in the sun.

Tap water is not safe to drink in most parts of the country; even the locals stick to bottled water, soft drinks, or beer.

Holidays
Government offices, schools, banks, and most stores close on the following national holidays. For a full list of festivals, see pp. 385–386.

Jan. 1 New Year's Day
Feb. (full moon) Makha Puja
April 6 Chakri Day
Mid-April Songkran
May 1 Labor Day
May 5 Coronation Day
Early May Royal Plowing Ceremony
May (full moon) Visakha Puja
July (full moon) Asanha Puja
Aug. 12 Queen's Birthday
Oct. 23 Chulalongkorn Day
Dec. 5 King's Birthday
Dec. 10 Constitution Day

Local Customs
The Thais favor a cool heart, or *jai yen*, so displays of anger and raised voices—and even kissing and hugging in public—are frowned upon. Yet formality is not required in addressing people—first names and nicknames are the norm.

The head is the most honored part of the body and the feet are despised, so don't sit with your feet pointing at someone or you may unwittingly be insulting them. Do not touch people (even children) on the head.

For temple etiquette, see p. 27.

Media
Newspapers
The Thai press is one of the freest in Southeast Asia and is

an excellent source of information. Two major English-language newspapers are published in Bangkok: the excellent *Bangkok Post* and the more opinionated *The Nation*. Both are morning newspapers and include special weekly supplements on tourism activities, tours, and special promotional events for visitors.

Magazines
Nearly all the big Western magazines are sold in Bangkok, along with specialized publications such as the *Far Eastern Economic Review*, *Asiaweek*, and *Time Asia*. Several of the major tourist destinations have local English-language newspapers and weekly magazines that provide insight and information such as promotions at neighborhood restaurants. They include the *Pattaya Mail*, the *Phuket Gazette*, and the *Chiang Mai News*. Excellent resources for Bangkok are *Big Chilli* and *Bangkok 101*, both published monthly.

Money Matters
Local Currency
The unit of currency is the baht, which is issued in a variety of coinage and paper units. Coins have been minted in several sizes over the last decade, often without any English labeling on the coin, and so can be confusing. The most commonly circulated coins are small, thin 1 baht coins, middle-size 5 baht coins, and slightly larger 10 baht coins. Paper currency comes in different sizes and colors: 10 baht (brown), 20 baht (green), 50 baht (blue), 100 baht (red), 500 baht (purple), and 1,000 baht (beige). The larger the note, the higher its value.

Exchange Rates
The baht floats in the 36–42 baht per dollar range. The airport money exchange desk is open 24 hours. Traveler's checks bring a

slightly higher exchange rate than cash. Exchanges can be made at banks, hotels, guesthouses, and exchange booths (found in tourist areas) Banks and guesthouses give a lower rate of exchange.

Many ATMs accept major credit cards and international ATM networks like Cirrus and Magellan. Banks will give cash advances on major credit cards. You will need your passport to change traveler's checks and to receive cash advances.

Security

As in any country, visitors should watch their valuables and use precautions such as money belts and hotel safes to guard them.

Tipping

A 10 percent service charge and 7 percent value added tax (VAT) is automatically added to all luxury hotel rooms and to most of the upscale restaurants that cater to tourists. The service charge makes it unnecessary to offer a tip in most restaurants. However, it remains thoughtful to offer a small gratuity to porters and chambermaids and small change as an additional tip to most other service personnel (10–20 baht). Leftover change is also appreciated in cafés, and by helpful taxi drivers or anyone else who provides a useful service.

Opening Times

Most private businesses keep similar hours to those in the West, while government offices open and close at more erratic hours (see below).

Banks Mon.–Fri. 8:30 a.m.–3:30 p.m. Some banks open on Saturday morning, while others have a mobile exchange trailer near the front door to provide exchange services for extended hours.

Museums National museums are open Wed.–Sun. 8:30 a.m.–noon and 1 p.m.–4:30 p.m.

State-run museums close Mon., Tues., and national holidays.

Government offices Most government offices (such as immigration) are open Mon.–Fri. 8:30 a.m.–noon and 1 p.m–4:30 p.m., and close on weekends and national holidays. The exception are tourist offices, which open daily except holidays 8:30 a.m.–4:30 p.m.

Shopping centers Large shopping emporiums are open daily 10/11 a.m.–9 p.m. year-round; many stay open on national holidays.

Rest Rooms

Few public buildings—aside from government facilities such as national museums and tourist offices—have restrooms. They are most easily found in large hotels and restaurants, as well as in nightclubs and other entertainment venues. Outside these places, the Thai-style facilities may seem primitive—usually a floor-level basin over which you squat. Toilet paper is available in establishments frequented by foreign visitors but not always in smaller restaurants and bars. Most shopping centers have clean toilets, but they often take a bit of finding.

Time Differences

There is only one time zone in Thailand. Thailand is seven hours ahead of Greenwich Mean Time (GMT +7). It is 15 hours ahead of the West Coast of the United States, 13 hours ahead of Chicago, 12 hours ahead of New York, 7 hours ahead of London, and 3 hours behind Sydney. Add one hour to these figures during summer daylight saving time. Thailand uses the 24-hour (military) clock.

Tourist Offices

The Tourism Authority of Thailand (TAT), or "Tawe Tawe Tawe" (TTT) in Thai, is an invaluable resource for travelers in Thailand. The Bangkok office, which is located on Petchaburi Road near

Sukhumvit 3, has information regarding all regions of Thailand, while smaller district offices have provincial brochures and maps, and can provide a wealth of verbal advice—their English skills are generally good. Particularly useful are the provincial brochures: mini-guidebooks that include maps and descriptions of attractions, interesting activities, festivals, regional cuisine, souvenirs, accommodations, and restaurants.

Thailand

Tourism Information Division, Tourism Authority of Thailand, 1600 Petchaburi Rd., Makkasan, Bangkok, tel 02-250-5500 or 1672, fax 02-250-5511, www.tourismthailand.org

TATs abroad include:

Australia

Sydney: National Australia Bank, 2nd fl., 75 Pitt St., Sydney, NSW 2000, tel 612/9247-7549, fax 612/9251-2465

Canada

Contact any TAT office in the United States (see below).

United Kingdom

London: 3rd fl., Brook House, 98-99 Jermyn St., London SW1Y 6EE, tel 44-207-925-2511, fax 44-207-925-2512

United States

New York: 61 Broadway, ste. 2810, New York, NY 10006, tel 212/432-0433, fax 212/269-2588

Los Angeles: 611 North Larchmont Blvc., Los Angeles, CA 90004, tel 213/461-9814, fax 213/461-9834

Visitors with Disabilities

Thailand is only just beginning to install special facilities for visitors with disabilities. While public restrooms with wheelchair access have yet to make an appearance, limited numbers of public phones for disabled users have been installed in Bangkok.

Hotels & Restaurants

Thailand has a superb range of hotels to suit all styles and budgets, from backpacker lodges with rooms for just a few dollars a night to five-star hotels offering world-class rooms and service with rates to match. Restaurants are also numerous, and you will never have to go far to find one that caters to your tastes and wallet.

Hotels

It is the top-end hotels and resorts, with their innovative architecture, memorable atmosphere, and high levels of service, that push Thailand consistently to the top of reader polls in magazines such as *Condé Nast Traveler* and *Travel & Leisure*. The real strength of Thai accommodations is that, no matter your budget, the country is prepared to welcome you with clean, comfortable, and well-designed facilities.

Accommodation Choices:
Although Thailand does not officially grade hotels, tariffs and a self-assigned star system act as an accurate guide.

Hotels with five stars are exceptional, invariably placed among the finest hotels in Asia and, in some cases, the world. The unaffected Thai friendliness of the staff in these places does not compromise service, which is exemplary. Amenities will include a large swimming pool with attentive staff ferrying food and drink to your lounge chair, world-class fitness and business centers, and laundry and pressing services.

Restaurants in these hotels in a lot of cases will be among the finest.

Guest rooms will be large and luxurious with top-quality, stylish furniture and fittings, crisp bed linens, and down comforters. There will be satellite TV, a DVD player with a sound system, two or more telephones with international direct dialing, a well-stocked minibar, high-speed Internet, and room service. Most also have executive floors with free laundry, butler service, a fax machine, personalized stationery, and a lounge offering coffee and snacks. Examples of hotels in this category are the Oriental Bangkok, the Peninsula, and the Sukhothai.

Four-star hotels differ from the five-stars by a less personal, but still friendly, efficient service. Rooms may be a little smaller, and the furnishings and fittings, while tasteful, will be less luxuriant. In-room amenities and services will be similar to those in five-star hotels, and the swimming pool and fitness center are free to guests. These establishments include the Marriott, Sheraton, Sofitel, and Hyatt.

Three-star hotels are called tourist hotels, and they mainly cater to the package tourist market. Service remains excellent, although many tend toward the perfunctory. Rooms have furniture and fittings more in the generic hotel mold. The TV will be smaller and have fewer channels. You'll still find a swimming pool, and the fitness center will be less elaborate than those found in four- and five-star hotels.

Choosing a two-star or budget hotel can be a lottery. While some offer services and facilities that are close to those of the three-stars mentioned above, others can be less appealing. It is a good idea to ask to see the room before checking in or book one for only one night initially. The upside is that they are cheap.

In beach resorts such as on Ko Samui, Ko Chang, and Ko Samet, many of the accommodations are "bungalows." These are groups of one-room (with a bathroom and small veranda or balcony), free-standing buildings just about always on or near the beach. Bungalows can vary from well-appointed to basic, but in most cases are clean and comfortable.

Serviced apartments and suites are a good deal if you're planning to stay in Bangkok for an extended period. The apartments are similar to the hotel rooms (a number of hotels have serviced apartment wings), but the usual amenities are not included. Substantial discounts are offered for stays of a month or more (in some cases, two weeks). Suites refer to serviced apartments with one or more rooms.

Hotels in Thailand have a standard checkout at noon. If you want to stay a few extra hours on the day you check out, this usually is allowed for no extra charge if you inform the front desk a day in advance.

Location: Hotels in Bangkok are congregated in the Sukhumvit area and along a section of the Chao Phraya river in eastern Bangkok. Many are conveniently located near the Skytrain and in the heart of the city's entertainment areas. Others are easily reached by an inexpensive taxi ride.

If you book a hotel from overseas, you can request limousine service from the airport, which is a stress-free way of settling into the city.

In the beach resorts of Phuket, Pattaya, and Ko Samui, hotels are either on or close to the beach. In Chiang Mai, a number of the city's better hotels are a few miles out of town, but easily reached by hotel shuttles or taxis.

Reservations: Reservations are advised during the high season (Oct.–March) in Bangkok and strongly advised year-round at the beach resorts on Phuket and Ko Samui. Hotels elsewhere experience relatively low occupancy rates year-round, and visitors who do not have reservations upon arrival can usually find a room without trouble, aside from major holidays and over New Year's vacation.

It is always a good idea to book your hotel in advance, however, as much to get a discount as to guarantee a room. Show up without a reservation, and you're likely to pay the full rate. In addition to the usual channels of telephone, fax or travel agent, most hotels take reservations online, either through the hotel's site or an international booking agent (*www.asiarooms.com* being one of the most biggest and most reputable). Thailand's service industry has become very Internet savvy over the last few years, with even guesthouses offering rooms over the Internet.

There is usually no need to pay in advance when booking, but you will need to furnish your credit card number. If you don't show up, you'll be automatically billed for one night. When you book a room over the Internet, you will receive a confirmation number that you will need to present on arrival at the hotel.

Booking over the Internet—either through an agent or the hotel itself—brings the best discounts, usually between 30 and 40 percent off the advertised room rate.

Booking also can be done over the phone, which precludes you from having to send your credit card number. This should not present a problem, because the hotel's desk staff usually speaks English.

If you have an itinerary, book your rooms before leaving home. If your schedule changes, most hotels will not have a problem changing your arrival and departure dates if given proper notice. Otherwise, once in Thailand, the tour desk at tourist hotels can book your future travel accommodations.

The Thai Hotels Association has a booking kiosk at the airport arrivals lounge with a list (and photos) of hotels covering most budgets. This offers a good, but fixed, discount off rack rates. On booking you pay for a night's accommodation and receive a receipt and voucher, which you hand to the hotel upon arrival.

Prices: Hotel room rates in Thailand—especially Bangkok—are bargains when compared with rates in the United States and Europe. The Oriental, which travel magazine readers' polls consistently rate as one of the top three or four hotels in the world, broke new ground a few years ago by lifting their rates above $200 a night. Only the Peninsula and the Sukhothai have rates approaching those of the Oriental. With advanced bookings, most four-star hotels have standard rooms for a little more than $100, while some very good deals are available at tourist-grade hotels with rates as low as $40.

Hotels have rack rates that are either placed on the front desk or are available upon request. These rates are only charged to guests who arrive without reservations. An advance booking usually comes with at least a 30 percent discount. When booking, establish whether the rate is "all inclusive," which means VAT (value-added tax; see p. 382) of 7 percent and a service charge of 10 percent are included in the price. Many hotels also include a buffet breakfast in the room charge.

Rates in Bangkok hotels remain stable throughout the year, except during the week between Christmas and New Year's, when they can rise sharply. However, rates at major tourist resorts fluctuate greatly depending upon the season. Rates during the tourist season (Nov.–Feb.) sometimes double and rise even more from the middle of December through mid-January. If you're staying in a hotel on Christ-

mas Day or New Year's Day, you could find a hefty surcharge for that evening's meal and party, whether you attend or not. Alternatively, during the off-season (especially May–Sept.), there are some very good deals to be had.

Hotels charge for the room, not the number of people staying in a room (although you will pay a surcharge for any additional beds). When asked if you require a single or double room, they are referring to the beds. A single room will have one king- or queen-sized bed, while a double will have two single beds.

Credit Cards: Most moderate and luxury hotels and resorts accept Visa (V) and Mastercard (MC), and, to a lesser degree, American Express (AE). Diners Club (DC) is only accepted at a handful of superior hotels. Many hotels post creditcard stickers near the front door so guests know which cards are accepted.

Hotel Groups: U.S. contact numbers:
Accor Group, tel 800/221-4542
Best Western, tel 800/780-7234
Hilton, tel 800/HILTONS
Dusit, tel 800/44-UTELL
Four Seasons, tel 416/449-1750
Holiday Inn, tel 800/HOLIDAY or 800/465-4329
Hyatt, tel 888/591-1234 or 800/228-9548
Leading Hotels of the World, tel 800/745-8883
Mandarin Oriental, tel 865/526-6567
Marriott, tel 800/932-2198
Meridien, tel 866/559-3821
Pan Pacific, tel 800/327-8585
Radisson, tel 800/333-3333
Regent, tel 888/201-1806
Shangri-La, tel 866/565-5050
Westin, tel 800/325-5555

Restaurants

Thailand has one of the world's most exotic cuisines; dining out is likely to be a highlight of your visit.

Types of Restaurants:

Thailand's restaurant scene is becoming more varied and sophisticated in Bangkok, Pattaya, Phuket, Ko Samui, and Hua Hin.

A fine homegrown cuisine, along with the parochial dining habits of even the most sophisticated Thais, may be reasons why Bangkok and other major tourist areas have not reached the great culinary heights when it comes to restaurants offering non-Thai cuisine. Bangkok is no Hong Kong, Singapore, or Sydney, but as home to one of the world's great cuisines, it doesn't really need to be.

While Thai food predominates in the tourist areas, there's no shortage of restaurants and cafés serving Western and other types of Asian foods, especially Japanese and Chinese. The best of these are often found in top-tier hotels.

Plenty of other countries and regions are represented, including Indian, Middle Eastern (mostly in the colorful Soi Middle East between Sukhumvit Road's Soi 3 and Soi 5), American, German, Danish, Mexican, Continental, and Vietnamese. Surprisingly good Irish and British pub food can be found in Bangkok's many bars themed on these countries. Equally surprising is that there are not many restaurants offering "fusion" (Thai/Asian and Western ingredients) cuisine.

Delis in some of the better hotels are good places for sandwiches and pastries, while the recent arrival of Subway has increased the options in that category. As usual in Asian cities, there is no shortage of McDonald's, and the arrival of Starbucks a few years back spurred an increase in the number of local coffee shops, both from chains and independents.

In the tourist resorts of Pattaya, Phuket, Hua Hin, and Ko Samui, restaurants, cafés, and bars offering Western fare predominate, and most are owned by Western expats. Bakeries that have been set up to serve the growth in this type of establishment have improved the quality and variety of breads, and they opened a market for British and Australian meat pies, pastries, and cakes.

From the best restaurants to roadside vendors' stalls, the quality of Thai food is consistently good—meaning it is rare to have a bad meal in the country. Often, the only differences between the same type of dish served in an expensive restaurant and a more humble establishment are price and presentation.

Many Thai restaurants in Bangkok and tourist areas will have a menu in English—even if they don't cater to tourists—as well as Thai. However, a lot of the time, the best you'll get is the Thai transliteration (translated into the Roman alphabet but still Thai). That is why it's handy to remember the Thai names of your favorite dishes.

Because of the liberal addition of chilies, Thai food can be intolerably hot for Westerners. Some restaurants, including a number of very good establishments that cater to a mainly Western clientele, make allowances and ease up on the chili count. In other places, the chilies can be kept to a minimum by asking that your order be *khaaw mai phet* (not spicy).

Some places offer guests the option of dining on cushions on the floor. This section of the restaurant will be raised. Thais traditionally eat while sitting on the floor, but restaurants compromise by using low tables.

Dining Hours:

Cafés and restaurants in most hotels follow familiar opening hours, with a buffet breakfast served from perhaps 6:30 a.m. to 10 a.m., lunch from 11:30 a.m. to 3 p.m., and dinner from 5:30 p.m. to about 10:30 p.m. Trendier independent restaurants in major tourist destinations often stay open nightly until midnight or later depending on demand and time of year. Outdoors, it's possible to find soups, noodle dishes, and fried rice almost any time, especially in larger urban areas and beach resorts.

Meals:

Thai food is designed to be eaten by groups rather than just one or two people. Various dishes are ordered and shared, with each person receiving his or her own plate of rice. The dishes rarely arrive at once, and no real attention is paid to the order of arrival, except in fancier Thai restaurants. People start eating after the first few dishes arrive.

The quality of the small restaurants and roadside vendors' stalls (sometimes a couple of tables have been set up for diners) is often very good and so inexpensive that you'll think you haven't been charged enough. A filling plate of tasty noodles or fried rice will set you back about one dollar. Many roadside vendors specialize in snacks and sweets; you'll rarely get something bad (even if it looks strange).

A meal usually consists of one type of dish, say chicken with basil, over a plate of rice, along with a fork and spoon (the food is pushed onto the spoon with the fork). If more than one dish is ordered, then the rice will come on a separate plate.

Paying & Tipping:

In better cafés and restaurants, a 7 percent VAT (see p. 382) and 10 percent service charge will be added to your bill, precluding the need to tip. But most establishments don't charge VAT or add a service charge. A tip isn't obligatory at these places, but appreciated; generally between 20 and 50 baht is adequate.

Restaurants in tourist destinations occasionally will try to overcharge Western customers; check your bill carefully before paying and inquire about any unknown

PRICES

HOTELS

An indication of the cost of double room in the high season is given by **$** signs.

$$$$$	Over $240
$$$$	$160–$240
$$$	$110–$160
$$	$70–1$10
$	Under $70

RESTAURANTS

An indication of the cost of three-course meal without drinks is given by **$** signs.

$$$$$	Over $65
$$$$	$50–$65
$$$	$30–$50
$$	$20–$30
$	Under $20

charges. If you are brought peanuts or other appetizers that you did not request, you may want to check about any possible charges before consuming them.

Important Notes

The hotels and restaurants below have been grouped according to region (by chapter), then alphabetically within price categories.

As the bus service in Thailand is notoriously inefficient and confusing, the best way to get to hotels is by taxi, although in Bangkok some are easily accessible by Skytrain.

All of the listed hotels have at least one café or restaurant, air-conditioning, and outdoor rather than indoor swimming pools. All multilevel (three floors or more) hotels and resorts have elevators.

All hotels offer both smoking and nonsmoking rooms. Smoking is banned in restaurants.

Finally, all of the listed hotels accept major credit cards.

Abbreviations:

L=Lunch   D=Dinner

■ BANGKOK

Hotels

⊞ BANGKOK MARRIOTT
¶ RESORT & SPA
$$$$$

257/1–3 CHAROEN NAKORN RD., THON BURI
TEL 02-476-0021
FAX 02-476-1120
www.marriott.com/bkkth

Situated on the opposite side of the river and about 3 miles (2 km) south of the Oriental, this resort in the city is the perfect place to visit Bangkok but enjoy the charms and character of more rural Thailand. The hotel has extensive grounds and a series of buildings. Dining options include an elaborate Chinese restaurant and a branch of Trader Vic's. You can also enjoy Japanese-American steaks at **Benihana's**, Chinese delicacies at the **Rice Mill**, and seafood at the **Market Restaurant**. Rooms are spacious and airy; many have tremendous views of the constant river activity—one of the wonders of Bangkok.

ℹ️ 416 + 15 suites 🅿️ � 🅂
🏊 🛡️ 🅂 All major cards

⊞ BANYAN TREE
¶ $$$$$

21/100 S. SATHORN RD.
TEL 02-679-1200
FAX 02-679-1199
www.banyantree.com/bangkok

This luxurious hotel caters to sophisticated travelers and businessmen who demand only the finest. The 60-story building lacks personality, but the hotel rooms—primarily those on the upper floors of the gray tower—provide unequaled city vistas. Amenities include a very complete business center, large spa, a rooftop Chinese restaurant that will take your breath away, and the **Rom Sai**, which serves Thai, Chinese, and other Asian specialties. Rooms have com-

puter ports and fax machines.

ℹ️ 216 suites 🅿️ 🅂 🛡️ 🅂 All major cards

⊞ FOUR SEASONS
¶ $$$$$

155 RATCHADAMRI RD.
TEL 02-250-1000
FAX 02-253-9195
www.fourseasons.com/bangkok

A few blocks from the shopping centers near Siam Square, this legendary hotel has a magnificent two-story lobby with an overwhelming amount of teak, polished marble, and silk furnishing, hovered over by one of the most attentive staffs in the city. Among the dining options are a Western grill with entertainment most evenings, the Italian **Biscotti** (see p. 365), a mezzanine coffee shop, a tea lounge for an afternoon break from the heat, a sushi bar, and the **Spice Market** restaurant. Rooms are stylish, large, and decorated in a restrained style.

ℹ️ 370 🚈 Skytrain: Ratchadamri
🅿️ 🅂 🅂 🏊 🛡️ 🅂 All major cards

⊞ IMPERIAL QUEEN'S
PARK
$$$$$

199 SUKHUMVIT SOI 22
TEL 02-261-9000
FAX 02-261-9530
www.imperialhotels.com/queenspark

The largest hotel in Bangkok looms over the mostly deserted Benjasiri Park in mid-Sukhumvit. The massive structure has everything imaginable within its walls, including almost a dozen cafés, restaurants, and pubs for diversion, a pair of swimming pools, and conference facilities for up to 3,000. Rooms are large, and standards are high.

ℹ️ 1,300 + 35 suites
🚈 Skytrain: Asoke 🅿️ 🅂 🅂
🏊 🛡️ 🅂 All major cards

NOVOTEL SIAM SQUARE
$$$$$
SIAM SQUARE SOI 6
TEL 02-209-8888
FAX 02-254-1328
www.novotel.com
This popular hotel lies right in the middle of Siam Square and within a few minutes' walk of the Central World Plaza and MBK shopping emporiums (see p. 382). Rooms are reasonably large and well appointed. As with most Novotel properties, it is popular with European visitors.
ⓘ 427 + 5 suites 🚆 Skytrain: Siam Square 🅿 🔄 📶 📶 📶 All major cards

NOVOTEL SUVARNA-BHUMI AIRPORT HOTEL
$$$$$
MOO 1 NONGPRUE BANG PHLI
TEL 02-131-1111
FAX 02-131-1188
www.novotelsuvarna
bhumi.com
The closest hotel to the airport is also the finest. A 24-hour shuttle provides service to and from the airport, and temporary rentals are also available. Wireless Internet and full-service business center cater to business travelers. Families benefit from family rooms that allow two children under 16 free stays including breakfasts. Multiple swimming pools, restaurants, and bars round out the hotel's comfort and convenience.
ⓘ 582 + 30 suites 🅿 🔄 📶 📶 📶 All major cards

SOMETHING SPECIAL

ORIENTAL
$$$$$
48 ORIENTAL AVE.
TEL 02-236-0400
FAX 02-659-9284 TO -5
www.mandarinoriental.com/
hotel/bangkok
One of the finest hotels in the world according to virtually every traveler's survey ever taken, the Mandarin Oriental is the ultimate accommodation and dining experience in Bangkok. Rooms are elegant and traditionally decorated, with a staggering range of facilities—including a spa—and outstanding personal service. Enjoy the **Sala Rim Nam** restaurant on the opposite bank of the river (see p. 364), the **China House** in a restored colonial residence, and the **Normandie,** one of the finest French restaurants in the country. The hotel dates from 1876 and has served as temporary home for a slew of movie stars and famous writers.
ⓘ 396 🅿 🔄 📶 📶 All major cards

THE PENINSULA
$$$$$
333 CHAROEN NAKORN RD.,
THON BURI
TEL 02-861-1111
FAX 02-861-2355
www.bangkok.peninsula.com
One of Bangkok's newest luxury hotels, the Peninsula invites guests to escape the traffic and pollution of the city and relax in a tranquil yet reasonably central location. The soaring 39-story structure has seven restaurants (including the **Mei Jiang**; see p. 364), lovely gardens set with palms and other tropical foliage, a riverside swimming pool, tennis courts, and some of the most spacious rooms in town.
ⓘ 370 + 60 suites 🅿 🔄 📶 📶 📶 All major cards

ROYAL ORCHID SHERATON HOTEL & TOWERS
$$$$$
2 CAPTAIN BUSH LN.
TEL 02-266-0123
FAX 02-266-9211
www.sheraton.com/bangkok
Another famous hotel magnificently situated on the riverbank. Though this hotel is older than many others in Bangkok, its recently refurbished rooms have larger double beds and all modern facilities. Restaurants include **Giorgio's** (see p. 365), a Thai restaurant, and a popular 24-hour coffee shop. Location, convenience, and expansive gardens are the main draws.
ⓘ 756 + 75 suites 🅿 🔄 📶 📶 📶 All major cards

SHANGRI-LA
$$$$$
89 SOI WAT SUAN PHU, OFF
CHAROEN KRUNG RD.
TEL 02-236-7777
FAX 02-236-8579
www.shangri-la.com/bangkok
The Shangri-La makes the most of its superb riverside setting with a glass wall in the lobby with stunning views over the river to Thon Buri. Dining options range from Thai and Japanese to the superb Italian restaurant **Angelini.** Rooms are fairly large and well furnished, and most have been renovated in recent years.
ⓘ 850 + 57 suites 🚆 Skytrain: Taksin Bridge 🅿 🔄 📶 📶 📶 All major cards

SHERATON GRAND SUKHUMVIT
$$$$$
250 SUKHUMVIT SOI 12
TEL 02-653-0333
FAX 02-649-8000
www.sheratongrande
sukhumvit.com
This fine hotel attracts guests with its wide range of facilities, luxurious appointments, and location near the Times Square shopping center, boutiques, and entertainment venues. No expense has been spared on the lobby and rooms, which each have an additional dressing room and marble bathroom. Among the hotel's eating places is **Riva's,** which serves lunch and dinner and converts into a nightclub.
ⓘ 445 🚆 Skytrain: Asoke 🅿 🔄 📶 📶 📶 📶 All major cards

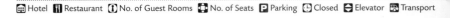

🏨 Hotel 🍴 Restaurant ⓘ No. of Guest Rooms 🪑 No. of Seats 🅿 Parking 🕐 Closed 🔄 Elevator 🚆 Transport

THE SUKHOTHAI

$$$$$

13/3 S. SATHORN RD.

TEL 02-344-8888

FAX 02-344-8822

www.sukhothai.com

Perhaps the most restrained and Zen-like sanctuary in Bangkok, this hotel is well removed from the traffic and noise that plagues most other districts in the city. The design emphasis is on simplicity, and artistic motifs recall the glorious days of Sukhothai. Museum-quality art abounds, while glass walls and enclosed carp ponds provide a feeling of perfect serenity. Dining options range from a Thai restaurant surrounded by lily ponds to an Italian outlet set on a lovely terrace. Rooms are spacious and neatly combine Thai styles with modern accents, along with antiques and fine arts. The floors are made of teak, and many of the fabrics are silk.

ⓘ 224 + 38 suites 🚆 Skytrain: Saladaeng 🅿 🚭 🛂 🏊 🅷

🅲 All major cards

SWISSÔTEL NAI LERT PARK

$$$$$

2 WITTHAYU RD.

TEL 02-253-0123

FAX 02-253-6509

www.bangkok-nailertpark
.swissotel.com

Tucked away on a relatively quiet street, this older property lacks the modernity or classic charm of other upscale hotels, but compensates with the city's largest gardens and hotel grounds. The lobby and halls are rather utilitarian, but **Ma Maison** café is among Bangkok's better French restaurants (see p. 364). Spacious rooms.

ⓘ 338 + 12 suites 🚆 Skytrain: Phayathai 🅿 🚭 🛂 🏊 🅷

🅲 All major cards

WESTIN GRANDE SUKHUMVIT

$$$$$

259 SUKHUMVIT RD.,

NEAR SOI ASOKE

TEL 02-207-8000

FAX 02-254-4431

www.starwoodhotels.com
/westin

Conveniently located opposite the Times Square shopping complex, this distinctive blue hotel is popular with group tours. Visitors are welcome in the seventh-floor lobby and can enjoy a gym, spa, and other facilities. Meals are served in the Mediterranean restaurant or Japanese café. The most popular spot is Horizons Sky Lounge with magnificent panoramic views and private karaoke rooms. Guest rooms are modern and reasonably spacious, yet unremarkably furnished.

ⓘ 364 🚆 Skytrain: Asoke 🅿 🚭 🛂 🏊 🅷 🅲 All major card

AMARI WATERGATE

$$$$–$$$$$

847 PETCHABURI RD.

TEL 02-653-9000

FAX 02-653-9045

www.amari.com/watergate

Rising unobtrusively near the Pratunam Market, this hotel is known for its friendliness and central location. The exterior is unremarkable, but the gaily decorated, lively lobby makes a good first impression. Dining options include an American-style bar and grill, and a fancy Italian café. Informality is the rule here, whether visiting the attached shopping center or just relaxing in one of the elegant rooms, which are among the largest in the city.

ⓘ 576 + 12 suites 🅿 🚭 🛂 🏊 🅷 🅲 All major cards

BEL-AIRE PRINCESS HOTEL

$$$$

SUKHUMVIT SOI 5

TEL 02-253-4300

FAX 02-255-8850

www.bel-aireprincess.com

This consistently popular mid-level hotel, tucked away in an alley just a few minutes' walk from busy Sukhumvit Road, is a good choice for peace and quiet. Facilities include a popular restaurant that serves Indian, Thai, and Western fare, a prettily landscaped pool, and a fitness center. Rooms are large and feature clean, minimalist decors, and the staff is friendly and efficient.

ⓘ 160 🚆 Skytrain: Nana 🅿 🚭 🛂 🏊 🅷 🅲 All major cards

DREAM HOTEL

$$$$

10 SUKHUMVIT SOI 15

TEL 02-254-8500

FAX 02-254-8534

www.dreambkk.com

The Dream exudes sophistication and style. Plush modern rooms have contemporary décor, plasma TVs, and Wi-Fi. Situated off Sukhumvit road, near BTS Nana, the hotel is surrounded by shopping, dining, and nightlife. Flava Lounge and Restaurant here are high-society hangouts and the pool features the occasional party.

ⓘ 165 – 30 suites 🚆 Skytrain: Nana 🅿 🚭 🛂 🅲 AE, D, V

DUSIT THANI HOTEL

$$$$

RAMA IV AT SILOM RD.

TEL 02-236-0450

FAX 02-636-3562

www.dusit-than.bangkok.com

This venerable hotel overlooks Lumphini Park. Its impressive lobby interiors are kept under constant renovation, and spacious rooms are outfitted with every possible amenity. The richness and profuse use of wood, marble, and silk, plus famous service from an experienced staff, make this hotel one of the best in town. Restaurants include **Hamilton's** (see p. 365) and an international restaurant on the roof that provides wonderful views.

ⓘ 520 + 15 suites 🚆 Skytrain: Saladaeng 🅿 🚭 🛂 🏊 🅷 🅲 All major cards

---

🅢 Nonsmoking   🅐 Air-conditioning   🅘 Indoor Pool   🅞 Outdoor Pool   🅗 Health Club   🅲 Credit Cards

🏨 GRAND HYATT ERAWAN BANGKOK
$$$$

494 RATCHADAMRI RD.
TEL 02-254-1234
FAX 02-254-6308
www.bangkok.grand.hyatt
.com
One of the largest and finest
hotels in the shopping district
near Siam Square, this 21-story
building has a soaring lobby
and naturally styled rooms in
pleasing timber tones. The
five restaurants serve Thai,
Chinese, and Continental food.
There is a bakery, a garden bar,
and a ballroom that has space
for 1,500 guests.
🛏 380 + 18 suites 🚈 Skytrain:
Chidlom 🅿 🔄 ❄ 🏊 🍸
🔱 All major cards

🏨🍴 HOLIDAY INN SILOM BANGKOK
$$$$

981 SILOM RD.
TEL 02-238-4300
FAX 02-238-5289
www.bangkok-silom.holiday-
inn.com
One of the premium Holiday
Inns, this hotel is well situated
between the nightlife enclave
of Patpong and the more luxurious properties on the river.
The gleaming 27-story tower
has a spacious lobby decorated
with marble and silk, a cozy
lounge for afternoon tea, and
several restaurants including
the **Tandoor,** one of the most
popular Indian spots in town
(see p. 365). Rooms are clean
and new; the best rooms are in
the Crowne Tower.
🛏 595 + 7 suites 🅿 🔄 ❄
🏊 🍸 🔱 All major cards

🏨 AMARI BOULEVARD
$$$

SUKHUMVIT SOI 5
TEL 02-255-2930
FAX 02-255-2959
www.amari.com/boulevard
This is a reasonably priced,
fairly luxurious hotel in the
middle of the Sukhumvit
nightlife district, with a cozy,

almost family feel. The pool
is smaller than at more expen-
sive hotels, and only a coffee
shop is found in the original
wing. Standard rooms are
stylish yet basic, while deluxe
rooms have private garden
patios. Service levels are high.
🛏 315 + 10 suites 🚈 Skytrain:
Nana 🅿 🔄 ❄ 🏊 🍸 🔱 All
major cards

🏨 GRAND CHINA PRINCESS
$$$

215 YAOWARAT RD.
TEL 02-224-9977
FAX 02-224-6999
www.grandchina.com
The only decent hotel in
Chinatown, this is the place for
the adventurous traveler who
wishes to explore this remarkable neighborhood. Simplicity
is the key, but all public areas
and rooms are kept clean and
functional, as are the Chinese
restaurant and the 24-hour
coffee shop. Best bet for relaxation is the rooftop revolving
bar, which guarantees great
views over Chinatown and
the river.
🛏 155 + 19 suites 🅿 🔄 ❄
🏊 🍸 🔱 All major cards

🏨 IMPERIAL TARA
$$$

SUKHUMVIT SOI 26
TEL 02-259-2900
FAX 02-259-2897
www.imperialhotels.com/tara
This hotel, conveniently located
on a quiet alley off Sukhumvit,
is popular with local and
Japanese travelers. Facilities
are good, and the rooms are
acceptable, though perhaps not
up to the standards of other
similarly priced properties.
🛏 165 + 6 suites 🚈 Skytrain:
Asoke 🅿 🔄 ❄ 🏊 🍸 🔱 All
major cards

🏨🍴 INDRA REGENT HOTEL
$$$

120 RATCHAPRAROP RD.
TEL 02-208-0022
FAX 02-208-0388

www.indrahotel.com
This venerable hotel has maintained good standards over the
years. The dirty exterior may
seem off-putting, but through
the doors is a hotel with professional staff, reasonable facilities,
the lovely **Sala Thai Restaurant**
with its 13th-century teak
pavilion and classical Thai
dancers, and decent rooms
that are all well appointed with
comfortable furnishings.
🛏 439 + 12 suites 🅿 🔄 ❄
🏊 🍸 🔱 All major cards

🏨🍴 INTERCONTINENTAL BANGKOK
$$$

973 PHLOEN CHIT RD.
TEL 02-656-0444
FAX 02-656-0325
www.bangkok.inter
continental.com
Located opposite the Erawan
shrine, this soaring white
wonder at the corner of
Ratchadamri Road is popular
with North American visitors.
Beyond the entrance lies a
grand lobby lined with marble.
The premier restaurants are
the **Espresso** (see p. 367) and
the **Chinese Summer Palace.**
Rooms are fairly large and
decorated in light earth tones.
There are great views from the
upper rooms.
🛏 381 + 39 suites 🚈 Skytrain:
Phloen Chit 🔄 ❄ 🏊 🍸
🔱 All major cards

🏨 J. W. MARRIOTT
$$$

4 SUKHUMVIT SOI 2
TEL 02-656-7700
FAX 02-656-9819
www.marriott.com/hotels
/travel/bkkdt-jw-marriott-
hotel-bangkok
This modern hotel is in an
excellent central location near
the shopping complexes of
Siam Square and Sukhumvit
Road. The exterior shows little
imagination, though the lobby
is spacious and inviting. The
modest-size rooms are decorated in a cheery and stylishly
modern design. Restaurants

🏨 Hotel 🍴 Restaurant 🛏 No. of Guest Rooms 🪑 No. of Seats 🅿 Parking 🕐 Closed 🔄 Elevator 🚈 Transport

offer Japanese, Thai, and Chinese cuisine, as well as an American-style steak house and coffeehouse with pastries.
🛈 435 rooms 🚇 Skytrain: Nana 🅿 🔄 🔃 🌊 🎖 🐾 All major cards

🏨 LANDMARK
🍴 $$$

138 SUKHUMVIT SOI 4
TEL 02-254-0404
FAX 02-254-2694
www.landmarkbangkok.com
This is one of the original luxury hotels in this central neighborhood, and years of constant refurbishing and renovation have kept it at the head of the pack, while providing a less expensive alternative to more recent hotels. Dining options include Thai, Japanese, Chinese, and Continental, and the rooftop restaurant, the **Hibiscus,** has outstanding views. Corner rooms are extra spacious. Service standards are some of the finest in town.
🛈 370 + 45 suites 🚇 Skytrain: Nana 🅿 🔄 🔃 🌊 🎖 🐾 All major cards

🏨 PAN PACIFIC
🍴 $$$

952 RAMA IV RD.
TEL 02-632-9000
FAX 02-632-9001
www.panpacific.com /bangkok
Situated within walking distance of the Patpong nightlife area, this hotel is unfortunately surrounded by expressways, mass transit schemes, and nonstop traffic jams—although the attentive staff does its best to greet guests and help them forget the world below. Most of the rooms are near the top of the building, with views over Lumphini Park. Dining choices include the Chinese restaurant **Hai Tien Lo,** dressed up in black marble, and **Keyaki** for Japanese fare.
🛈 235 + 14 suites 🚇 Skytrain: Saladaeng 🅿 🔄 🔃 🌊 🎖 🐾 All major cards

🏨 ROYAL PRINCESS LARN LUANG
$$$

269 LARN LUANG RD.
TEL 02-281-3088
FAX 02-280-1314
www.bangkok.com/royal princess-larnluang
This decent hotel is conveniently located near the Royal Palace, Sanam Luang, and the Banglamphu backpacker's district. Facilities include surprisingly large rooms with modern furnishings, cafés and restaurants, and a fitness room.
🛈 166 + 5 suites 🅿 🔄 🔃 🌊 🎖 🐾 All major cards

🏨 SOFITEL SILOM BANGKOK
$$$

188 SILOM RD.
TEL 02-238-1991
FAX 02-238-1992
www.sofitel.com
A 38-story high-rise hotel, this competes well beside the more recognized properties in the same neighborhood, and is within walking distance of Patpong and the shops on Silom Road. Facilities include a health club and business center, and restaurants include Japanese and French, along with a famous Chinese option on the rooftop. Good value for mid-level travelers.
🛈 454 + 32 suites 🚇 Skytrain: Saladaeng 🅿 🔄 🔃 🌊 🎖 🐾 All major cards

🏨 BAIYOKE SUITE HOTEL
$$

130 RATCHAPRAROP RD.
TEL 02-255-0330
FAX 02-254-5553
www.baiyokehotel.com /baiyokesuite
Located in Thailand's second tallest building, this all-suite hotel is easily reached by taxi. You can't miss the distinctive rainbow-hued exterior. There are tremendous views from all of the upper rooms, which ascend the 43 floors to a rooftop observation deck

and restaurant with equally remarkable vistas. Good value for families.
🛈 255 suites 🅿 🔄 🔃 🌊 🎖 🐾 All major cards

🏨 NARAI
🍴 $$

222 SILOM RD.
TEL 02-237-0100
FAX 02-235-6781
www.naraihotel.com
In an excellent location almost midway between Patpong and the river, this 15-story hotel provides a very reasonable alternative to the much more luxurious and expensive hotels in the neighborhood. The hotel is basic but has all the standard facilities. Rooms are decorated in a pleasing, clean, modern style. There are several restaurants on the main floor, and the revolving option, **La Rotonde Grill,** on the 15th floor, is great fun.
🛈 409 + 20 suites 🚇 Skytrain: Surasak 🅿 🔄 🔃 🌊 🎖 🐾 All major cards

🏨 SILOM CITY INN
$

SILOM SOI 22 AT 72 SOI PRA-CHUM
TEL 02-635-6211 TO -14
FAX 02-365-9215
www.bangkok.com/silom cityinn
This simple hotel offers excellent value within a few blocks of the shops, boutiques, and nightclubs of the Silom-Surawong district. Often overlooked by Western visitors, this small gem has most of the necessary facilities, such as an exercise room and acceptable deluxe rooms. The interior is stylish, and the staff is exceptionally willing to help.
🛈 70 + 12 suites 🅿 🔄 🔃 🌊 🎖 🐾 All major cards

🚭 Nonsmoking 🔃 Air-conditioning 🔄 Indoor Pool 🌊 Outdoor Pool 🎖 Health Club 🐾 Credit Cards

The Best of the best

Best Thai Restaurant in a hotel

Celadon (The Sukhothai)
Ruen Thai (Grand Hyatt Erawan Bangkok)
Spice Market (The Regent)
Salathip (Shangri-La)

Best Chinese Restaurant in a hotel

Mei Jiang (Peninsula)
Bai Yun (Banyan Tree)
The Chinese Restaurant (Grand Hyatt Erawan Bangkok)
Mayflower (Dusit Thani)

Best Brunch Buffet

Marriott Cafe (J. W. Marriott)
The Captain's Table (Grand Pacific)
Colonnade (The Sukhothai)
The Dining Room (Grand Hyatt Erawan Bangkok)
Trader Vic's (Bangkok Marriott Resort & Spa)
Mei Jiang (Peninsula)

Best Restaurant with Thai Dance Performance

Baan Thai
Sala Rim Nam (Oriental)

Restaurants

Best Bangkok Restaurants

Bangkok has hundreds of restaurants serving virtually every form of food on the planet, and many of these restaurants change ownership, names, and cuisines with the seasons. The most accurate listing of current offerings can be found in *Metro*, a monthly English-language magazine that divides Bangkok restaurants into categories based on nationality. *Metro* also sponsors a yearly contest that names the best restaurants in town. Based on their latest recommendations, here are some recent winners:

🍴 CAFÉ SIAM
$$$$
4 SOI SRIAKSON
TEL 02-671-0030
FAX 02-671-0031
Difficult to find, but worth the effort (call them first so they can fax you a map). The menu offers mostly French cuisine, although it also has a good selection of popular Thai curries, plus a reasonable list of wines and cocktails.
🔢 120 🚇 Skytrain: Saladaeng 🚫 🅿 🕐 Closed 2 p.m.– 6 p.m. 💳 All major cards

🍴 BUSSARACUM
$$$
425 SOI PHIPAT 2, SILOM RD.
TEL 02-266-6312
FAX 02-266-6312 TO -6
One of the original upscale Royal Thai restaurants, Bussaracum is known for its quiet setting and fine dining. Bussaracum aims for authenticity in its dishes, which range from seafood and curries to spicy vegetarian options. Advance reservations are essential.
🔢 45 🅿 🕐 Closed L Mon. 💳 All major cards

🍴 LOY NAVA DINNER CRUISES
$$$
1367 CHAROEN NAKORN RD., KLONGSAN
TEL 02-437-4932 & 02-437-7329
FAX 02-438-3098
Five-star dining on the *Tahsaneeya Nava,* the only antique teak rice barge in Bangkok. This is a good chance to get away from the noise while seeing the historical landmarks as you cruise along the Chao Phraya river. The menu offers a choice of Thai, vegetarian, and seafood dishes in set-menu style. While the range is not fantastic, the meals are authentic.
🔢 55 🅿 💳 All major cards

🍴 MA MAISON
$$$
SWISSÔTEL NAI LERT PARK
2 WITTHAYU RD.
TEL 02-253-0123
FAX 02-253-6509 OR 02-253-6513
A favorite of high society and local power brokers, Ma Maison, in the Swissôtel (see p. 361), is known for its elegant yet unpretentious interior design, its extensive wine list, and its innovative French dishes.
🔢 65 🚇 Skytrain: Phayathai 🅿 💳 All major cards

🍴 MEI JIANG
$$$
PENINSULA HOTEL
333 CHAROEN NAKORN RD., THON BURI
TEL 02-861-2888
FAX 02-861-1112
Inside the Peninsula, one of Bangkok's finest hotels (see p. 360), is this esteemed Chinese restaurant, which has smartly avoided tired clichés in its decor and style of cuisine. The restaurant is like an elegant, understated club, and the food emphasizes lightness and health. Views across the Chao Phraya to Bangkok are outstanding, while service is up to lofty Peninsula standards.
🔢 60 🚇 Ferry from the Oriental 🅿 💳 All major cards

SOMETHING SPECIAL

🍴 SALA RIM NAM
$$$
ORIENTAL HOTEL
48 ORIENTAL AVE.
TEL 02-437-3080
FAX 02-439-7590
This elegantly designed restaurant, across the river from (and owned by) the Oriental (see p. 360), is the best place to enjoy an evening of exceptionally fine Thai cuisine and impressive classical dance entertainment. Lunch is also served, though most visitors opt for the dinner, which is an outstanding fixed menu of Royal Thai cuisine. Reservations

PRICES

HOTELS

An indication of the cost of double room in the high season is given by **$** signs.

$$$$$	Over $240
$$$$	$160–$240
$$$	$110–$160
$$	$70–$110
$	Under $70

RESTAURANTS

An indication of the cost of three-course meal without drinks is given by **$** signs.

$$$$$	Over $65
$$$$	$50–$65
$$$	$30–$50
$$	$20–$30
$	Under $20

are recommended.
🛏 75 🚠 Ferry from the Oriental 🅿 🕐 Closed national holidays 💺 🏧 All major cards

---

🍴 SALATHIP
$$$
SHANGRI-LA HOTEL
89 SOI WAT SUAN PHU
TEL 02-236-7777
FAX 02-236-8579 TO -82
While the dining can be enjoyed indoors in air-conditioned comfort at this romantically designed venue in the Shangri-La (see p. 360), the most memorable choice is to reserve a table on the outside veranda. Arrive early enough to take in the spectacular sunset over the Chao Phraya river.
🛏 95 🚠 Skytrain: Taksin Bridge 🅿 💺 🏧 All major cards

🍴 BISCOTTI
$$–$$$
FOUR SEASONS
155 RATCHADAMRI RD.
TEL 02-250-1000
FAX 02-650-2690
Bangkok has been mad about Italian cuisine for decades, and the current favorite is this unpretentious venue in the upscale Four Seasons (see p. 359). Meals are acclaimed as some of the finest Continental fare in town, and the decor is lively and fun. The place is filled with music and conversation, and it has an open kitchen where you can watch the chefs preparing the pasta and veal specialties.
🛏 70 🚠 Skytrain: Ratchadmri 🅿 💺 🏧 All major cards

🍴 GIORGIO'S
$$–$$$
ROYAL ORCHID SHERATON HOTEL & TOWERS
2 CHAROEN KUNG SOI 30
TEL 02-266-0123
FAX 02-236-8320
The signature restaurant at the riverside Royal Orchid Sheraton (see p. 360) attracts diners for its lunchtime buffet and more sophisticated à la carte choices in the evening. Italian dishes and other Continental fare are prepared with great style. Reservations are recommended to ensure a table on the terrace with views over the river.
🛏 80 🅿 💺 🏧 All major cards

🍴 HAMILTON'S
$$–$$$
DUSIT THANI HOTEL
946 RAMA IV RD.
TEL 02-236-0450
FAX 02-236-6400
This small but elegant restaurant in the upscale Dusit Thani (see p. 361), is named after the first U.S. ambassador to Thailand, and is furnished in mid-19th-century style. Western fare is the theme here, with excellent steaks, lobster, and regional dishes such as Cajun and Tex-Mex.
🛏 40 🚠 Skytrain: Saladaeng 🅿 🕐 Closed Sun. 💺 🏧 All major cards

🍴 TANDOOR
$$–$$$
HOLIDAY INN SILOM BANGKOK
981 SILOM RD.
TEL 02-238-4300
FAX 02-238-5289
Bangkok's finest Indian cuisine can be enjoyed in this gracious restaurant, in the Holiday Inn (see p. 362) in the middle of the city's traditional Hindu district. The emphasis is on the flavors of northern India, including the tandoori style of preparation. The kitchen is led by a famous chef from New Delhi, who maintains excellence in both the vegetarian and non-vegetarian selections.
🛏 75 🅿 💺 🏧 All major cards

SOMETHING SPECIAL

🍴 CABBAGES & CONDOMS
$$
10 SUKHUMVIT SOI 12
TEL 02-229-4610 TC -28
FAX 02-229-4610
This world-famous restaurant, tucked away in an alley off busy Sukhumvit, is the brainchild of Thailand's former family planning director, Khun Meechai, to raise funds for birth control and AIDS programs. Despite the odd name and unusual merchandise sold at the front desk (condom key chains and the like), the classic Thai dishes are excellent and the decor (almost exclusively condom-related) adds to the charm.
🛏 50 🚠 Skytrain: Asoke 🅿 💺 🏧 All major cards

🍴 CAFÉ BONGO
$$
44 CONVENT RD.
TEL 02-266-3534 (EVENING TIME)
This cozy café, bakery, wine bar, and restaurant off Silom Road is known for its innovative preparation of Western dishes along with a limited selection of local fare. Specialties include paella, tapas, and osso buco. Keep walking down the street for similar operations popular with local trendsetters and office workers from the

---

nearby financial district.

🔲 30 🕐 Closed Sun. 🈂️
🈂️ All major cards

🍴 CIRCLE
$$
20/27–29 RUAM RUDEE VILLAGE,
SOI RUAM RUDEE
TEL 02-650-8047
FAX 02-650-8049
Near the shopping centers at
Siam Square, the Circle has
California-fusion cuisine with
a range of highly innovative
dishes. Classic Thai dishes add
to the eclectic mix.
🔲 55 🚆 Skytrain: Phloen Chit
🅿️ 🕐 Closed L daily 🈂️ 🈂️ All
major cards

🍴 HARMONIQUE
$$
22 CHAROEN KRUNG RD.
SOI 34
TEL 02-237-8175 OR 02-630-6763
Somewhat removed from the
tourist scene, this popular café
is set in a lovely, quiet courtyard
among old terrace houses.
Indulge yourself with the tasty
Thai delicacies either on the
outside patio or indoors.
🔲 45 🅿️ 🈂️ 🈂️ All major cards

🍴 LOT 24
$$
93 SUKHUMVIT SOI 24
TEL 02-259-5170
This popular, trendy restaurant
in the heart of the Sukhumvit
district offers classic Thai
dishes at reasonable prices.
The environment is high-tech
with an attractive black-and-
white theme. The *tom yam*
soups, *gaeng* curries, and other
staples attract large parties.
🔲 40 🚆 Skytrain: Phrom Pong
🈂️ 🈂️ All major cards

🍴 THE MANGO TREE
$$
37 SOI TANTAWAN, SURA-
WONGSE RD.
TEL 02-236-2820
FAX 02-238-2649
Located in the heart of the
Silom business district and laid
out with plenty of greenery,

this is a classical Thai house
that is about 100 years old. The
owner, Khun Pitaya, has delib-
erately made few changes to
the original house, which gives
you a range of settings from
which to choose: Dine indoors
or among the foliage of the
garden. There is an excellent
range of curries and food from
all around Thailand, with such
specialties as garlic and pepper
duck and *tom yum ruam mit*, a
traditional spicy soup. Feel free
to let the cook know if you
want a dish specially prepared.
🔲 200 🚆 Skytrain: Saladaeng
🈂️ 🅿️ 🈂️ 🈂️ All major cards

🍴 RIVER CITY BBQ
$$
RIVER CITY COMPLEX
YOTA RD.
TEL 02-237-0077, EXT. 239 OR 466
While there are also outlets
of this famous self-service
Mongolian barbecue on Royal
City Avenue and in the Tower
wing of the Ambassador hotel
on Sukhumvit Road, the best
choice is the original location
on the top floor of the River
City Complex. Enjoy superb
views over the river while
cooking your own meal of
meats, chicken, fish, and vegetables in a pot of broth.
🔲 85 🕐 Closed L daily 🈂️
🈂️ All major cards

🍴 SALA ROSSA
$$
29/1 SALADAENG SOI 1
SILOM
TEL 02-234-5653
FAX 02 233-6912
A longtime favorite with
visitors, who can enjoy dinner
followed by a performance of
Thai classical dance around
9 p.m. The food has been
tempered for sensitive palates,
and the theater performance
is inferior to that at the Sala
Rim Nam (see p. 364). That
said, the prices are reasonable, and this an acceptable
introduction to traditional
Thai food and dance.

🔲 140 🚆 Skytrain: Thong Lo
🅿️ 🈂️ 🈂️ All major cards

🍴 COFFEE BEANS BY DAO
$–$$$
20/12-15 SOI RUAM RUDEE
TEL 02-391-9815
The second branch of this
popular Thai restaurant is far
more accessible to visitors, located on Soi Ruam Rudee, near
BTS Phloen Chit. Classic and
creative Thai and Italian cuisine,
as well as renowned desserts,
have developed a following.
🔲 75 🈂️ 🈂️ All major cards

🍴 HIMALI CHA CHA
$–$$
SILOM SOI CONVENT.
TEL 02-637-0508
The founder was chef to an
Indian Ambassador for two
decades and today his son overseas this chain of restaurants,
with several locations around
the city, including this one
located near BTS Sala Daeng,
down the street from California
Wow. Serving Indian and Halal
meat and vegetarian dishes,
the food is outstanding and the
atmosphere is uniquely Indian.
🈂️ All major cards

🍴 TAWAN DAENG
$–$$
462/61 RAMA 3 RD.
TEL 02-678-1114
Tricky to find—near the
intersection of Narithiwat and
Rama 3—but worth the trip,
Tawan Daeng is the largest
beer hall in Thailand. The
lagers are handcrafted by a
German brewer and come
in sampler sizes and five liter
towers. The cuisine is both
German, including sauerkraut
and pork knuckle, and outstanding Thai, particularly seafood. Nightly entertainment
includes famous singers and
choreographed performances.
🔲 335 🈂️ No cards

🍴 BOURBON STREET
$
29/4–6 WASHINGTON SQ.,

SUKHUMVIT SOI 22
TEL 02-259-0328
FAX 02-259-4318
Local American expatriates often fill this restaurant and bar—in the low-key entertainment district known as Washington Square—lured by the American-style breakfasts and Louisiana Cajun dishes that dominate the dinner menu. Tex-Mex and other North American specialties are served on a rotating basis throughout the week.
🍴 35 🚇 Skytrain: Phrom Pong 🅿 🅲 All major cards

🍴 BUG & BEE
$
SILOM SOI 2
TEL 02-233-8118
This multistory, 24-hour café cum restaurant features free Wi-Fi, making it a popular hangout for students and journalists. It is also popular among the gay expat and local communities. The menu features mostly crepe-based entrees and pan-Asian cuisine, though it may be most famous around town for its fruit smoothies.
🍴 60 🅲 MC, V

🍴 CHALERMBURI
$
113 SONG SAWAT RD.
TEL 02-222-3029
Chinatown has dozens of excellent cafés offering Cantonese specialties, including this small outlet chiefly known for its bird's nest and shark's fin soups. Goat and steamed prawns are also specialties. Crab claws and other seafood items are prepared in both sweet and pungent black bean sauces. It also has Thai dishes.
🍴 30 No cards

🍴 CHOKCHAI STEAK HOUSE
$
SUKHUMVIT SOI 23
TEL 02-259-9596
FAX 02-259-9609
Part of Bangkok's famous chain of steak houses, Chokchai's central location makes it a favorite of Western visitors. Choose from a variety of steaks, including T-bones and spicy pepper steaks.
🍴 50 🚇 Skytrain: Asoke 🅲 All major cards

SOMETHING SPECIAL

🍴 ESPRESSO
$
INTERCONTINENTAL BANGKOK
973 PHLOEN CHIT RD.
TEL 02-656-0444
A classy buffet with outstanding food, Espresso is in the Intercontinental Bangkok, one of the neighborhood's most elegant hotels (see p. 362). A French chef oversees the cooking, with innovative Continental fare rarely found elsewhere in Bangkok. Reservations are recommended for the Sunday buffet.
🍴 65 🚇 Skytrain: Phloen Chit 🅿 🅲 All major cards

🍴 LANG SUAN BALCONY
$
2ND FL., SOI LANG SUAN
TEL 02-251-9822
Thai and international cuisine with one of Bangkok's best wine selections. Depending on the kind of atmosphere you would prefer, you can choose between a table in the cozy dining room or on the balcony overlooking busy Soi Lang Suan. *Gaeng keeyo wahn maprao orn* (green curry with coconut) is a favorite here, though there are many other authentic dishes from which to choose, as well as a good range of Western fare.
🍴 40 🚇 Skytrain: Chidlom 🅿 🅲 All major cards

🍴 RATSSTUBE
$
18/1 SATHORN SOI 1, SOUTH SATHORN RD.
TEL 02-286-4258
FAX 02-679-7274
Some of the best German cooking in town is found at the café at the Goethe Institut, where homemade sausage, sauerkraut, and fried potatoes are on the menu. The atmosphere is often enhanced with German-language films, which attract a surprising number of Thais along with the local German-speaking community.
🍴 55 🅿 🅲 All major cards

🍴 SUN FAR MYANMAR FOOD CENTRE
$
107/1 PAN RD., OFF SILOM RD.
TEL 02-266-8787
This inexpensive Burmese café, on the same street as the Myanmar Embassy, serves regional dishes such as the famous tea-leaf salad.
🍴 25 No cards

🍴 TAKIANG
$
62 CHOCKPADIPONG RD.
TEL 02-281-2837 OR 02-282-4524
The cozy character of this restaurant, popular with locals, creates an intimacy that would not be particularly appropriate for large groups. Lots of timber and a well-thought-out design are the main attractions here, though the food is also excellent and authentic.
🍴 50 🅿 🅲 All major cards

🍴 TONY ROMA'S
$
SUKHUMVIT SOI 3
TEL 02-254-2912
This longtime favorite almost single-handedly introduced American cowboy decor to the city and claims its culinary fame from its barbecued baby back ribs, along with all the other American staples. Salads are enormous.
🍴 65 🚇 Skytrain: Nana 🅲 All major cards

🍴 VEGAS GRILL STEAK & SEAFOOD
$

TRINITY COMPLEX
SILOM SOI 3
TEL 02-231-5360 OR 02-231-5265
Popular with office workers
and the occasional tourist, this
restaurant offers seafood and
steak dishes at reasonable prices. Selections include imported
Alaskan king crab and both
domestic and imported steaks,
all cooked to perfection.
🪑 45 🚈 Skytrain: Saladaeng
⚅ 🚙 All major cards

■ AROUND BANGKOK

AYUTTHAYA

🏨 AYUTTHAYA GRAND
$$
75/5 ROTCHANA RD.
TEL 035-335483
FAX 035-335492
www.ayutthayagrand.com
East of town, this mid-level
hotel attracts businessmen and
the occasional tourists with
decent, if standard, rooms,
a coffee shop, a utilitarian
restaurant with Thai and West-
ern dishes, and a nightclub for
evening diversion.
ⓘ 145 🅿 ⚅ 🏊 🚙 All major
cards

🏨 KRUNGSRI RIVER
$$
27/2 ROTCHANA RD.
TEL 035-244483
FAX 035-243777
www.krungsririver.com
Most visitors visit Ayutthaya as
a day trip from Bangkok, which
is a pity since the ruins are at
their best near sunset and sunrise. A half dozen guesthouses
are located near the market,
and a few moderately priced
hotels are near the river. None
is world class, but the Krungsri
River is decent and has clean
rooms with private baths.
Request a room with a river
view and be sure to explore
the market in the evening.
ⓘ 206 + 18 suites 🅿 ⚅ 🏊
🚙 All major cards

KANCHANABURI

🏨 FELIX RIVER KWAI RESORT
$$$
9/1 MUY 3 THAMAKHAM
TEL 034-551000
FAX 026-344595
www.felixriverkwai.co.th
This hotel has a good location
just 100 yards (91 m) from
the famous bridge and within
walking distance of all the
cafés and souvenir shops.
The resort has spacious and
relaxing grounds that have
been developed into some of
the most outstanding gardens
in this part of the country.
The lobby is comfortable,
and there are several decent
restaurants, a cocktail lounge,
a small but adequate fitness
center, and even a business
center. Rooms, which are well
stocked with amenities, are
decorated in pastel tones.
ⓘ 255 🅿 ⚅ 🏊 🎥 🚙 All
major cards

🏨 RIVER KWAI HOTEL
$
284/15-16 SAENG CHUTO RD.,
MUANG DISTRICT
TEL 02-216-5164 TO -5 OR 034-
510111 OR 034-511184
FAX 02-677-6246
www.riverkwai.co.th
The River Kwai Hotel is set
back from the river, which is
not such a bad thing in the
long run; although you have to
sacrifice the picturesque river
view, you won't have to suffer
the earsplitting noise from
the late-night floating discos.
Deluxe single bedrooms or
double-bed suites are available.
Service here is very friendly
and of a high standard.
ⓘ 169 🅿 ⚅ 🏊 🚙 All major
cards

LOP BURI

🏨 LOPBURI INN
$
28/9 NARAI MAHARAT RD.

TEL 036-412300
FAX 036-412457
www.lopburiinn.com
Lop Buri receives few over-
night visitors, and the town's
only hotel with air-conditioned
rooms is the Lopburi Inn. Little
more than a motel, it has clean
rooms and hot showers, and is
a step above the budget hotels
around the old town.
ⓘ 136 🅿 ⚅ 🚙 All major
cards

■ EAST COAST

PATTAYA

🏨 MONTIEN HOTEL PATTAYA
$$$$$
PATTAYA 2 RD.
TEL 038-428155 OR 038-428156
FAX 038-423155 OR 038-428311
www.montien.com/pattaya
Tucked away between Beach
Road and Pattaya 2 Road, this
15-story hotel is surprisingly
sophisticated. It is surrounded
by delightful tropical gardens,
which complement the refined
furnishings of the public
rooms. Restaurants are top-
notch, as are the hotel facilities
and immaculate rooms.
ⓘ 300 + 12 suites 🅿 ⚆ ⚅
🏊 🎥 🚙 All major cards

🏨 PATTAYA MARRIOTT RESORT AND SPA
$$$$$
218 BEACH RD.
TEL 038-412120
FAX 038-429926
www.marriott.com/pyxmc
Visitors who seek a quality
mid-level hotel within walking
distance of the cabarets and
nightclubs in south Pattaya
stay here, a five-minute stroll
from the so-called Walking
Street. The lobby is surpris-
ingly modest for such a large
property, and the restaurants
are hardly spectacular, but many
directly facing the beach are
absolutely wonderful. Adjacent
to the resort is Pattaya's best

shopping complex, a great place to dine and shop in air-conditioned comfort.

(i) 292 P S G S V
S All major cards

SOMETHING SPECIAL

ROYAL CLIFF BEACH RESORT
$$$$$

ROYAL CLIFF BAY
TEL 038-250421
FAX 038-250884
www.royalcliff.com

This series of cliffside towers midway between Pattaya and Jomtien is the finest hotel on the eastern seaboard and one of the best in the country. After a few years of shortcomings, this resort seems to have returned to form with a renewed spirit among the staff and major additions to the property such as the convention center. The complex has almost a dozen restaurants, cafés, lounges, and music venues. Rooms range from utilitarian to splendid.

(i) 921 + 110 suites P S G
S V S All major cards

AMARI ORCHID RESORT
$$$$

BEACH RD.
TEL 038-428161
FAX 380-418410
www.amari.com/orchid

The Amari Orchid occupies a large piece of land a few hundred yards south of the Dusit. Perhaps the most striking aspects here are the spacious, manicured gardens that separate the hotel from the beach. The superb dining options range from the Italian **La Gritta** restaurant to the colorful colonial-style **Henry J. Bean's** (see right) by the beach. Rooms vary in quality according to the building; the Loggia Suites are best.

(i) 236 P S G S V S All major cards

DUSIT THANI PATTAYA
$$$$

240/2 BEACH RD.
TEL 038-425611 TO -17
FAX 038-428239
www.dusit.com

Clinging to a small cliff at the northern end of the main beach is this outlet of Thailand's largest hotel chain. The grounds are lovely, and the four-story lobby atrium is the most impressive bit of architecture in Pattaya. Among the facilities, restaurants include a Chinese room and three cocktail lounges. Windsurfing and sailing are available. Rooms have chic Thai-Western motifs.

(i) 464 + 26 suites P S G
S V S All major cards

NEW SEAVIEW RESORT HOTEL
$$

SOI 18 PATTAYA–NAKLUA RD.
TEL 038-429317
FAX 034 423668
www.newseaviewresort.com

Comfortable air-conditioned rooms with easy beach access. The hotel is well located for trips into Pattaya or Jomtien.

(i) 155 S S S All major cards

SAWASDEE SEA VIEW HOTEL (WING B)
$

SOI 10 PATTAYA RD.
TEL 038-711071 OR 038-711079
FAX 038-711078
www.sawasdee-hotels.com

The rooms here are tidy, very colorful, and comfortable, with TVs. There is a restaurant. Room rates are good, and the hotel is close to the beach.

(i) 30 P S G S MC, V

CASA PASCAL
$$$

485/4 MOO 10, 2ND RD.
TEL 038-723660

Casa Pascal is fine dining in a fairly casual atmosphere, ideal for a beach vacation. Yet Chef Pascal Schnyder's European cuisine is worthy of the most

formal occasion, or simply for a relaxing Sunday brunch.

56 S S All major cards

BRUNO'S RESTAURANT & WINE BAR
$$

463/77 SRI NAKORN CENTRE
NORTH PATTAYA
TEL 038-361073

One of Pattaya's more famous restaurants, Bruno's serves French and Swiss dishes under the direction of the former manager of the Royal Cliff Beach Resort. Thai and international food also feature on the menu. The upstairs wine "cellar" is considered the most extensive on the east coast.

45 P S S All major cards

SOMETHING SPECIAL

CAFE NEW ORLEANS
$$

BEACH RD. SOI
PATTAYALAND 2
TEL 038-710805 OR 038-710806
FAX 038-610826
www.cafeneworleans.info

Some consider this cozy café the best addition to the Pattaya food scene in several years, especially for the high quality of its Western dishes, such as the famous baby back ribs. There are also Thai dishes offered, and the service is top-notch.

40 S S All major cards

HENRY J. BEAN'S BAR & GRILL
$$

AMARI ORCHID RESORT
BEACH RD.
TEL 038-428161
FAX 038-418410
www.amari.com

Western and Thai dishes, a wide range of brews, and nightly entertainment make this romantically restored old house (part of the Amari Orchid Resort; see left) one of Pattaya's most special evening venues.

65 P S S All major cards

S Nonsmoking S Air-conditioning S Indoor Pool S Outdoor Pool V Health Club S Credit Cards

SOMETHING SPECIAL

🍴 HOPF BREW HOUSE
$$
219 BEACH RD., SOUTH PATTAYA
TEL 038-710650 OR 038-429008
This immense operation has been the most successful new restaurant here in recent years, consistently drawing the crowds for its excellent German and Italian food, variety of beers and spirits, and entertainment. The latter ranges from ragtime bands to jazz combos, and the family atmosphere makes this one of the best places in town.
🔲 90 🅿 💲 🕙 All major cards

🍴 LOBSTER POT
$$
228 BEACH RD., SOUTH PATTAYA
TEL 038-426083
FAX 038-424389
Overlooking the water at the southern end of town, this restaurant is located on a section of road known as the Walking Street. Diners choose their fish or seafood from open displays and then have their selection cooked in any variety of ways, from steamed to fried with scallions and black bean sauce. The terrace is perfect for sunsets, so arrive early.
🔲 90 💲 🕙 All major cards

🍴 REVOLVING RESTAURANT
$$
PATTAYA WATER PARK 345, JOMTIEN BEACH RD.
TEL 038-251201
A few miles south of Pattaya, at Jomtien Beach, is a huge tower topped with a revolving restaurant. While the food (Thai and Western dishes) isn't spectacular, the views over the Gulf of Thailand are.
🔲 95 🅿 💲 🕙 All major cards

🍴 RUEN THAI RESTAURANT
$$
485/3 SOI 2
SOUTH PATTAYA RD.
TEL 038-425911
FAX 038-425273
www.thepattayacity.com
Ruen Thai is set up amid a tropical garden. Here they serve the usual Thai dishes (Western food is also available), though the main draw is classical dancing in the evenings.
🔲 400 💲 🕙 All major cards

🍴 SUGAR HUT
$$
PATTAYA–JOMTIEN RD.
TEL 038-251686
FAX 038-251689
www.sugar-hut.com
Perhaps the most elegant Thai restaurant in Pattaya, this collection of teak pavilions is situated on the undulating road that leads south from Pattaya to Jomtien Beach. Specialties here include *sai krok* (Thai sausage) and *kar mu* (leg of pork). This place has superb atmosphere and is well worth the taxi ride from central Pattaya.
🔲 85 🅿 💲 🕙 All major cards

🍴 CAPTAIN'S CORNER STEAK HOUSE
$
PATTAYA–JOMTIEN RD.
TEL 038-364318
FAX 038-364450
www.theresidentgarden.com
A few miles south of Pattaya on the road to Jomtien, this spacious garden restaurant is known for its all-you-can-eat Texas-style barbecues, which draw the crowds every night.
🔲 75 🅿 🕙 Closed L 💲 🕙 All major cards

🍴 MOON RIVER PUB
$
NORTH PATTAYA RD.
TEL 038-370614
FAX 038-426198
www.thaigarden.com
This restaurant/nightclub, near the Thai Garden Resort, is very popular with the local expatriate community and is one of the friendliest gathering places in town. The food includes Thai and Western dishes.
🔲 55 🅿 💲 🕙 All major cards

🍴 MOTTA MAHAL
$
323/26 SOI SAEN SAMRAN, SOUTH PATTAYA
Pattaya has several standard Indian restaurants with exotic decors and sitar music playing on the stereos. The huge menu here runs the gamut from southern *thali* combinations to classic tandooris. Dishes tend to be mild.
🔲 35 🕙 Closed L daily 💲 🕙 All major cards

🍴 PIC KITCHEN
$
PATTAYA 2 RD. SOI 5
TEL 038-428374
www.pic-kitchen.com
Pic Kitchen is an old favorite. Superb Thai dishes in a romantic setting, enhanced by jazz entertainment and classical dance several times a week. Dishes are prepared mild but can be spiced up on request.
🔲 65 🅿 💲 🕙 All major cards

🍴 THAI HOUSE
$
171 NORTH PATTAYA RD.
TEL 038-370579
www.patayacity.com/thaihouse
This upscale Thai restaurant is one of the best places to eat in Pattaya, and classical Thai dance performances are given most nights starting around 8 p.m. A taxi is necessary to reach this isolated restaurant.
🔲 60 🅿 💲 🕙 All major cards

🍴 VIENTIANE
$
185 PATTAYA 2 RD.
TEL 038-411298
FAX 038-373374
As the name implies, this restaurant serves Laotian and Issan dishes, along with a wide selection of Thai, Chinese, and

PRICES

HOTELS

An indication of the cost of double room in the high season is given by **$** signs.

$$$$$	Over $240
$$$$	$160–$240
$$$	$110–$160
$$	$70–1$10
$	Under $70

RESTAURANTS

An indication of the cost of three-course meal without drinks is given by **$** signs.

$$$$$	Over $65
$$$$	$50–$65
$$$	$30–$50
$$	$20–$30
$	Under $20

Western standards. Vientiane's atmosphere is somewhere between a rustic open-air café and a more formal restaurant. 🍴 50 📵 🗝 All major cards

🍴 YAMATO
$

219/51 SOI YAMATO, SOUTH PATTAYA
TEL 038-429685
FAX 038-425673

This longtime favorite has been here for so many years that locals now call its street Soi Yamato. An older establishment with rustic decor, it serves standard Japanese dishes. 🍴 35 🕐 Closed L daily 📵 🗝 All major cards

■ NORTHEAST THAILAND

KHON KAEN

🏨 SOFITEL RAJA ORCHID
$$$$

9/9 PRACHA SUMRAN RD.
TEL 043-322155
FAX 043-322150
www.sofitelkhonkaen.com
This reasonably priced hotel is the best option in town. At 22 stories, the gleaming structure almost completely dominates Khon Kaen. Marble, flowers, and richly upholstered furniture characterize the lobby, which leads to restaurants serving Thai, Chinese, Japanese, Western, and even Vietnamese cuisine. The hotel's biggest draw is the underground entertainment plaza, where lounges, nightclubs, and a German microbrewery attract locals. Immaculate rooms have been equipped with every gadget conceivable. ℹ️ 293 📵🗝📵🗝🗝 🗝 All major cards

NAKHON RATCHASIMA (KHORAT)

🏨 ROYAL PRINCESS KORAT
$$$

1/37 SURANARI RD.
TEL 044-256629
FAX 044-256601
www.dusit.com
Khorat has relatively new accommodations, one of which is this edifice located a few miles outside town but just a few minutes by taxi from the central market. Facilities are limited, but the Royal Princess has clean, brightly decorated rooms with televisions, minibars, and other modern conveniences. ℹ️ 188 📵🗝📵🗝🗝🗝 🗝 All major cards

🏨 SIMA THANI HOTEL
$$

2112/2 MITTRAPHAP RD.
TEL 044-213121
FAX 044-213100
www.simathani.com
Another 1990s addition to the Khorat hotel scene is this reasonably luxurious hotel also situated a few miles outside town. Although the public spaces and rooms have deteriorated somewhat, the hotel has decent restaurants and an efficient staff. The pool, health club, and nightclub make this the best choice in town. Guests may get traditional Thai massages here. ℹ️ 144 📵🗝📵🗝🗝 🗝 All major cards

NONG KHAI

🏨 ROYAL MEKONG
$$

222 CHOMANEE RD.
TEL 042-420024
FAX 042-421280
www.royalmekong.com
Nong Khai is a sleepy town near the Friendship Bridge. The client shortage has forced cutbacks in staff, but rooms remain in decent condition with all the modern facilities you would expect. ℹ️ 199 📵🗝📵🗝🗝🗝 🗝 All major cards

■ CENTRAL THAILAND

PHITSANULOK

🏨 AMARIN NAKHON
$

3/1 CHAO PHRAYA RD.
TEL 055-219069 TO -73
FAX 055-258945
www.amarinnakorn.com
This hotel is probably the best in town, but basic is the key word for all hotels in Phitsanulok. It is characterized by acceptable rooms, friendly staff, a popular coffee shop, and a popular nightclub. ℹ️ 146 📵🗝📵🗝🗝 🗝 All major cards

🏨 PAILYN
$

36 BOROMATRAILOKART RD.
TEL 055-252412
FAX 055-225237
www.pailynhotelgroup.com
One of the newer hotels, this is in a central location within walking distance of the riverside cafés. It has a coffee shop, restaurant, small convention center, and a nightclub

that competes with the older venue at the Amarin Nakhon (see above). Rooms are in good condition with basic decor, and the staff is the best in town.
ⓘ 134 🅿 ⬒ 🄯 🌊 🅶 All major cards

SUKHOTHAI

🏨 SUKHOTHAI HERITAGE HOTEL
$$$
999 MOO 2, T. KLONGKRAJONG
TEL 055-647564
FAX 055-647575
www.sukhothaiheritage.com
An expansive resort situated beside the Sukhothai airport, halfway between Sukhothai and Si Satchanalai, the Sukhothai Heritage mimics the styles of the ancient cities near which it is located. Redbrick walkways and white stucco walls lead away from the wooden *sala* surrounded central courtyard. Rooms in both wings face inward toward swimming pools and feature earth tone interiors accentuated by colorful silk pillows. A short bike ride to the airport allows guests to learn about Thai handicrafts and visit an orchid greenhouse.
ⓘ 61 + 7 suites 🅿 🄯 🌊 🅶 All major cards

🏨 PAILYN SUKHOTHAI
$
1003 CHAROD VITHITHONG RD.
TEL 055-613310
FAX 055-613317
www.pailynhotelgroup.com
Most visitors find a budget hotel or guesthouse in old Sukhothai, but tour groups and upscale travelers sometimes select this large hotel 5 miles (8 km) east of town. It is an almost luxurious, if rather poorly planned, hotel, and it has several restaurants and a health club.
ⓘ 245 🅿 ⬒ 🄯 🌊 🍸 🅶 All major cards

■ NORTHERN THAILAND

CHIANG MAI

🏨 FOUR SEASONS CHIANG MAI
$$$$$
MAE RIM–SAMOENG OLD RD.
TEL 053-298181
FAX 053-298190
www.fourseasons.com/chiangmai
One of Thailand's most exclusive and stylish resorts is magnificently situated about 12 miles (18 km) northwest of Chiang Mai on a hillside overlooking rice fields, with soaring mountains in the distance. This extraordinary place was built in traditional northern Lanna style in its Pavilion Suites and private villas, of which a limited number are available to overnight guests. The levels of service are extraordinary. Many guests come solely for the world-class spa, while others enjoy any of the four nearby golf courses, or perhaps mountain-bike riding in the hills. If you can afford the rate, this is one of the finest experiences in Thailand.
ⓘ 64 suites + 11 villas 🚐 Hotel taxi from Chiang Mai 🅿 🄯 🌊 🍸 🅶 All major cards

SOMETHING SPECIAL

🏨 MANDARIN ORIENTAL DHARA DHEVI
$$$$$
51/4 CHIANG MAI-SANKAMPAENG RD., MOO 1
TEL 053-888888
FAX 053-888999
www.mandarinoriental.com
Exploring the grounds of the 60-acre Dhara Dhevi on a complimentary bicycle, its easy to get lost, not simply because it's so expansive but because it all seems so real; the working rice fields, antique houses, and grandiose temples draw one back in time to a mystical

world of yesteryear. Combining all the stylistic influences that affected Lanna culture through the ages, the resort features majestic re-creations of historic architecture that house genuine antiques from the hotel owner's private collection. World class spa, luxurious accommodation, delectable cuisine, and the friendliest Thai service are a few of the many more features of this truly unique Thai destination resort.
ⓘ 123 suites & villas 🅿 🄯 🌊 🍸 🅶 All major cards

🏨 D2
$$$$
100 CHANG KLAN RD.
TEL 053-999999
FAX 053-999900
www.dusit.com
The next level of sophistication in Chiang Mai, D2 is operated by the standard-bearers of five-star Thai service, Dusit International. D2 features contemporary decor with traditional Thai flair, such as modern rattan furniture. Located beside the night bazaar, it's both convenient and comfortable. Outdoor beer garden, first class spa, and stylish business lounge are additional facilities.
ⓘ 102 + 29 suites 🅿 ⬒ 🄯 🌊 🍸 🅶 All major cards

🏨 FONDCOME VILLAGE
$$$$
333 MOO 11 NAMPHRAE
TEL 053-125333
FAX 053-125340
www.fondcome.com
Just over the hill from town, on the fringe of Doi Suthep National Park, Fondcome is a ten-minute drive from downtown Chiang Mai. A unique resort that is as much a cultural experience as a hotel, the "village" consists of theme rooms that represent northern Thailand's various ethnic groups, and staff, who dress

in tribal costumes, are led by the hospitable village "chief." The cuisine draws upon native ingredients and the staff treats guests like family.
🛏 48 + 2 suites 🅿 🍴 ♨ 🅂 MC, V

🏨 AMARI RINCOME HOTEL
$$$
1 NIMMANHAEMINDA RD.
TEL 053-221130
FAX 053-221915
www.amari.com/rincome
This seven-story "garden hotel" is well maintained. It has a café and restaurant serving Thai and Western dishes, two pools, a tennis court, and a business center. Guest rooms are attractive and refurbished on a regular schedule, making this Chiang Mai's best-value hotel in the luxury category.
🛏 158 🅿 🍴 🛎 ♨ 🅂 All major cards

🏨 CHIANG MAI ORCHID
$$
23 HUAY KAEW RD.
TEL 053-222099
FAX 053-221625
www.chiangmaiorchid.com
This modestly priced hotel, about 3 miles (5 km) from downtown Chiang Mai, is surprisingly stylish. There are three dining options: a café, a basic Chinese outlet, and a fancy French restaurant for a splurge. The hotel has a nightclub that hosts live bands. The clean guest rooms are decorated in pastel shades.
🛏 267 🅿 🍴 🛎 ♨ 🅂 All major cards

🏨 CHIANGMAI HILLS
$
13 HUAY KAEW RD.
TEL 053-210030
FAX 053-210035
www.chiangmaihills.com
An older hotel in the budget category that caters to large tour groups and local conventions. The public areas, Japanese café, and

basic furnishings in the rooms should prove adequate to those on a budget.
🛏 249 🅿 🍴 🛎 ♨ 🅂 All major cards

🏨 ROYAL PRINCESS CHIANG MAI
$
112 CHANG KLAN RD.
TEL 053-281033
FAX 053-281044
www.dusit.com
Conveniently located in the center of town opposite the night bazaar, this nine-story property is very good value and is popular year-round. The lobby decor and general ambience are basic but acceptable, and the hotel has three restaurants and a basement nightclub. Rooms are well maintained.
🛏 198 🅿 🍴 🛎 ♨ 🅂 All major cards

SOMETHING SPECIAL

🍴 THE GALLERY
$$
25 CHAROEN RAT RD.
TEL 053-248601
On the eastern bank of the Ping River, this combined art gallery and restaurant serves superb Thai food. The atmosphere is marvelous, especially in the early evening as the sun sets over the river and Doi Suthep. Romantic types will love the intimate alcoves and decks, which cling to the side of the river and provide a great deal of privacy.
🍴 40 🅿 🅂 All major cards

🍴 THE GOOD VIEW
$$
13 CHAROEN RAT RD.
TEL 053-241866
FAX 053-249029
www.goodview.co.th
This restaurant is in a teak mansion on the eastern bank of the river. It has a creative menu (specialties include *yum woon sen*, or jellied noodles, and *bo bria*, or spring rolls), a

superb environment, and great views. Arts and home furnishings are sold here.
🍴 30 🅿 🅂 All major cards

🍴 NANG NUAL SEAFOOD RESTAURANT
$$
27 KO KLANG RD.
TEL 053-281961
FAX 053-281972
Chiang Mai's largest restaurant, 5 miles (8 km) south of the city center, specializes in seafood and ostentatious decor at a wonderful location on the riverbank. Try the *pla raad prik* (fish grilled with chili).
🍴 240 🅿 🅂 All major cards

🍴 OLD CHIANG MAI CULTURAL CENTER
$$
185 WULAI RD.
TEL 053-202993 TO -
FAX 053-274094
www.oldchiangmai.com
The venerable cultural hall, south of town in a residential neighborhood, specializes in traditional *kun toke* (northern-style) dinners. Food is served in a teak dining hall, and dance performances take place next door in an amphitheater.
🍴 250 🅿 🕐 Closed L daily 🅂 All major cards

🍴 PICCOLA ROMA
$$
3/2 CHAROEN PRATHET RD.
TEL 053-271256
FAX 053-820297 TC-8
www.piccolaromapalace.com
This is perhaps the best Italian restaurant in town, offering a wide choice of pastas, veal, and chicken dishes that are prepared by the resident owner/chef, who hails from northern Italy. Although the atmosphere is a little jaded, the food remains excellent.
🍴 40 🅂 🅂 All major cards

🅂 Nonsmoking 🅂 Air-conditioning 🛎 Indoor Pool ♨ Outdoor Pool 🅆 Health Club 🅂 Credit Cards

🍴 THE PUB
$$

88 HUAY KAEO RD.
TEL 053-211550
FAX 053-211550
www.thepubchiangmai.com
Decorated in an Old English style, this establishment has been a focal point for the Chiang Mai expatriate community for more than 20 years. The food emphasizes English and French cuisine, while the atmosphere shines with homey touches such as a roaring fire most evenings.
🪑 50 🅿 🈂 🌀 All major cards

SOMETHING SPECIAL

🍴 THE RIVERSIDE BAR & RESTAURANT
$$

9 CHAROEN RAT RD.
TEL 053-243239
www.theriversidechiang
mai.com
Some of the most romantic restaurants in Chiang Mai are along the east bank of the Ping River. The Riverside is one such restaurant, where virtually every table has a river view. It serves decent Thai and Western dishes (specialties include *yum woon sen*, or jellied noodles, and green chicken curry) but is especially recommended for its live entertainment, which starts about 9:30 p.m.
🪑 65 🅿 🈂 No cards

🍴 WHOLE EARTH
$$

88 SRI DONCHAI RD.
TEL 053-282463
One of the oldest restaurants in town, this is also one of the most romantic, in a lovely teak house almost completely surrounded by gardens and lakes. The food is primarily Indian with an emphasis on vegetarian dishes, although a few seafood and meat items are included.
🪑 40 🌀 🈂 No cards

🍴 AROON RAI
$

45 KOTCHASAN RD.
TEL 053-276947
The atmosphere may be lacking, but this open-air café just south of Tha Phae Gate has been serving the finest Issan food in Chiang Mai for years. Among the regional specialties are pork curry, a spicy salsa called *nam prik*, sticky rice, fried bamboo shoots, and sausage stuffed with pork.
🪑 80 🈂 No cards

🍴 BIERSTUBE
$

33/6A MOON MUANG RD.
TEL 053-278869
Although German food is the primary emphasis at this simple café in the center near Tha Phae Gate, it also prepares excellent Thai dishes. All are served by some of the friendliest waitresses in town.
🪑 30 🈂 No cards

🍴 DIAMOND RIVERSIDE HOTEL RESTAURANT
$

33 CHAROEN PRATHET RD.
TEL 053-270081
www.diamondriverside.com
This is the most elegant place in town to enjoy a traditional *kun toke* (northern-style) dinner followed by a short performance of Thai classical dance and theater. While more expensive than similar offerings at the Old Chiang Mai Cultural Center (see p. 373), the intimate setting ensures superior views, and the food is a few notches above its rival.
🪑 80 🅿 🕐 Closed L daily
🈂 🌀 All major cards

🍴 GALAE
$

65 SUTHEP RD.
TEL 053-278655
FAX 053-278655
Visitors with private transportation may enjoy a stop at this popular café, wonderfully

situated a few miles west of town at the base of the road that leads up to Doi Suthep. Although the food is nothing special, the views of the valley are superb.
🪑 45 🅿 🈂 No cards

🍴 GALARE FOOD COURT
$

NIGHT BAZAAR,
CHANG KLAN RD.
TEL 053-272067
The Galare Food Court has an excellent range of inexpensive stalls serving all different kinds of food from around Southeast Asia, India, and China. The lively atmosphere of the night bazaar is enhanced by the classical dancing and northern Thai music, which are performed here every night free of charge.
🪑 200 🅿 🈂 No cards

🍴 JUST KHAO SOY
$

108/2 CHAROENPRATHET RD.
TEL 053-818641
Select Burmese or Chiang Mai style, choose chicken, beef, or vegetarian, and then indicate preferred spiciness. Your steaming bowl of *khao soy* is served with various condiments: chili, fish sauce, coconut milk, shallots, pickled cabbage, lime, and banana. Far from the alleys of Chiang Mai where khao soy grew up, but an ideal introduction to a classic northern dish.
🪑 72 🈂 🌀 MC, V

CHIANG RAI

🏨 DUSIT ISLAND RESORT
$$$

1129 KRAISORASIT RD.
TEL 053-715777
FAX 053-715801
www.dusit.com
This is a very impressive nine-story hotel just outside town on an island in the Mae Kok River. Visitors stay here for the immaculate marble-

covered public areas, the three restaurants (including a wonderful rooftop option that serves Continental and Asian cuisines), and facilities such as tennis courts and an 18-hole golf course. Rooms are spacious; those on the upper floors have superb views over the mountains.

🛏 271 + 12 suites 🅿 🔁 💲
🏊 📺 🔖 All major cards

WIANG INN
$$$
893 PHAHOLYOTHIN RD.
TEL 053-711543
FAX 053-711877
www.wianginn.com
This basic mid-level hotel has been serving the needs of travelers for more than 20 years. Although there is nothing fancy about the place, its central location and decent facilities make it the preferred choice for informed visitors.

🛏 258 🅿 🔁 💲 🏊 🔖 All major cards

GOLDEN TRIANGLE

ANANTARA RESORT & SPA GOLDEN TRIANGLE
$$$$$
229 M.1, CHIANG SAEN
TEL 053-784084
FAX 053-784090
www.anantara.com
One of the most attractive resorts in northern Thailand, this luxurious place lies east of Chiang Saen, near the intersection of Thailand, Laos, and Myanmar. Remote, exclusive, and always struggling for improved business, this wonderfully designed escape provides the perfect base to explore the region and retreat to sheer luxury each evening. Two restaurants and three levels of rooms make this an amazing destination in one of Thailand's remoter areas.

🛏 110 🅿 🔁 💲 🏊 📺 🔖 All major cards

MAE HONG SON

THE IMPERIAL TARA MAE HONG SON
$$–$$$
149 MU 8, MAIN HIGHWAY
TEL 053-684445
FAX 053-684440
www.imperialhotels.com
Upscale tourists choose this semi-luxurious hotel at the south end of town. Owned by one of the largest hotel chains, it provides excellent food and lodging at reasonable prices. Tropical design typifies the public areas, while northern-Thai style carries through in the restaurant, which serves Thai, Chinese, and Western dishes. Rooms are simple and feature local materials such as bamboo and rattan.

🛏 104 🅿 🔁 💲 🏊 📺 🔖 All major cards

SOUTHERN THAILAND

HUA HIN & CHA-AM

CHIVA-SOM SPA & RESORT
$$$$$
73/4 PETCHKASEM RD., HUA HIN
TEL 032-536536
FAX 032-511154
www.chivasom.com
As with the rest of the world, Thailand has gone mad with "spa fever," and spa resorts are opening across the country. The Chiva-Som is widely considered the finest dedicated spa resort in Thailand. All the standard treatments are available with Asian-Thai twists, along with the requisite tranquil setting, healthful meals, and cultural pursuits such as music. Guest rooms are available either in the ocean-view building or in individual chalets surrounded by gardens and lakes.

🛏 295 rooms 🅿 💲 🏊 📺 🔖 All major cards

HILTON HUA HIN RESORT & SPA
$$$$$
33 NARESDAMRI RD., HUA HIN
TEL 032-538999
FAX 032-538990
www.huahin.hilton.com
The sleepy town of Hua Hin changed dramatically in the early 1990s with the construction of this 15-story hotel complex directly over the central part of the principal beach. Today, the hotel provides the most luxurious and conveniently located accommodations around. Enjoy the extensive recreational facilities, and dine at top-notch restaurants such as the Mediterranean Goya. Request a room facing the ocean.

🛏 295 + 10 suites 🅿 🔁 💲 🏊 📺 🔖 All major cards

ANANTARA RESORT & SPA HUA HIN
$$$$
43/1 PHETKASEM BEACH RD.
TEL 032-520230
FAX 032-520259
www.anantara.com
The Anantara Resort creates its ambience with traditional Thai architecture, vast landscaped gardens filled with flowers and native shrubs, and an open-air Thai restaurant for evening repasts. Dining options also include a café facing the gardens and beach, and weekly barbecues by the pool. All the standard sports facilities are available. Rooms are elaborate, but are tastefully decorated.

🛏 162 🅿 💲 🏊 📺 🔖 All major cards

DUSIT RESORT, HUA HIN
$$$$
1349 PETCHKASEM RD., CHA-AM
TEL 032-520009
FAX 032-520296
www.dusit.com
This exclusive resort is the premium choice for the

🔖 Nonsmoking 💲 Air-conditioning 🏊 Indoor Pool 🏊 Outdoor Pool 📺 Health Club 🔖 Credit Cards

discriminating traveler. It is centered around the neighboring polo club, where visitors can indulge their love of the game and spend time in the various restaurants or multiplicity of cocktail lounges and bars. Those who are not inclined to ride horses while swatting at a ball can swim, play tennis, unwind at the spa, or enjoy golf. Rooms are available in four levels from standards to studio apartments.

ⓘ 302 🅿 ⮀ 🅖 ⛴ 🎔 ⓢ All major cards

HOTEL HOLIDAY INN RESORT REGENT BEACH CHA-AM
$$$$
849/21 PETCHKASEM RD., CHA-AM
TEL 032-451240 TO -9
FAX 032-471491 TO -2
www.chaam.holidayinn.com
Set on a long stretch of white-sand beach, midway between Hua Hin and Cha-am, this resort is the largest property in the region and a popular destination for families and groups. All possible forms of recreation are available, from volleyball and tennis to diving and sailing. There is a wide choice of restaurants and bars. Rooms vary from tacky cubicles to deluxe chalets.

ⓘ 670 🅿 ⮀ 🅖 ⛴ 🎔 ⓢ All major cards

HOTEL HUA HIN MARRIOTT RESORT & SPA
$$$$
107/1 PETCHKASEM BEACH RD.
TEL 032-511881
FAX 032-512422
www.marriott.com/hhqmc
Three miles (5 km) north of Hua Hin, this popular resort has excellent facilities, superb management, and wonderful rooms at reasonable prices. Rooms are decorated with a tropical theme. Restaurants include Italian, Thai, and a steak house. A gym, children's playground, and golf on two

nearby courses are among the facilities here.

ⓘ 220 🅿 🅖 ⛴ 🎔 ⓢ All major cards

SOMETHING SPECIAL

HOTEL RESTAURANT SOFITEL CENTRAL HUA HIN RESORT
$$$–$$$$
1 DAMNOEN KASEM RD., HUA HIN
TEL 032-512021
FAX 032-511014
www.centarahotels resorts.com
Formerly the Railway Hotel, this grand old lady is one of the most historic hotels in Southeast Asia, with a legacy that rivals the Oriental in Bangkok and Raffles in Singapore. It was constructed in 1923 to host the royal family and other wealthy residents of Bangkok who fled the city and established Hua Hin as the original beach resort in Thailand. After years of neglect, the hotel was tastefully restored in 1986. The gardens are large and lovely, while the interior is decorated with oriental rugs, gleaming chandeliers, and polished marble floors. Royal Thai cuisine (using coconut cream, plenty of spices, and exotic ingredients such as shark's fin) is served in the acclaimed **Salathai** restaurant, while further refreshments are available in a beachfront chalet and a café that resembles an old railway car. Rooms are superbly furnished with period accents. The history, setting, and refined service make this an outstanding resort.

ⓘ 218 + 38 villas 🅿 ⮀ 🅖 ⛴ 🎔 ⓢ All major cards

KO SAMUI

HOTEL BAAN TALING NGAM RESORT & SPA
$$$$$
295 MU 3, THALING NGAM,

SOUTHWEST SAMUI
TEL 077-423019
FAX 077-423220
www.baantaling-ngam.com
The finest resort on Ko Samui is also one of the most elegant in Southeast Asia. More than just a pricey escape from the crowds, this oasis of tranquility transports you to another world. The resort is elevated on a mountainous outcrop that provides unforgettable views over the ocean. Public rooms are sumptuously decorated, with good use of natural materials and open-air architecture designed to maximize the views in all directions. Along with a breezy dining venue and stylish cocktail lounge, the resort has a restaurant with Mediterranean fare, and a beachfront café for seafood and Italian cuisine. All forms of water sports are available at the beach. Rooms range from deluxe *salas* to cliff villas, resplendent with art and antiques.

ⓘ 72 rooms 🅿 🅖 ⛴ 🎔 ⓢ All major cards

HOTEL CENTARA GRAND BEACH RESORT SAMUI
$$$$$
38/2 MU 3, CENTRAL CHAWENG BEACH
TEL 077-230500
FAX 077-422385
www.centarahotels resorts.com
Visitors seeking luxury accommodations in the middle of the best beach should head directly to this property on Chaweng Beach. The Centara ensures a high level of comfort in an ideal location, tucked behind a formidable wall that blocks all street noise. It has vast manicured lawns and gardens, and a stunning beach. The building style is 19th-century British colonial, but Thai influence is seen in the dining outlets and the attentive service. Dining options include an enormous main restaurant, a smaller Thai

🏨 Hotel 🍴 Restaurant ⓘ No. of Guest Rooms ➕ No. of Seats 🅿 Parking 🕐 Closed ⮀ Elevator 🚉 Transport

outlet, and a cocktail bar on the second floor with views over the entire estate. Guest rooms are immaculate. 🛈 208 🅿 🔄 🅰 🏊 🏋 🐾 All major cards

🏨 IMPERIAL SAMUI HOTEL
$$$$$
86 MU 3, SOUTH CHAWENG BEACH
TEL 077-422020
FAX 077-422396
www.imperialhotels.com/samui

At the southern end of Chaweng, this Mediterranean-style resort has whitewashed walls, arched hallways, and roofs of glazed terra-cotta tiles. The location provides a degree of privacy, though rooms in the additional wing across the road lack ocean views or easy access to the pool. Guest rooms have tropical touches, with lots of bamboo. Facilities include two restaurants serving Thai and Western dishes, a saltwater and freshwater pool, limited shopping, and two bars. 🛈 155 🅿 🔄 🅰 🏊 🏋 🐾 All major cards

🏨 POPPIES SAMUI
$$$$$
28/1 MU 3, SOUTH CHAWENG BEACH
TEL 077-422419
FAX 077-422420
www.poppiessamui.com

One of the most attractive hotels in Thailand, Poppies is an offshoot of the famed hotel on Kuta Beach in Bali. This tiny and immaculately designed escape is an unadulterated delight, from the charming guest rooms to the tropical gardens. Fish ponds, Thai sculpture, and gurgling streams add to the tranquility of the Poppies experience. Amenities are limited to a small swimming pool, an open-air bar and lounge, and a regally decorated restaurant known for its royal Thai cuisine. Guests

are ensconced in luxurious cottages decorated with teak and silk. 🛈 24 🅿 🔄 🅰 🏊 🏋 🐾 All major cards

🏨 SALA SAMUI
$$$$$
10/9 MOO 5, BAAN PLAI LAEM
TEL 077-245888
FAX 077-245889
www.salasamui.com

While the Sala Samui doesn't feature the total isolation that other romantic retreats in its class provide, the ability to walk to neighboring properties along Choeng Mon Beach for dinner or drinks is an advantage. Regardless, the resort leaves little reason to leave its grounds; the guest rooms, especially the ultra-luxurious pool salas, are ideal for your honeymoon hideaway, the beachside pools have shady *salas* of their own, and the restaurant serves exquisite cuisine along with regular theme nights. 🛈 16 + 53 suites 🅿 🔄 🅰 🏋 🐾 All major cards

🏨 SANTIBURI GOLF RESORT
$$$$$
12/12 MU 1, MAENAM BAY, NORTH SAMUI
TEL 077-425031 TO -8
FAX 077-425040
www.santiburi.com

Santiburi is the second most exclusive property on Ko Samui, offering the widest range of water sports on the island. This is a very polished resort, used to pampering its guests. The architecture lacks imagination and resembles a generic international style. That aside, this north shore escape boasts a fine Thai restaurant, as well as a Continental one. Rooms are either in villas or suites, and adorned with silk, reproduction antiques, and spacious baths. Service is impeccable, but the isolation may not suit all visitors.

🛈 73 🅿 🔄 🅰 🏊 🏋 🐾 All major cards

SOMETHING SPECIAL

🏨 TONGSAI BAY COTTAGES & HOTEL
$$$$$
84 MU 5, TONGSAI BAY, NORTH-EAST SAMUI
TEL 077-425015
FAX 077-425462
www.tongsaibay.co.th

This fabulous resort between Chaweng and Bophut beaches provides the best combination of luxury and location on the island, with friendly service thrown in. Tongsai is tucked away on its own cove with a beach, manicured gardens, and comfortable chalets arranged to provide views for all guests. The principal building is an open-air affair, with lounges and the main restaurant. Below is an outstanding pool and beachfront restaurant. Recreation is limited, although water sports can be arranged through the front desk. Individual chalets are decorated in warm colors with rattan furniture.

🛈 72 units 🅿 🔄 🅰 🏋 🐾 All major cards

🏨 CORAL BAY RESORT
$$$$
9 MOO 2, YA NOI BAY, CHAWENG BEACH
TEL 077-234555
FAX 077-234558
www.coralbay.net

Two miles (3 km) north of Chaweng Bay, this unusual resort is in the middle of a coconut plantation. More curious than luxurious, it appeals to visitors wishing to retreat into the jungle. Basic facilities include a lounge, a bar, a gift shop, and a restaurant serving reasonably priced Thai, Chinese, and Western fare. The best place to relax is on the elevated terrace. The beach can vary from muddy shoals to sandy islets spotted with

🚭 Nonsmoking 🅰 Air-conditioning 🏊 Indoor Pool 🏊 Outdoor Pool 🏋 Health Club 🐾 Credit Cards

coral reefs. Guests are housed in well-maintained, but basic, individual bungalows on stilts. 🛈 42 🅿 🚫 🏊 🛍 All major cards

🏨 BLUE LAGOON HOTEL
$$$
99 MU 2, NORTH CHAWENG BEACH
TEL 077-422037
FAX 077-422401
www.bluelagoonhotel.com
Some of the best sand on Samui is found at the northern end of Chaweng in front of this budget hotel. Motel-like buildings are set around gardens and lawns that lead to the swimming pool and the beach. Rooms are fairly large and adequately furnished. Some superior rooms face the beach. A rather ordinary restaurant serves Western and *kow tom* (rice soup) breakfasts and other Thai specialties.
🛈 71 🅿 🚫 🏊 🛍 All major cards

■ FAR SOUTH

PHUKET

SOMETHING SPECIAL

🏨 AMANPURI
🍴 $$$$$
118/1 M.3 SRISOONTHORN RD., PANSEA BEACH
TEL 076-324333
FAX 076-324100
www.amanresorts.com
The Aman hotel chain is world famous, and this is where it all started. Set in tropical splendor over a near-private beach, this jewel has welcomed Hollywood stars and heads of state since its opening more than 20 years ago. The resort has aged well. Amanpuri melds the traditional architecture of Bali, Myanmar, and Thailand. Public areas are open-air, with lofty ceilings, while lounges and restaurants maximize the views. Both restaurants—one Thai, one Italian—are first-class.

You can even cruise on the hotel's private yacht. Guest rooms are filled with antiques and interesting artifacts.
🛈 70 🅿 🚫 🏊 🛍 All major cards

🏨 BANYAN TREE PHUKET
🍴 $$$$$
33 M.4 SRISOONTHORN RD., BANG TAO BAY
TEL 076-324374
FAX 076-324375
www.banyantree.com
Bolstered by accolades from around the world, this hyper-elegant newcomer has made a serious challenge to the Amanpuri (see left). The resort is based on Zen minimalism, and lakes provide calm. It offers all forms of spa therapy, from herbal saunas to mud baths. Facilities include tennis courts, an 18-hole golf course, a cocktail lounge, and several restaurants, including an Asian seafood option. Individual chalets are widely scattered, and golf carts shuttle guests.
🛈 110 🅿 🚫 🏊 🛍 All major cards

🏨 THE CHEDI, PHUKET
$$$$$
118 M.3 CHOENG TALAY
TEL 076-324017
FAX 076-324252
www.ghmhotels.com
The Chedi creates a close imitation of the Amanpuri (see left), with its breezy buildings, Continental restaurant, and outstanding sea views. The elegant cottages are comfortable. Leisure facilities include a billiards room, two bars, a well-stocked library, and water sports (the core activity here).
🛈 110 🅿 🚫 🏊 🛍 All major cards

🏨 DUSIT THANI LAGUNA PHUKET
$$$$$
BANG TAO BAY
TEL 076-6362999
FAX 076-6362900

www.dusit.com
This mid-size resort is the main hotel at the immense planned community at Bang Tao Bay. Surrounding landscaped hills form part of the golf course. Everything is on a grand scale: a huge lobby, spacious restaurants, long corridors, and big rooms and bathrooms. The beach is a short walk away; facilities include tennis courts and a giant chessboard. Six restaurants range from Italian to an American grill.
🛈 226 + 12 suites 🅿 🚫 🏊 🛍 All major cards

🏨 HILTON PHUKET ARCA-
DIA RESORT & SPA
$$$$$
333 KATA RD., KARON BEACH
TEL 076-396433
FAX 076-396136
www.hiltonphuket.com
Few hotels on Karon Beach are larger than this group of circular towers. Popular with tour groups, the hotel does an excellent job for its size. The large rooms are well maintained. Restaurants range from noodle shops to refined Italian emporiums. Boasts three swimming pools, squash and tennis courts, miniature golf, and a water-sports center.
🛈 685 🅿 🚫 🏊 🛍 All major cards

🏨 LE MERIDIEN PHUKET
BEACH RESORT
$$$$$
RELAX BAY
TEL 076-340480
FAX 076-340479
www.lemeridien.com/phuketbeachresort
This property, set on a private cove and featuring a range of activities for children, is ideal for families. Rooms are ordinary but functional. The wonderful beach is reserved for guests; two enormous swimming pools cover almost the entire area between the hotel towers. Restaurants include Thai, Japanese, Italian,

---

🏨 Hotel 🍴 Restaurant 🛈 No. of Guest Rooms 🪑 No. of Seats 🅿 Parking 🕐 Closed 🛗 Elevator 🚆 Transport

PRICES

HOTELS

An indication of the cost of double room in the high season is given by **$** signs.

$$$$$	Over $240
$$$$	$160–$240
$$$	$110–$160
$$	$70–$110
$	Under $70

RESTAURANTS

An indication of the cost of three-course meal without drinks is given by **$** signs.

$$$$$	Over $65
$$$$	$50–$65
$$$	$30–$50
$$	$20–$30
$	Under $20

Continental, and French options. Oustanding recreational facilities include a children's club, a dive shop, and a yacht that cruises to nearby islands.
[1] 477 P 🔊 🅰 🏊 💪 🅲 All major cards

🏨 MARINA PHUKET
$$$$$
47 KARON ROAD, KARON BEACH
TEL 076-330625 OR 330493 TO -37
FAX 076-330516 & 330999
www.marinaphuket.com
On a hilltop separating Karon and Kata beaches, this alluring collection of cottages is set among spacious gardens above a private beach. The prices are steep considering the simplicity of the facilities and rooms, but otherwise this operation is a winner. A pair of casual restaurants provides sustenance; a lounge has ocean views.
[1] 104 P 🅰 🏊 💪 🅲 All major cards

SOMETHING SPECIAL

🏨 THE ROYAL PHUKET YACHT CLUB
$$$$$
NAI HARN BEACH

TEL 076-380200 TO -19
FAX 076-380280
www.theroyalphuket
yachtclub.com
This resort at the island's southwest corner perches on a cliffside, with fabulous views to Cape Promthep. The one sign of civilization is a wind turbine. The resort appears buried in the jungle; only the balconies of the rooms and chalets peek out. Enormous rooms are adorned with beautiful wood, huge bathrooms, and extravagant furniture. Diners can linger in the open-air Mediterranean restaurant or in the Regatta (Italian fare).
[1] 110 + 10 suites P 🔊 🅲 🏊 💪 🅰 All major cards

🏨 SHERATON GRANDE LAGUNA PHUKET
$$$$$
10 M.4 SRISOONTHORN RD., BANG TAO BAY
TEL 076-324101
FAX 076-324108
www.starwoodhotels.com/phuket
While the exterior of Phuket's largest resort leaves much to be desired, the guest rooms are lovely. Among the seven restaurants are a Thai outlet by the beach, a traditional steak and lobster grill, and a Chinese affair. You can use the tennis courts, health center, entertainment room, or spa, or stroll to the beach for water sports.
[1] 325 + 18 suites P 🔊 🅲 🏊 💪 🅰 All major cards

🏨 INDIGO PEARL HOTEL
$$$$–$$$$$
NAI YANG BEACH
TEL 076-327006
FAX 076-327338
www.pearlvillage.co.th
The former Pearl Village Hotel underwent a 2006 upgrade from a rustic seaside retreat to a sophisticated getaway. Nestled beside Sirinath National Park, the resort still benefits from the natural beauty of Nai

Yang beach, but now features a five-star spa and international cuisine, including Japanese, Thai, and Spanish restaurants. Rooms, and villas with private pool pavilions, fuse classic and contemporary Thai decor.
[1] 270 + 7 suites P 🔊 🅰 💪 🅲 All major cards

🏨 AMARI CORAL BEACH RESORT
$$$$
PATONG BEACH
TEL 076-340106 TO -14
FAX 076-340115
www.amari.com/coralbeach/
This elegant yet informal hotel is a white stucco affair set on the rocks at the southern end of Patong Beach. Rooms are decorated in Mediterranean colors. Restaurants include Thai and Italian outlets, but the café at the hotel pier is the place to go at sunset. There are plenty of recreational opportunites here: two pools, tennis courts, and a variety of water sports.
[1] 190 + 7 suites P 🔊 💪 🅲 All major cards

🏨 CAPE PANWA HOTEL
$$$$
27 M.8 SAK DI DETH
CAPE PANWA
TEL 076-391123
FAX 076-391177
www.capepanwa.com
This romantic hotel on the island's isolated southeast corner is highly regarded: Leonardo DiCaprio stayed here during the filming of *The Beach*. Lovely chalets step down an incline from the main building toward the ocean. Restaurants include Italian and French options, plus a Thai restaurant in an old house.
[1] 219 + 12 suites P 🔊 🅲 🏊 💪 🅰 All major cards

🏨 KATATHANI THANI RESORT & SPA
$$$$
KATA NOI BEACH
TEL 076-330124
FAX 076-330426

🚭 Non-smoking 🅰 Air-conditioning 🏊 Indoor Pool 🏊 Outdoor Pool 💪 Health Club 🅲 Credit Cards

www.katathani.com
Beach lovers will be thrilled with the quality of the sand here, and all can enjoy the spacious landscaped lawns and gardens. Several restaurants provide fine food at reasonable prices, including a seafood grill on the beach and a Thai restaurant with garden views.
🛈 265 🅿 🔄 ⛱ 🏖 🍴 🛗 All major cards

🏨🍴 MOM TRI'S BOATHOUSE
$$$$
182 KOKTANON, KATA BEACH
TEL 076-330015 TO -7
FAX 076-330561
www.boathousephuket.com
This old favorite has received rave reviews since it opened its doors in the early 1980s. Diners flock to its open-air restaurant for cocktails and seafood at sunset. The property is small, however, and the years have not been kind. Renovation has been haphazard, and the two swimming pools have fallen into disuse. The restaurant is still a winner, though, and the chief reason to stay here.
🛈 36 🅿 🔄 🏖 🍴 🛗 All major cards

🏨 AMORA BEACH RESORT
$$
322 M.2, BANG TAO BEACH
TEL 076-324021
FAX 076-324243
www.phuket.com/amora
Travelers on a budget who wish to avoid the touristy parts of Phuket can go to this modest place on the island's northwest side. Dining choices include a Thai restaurant, but most of the guests staying here eagerly wait for the nightly barbecue on the beach.
🛈 115 🅿 🔄 🏖 🍴 🛗 All major cards

🏨 METROPOLE PHUKET
$$
1 SOI SURIN, MONTRI RD.

PHUKET TOWN
TEL 076-215050
FAX 076-215990
www.metropolephuket.com
This hotel is truly luxurious and represents the best value on Phuket. It is an international affair with marble, sculpture and silk in the public rooms. Guest rooms are modern with a nod to Thai tastes.
🛈 228 + 20 suites 🅿 🔄 🔄 🏖 🍴 🛗 All major cards

🍴 BAAN RIM PA
$$
PATONG–KAMALA BEACH RD.
PATONG BEACH
TEL 076-340789
FAX 076-290267
www.baanrimpa.com
At this upscale Thai restaurant on the rocky cliff at the north end of Patong Beach, dishes are imaginative, if somewhat tame. The water views from the veranda are amazing.
🪑 145 🛗 All major cards

🍴 OLD SIAM
$$
THAVORN PALM BEACH RESORT, KARON BEACH
TEL 076-396090 TO -1
Perhaps the loveliest dinner-dance show venue on the island, Old Siam has Thai dance and dramatic performances on Wednesday and Sunday evenings. There is indoor and outdoor dining on a terrace.
🪑 120 🔄 🛗 All major cards

KO PHI PHI

🏨 HOLIDAY INN RESORT PHI PHI ISLAND
$$$
PHI PHI ISLAND
TEL 076-261860
FAX 076-261866
www.phiphi-palmbeach.com
This resort is on a private beach on the island's northeastern tip; transportation must be arranged with the hotel in advance. Individual cottages are arranged around the central hall, which has a

lounge and a restaurant.
🛈 77 🚐 Boat 🔄 🏖 🛗 All major cards

🏨 PHI PHI NATURAL RESORT
$$
MU 8, LAEMTONG
TEL 075-613010 TO -11
FAX 075-613000
www.phiphinatural.com
Set in a lush tropical paradise, tastefully decorated cottages perch near a gorgeous white-sand beach. The resort's central building has a cocktail lounge, a decent restaurant serving Thai seafood and Western dishes, and an entertainment room with pool and video games.
🛈 70 units 🚐 Boat 🔄 🏖 🛗 All major cards

KRABI

SOMETHING SPECIAL

🏨 RAYAVADEE RESORT
$$$$$
214 M.2 AONANG, 67 MU 5,
SAI THAI–SUSAN HOY RD.,
PHRA NANG
TEL 075-620740 OR
075-620740 TO -3
FAX 075-620630
www.rayavadee.com
The prime real estate at the cape's southern tip is almost completely taken up with the ultra-luxurious Rayavadee, poised in a stunning natural environment of limestone pinnacles, turquoise sea, and white sand. The rooms are superb. Guests can take cruises to nearby islands or snorkel. Posh spa and a restaurant specializing in royal Thai cuisine.
🛈 100 🚐 Boat 🔄 🏖 🍴 🛗 All major cards

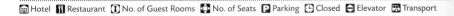

Shopping in Thailand

Shopping is one of the delights of Thailand, and there is a staggering range of items from which to select: fine jewelry set with sparkling rubies and sapphires, carved Buddhist effigies, clothing made from Thai silk and fine cottons, silverwork bowls and utensils, brass cutlery, reproductions of classic European furniture, and, of course, all those carved elephants. You can also add to this list temptations such as authentic and "instant" antiques, precious art, delicate ceramics. leather coats, and suits made in 24 hours.

Bargaining

Prices for most of these goods are surprisingly reasonable considering the time and craftsmanship that goes into their manufacture. Bargaining is expected in many small shops and from individual artisans, especially in the tourist zones of Bangkok, Chiang Mai, and Phuket. The general rule is to offer half the price quoted by the merchant and then slowly move toward a middle price that reflects a discount of 25 to 33 percent. You might expect a discount of at least 50 percent from street merchants and tourist shops selling souvenirs. Prices are generally fixed in larger shopping centers.

Cautions

Shoppers should exercise caution as rules are different in Thailand. Generally, refunds are rarely given and, once a product is purchased, there will be no exchanges. Receipts are often provided upon request, but do not guarantee exchange or refund privileges, so examine all items carefully before you hand over your cash or credit card. Deposits are nonrefundable.

You should also be wary of touts, who are paid generous commissions for bringing customers into stores. There is absolutely no reason to allow anyone to take you around town on a shopping expedition, no matter how great the promised savings—especially if it's a "special one-day jewelry sale."

Thailand produces convincing counterfeits: Rolex watches, Louis Vuitton handbags, Nike running shoes, Levi's jeans, and Oakley sun-glasses are just a few of the famous brands found in vendors' stalls in parts of the city. The fake-goods market is not as rampant as it once was, thanks to a more concerted effort by Thai authorities (after prompting from the United States) to enforce the law.

Fake gem scams have been going on in Bangkok for decades with many of the same retailers involved. If a *tuk-tuk* driver offers to take you on a "free tour" or one for a small charge, you'll likely end up at one of these places, along with half a dozen other outlets selling various overpriced goods. Don't buy gemstones unless you are knowledgeable about the trade. Most of the so-called antiques sold in the country are also clever fakes.

Shopping Centers

The best introduction to shopping in Thailand is to visit one of the huge shopping centers in Bangkok, many of which are located in the easily accessible Siam Square area. By spending a few hours exploring stores such as the middle-market Central department store and the down-town market MBK, you'll have a good idea of what most things cost—and be pleasantly surprised. While prices are fixed, always ask if there is a discount available, and you may get lucky; 10 percent is the norm.

The Central store chain has an off-and-on tourist promotion that gives visitors between 5 and 10 per-cent off. You'll probably have to ask to apply. Also, the store has a few discount bins, mainly for clothing that you can rummage through for some excellent bargains. The best buys are clothing and accessories, men's and women's shoes, name-brand athletic shoes, leather goods such as wallets, belts, and handbags, and good quality knickknacks.

Department stores are usually attached to large shopping malls that give much of their space to vendors who sell inexpensive and impressively made handicrafts.

The government's "one village, one product" scheme, OTOP, encourages villagers to make objects with a Thai flavor. The results, in the form of handicrafts, processed foods, knickknacks, and clothing, turn up in vendors' stalls in malls and department stores. All these goods have OTOP tags on them.

Modern shopping centers are usually air-conditioned and provide a welcome relief from the heat and humidity. Food courts—with lots of delicious options—and small enter-tainment venues are often located on the top floor or in the basement.

Markets

Old-fashioned traditional markets still dominate the smaller towns. They may appear dark and dank and smell awful, but they com-pensate with all the local color and vibrancy of authentic Thai life. Most towns have one central mar-ket that is open daily until around 4 p.m. They have an indoor sec-tion for meats and other valuable food items and an outdoor sec-tion for fruit and vegetables.

If your stomach is not prepared for the often strange, smelly world of the interior market, stick to the outdoor sections where you can watch the merchants in action.

Specialties

Thailand produces a large variety of handicrafts that are unique to the country; certain products are best purchased near their area of origin. Thai silk traditionally has been produced in the northeast or Issan region, and those searching for shell or coconut items will be best rewarded in the south, around Phuket and Ko Samui. Ayutthaya has long been known for sculpted stonework, which is sold in outdoor markets near the ancient capital's historic buildings, while ceramics are closely associated with the Sawankalok tradition near Sukhothai.

The greatest concentration of handicrafts is found in and around Chiang Mai. Woodcarving, silverwork, silk weaving, and furniture are produced in hundreds of small shops and factories around the city. In fact, if you are going to Thailand chiefly to shop, save most of your time and money for the bargains of Chiang Mai.

What to Buy

Products produced in Thailand will be cheaper than in the United States, while imported items such as Japanese electronics will be less expensive back home, as import duties in Thailand remain high. The most popular craft items are silk, precious stones, "instant" antiques (reproductions), carved wooden images, hill-tribe handicrafts, bronzes cutlery, nielloware, celadon pottery, and lacquerware.

Thai silk is perhaps the most famous national product. It can be 100 percent silk or interwoven with synthetic fibers to improve wearability and reduce the naturally rough texture of pure, raw silk. Beware of fake silk made entirely from rayon or of a composite of synthetics and cotton.

Most antiques sold here are actually modern reproductions cleverly made to appear old and sometimes sold under false pretenses.

Unless you are an expert, it's best to assume that all antiques are modern fakes and negotiate accordingly.

It is illegal to export any authentic antique and also to export any image of the Buddha, unless you are Buddhist yourself. Most images that appear to be Buddhas, however, are actually figures of kneeling monks or female deities, often modeled after Burmese prototypes.

Payment

Department stores and most retail outlets accept major credit cards. Some of the smaller stores charge you an extra 3 to 5 percent if you pay with a card. Vendors at markets only take cash. And very few, if any, retailers or department stores take travelers' checks. You'll need to cash these at a bank or foreign-exchange kiosk.

Value-added Tax

Although value-added tax (VAT) is required on all purchases in Thailand, it is not always collected. Only department stores and some retailers in malls and up-market hotels collect the 7 percent tax.

Special arrangements allow travelers to obtain a VAT refund when all legal conditions are fulfilled. Visitors who depart Thailand by air from an international airport and have not been in the country more than 180 days in a calendar year qualify for a refund. VAT refunds apply only to goods taken out of the country within 60 days from the date of purchase, and all goods must be purchased from stores that display the "VAT Refund for Tourists" sticker. You must spend at least 2,000 baht in a single day, and the total amount of goods purchased must be not less than 5,000 baht. VAT refund forms are filled out in the store and then presented at the VAT refund counter in the departure lounge of the airport. Gems do not qualify for a VAT refund.

■ BANGKOK

Bangkok's major shopping centers are chiefly located in the Siam Square–Ploen Chit–Rama 1 district, and along Sukhumvit Road between Sois 10 and 24. Small tourist shops are abundant along Silom and Sukhumvit Roads near the inner sois from Soi 4 to Soi 12 (note that soi means "alley" and thanon, "road").

Shopping Centers
Central Bangkok

Amari Plaza & Tower Phloen Chit at Ratchadamri Rd., tel 02-256-9111. Another upscale shopping center offering designer fashion, plus some very slick restaurants. The primary anchor here is the Japanese department store Sogo, while the most distinctive element is the extravagant Romanesque exterior architecture.

Central Chidlom Phloen Chit at Chidlom Rd., tel 02-655-7777. This newest branch of the Central group, Thailand's largest department store chain, specializes in moderately priced clothing and household goods. The extensive collection of Thai handicrafts is priced lower than in most comparable stores.

Central World Plaza Rama 1 at Ratchadamri Rd., tel 02-255-9400. Bangkok's largest shopping center boasts six floors of shops, restaurants, grocery stores, Internet cafés, and an ice-skating rink, all anchored by the mid-priced Zen Central at one end and the upscale Isetan at the other. It's a great place to wander in air-conditioned comfort.

Gaysorn Plaza Phloen Chit at Ratchadamri Rd., tel 02-656-1149. A small, upscale complex with pricey boutiques and quality handicraft shops on the second floor. The handicraft emporium Narayana Phand completes the scene.

Mahboonkrong (MBK) Center Rama 1 at Phaya Thai Rd., tel 02-217-9119. An older but nevertheless impressive shopping center with less expensive and less exclusive offerings, just across the road from the Central World Plaza. Popular with teenagers and budget shoppers, the immense eight-level complex has restaurants and cafés on the ground floor, several popular jazz nightclubs upstairs in the back, six cinemas, and hundreds of small shops selling everything from trinkets to designer jewelry.

Peninsula Plaza Ratchadamri, just south of Phloen Chit Rd., tel 02-253-9762. Somewhat off the beaten track, but excellent for antiques shops, boutiques, and a large Asia Books outlet.

Siam Center Rama 1 Rd., tel 02-658-1000. A reasonably priced shopping center popular with teenagers and well stocked with trendy clothing and other merchandise.

Siam Paragon 991/1 Rama 1 at Phaya Thai Rd., tel 02-690-1000. Although shopping centers are built in Bangkok at a breakneck pace, it will be some time before one surpasses Siam Paragon. In the heart of Siam Square, it features international clothing companies, auto showrooms, bookstores, electronics stores, an aquarium, a gourmet market, dozens of restaurants, a fitness club, and a 21-screen movie theater with IMAX. Soon it will be joined by a five-star hotel, serviced apartments, and Thailand's first opera house.

Siam Square Rama 1 at Phaya Thai Rd. Bangkok's oldest shopping center in Bangkok, constructed in an open-air style in the 1960s, is now filled with inexpensive stationary stores, hardware shops, and other utilitarian outlets. The Novotel Siam Square (see p. 360) and dozens of small restaurants are also here.

Silom Road

Central Department Store Silom, near Pramuan Rd., tel 02-233-6930. The neighborhood's oldest shopping center lacks trendiness but offers reasonably priced clothing, household items, and other basics. On the upper floor is a

selection of local handicrafts.

Oriental Place Oriental Ln., tel 02-266-0186. Linked with the Oriental hotel (see p. 360), this upscale emporium has clothing boutiques and exclusive antiques. The striking building has a handsome facade and elegant interiors.

Silom Village Silom, near Pramuan Rd., tel 02-234-4448. A small complex's good selection of shops caters almost exclusively to visitors.

Sukhumvit Road

The Emporium Sukhumvit Soi 24, tel 02-268-1000, ext. 1726 to -7. One of the neighborhood's newest shopping centers, aimed at the rich with designer-name shops and pricey cafés in a monolithic building set with tons of marble.

Ploenchit Center Sukhumvit Soi 2, tel 02-656-8600. A fairly small and well-stocked shopping center, beside the J. W. Marriott Hotel (see p. 362). Moderately priced Asian restaurants occupy the second floor; clothing sales are held regularly in the basement.

Street Markets

Chatuchak Weekend Market Off Paholyothin Rd., tel 02-272-4631. Thailand's largest flea market takes place every weekend in the eastern part of town and is now reachable by Skytrain (Morchit station). Spread over 35 acres (14 ha), it is loosely organized by the type of goods. It's a baffling wonderland of everything from antiques and fine clothing to old magazines and pure junk. For a quick tour, explore along Sois 1 through 4, where you find amulets and religious articles, handicrafts and antiques, textiles both old and new, souvenirs, stamps and coins, and hill-tribe crafts. Chatuchak also has outdoor cafés, a post office, small tourist information center, and several banks.

Pak Khlong Market Memorial Bridge at the Chao Phraya river. A huge vegetable-and-fruit market

inside an old warehouse, where hundreds of merchants sell to thousands of daily shoppers. The smell can be overwhelming but the color and cacophony are thrilling.

Pratunam Market Petchaburi and Ratchaprarop Rds. Just two blocks west of Central World Plaza is Thailand's largest clothing emporium, a confusing but fascinating warren of tiny shops selling all types of clothing at bargain basement prices. The quality may leave something to desire, but the range of goods and authentic atmosphere make this a great experience.

Sampeng Lane Chinatown. This narrow, crowded alley in Chinatown near the Chao Phraya is just a crazy place, with great atmosphere, hordes of people, and great bargains in clothing and household goods.

Other Outlets

Antiques

Elephant House 67/12 Soi Pra Phinit, tel 02-286-2780. This old antiques shop in an odd location off Sathorn Tai Road in the Silom district is known for decorative artwork and carved wooden artifacts, including Burmese antiques and modern reproductions.

Prayer Textile Gallery, 197 Phayathai Rd., tel 02-251-7549. Traditional and ethnic textiles from Laos, Cambodia, and Thailand, some more than 100 years old.

Rasi Sayam Sukhumvit Soi 23, tel 02-286-5592. One of many intriguing shops that generally sell "instant" antiques, with a scattering of authentic items thrown in for good measure. This particular shop offers higher quality than most.

River City Shopping Complex Sri Phaya Rd., tel 02-237-0077. Thailand's largest and most famous group of antiques stores spreads over several floors, alongside less expensive shops for imitation antiques. Monthly auctions are held in this gargantuan building next door to the Royal Orchid Sheraton Hotel & Towers (see p. 360).

Handicrafts

Chitralada This handicraft center enjoys royal support and distributes most profits back to the artisans, often handicapped Thais, rather than middlemen. Chitralada has shops at the Oriental Plaza, Grand Palace, Vimanmek, Thaniya Plaza, Amari Watergate hotel, and Bangkok Marriott Resort & Spa.

Narayana Phand 295/2 Ratchaprarop Rd., tel 02-252-4670. A huge, privately owned handicraft center under the patronage of the royal family. A high proportion of its proceeds go directly to the artisans, often impoverished hill-tribe people. Stocks every handicraft sold in Thailand at fixed, reasonable prices.

Silk

Anita Thai Silk 294/4-5 Silom Rd., tel 02-234-2481. With 50 years in the business, 30 at this location, Anita Thai is a top manufacturer, wholesaler, and tailor of women's clothes. Thousands of prints are available.

Jim Thompson Silk 9 Surawong Rd., tel 02-234-4900. The most famous name in silk has outlets on Surawong Road near Rama IV Road, in the Oriental hotel (see p. 360), in Isetan at Central World Plaza (see p. 382), and at the Grand Hyatt Erawan Bangkok hotel (see p. 362). Quality is the highest in the country, with prices to match.

Shinawatra Silk Thailand's second most famous silk merchant has shops on South Sathorn Road in the Silom district and at Sukhumvit Soi 23, tel 053-221076.

■ CHIANG MAI

Chiang Mai has Thailand's greatest array of handicrafts. Most of the shops are just east of town on the road to the village of San Kamphaeng. The sheer number of shops and factories along this route precludes detailed descriptions. Among the more famous and respected are Jolie Femme Silk, Thai Shop, Chiang Mai Silver,

Iyara Art, Borisoothi Antiques, Shinawatra Thai Silk, Nakorn Ping Leather, Chiang Mai Treasure, the umbrella village of Borsang, San Kamphaeng Kilns, and another Shinawatra Silk Factory just before Highway 1006 splits.

Shopping Centers

Kaed Sua Kaew (KSK) Huay Kaew Rd., tel 053-224444. The largest modern, air-conditioned shopping center in town, with five floors of shops, fast-food outlets, and several cinemas.

Tantrapan An older but serviceable shopping center with branches on Tha Phae Road, at the airport, and near Chang Puak Gate. Prices tend to be lower than at KSK.

Other Outlets

Hill-tribe Handicrafts

Hill-tribe crafts are best purchased from nonprofits, which return most of the funds they make to the craftsperson rather than the shop owner or middleman.

Hill Tribes Product Foundation 21/17 Suthep Rd., near Wat Suan Dok, tel 053-277743.

Thai Tribal Crafts 208 Bumrungrat Rd., near McCormick Hospital, tel 053-241043.

Antiques

Antiques Corner Chiang Mai Night Bazaar, Chang Klan Rd. A group of antiques shops tucked away on the second floor of the shopping complex beside the Chiang Inn. They include Yonok Treasure, The Lost Heavens, Oriental Spirit, and Lanna Antiques.

Chiang Saen Art Souvenirs 68–70 Rat Chiang Saen Rd., tel 053-273176. Antiques and modern reproductions in bronze, stone, silver, and wood, with a special emphasis on Buddhist amulets.

Ceramics

Ban Phor Liang Muen 36 Phra Pok Klao Rd., tel 053-278187.

An unusual ceramic and terracotta factory set around a lovely old teak house and expansive gardens, producing kitschy but fun items. Situated in the southwest corner of old Chiang Mai.

Mengrai Kilns 79/2 Arak Rd. Soi Samlarm 6, tel 053-272063. An outstanding range, including their famous celadons fashioned after prototypes discovered at Sawankalok near Sukhothai. Their retail shop is also located in the southwest corner of the historic walled town.

Silverwork

Silverwork was first produced here in small shops along Wualai Road, on the southern edge of town. The city sprawl has since completely enveloped the silversmiths.

Siam Silverware 5 Wualai Rd. For more than 50 years this shop has been producing some of Thailand's best silverwork, still superior to that in the shops east of town.

Sipsong Panna Nantawan Arcade, 95/19 Nimanhemin Rd., tel 053-216096. Another established favorite with an excellent reputation, now in this arts and crafts shopping arcade.

Textiles

Duangjitt House Nantawan Arcade, 95/10 Nimanhemin Rd., tel 053-283085. Both antiques and fine textiles are sold in this long-running shop, which also maintains an outlet on the third floor of the Chiang Inn Plaza.

The Loom 27 Ratchamankha Rd., tel 053-283085. A quality store with fabrics from all regions of Thailand, plus samples imported from Cambodia, Laos, and Myanmar—all displayed in a lovely teak house a few blocks south of Tha Phae Gate.

Naenna Textile Studio 138 Soi Chang Kian, tel 053-226042. Quality textiles designed by the owner, Patricia Cheesman Naenna. An expert on Thai textiles, she wrote several books on the subject.

Entertainment & Activities

Bars and nightclubs in the major urban areas are a familiar scene, but Thailand also has a number of cultural venues where visitors can see traditional performance arts of dance and drama. For an authentic experience, you may find it more rewarding to attend any of the annual festivals described below. Details of the main sporting activities—water sports and golf—are also listed below.

Performing Arts

Bangkok has the only formal performing halls in the country. In addition, some restaurants sponsor dinner-dance performances almost every night.

Chalern Krung Royal Theatre 66 Charoen Krung Rd., tel 02-221-6239. Thailand's newest venue for performing arts, including the *khon* and *lakhon*, is this renovated cinema just four blocks from the Grand Palace.

Erawan Hotel Shrine Phloen Chit at Ratchadamri Rd. Free outdoor dance performances can be seen daily at this famous shrine on the grounds of the Grand Hyatt Erawan hotel (see p. 362).

National Theater Chao Fa Rd., tel 02-224-1342. Bangkok's original cultural hall puts on lavish dance spectacles several times a year, plus weekly Sunday afternoon shows.

Thailand Cultural Centre Ratchadphisek Rd., tel 02-247-0028. This all-purpose hall sponsors events from classical music to traditional Thai dramas.

Major Festivals

Thailand has many festivals; the following highlights often include a spectacular parade, followed by evening performances of classical dance and drama.

January
Don Chedi Memorial Fair Suphanburi. A weeklong festival; celebrates Prince Naresuanthe's victory over the Burmese. *(Late Jan.)*

King Mengrai Festival Chiang Rai. Northern festival to honor King Mengrai, founder of the Lanna Kingdom, with parade and sound-and-light show. *(Late Jan.)*

Nakhon Phanom Prathat Phanom Festival Nakhon Phanom. A weeklong fair held at the most honored stupa in the northeast. *(Late Jan.)*

February
Chinese New Year Nationwide. Asia's most important festival for the Chinese community is best observed in predominantly Chinese towns such as Nakhon Sawan, a few hours north of Bangkok. *(Late Jan.–mid-Feb.)*

Chainat Giant Straw Birds Chainat. A southern event that features giant models of birds constructed with dried rice stalks. *(Early Feb.)*

Chiang Mai Flower Festival Chiang Mai. The northern city honors its chief product with processions, floats, and beauty contests. *(Early Feb.)*

Makha Puja Nationwide. Important Buddhist festival with candlelight processions around major temples. *(Feb. full moon)*

March
Wat Phra Buddhaphat Fair Saraburi. Thousands of pilgrims flood this small town to honor a giant imprint of the foot of Buddha. *(Early March)*

Singing Dove Festival Yala. Southern festival with bird displays and birdsong contests. *(Mid-March)*

Thao Suranari Fair Nakhon Ratchasima. The female military hero is honored for her spirited resistance against Lao forces during a siege from Vientiane. *(Late March)*

April
Pattaya Festival Pattaya. Major weeklong festival at Thailand's original beach resort, three hours from the capital, with both cultural and hedonistic offerings. *(Early April)*

Songkran Nationwide. The Thai New Year is also known as the "water festival," when everyone is drenched by friends, family, and strangers—a welcome respite from the heat. *(Mid-April)*

Si Satchanalai Ordinations Si Satchanalai. Dozens of young monks are ordained into the Buddhist priesthood after a colorful and photogenic parade. *(Late April)*

May
Royal Plowing Ceremony Bangkok. Hindu ceremony held annually at Sanam Luang to ensure good fortune for the nation's farmers. *(Early May)*

Visaka Puja Nationwide. This major Buddhist holiday commemorates the birth, death, and enlightenment of the Buddha with candlelight processions around the temples. *(Early May)*

Rocket Festival Northeast Thailand. Rockets are fired into the air to bring rain is fired throughout the northeast, the display in Yasothan is the most spectacular. *(Mid-May)*

July
Candle Festival Ubon Ratchathan. Parade with more than 100 lavishly decorated floats, dance performances, traditional Issan music, and other cultural shows. *(Mid-July)*

Khao Phansa Nationwide. A big day for young men to enter the Buddhist priesthood at the beginning of the "rains retreat." *(Mid-July)*

Asanha Puja Buddha's first sermon is celebrated in temples throughout Thailand. *(July full moon)*

September

Phichit Boat Races Phichit. Long-tail boat races are held around the country at the height of the rainy season. Other famous venues are Nan, Phimai, and Nakhon Phanom. *(Early Sept.)*

Narathiwat Fair Narathiwat. A weeklong Muslim fair with boat races, singing-dove competitions, and demonstrations of traditional martial arts. *(Late Sept.)*

October

Phuket Vegetarian Festival Phuket town. Major Chinese festival with a parade, cultural performances, and men who pierce their body with needles, knives, and sharpened steel blades. *(Late Sept.–early Oct.)*

Sakhon Nakhon Wax Candle Festival Sakhon Nakhon. The end of Buddhist Lent and the rains retreat is marked with boat races and a parade of floats, giant candles, and beauty queens. *(Mid-Oct.)*

Ok Phansa Nationwide. End of the three-month Lenten season, when Buddhists present new robes to monks. *(Mid–late Oct.)*

November

Loy Krathong Nationwide. Delightful festival with beauty contests, daylong parades, and event honoring the ancient water spirit of Mae Kong Ka. *(Mid-Nov.)*

Wat Saket Fair Bangkok. The city's largest temple fair, with folk dance and drama, modern entertainment, and a candlelight procession around the Golden Mount of Wat Saket. *(Mid-Nov.)*

River Kwai Historical Week Kanchanaburi. A weeklong remembrance of the events of World War II, with exhibitions, memorial services, and a sound-and-light show over the famous bridge. *(Late Nov.)*

Surin Elephant Roundup Surin. Thailand's most famous animal and national symbol is honored with staged elephant hunts, rodeos, and elephant polo. *(Late Nov.)*

December

King's Birthday Bangkok. King Bhumibol Adulyadej is honored with a parade down Rachadamoen Klang Avenue. *(Dec. 5)*

Chiang Mai Winter Fair Chiang Mai. Major cool-season festival with cultural activities, beauty contests, and a grand parade. *(Late Dec.)*

Activities

Activities include all forms of watercraft, parasailing, and, for snorkeling and diving enthusiasts, some of the best underwater viewing that nature has to offer.

If you are heading north to Chiang Mai, Chiang Rai, or Mae Hong Son, you will find plenty of opportunities to get out into the mountains and away from the busy atmosphere of the cities and popular seaside resorts. There are several options to help you decide just how you'd like to get away from it all.

Wherever you are in Thailand, packages for every activity available locally can be organized direct through your guesthouse or hotel tour desk; simply tell them what you want to do, and they'll set it up for you. Storefront travel agents are found in large numbers in all tourist centers and offer similar services. In general, their tours are well organized and excellent value. Never accept tour offers from street touts, or tuk-tuk or taxi drivers.

Adventure Sports

Thailand provides a wide range of adventure sports, though the base centers for these may often be located far apart.

Bungee jumping Tarzan's Jungle Bungee Jump in the village of Kata, Phuket, is set in beautiful natural surroundings. The jump is a 160-foot (50 m) drop from a man-made tower suspended above a lake that used to be an open gem mine.

Microlighting You can go up in a microlight at Chiang Mai, on the road to Doi Saket. Though the immediate scenery here is nothing spectacular, if you are looking for a bird's-eye view of water buffaloes working the rice paddies and of Thai village life, then this is the best way to do it. Rates start at 1,700 baht for 15 minutes, although this should be negotiable. Call Discovery Adventure International Co. Ltd. *(tel 053-868460).*

Personal watercrafts Some consider motoring around in personal watercrafts such as Jet Skis more of an irritation than an activity, but they are popular among tourists on the beaches of Phuket, Samui, and Pattaya. Most places have few controls over where the machines can be used, and so they're often found zooming through the water a few feet from swimmers. Tourists can rent the crafts on beaches for 30 minutes of noisy adventure.

Sea canoeing While once an incredible experience, canoeing in sea caves (or *hwangs*) hidden inside the giant karsts in Phangnga Bay became so popular that the activity was close to self-destructing. The number of sea canoe tour companies, many of which had scant regard for the karsts' delicate ecosystems—went from just a few to dozens, and hundreds of tourists were carted out to the bay daily. Since then, a few of the more reputable companies have led excursions in other less-crowded areas.

Paddling tours also venture into mangrove channels where you can get a closer look at estuarine wildlife. Sea Canoe Thailand *(tel 076-528839)* the original operator of these eco-tours and winner of many tourism awards, is still regarded as the best.

Snorkeling Snorkelers will find plenty of coral patches a few meters offshore from some of Krabi's mainland beaches and islands, and the Ko Phi Phi island group. Other favorite places for snorkeling are the islands in the Ko Samui group; Phuket and the islands near it; and Pattaya's off-shore islands. Coral patches off Ko Chang are also suitable for snorkeling. For snorkeling excursions contact a local outfitter. Another option is to hire a local long-tail boat operator; they know where to go and will charge a reasonable price.

Cycling/Mountain-biking Tours

With a good bike, a fair degree of fitness, and a recommended guide, there is a lot of fun to be had out there. If you just want to get away from Chiang Mai on a day trip, then you can pick up a bike and a map of Doi Suthep, and rent a pickup (songthaew) to take you to the summit, just 30 minutes' drive from the center. From here you can spend the day exploring the trails, waterfalls, and hill-tribe villages dotted around the mountain as you wind your way back down to Chiang Mai.

Elephant Safaris

Symbolically, the elephant is Thailand's national animal. Elephants play a large part in traditional culture and are also a popular draw at shows and festivals. While the introduction of modern technology has seen a decline in the use of elephants for logging, some operations do still use elephants that have been trained at specialized camps (parng chang). There are several such camps around the northern provinces that can be visited, where you can see elephants and their riders (mahouts) showing off their skills and versatility, after which you can take an elephant ride yourself. Most camps or trekking companies will gladly arrange for longer safaris, or you may wish to include an elephant ride with a trekking tour (see below)

Golf

Thailand has hundreds of golf courses, most of which were built during the economic boom of the late 1980s and mid-1990s. Major tourist areas as well as Pattaya, Hua Hin, and, to a lesser extent, Phuket, have lots of courses, many of which were built to international standards. Visitors from Singapore and Hong Kong head to Thailand specifically to play golf because they can avoid paying the high greens fees they're used to paying at home. Pattaya leads the way with about 30 golf courses. Hua Hin has about 20, and Phuket has about 5.

Thailand has played host to a number of international tournaments, and some of its courses are part of the Asian professional golfing circuit. Golf's image has also received a boost with the rise to fame of Tiger Woods; born to a Thai mother, he was awarded honorary citizenship despite never having lived in Thailand. While golf still remains the domain of the more wealthy, the greens fees and equipment rental in Thailand are among the cheapest in the world. Many golfing operators are now established in the kingdom, and the range of options to suit your preference and time frame is unlimited.

Rafting

There are two types of rafting available, and both are in the north. Whitewater rafting is centered on Pai, in Mae Hong Son, and is available from the onset of the wet season (July–Feb.). The more placid form—bamboo rafting—can be found along the Thai-Laotian border (on the Mekong River), departing from Chiang Rai (on the Mae Kok), or west of Bangkok in Kanchanaburi province. All-inclusive tours lasting up to three days (depending on location and time of year) can be arranged with tour companies, which provide large "house rafts" for you to sleep on. Again, for reasons of safety, it is recommended you ask at the tourist office for a reputable company.

Rock Climbing

Rock climbing has taken off in recent years, especially in Krabi, where the limestone formations of the coast and islands provide steep walls and overhangs to give even the more experienced climbers a challenge worth scaling. There is a number of rock-climbing schools in Krabi for beginners and intermediates. Equipment and guides can be hired for a reasonable cost.

Scuba Diving

With some 1,355 miles (2,170 km) of coastline on the Gulf of Thailand and the Andaman Sea, Thailand offers a wide variety of dive possibilities among some of the world's richest marine fauna.

This is a tropical country with warm waters, and a wet suit is not required to explore the exceptionally clear waters on either side of the Thai peninsula. The relatively high water temperature also encourages the growth of marine life and sustains coral beds. From major dive destinations such as Phuket in the Andaman Sea and Ko Tao in the Gulf of Thailand, you can do quick offshore dives, conduct full-day dive excursions to nearby islands and reefs, or even join live-aboard dive boats for longer expeditions to additional dive destinations such as the Surin and Similan Islands.

Thailand offers something for every level of diver. Novices can earn PADI or NAUI certification from accredited dive schools located at all major dive destinations, while more seasoned divers can explore wrecks and coral canyons or sign up for advance classes to further their dive education.

Diving Seasons

Ideal dive conditions exist throughout the year at various beaches and islands, depending on their location in relation to the annual monsoons. Phuket and other islands on the west side of the peninsula are subject to storms and rainfall during the June to November monsoons, but generally enjoy dry, clear weather for the remainder of the year. Across the peninsula are the dive destinations of Ko Samui, Ko Tao, and Chumphon, which are dry and clear from June to November, but receive modest rainfall during the milder northeast monsoons from November to May. So to escape the rain, just move to the other side of the peninsula. East coast dive spots such as Pattaya and Ko Si Chang rarely witness monsoons, and so diving is possible here all year.

Even at the peak of the rainy season in Phuket, periods of sunshine will allow divers to make day excursions to nearby islands and reefs to enjoy calm seas and decent visibility. Dive operators survey weather conditions daily and base decisions on long-term forecasts.

Southwest Thailand Dive Destinations

Phuket is the dive capital of Thailand in terms of number of dive companies and variety of dive opportunities. Pattaya continues to sell more individual divers owing to its location; it is just two hours from Bangkok. Serious divers tend to head directly to Phuket or perhaps across the peninsula to Ko Samui, from where they continue north up to Ko Tao.

Phuket Thailand's largest island has dive opportunities ranging from easy day trips to longer multiday excursions to the Similan and Surin Islands. Several dive companies also offer escorted dive trips beyond the Surin Islands into Myanmar waters around the

so-called Burmese Banks. Phuket has more than 20 dive operators, who rent equipment and provide professional instruction for a variety of PADI certifications.

Ko Lanta & Trang South of Phuket and Krabi, several islands and beach towns with promising dive sites are just making their impact on the scuba scene. Dive companies on Phuket can help with details.

Ko Phi Phi Islands south of Phuket are often limestone karsts that drop sharply into the sea and provide unique underwater vistas for divers. Ko Phi Phi Don and Ko Bida Nok are the favored dive sites.

Similan Islands This nine-island archipelago is one of the premier dive sites in Southeast Asia for its varied topography and rich sea life. As the Similans are about four hours from Phuket, they are best visited with a live-aboard vessel.

Surin Islands North of the Similans and 94 miles (150 km) from Phuket is the final dive archipelago before you enter Myanmar's waters. The Surin Islands are chiefly known for their superb corals, inhabited by sailfish and large pelagics.

Southeast Thailand Dive Destinations

Chumphon Bustling Chumphon marks the point where corals and fringe reefs make their appearance in Thailand, and it is popular with local divers and more intrepid visitors.

Ko Samui & Ko Tao Samui may be the second most popular resort in the country, but divers head two hours north to the tiny island of Ko Tao, which has the best diving in the Gulf of Thailand. Dive shops on Samui organize multiday dive excursions.

East Coast Dive Destinations

Ko Chang The marine national park near the Cambodian border includes many small islands with

superb corals, and calm dive conditions prevail throughout most of the year. Skin- and scuba-diving shops are located at White Beach.

Pattaya Thailand's oldest beach resort continues to draw thousands of divers annually to its offshore islands, which may not be as spectacular as those in the Andaman Sea or near Samui, but are conveniently reached from Bangkok in just a few hours. Pattaya has about a dozen dive shops.

Other Water Sports

Surfing This is really only an option on certain beaches in Phuket (Kara, Niaharn, and Karon) during the June-October monsoon season. (It's not an organized activity there, however.) Most surfers are expatriates living on Phuket, although more and more locals are taking up the sport.

Windsurfing Wind conditions and equipment rentals are best at Pattaya and Jomtien Beach, which has been the country's windsurfing capital for many years. Breezes blow strongest during the northeast monsoon season from February to May. Phuket gets decent wind during the summer months.

Trekking

Dozens of tour companies in Chiang Mai, Chiang Rai, and Mae Hong Son districts offer trekking (hiking) tours in the mountains of the north. A typical trek lasts two to three days (though shorter or longer treks can be arranged) and will include overnight accommodation at a hill-tribe village, where you can experience local traditions and food and drink. You may or may not get to sleep on a soft mattress, though after a tough day's trek you probably won't notice the hardness of a bamboo floor anyway. Trekking tour standards can vary widely, so be sure to deal with a licensed operator recommended by your hotel or by the local TAT office.

Language Guide & Menu Reader

Thais really appreciate it when visitors to their country make an effort to speak their language. Learning even just a few basic greetings and how to say "thank-you" usually makes a big difference to how locals react to you, and using a bit of Thai when bargaining in the market often helps to bring the price down. As you travel farther off the tourist path you will find it more necessary to speak Thai, though most younger Thais have a rudimentary knowledge of English.

For men, the pronoun *pom* is used for "I," and the word *krup*, or the less formal *kap*, is added at the end of a sentence to make the phrase politer, or to show respect. For women, the first person pronoun *dichan* is used, while the word *koa* is added in the place of *krup*.

For example:

Man: *Khun sabai dee mai krup?* (You are fine, no?)

Woman: *Dichan sabai dee, kawb khun koa* (I'm fine, thank-you). (Note: Adults generally don't use the terms *krup* or *koa* when speaking to children.)

Above all else, if words fail you and there seems to be a breakdown in communication, just smile and try to laugh about it—a common Thai response.

Note that the Thai words/phrases below have been transliterated to give as clear a guide to pronunciation as possible. Words may be spelled differently on signs, menus, maps, etc.

General Conversation

Hello *sawadee krap* (used by men)
    sawadee koa (used by women)
How are you? *pen yangai?*
I'm fine *sa bai dee*
May I have *kawe*
Thank-you *kawp khun*
Excuse me *khaw tote*
What is your name *khun cheu arrai?*

My name is *pom cheu* (spoken by male)
My name is *dichan cheu* (spoken by female)
I come from *pom maa jaak* (spoken by male)
I come from *dichan maa jaak* (spoken by female)
America/Canada/Australia *Ameriga/Kanada/Australia*
I'm just going out *pbai teeyao*
I had/am having a great time *sanuk dee*

Language Difficulties

I speak little Thai *puut pasa Thai nitnoy*
I don't understand *mai kow jai*
Do you understand? *kow jai mai?*
It doesn't matter *mai pen rai*

General Conversations & Questions

yes *chai*
no *mai*
okay *oh-kay*
don't want *mai ao*
don't have *mai mee*
sorry *kawe tote*
I want *pom tong gau* (spoken by male)
I want *dichan tong gau* (spoken by female)
I don't know *mai loo*
no good *mai dee*
What's this called in Thai? *nee pasa Thai riak waa arrai?*
where is? *yoo tee nai?*
when? *meua rai?*
how much? *tai lai?*

Directions

I'm going to *ploai*
Where can I get a map? *seu pantee dai tee nai?*
How far is it to? *pai taorai?*

Transportation

air-conditioned bus *rote toca*
ordinary bus *rote tammada*
bus station *sattani rote may*
minibus *rote dtoo*
ticket *tua*

timetable *talang wayla*
railway station *sattani rote fai*
train *rote fai*
express *duan*
sleeper *rote nawn*
seat *tee nung*
airport *sanam bin*
airline office *tee tam ngan saai kam bin*
plane *krueng bin*
boat *rua*
boat dock *tah rua*
long-tail boat *rua harng yao*
ferry *rua doy sarn*
ferry pier *tha*
taxi *teksi*
bicycle *rot jakrayan*
motorcycle *motosai*

Geography & Places

tourist office *samnakngan karn tong tiao*
embassy *sathan toot*
post office *praisinee*
bank *tanakan*
market *talaat*
museum *pipitapun*
police station *sattani tamruat*
beach *haht*
island *ko*
archipelago *mu ko*
village *ban*

Temple Architecture

wat temple complex
bot rectangular meeting hall
chedi bell-shaped structure housing Buddha relic
wihan secondary meeting hall
prang decoratively carved tower
prasat sanctuary tower
sala open-sided building used as community hall

Hotels & Restaurants

hotel *rong raem*
guesthouse *guest how*
men's toilet *hong nacm chai*
women's toilet *hong nacm ying*
restaurant *raan aahaan*
café *raan garfay*
night market *talaat toh nung*

Please bring me the menu *kor doo menu*
May I have? *kawe?*
The food is delicious *ahan arroi*
The bill please *kawe check bin*

Shopping
How much is this? *nee taolai?*
Do you have...? *mee...mai?*
too big *yai gern pai*
too small *lek gern pai*
too expensive *paeng pai*

Emergencies
I need a doctor *tong haa mawe*
I need a dentist *tong haa mawe fun*
please help *chuay duay*
emergency *chook chern*
hospital *rong payabarn*

Time
What is the time? *gee moong laew?*
today *wan nee*
yesterday *meaua wan nee*
tomorrow *prung nee*
morning *ton chao*
afternoon *bai*
evening *yen*

Days of the Week
Sunday *wan aathit*
Monday *wan jahn*
Tuesday *wan ungkarn*
Wednesday *wan poot*
Thursday *wan paruhad*
Friday *wan sook*
Saturday *wan sao*

Numbers
1 *neung*
2 *song*
3 *saam*
4 *sii*
5 *haa*
6 *hok*
7 *jet*
8 *bpat*
9 *gow*
10 *sip*
15 *sip-haa*
20 *yeesip*
25 *yeesip-haa*
100 *neung loi*
1,000 *neung pun*

Menu Reader
Glossary of Popular Thai Dishes
(See also pp. 34–37)
kow pud fried rice
pad-thai Thai-style fried noodles
pad see yoo Chinese-style noodles in soya sauce
tom yum goong sour and spicy prawn soup
kow soi gai spicy northern chicken curry
panang red Thai curry
tom ka gai sour and spicy chicken soup
yum woon sen jellied noodles with sour sauce
kwe-teeyo noodles in soup
som tam papaya salad (an Issan dish)
khan toke classic meal of the north

General Food Terms
to eat *gin*
to drink *duem*
salt *gleua*
sugar *naam tan*
egg *kai*
bread *kanom pung*
liquid, as in curry or soup *gaeng*
dry, without soup *haeng*
spicy, pungent, peppery *pet*
not hot *mai pet*

Meats & Seafood
chicken *gai*
spiced ground beef *larb*
meatball *luke chin neaua*
pork *mu*
spicy sausages *nam*
beef *neua*
duck *bet*
fish *pla*
crab *pu*
shellfish *hoi*
prawn *goong*
dried fish *pla hang*

Fruits
banana *kluay*
coconut *maprow*
durian *toorian*
guava *falang*
jackfruit *kanoon*
lime *manao*
mango *mamuang*
mangosteen *mangkut*
papaya *malagawe*
pineapple *sap-parot*
rambutan *ngaw*

Drinks
drinking water *naam deum*
purified bottled water *naam plow kuat*
milk *nom*
tea *naam cha*

INDEX

ILLUSTRATIONS CREDITS

Cover, R. Ian Lloyd; 2-3, Jodi Cobb/NGS; 4, Pictures Colour Library; 9, Gerald Cubitt; 11, TravelStock44/Alamy; 12, Jerry Alexander/Getty Images; 13, James Morris/Axiom Photographic Agency Ltd.; 15, Kevin R. Morris/CORBIS; 16, Paul Quayle/Axiom Photographic Agency Ltd.; 19, Jacob Halaska/Jupiter Images; 20, R. Ian Lloyd; 23, James Marshall/CORBIS; 24, Luca Tettoni; 26, Jeremy Horner/Getty Images; 29, R. Ian Lloyd; 31, R. Ian Lloyd; 32-33, Paul Chesley/Getty Images; 35, Will & Deni McIntyre/Getty Images; 36, Ben Davies; 39, Luca Tettoni; 40, Gerald Cubitt; 42-46 (all), Luca Tettoni; 49, Royal Household Bureau/Handout/epa/CORBIS; 51-56 (all photos), R. Ian Lloyd; 60, Luca Tettoni; 63, Jim Holmes/Tourist Authority of Thailand; 64, Kris LeBoutillier; 68, Luca Tettoni; 70, Luca Tettoni; 72, Robert Holmes/CORBIS; 74, Michael S. Yamashita/CORBIS; 77, Luca Tettoni; 80, A. Hartley/Travel Ink; 84, Luca Tettoni; 86, Kevin R. Morris/CORBIS; 89, R. Ian Lloyd; 93, Frederic J. Brown/Getty Images; 94, R. Ian Lloyd; 97, David Henley/CPA Media; 98, Jim Holmes/Axiom Photographic Agency Ltd.; 100, R. Ian Lloyd; 103, James Marshall/CORBIS; 104, Anders Blomqvist/The Seeing Eye; 106, Paul Chesley/Getty Images; 109, Kevin R. Morris/CORBIS; 110, Pornchai Kittiwongsakul/Getty Images; 112, Ron Dahlquist; 115, Kevin R. Morris/CORBIS; 117, Yann Arthus-Bertrand/CORBIS; 118, R. Strange/AA Photo Library; 120, Nik Wheeler/CORBIS; 122, Jan Butchofsky-Houser/CORBIS; 124, Tourist Authority of Thailand; 127, Robert Holmes/CORBIS; 128, Gerald Cubitt; 129, Robert Holmes/CORBIS; 130, Gerald Cubitt; 132, Luca Tettoni; 135, Kevin R. Morris/CORBIS; 136, Kevin R. Morris/CORBIS; 139, Eye Ubiquitous; 141, Luca Tettoni; 143, John Everingham; 144, Jodi Cobb/NGS; 147, R. Strange/AA Photo Library; 150, R. Strange/AA Photo Library; 152, Nicholas Pitt/Alamy; 154, Gerald Cubitt; 156, Charcrit Boonsom/Travel Ink; 158, Paul Almasy/CORBIS; 159, R. Strange/AA Photo Library; 160, Gerald Cubitt; 162, R. Strange/AA Photo Library; 163, Paul Chesley/Getty Images; 166, R. Strange/AA Photo Library; 168, Cris Haigh/Alamy; 170, R. Strange/AA Photo Library; 172, R. Ian Lloyd;

174, Mark Williams/Getty Images; 177, Gerald Cubitt; 178, Wolfgang Kaehler/CORBIS; 180, Gerald Cubitt; 181, Gerald Cubitt; 182, Wolfgang Kaehler/CORBIS; 183, Eye Ubiquitous; 185, G P Bowater/Alamy; 188, Tourist Authority of Thailand; 191, Image State; 192, R. Ian Lloyd; 194, R. Strange/AA Photo Library; 195, Wolfgang Kaehler/CORBIS; 198, R. Ian Lloyd; 201, R. Ian Lloyd; 202, Luca Tettoni; 204, Dave G. Houser/CORBIS; 206, Luca Tettoni; 208, R. Strange/AA Photo Library; 209, Gerald Cubitt; 211, R. Ian Lloyd; 212, Yann Arthus-Bertrand/CORBIS; 214, R. Ian Lloyd; 217-220 (all), Luca Tettoni; 223, Eye Ubiquitous; 225, Anders Ryman/CORBIS; 226, Luca Tettoni; 229, R. Ian Lloyd; 230, Kevin R. Morris/CORBIS; 233, Luca Tettoni; 234, Owen Franken/CORBIS; 239, Image State; 240, R. Ian Lloyd; 243, Luca Tettoni; 244, R. Ian Lloyd; 246, Dave G. Houser/CORBIS; 249, R. Ian Lloyd; 250, R. Ian Lloyd; 253, Luca Tettoni; 254, Michael Freeman/CORBIS; 255, Galen Rowell/CORBIS; 257, Luca Tettoni; 258, Hugh Sitton/Getty Images; 260, David Henley/CPA Media; 261, Royalty-Free/CORBIS; 262, R. Strange/AA Photo Library; 264, John F. Sims; 266, Luca I. Tettoni/CORBIS; 268, Philip Game/Lonely Planet Images; 271, Gerald Cubitt; 272, Gerald Cubitt; 274, R. Strange/AA Photo Library; 275, Rainer Krack/CPA Media; 276, Jean-Leo Dugast/Luca Tettoni; 278, Michael Freeman; 281, Luca Tettoni; 282, Gerald Cubitt; 284, Michael Freeman; 285, Kevin R. Morris/CORBIS; 286, Earl & Nazima Kowall/CORBIS; 288. Luca Tettoni; 290, Image State; 295, Luca Tettoni; 296, Michele Falzone/Alamy; 299, Paul Quayle/Axiom Photographic Agency Ltd.; 300, Neil McAllister; 303, Gerald Cubitt; 304, Hakan Johansson/Guttsman Foto; 307, Frederic J. Brown/Getty Images; 308, Gerald Cubitt; 310, David Henley/CPA Media; 313, Oliver Hargreave; 314, Ben Davies; 316, Michael Freeman/CORBIS; 318, Gerald Cubitt; 320, R. Strange/AA Photo Library; 322, Luca Tettoni; 327, R. Ian Lloyd; 328, Chris Noble/Getty Images; 331, Luca Tettoni; 334, Ron Dahlquist; 337, Kevin R. Morris/CORBIS; 338, Saeed Khan/AFP/Getty Images; 341, Gerald Cubitt; 343, Gerald Cubitt; 344, Ben Davies; 347, R. Ian Lloyd.

National Geographic

TRAVELER
Thailand

Published by the National Geographic Society

John M. Fahey, Jr., *President
and Chief Executive Officer*
Gilbert M. Grosvenor, *Chairman of the Board*
Tim T. Kelly, *President, Global Media Group*
John Q. Griffin, *President, Publishing*
Nina D. Hoffman, *Executive Vice President,
President, Book Publishing Group*

Prepared by the Book Division

Kevin Mulroy, *Senior Vice President and Publisher*
Leah Bendavid-Val, *Director of Photography Publishing
and Illustrations*
Marianne R. Koszorus, *Director of Design*
Barbara Brownell Grogan, *Executive Editor*
Elizabeth Newhouse, *Director of Travel Publishing*
Carl Mehler, *Director of Maps*
Barbara A. Noe, *Series Editor*
Cinda Rose, *Series Art Director*

Staff for 2009 Edition

Barbara A. Noe, Deb Antonini, *Project Managers*
Kay Kobor Hankins, *Art Director*
Linda Johansson, *Designer*
Paula Kelly, *Text Editor*
Steven D. Gardner, Michael McNey, Nicholas P.
Rosenbach, and Mapping Specialists
Map Research & Production
Al Morrow, *Design Assistant*
Richard Wain, *Production Project Manager*
Meredith Wilcox, *Illustrations Specialist*
Bridget A. English, Christina Solazzo, Elliana Spiegel,
Jane Sunderland, Maura Walsh, *Contributors*
Bonnie Hanks, *Indexer*

Jennifer A. Thornton, *Managing Editor*
R. Gary Colbert, *Production Director*

Manufacturing and Quality Management

Christopher A. Liedel, *Chief Financial Officer*
Phillip L. Schlosser, *Vice President*
Chris Brown, *Technical Director*
Nicole Elliott, *Manager*
Monika D. Lynde, *Manager*
Rachel Fauise, *Manager*

Area maps drawn by Chris Orr Associates,
Southampton, England

Cutaway illustrations drawn by Maltings
Partnership, Derby, England

National Geographic Traveler: Thailand
(Third Edition) ISBN: 978-1-4262-0408-1

First edition: Edited and designed by AA Publishing (a
trading name of Automobile Association Developments
Limited, whose registered office is Norfolk House,
Priestley Road, Basingstoke, Hampshire, England RG24
9NY. Registered number: 1878835).

Founded in 1888, the National Geographic Society is
one of the largest nonprofit scientific and educational
organizations in the world. It reaches more than 285
million people worldwide each month through its
official journal, *National Geographic*, and its four other
magazines; the National Geographic Channel; television documentaries; radio programs; films; books; videos and DVDs; maps; and interactive media. National
Geographic has funded more than 8,000 scientific
research projects and supports an education program
combating geographic illiteracy.

For more information, please call 1-800-NGS LINE
(647-5463) or write to the following address:

National Geographic Society
1145 17th Street N.W.
Washington, D.C. 20036-4688 U.S.A.

Visit us online at www.nationalgeographic.com/books.

For information about special discounts for bulk
purchases, please contact National Geographic Books
Special Sales: ngspecsales@ngs.org.

For rights or permissions inquiries, please contact
National Geographic Books Subsidiary Rights: ng-
bookrights@ngs.org.

Printed in China

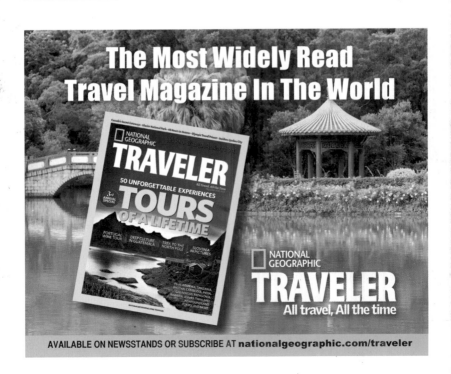